RENDER UNTO THE SULTAN

Render unto the Sultan

Power, Authority, and the Greek Orthodox Church in the early Ottoman Centuries

TOM PAPADEMETRIOU

OXFORD
UNIVERSITY PRESS

OXFORD
UNIVERSITY PRESS

Great Clarendon Street, Oxford, OX2 6DP,
United Kingdom

Oxford University Press is a department of the University of Oxford.
It furthers the University's objective of excellence in research, scholarship,
and education by publishing worldwide. Oxford is a registered trade mark of
Oxford University Press in the UK and in certain other countries

First Edition published 2015

Published in the United States of America by Oxford University Press
198 Madison Avenue, New York, NY 10016, United States of America

British Library Cataloguing in Publication Data
Data available

Library of Congress Control Number: 2014950838

ISBN 978–0–19–871789–8

Acknowledgments

On my initial trip to Istanbul in 1989, I entered the Library and Archives of the Ecumenical Patriarchate of Constantinople for the first time. I was excited because I had been selected to assist a scholar of Byzantine history to research philanthropic institutions of the Ecumenical Patriarchate during the Ottoman period. Having grown up as the son of a Greek Orthodox priest, and later as a seminary student at Hellenic College/Holy Cross Greek Orthodox School of Theology, I had been immersed in the glory and legacy of Byzantium both in my history courses, as well as in the living church tradition of the Greek Orthodox Church. On that trip, I set out to discover Constantinople, and I unearthed Istanbul.

Day after day, I walked into the humble patriarchal compound that at the time was finally being rebuilt after a devastating fire in 1941, past the gate where Patriarch Gregory V had been hung at the start of the Greek Revolution in 1821 (a gate that has since been sealed), and each day I began to see the Patriarchate of Constantinople in its own context and in realistic terms. What became most obvious as we sat quietly working in the Archives was the call of the muezzin from the nearby mosque. It became clear to me then that it was just as important to understand the Ottoman layer of the history of the Church as the early Christian or Byzantine layers, and in some respects was more directly linked to today's realities.

There is a tendency for people of Greek Orthodox heritage to focus on the rise of Christianity, the Patristic age, or the glory of Byzantium, and ignore the Ottoman period as a period of enslavement full of evil oppression. Since this was the last period in the history of the Church before everything radically changed in the twentieth century, it seems as if it should also be the most well understood period. However, this is not the case. Rather, it is perhaps one of the most misunderstood periods.

Within the archives, the libraries, and in the city of Istanbul itself, I discovered a truly dynamic Greek Orthodox world in the midst of the Ottoman Empire that had amazing brilliance, both in theological and intellectual activity, but also in supporting community institutions, schools, and churches that are unparalleled in the same period anywhere in the world, except perhaps Russia. From that moment, I set out to uncover that world.

This book is the result of that initial search as well as a later collective vision shared by a number of colleagues and friends who studied together in Princeton University's Department of Near Eastern Studies. Together we sought to confront the received wisdom about how the Ottomans ruled their subject populations and challenge entrenched historical conceptions. The open and supportive working environment allowed us to formulate our ideas and propose our plans to examine important aspects of the long-lasting, territorially large, multi-ethnic, multi-religious, and multi-racial Ottoman Empire. As a beneficiary of this open environment, I owe my primary debt of gratitude to the Department of Near Eastern Studies, and the Program in Hellenic Studies, that in this same spirit continue to provide combined support to graduate students. I am grateful to Heath W. Lowry who encouraged me even before I arrived at Princeton to see for its own sake the richness of the Ottoman world, and helped me grow confidant as an Ottomanist in search of continuity and change from the Byzantine period. His long experience in Ottoman studies helped me navigate through the conceptual as well as technical terrain. Molly Greene provided the example of how one can move seamlessly between Ottoman and Greek sources to arrive at a more genuine picture of Greeks in Ottoman society. Her command of the historiographical issues involved in this work also was invaluable for helping me formulate my own thoughts and ideas. I am also grateful to Norman Itzkowitz and Şükrü Hanioğlu who instilled in me a great appreciation for the richness of Ottoman administration and the administrative documents.

I would also like to acknowledge other colleagues and friends who made a tremendous impact on my approach to Ottoman history, whether in the broader theoretical formulations, or in its more concrete applications. My first true teacher of history, Stephen W. Reinert, not only set high standards for historical scholarship, but also was equally gracious to his students by keeping their interests at heart. I would never have imagined the present book without his genial encouragement to move into the post-Byzantine world. Rifa'at Abou-El-Haj challenged me always to consider larger issues of Ottoman social history when looking at specific events. Nejat Göyünç's mastery as an archivist and generosity as a teacher and friend gave me the confidence to approach the demands and intricacies of the Ottoman scripts. Elizabeth Zachariadou helped me narrow and define my questions through early conversations, and her vast scholarship continues to lead the way through difficult terrain. I am also appreciative of other influential and helpful colleagues including Rev. Dr. Demetrios J. Constantelos, Nenad Filipoviç, Dimitri Gondicas, Baki Tezcan, Christine Philliou, Mustafa Aksakal, Phillip Allen, Bob Crews, Macit Kenanoğlu, Abdelhafid Tbaili, Dimiter Angelov, Kostes Smyrlis, Shirine Hamadeh, Rev. Dr. N. M. Vaporis, Ilan Karmi, Vasilios Stavrides, Nikiforos Metaxas, and my colleagues of the Historical Studies Program of the Richard Stockton College of New Jersey. Each individual listed provided, at various points in this work, scholarly perspective, balance, expertise as well as friendship to encourage me to continue.

I am forever grateful to the directorship and staff of the Osmanlı Başbakanlık Arşivi in Istanbul, Turkey for granting full access to the rich collection of fifteenth and sixteenth century Ottoman documents. Their energy and interest in my project, made working in the archives a fruitful and pleasurable experience.

Special appreciation is directed to His All Holiness, Ecumenical Patriarch Bartholomew, and the members of the Holy Synod, who provided me with access to the archives and library of the Ecumenical Patriarchate in the Fener and the Halki Theological School Library on Heybeliada, in Istanbul. I am also grateful to the Chief Archivist, Fr. Nicholas Petropelis and the Librarian, Grand

Archimandrite Athenagoras as well as Mr. Yorgo Benlisoy, who extended their hospitality during my research.

I benefited greatly from the generous support of many different institutions that funded and facilitated my research and writing. I am grateful to the people of these institutions who were able to identify something of value in the project I set before them. My work was funded in part by the Social Science Research Council—Near and Middle East Fellowship, the American Research Institute in Turkey Dissertation Fellowship, as well as grants from the Princeton University Graduate School, the Program in Near Eastern Studies, and Program in Hellenic Studies. I was also the lucky beneficiary of a wonderful year in residence at the Dumbarton Oaks Research Library and Collection (Trustees of Harvard University) in Washington, DC. At the Richard Stockton College of New Jersey, I benefitted from the Research and Professional Development grant, as well as funding provided by the Constantine and Georgean Georgiou Endowed Professorship in Greek History of the Interdisciplinary Center for Hellenic Studies.

Finally, I would like to offer my deep gratitude to my family. My parents, brother, and sister constantly encouraged my research and writing, even when it challenged some of their most fundamental historical assumptions. Their example of academic excellence and care for my development continue to inspire me in my own work. I owe my greatest debt to my wife, Dorrie, who had the stamina and patience to endure what has been an arduous and lengthy process. She, and my two sons, George and Roman, have borne the adventures of this book, of living as academic nomads in Istanbul, New Jersey, Washington, DC, Michigan, and back to New Jersey, as well as the anguish and uncertainty that accompanies any creative enterprise. It is to Dorrie, George, and Roman that I dedicate this book.

I now have returned again to the Fener in Istanbul, years later, to complete this book. At the vespers of Feast of the Holy Transfiguration, high on a hilltop on the island of Heybeliada (Halki), His All Holiness Ecumenical Patriarch Bartholomew spoke about the small number of Rum (Greek Orthodox) remaining in Istanbul, remarking about the few who had gathered for the vespers. He went on to list many significant Greek Orthodox people, lay and clerics, who over the centuries had lived, worked, studied, and prayed in that very place. He explained that these people, some of whom are written about in the pages of this book, are present today, as they survive in the memory of the Church. Their presence, whether in the churches, as Ecumenical Patriarch Bartholomew explained, or in archives and historical accounts, continues to offer insight into how the Church transitioned from Byzantine to Ottoman rule. This, therefore, is the story that follows.

August 6, 2012
Feast of the Holy Transfiguration
Fener-Haliç (Golden Horn)

For Dorrie, George, and Roman

Contents

List of Figures and Tables xiii
Note on Transliteration and Place names xv

I. THEORETICAL AND HISTORICAL BACKGROUND

Introduction 3

1. The *Millet* System Revisited 19
2. İstimâlet, Ottoman Methods of Conquest, and the Greek Orthodox Church 63

II. THE PATRIARCHAL TAX FARM

3. The All-Holy Tax Farmer: The *İstanbul Rum Patriği* as *Mültezim* 107
4. Ottoman Tax Farming and the Greek Orthodox Church 139

III. CONTESTED POWER AND AUTHORITY

5. Competition and Corruption: Sultan, Patriarch, and Greek Elite 179
6. Conclusion: Continuity Beyond the Sixteenth Century 214

Glossary 221
Bibliography 223
Index 247

List of Figures and Tables

FIGURES

1.1. Contemporary mosaic of Sultan Mehmet II and the investiture of Patriarch Gennadios on display at the Ecumenical Patriarchate of Constantinople, Fener, Istanbul, Turkey 25

2.1. Ottoman Sultan Selim II (r.1566–1574) in procession 102

3.1. Courtyard of the Patriarchate of Constantinople at the Monastery of the Pammakaristos 118

4.1. The daily dress of the Patriarch of Constantinople and his court. 163

4.2. The daily dress of Greek Orthodox priests 164

4.3. Greek Orthodox metropolitans in liturgical vestments 170

4.4. Greek Orthodox Patriarch with villagers 170

5.1. The procession of the Great Entrance during the Greek Orthodox Divine Liturgy 183

5.2. The Greek Orthodox Christian brother of Alexander II, the Voivode of Wallachia, on horseback serving as an envoy (müteferrika) with a Turkish envoy on horseback 196

TABLES

4.1. Estimated Number of Households and Clergy in Patriarchal Jurisdiction 162

5.1. Mid-Sixteenth Century Patriarchs Supported by the Kantakouzenos family 204

Note on Transliteration and Place names

Foreign terms are italicized throughout the text. When transliterating Ottoman words, Turkish orthography is used. Greek words, whether Byzantine or modern, are transliterated according to the Library of Congress system. In cases of words well known in English, English spelling is preferred. English usage is also preferred for geographical names that are common in English, otherwise the Turkish place-names are used.

PART I

THEORETICAL AND HISTORICAL BACKGROUND

Introduction

The theologian may indulge the pleasing task of describing Religion as she descended from Heaven, arrayed in her native purity. A more melancholy duty is imposed on the historian. He must discover the inevitable mixture of error and corruption, which she contracted in a long residence upon earth, among a weak and degenerate race of beings.

Edward Gibbon, *Decline and Fall of the Roman Empire*

The institutions of Christianity, however divine their inspiration, have been ordered and governed by men and are affected by the temporal processes to which man is subject.

Stephen Runciman, *The Great Church in Captivity*

Standing beside a deep well, Patriarch Ioasaph, the Patriarch of Constantinople from 1464 to 1466, was about to jump in to kill himself. Undoubtedly running through his mind as he stood at the edge were thoughts of scandal, corruption, injustice, and unrestrained power. After he jumped, nearby Christians heard the loud splash and rushed to see what had happened. Reaching down to save him, they recovered the soaking wet bishop, who, they later realized, was the patriarch himself. Severely battered from his fall, Patriarch Ioasaph had swallowed enormous amounts of water, but with the tireless efforts of his doctors he recovered.[1]

Immense pressure and hopelessness weighed heavily on Patriarch Ioasaph's shoulders, enough to wish to sin against Church law forbidding suicide. The Greek sixteenth-century chronicler who recorded this event recounted that, by surviving, Ioasaph was fortunate to be spared "eternal hell-fire" even though his poor judgment might have actually led him to a certain and eternal damnation. Ioasaph was, after all, the Ecumenical Patriarch of Constantinople, the leading bishop of the Eastern Christian Church whose predecessors crowned, counseled, and sometimes chastized Byzantine emperors. Patriarch Ioasaph was the third bishop to hold this position after the conquest of Constantinople by the Ottomans

[1] Martin Crusius, ed., *Turco-Graeciae, Libri Octo* (Basle, 1584), 120–123. See also Immanuel Bekker, ed., *Historia politica et patriarchica Constantinopoleos: Epirotica,* Corpus Scriptorum Historiae Byzantinae (Bonn: Impensis Ed. Weberi, 1849), 95–101.

in 1453. Now with a sultan instead of an emperor in power, his position, role, and function in society had changed from when the Byzantines were in charge. How could things have become so difficult to have led Ioasaph to such an extreme act?

Moments such as this, considered by European and Balkan historians, have traditionally been read within the context of an Ottoman "Dark Ages" that included the enslavement of the Greek Orthodox Christians by the Ottomans.[2] This enslavement, it is alleged, began with the earliest Ottoman conquests, lasted for over 400 years, and ended in national liberation in the nineteenth and twentieth centuries. For the Greeks this meant an independent modern state in 1830, for the Serbs in 1848, for Bulgaria in 1878, and for Albania as late as 1919. The legacy of Ottoman rule, however, remains strong in each of these societies. Before historical revisionism transformed Ottoman historiography, the standard interpretation by nationalist historians, therefore, placed all unsavory events within a dichotomous interpretive framework that sees only good and evil, honesty and corruption, or integrity and deceitfulness. They concluded that people only acted immorally because they were under the duress of Ottoman oppression, and the "Turks" were completely to blame for this state of affairs. Patriarch Ioasaph, for example, was clearly subjected to wickedness out of his control, which he sought to end, if by killing himself. Although there is a sense that there were strong political and social forces pushing and pulling Ioasaph to his fate, the entire period takes on the gloomy disposition of "captivity" and "slavery."

The classic work dealing with the Church under Ottoman rule is Sir Steven Runciman's *The Great Church in Captivity: A Study of the Patriarchate of Constantinople from the Eve of the Turkish Conquest to the Greek War of Independence.* In the first lines of this book, Runciman announced, "of all the roads that a historian may tread none passes through more difficult country than that of a religious historian."[3] He declared this caveat less to shield himself from readers' possible reproach and more as a warning to himself as a historian who must deal with the prickly subject of Greek Christians under Ottoman rule. Through his long experience studying the Byzantine world, he knew well the difficulty of characterizing the Eastern Christian tradition with the precision one might expect from examining the Western Church. He understood that writing a history of the Eastern Church requires more than empirical knowledge. To make it comprehensible to a wider non-Orthodox Christian audience, he felt it required an intuitive gift and awareness of a Church that allowed for "tolerance and elasticity" and overlooked or even condoned "minor errors in belief or liturgical practice and minor breaches in canonical correctitude ... for the greater good of Christendom."[4]

Even with these challenges to understanding the Eastern Church, Runciman focused his attention on the Great Church of Christ, the center of which was the patriarchal see of Constantinople, the spiritual center of the Byzantine world. For

[2] Maria Todorova, "Ottoman Legacy in the Balkans," in *Imperial Legacy: The Ottoman Imprint on the Balkans and the Middle East*, ed. L. C. Brown (New York: Columbia University Press, 1996), 71.

[3] Steven Runciman, *The Great Church in Captivity* (Cambridge: Cambridge University Press, 1968), 3.

[4] Runciman, *Great Church in Captivity*, 5.

Runciman, the Great Church of Christ survived "in captivity" during the period of Ottoman rule. The sympathy with which Runciman dealt with the Greek Christian community and Church from the eve of the Turkish conquests, demonstrates his intimate awareness and deep connection with the subject. Historian Peter Brown explained in his review of *The Great Church in Captivity* that "one can always blame the Turks and with good reason. But the terms on which a religion survives in a hostile environment depends, also, on what the religion itself can offer in the daily life of men in hard times."[5] With this in mind, we turn again to Ioasaph to ask why he was desperate to drown himself. As a hierarch and as a man, perhaps Patriarch Ioasaph doubted what his own religion could offer as he faced extremely hard times. What, after all, could his Church offer Christians like himself who lived under the stress of Ottoman religious, social, political, and cultural domination?

Considered by his peers a peaceful man who abhorred scandals, Patriarch Ioasaph was thought to be a just man worthy to sit on the patriarchal throne. The local clergy who served under him, however, were reported to have behaved disgracefully, and unbefitting of clergy, dishonoring both the Church and Ioasaph. As he grew weary and could no longer bear the pressure, he decided that his only solution was to kill himself. While we may not be told directly by the chronicler what unseemly behavior Ioasaph's clergy engaged in, we are told elsewhere, and multiple times, about the brokering of power, of office buying and selling, and ultimately, about the abuse of influence and authority.

The setting for these events in Constantinople was a society that experienced a dramatic social rupture; a population distressed by conquest and dislocation following the conquest of the city. It was a society that had been overcome by new rulers, and changed from Byzantine Christian leaders to Ottoman Muslim masters. This conquest created a new reality that required adjustment to a new social and political order. Patriarchs, bishops, priests, and deacons had to face a new set of social and political rules.

Part of Patriarch Ioasaph's problem was in accepting this new reality. His disappointment and disillusionment came not at the hands of the "Turks," but from important members of the Greek community who were powerful within Greek circles, but also had enormous influence among the Ottoman authorities. The one with whom Patriarch Ioasaph had to contend was the former chief minister (*Protovestiarios*) of the Komnenian Emperor of Trebizond, George Amiroutzes.[6] Amiroutzes was charged with inviting the Ottomans to attack Trebizond, the city on the Black Sea that held out and remained unvanquished until 1462, convincing the Emperor David Komnenos to surrender. Clearly of noble Byzantine lineage, Amiroutzes was

[5] Peter Brown, "Review of the Great Church in Captivity: a Study of the Patriarchate of Constantinople from the Eve of the Turkish Conquest to the Greek War of Independence, by Steven Runciman," in his *Religion and Society in the Age of St. Augustine* (London: Faber and Faber, 1972), 155.

[6] Alice Mary Talbot, "Amiroutzes, George," *The Oxford Dictionary of Byzantium* (New York: Oxford University Press, 1991) I, 77–78. *Protovestiarios* was originally the Keeper of the Imperial Wardrobe, but the office later took on the role as a chief minister. See A. Kazhdan, "Protovestiarios," *The Oxford Dictionary of Byzantium*, III, 1749.

the cousin of the Ottoman Grand Vizier Mahmud Pasha (1456–68 and 1472–74) also of noble lineage, of the Angelović family.[7] Mahmud Pasha was brought into Ottoman service via the child-levy (*devşirme*), ultimately serving Sultan Mehmet II and accompanying him on many campaigns. Amiroutzes settled in Constantinople and immediately immersed himself in the life and intrigues of the Greek community as he became acquainted with the Ottoman court. He became very powerful due to his intimate Ottoman connections.

As with many stories of power, intrigue, and conflict, the conflict between Amiroutzes and Patriarch Ioasaph was personal. Amiroutzes, a married man, had fallen in love with the widow of Franco II Acciajuoli, the last Duke of Athens. She had been captured in the Ottoman conquest of Athens and brought to Constantinople. Amiroutzes relied on his cousin Mahmud Pasha's influence to gain possession of her and marry her. The problem was that he was already married with children. It was forbidden by the Church to engage in a forbidden union, to divorce one's wife, and abandon one's children. Nevertheless, Amiroutzes sent his wife and children away. Patriarch Ioasaph responded by vehemently opposing Amiroutzes' actions. In response, Amiroutzes tried to offer the Grand Sacristan (*Megas Ekklesiarches*), the patriarch's assistant, secret gifts in order to influence him; but was refused. Having no alternative, Amiroutzes, once again, enlisted the aid of Mahmud Pasha to influence the patriarch's opinion more forcefully. On Amiroutzes' bidding, Mahmud Pasha "acted like the sultan and cut the Patriarch's beard and sliced the Great Ecclesiarch's nose on both sides."[8] Through Mahmud Pasha, Amiroutzes bullied the churchmen to get his way, thereby exploiting the power of the Ottoman court. Amiroutzes eventually did get his way as he violated Canon Law, disposed of his wife and children and married the widow, ultimately with the sanction of the Church.

This incident, which is recounted by the patriarchal chronicles, details an extremely challenging moment in the life of one of the post-conquest patriarchs. As with other moral lessons recounted by chronicles, divine retribution repays evil deeds. The chronicle inserts the account of Amiroutzes' death. Amiroutzes one day was sitting in the midst of other leading men of Greek society (*archons*), and while he was playing dice, "He stretched out his hand to grab the dice and throw them. And when he stretched out his hand, he died right there, wildly and fearfully grinding his teeth."[9] From the standpoint of the chronicle, and of Patriarch Ioasaph, God repaid his great tormentor with just retribution.

Typically, a story like Ioasaph's, where violence is vividly perpetrated by Ottomans on Greek Christians, has led historians to focus either on individual morality stories, or on ethnic or religious oppression. Accepting the testimony of chroniclers at face value as Runciman and others who write about this subject

[7] Theoharis Stavrides, *The Sultan of Vezirs: The Life and Times of the Ottoman Grand Vezir Mahmud Pasha Angelović (1453–1474)* (Leiden: E. J. Brill, 2001), 86–90.

[8] *Historia Patriarchica*, ed. Bekker, 98. On the sources of this relationship see Stavrides, *Sultan of Vezirs*, 88–89, n. 70.

[9] *Historia Patriarchica*, ed. Bekker, 100.

do, leads to writing about the "dark period" where cases of scandal, intrigue, corruption, and unrestrained power influence peoples' behavior. From this perspective, the religious history of this period would result in a listing of bishops behaving badly, and lay people making power plays for influence in the Church. This type of analysis is extremely limiting, as the "dark period" filter colors each event and each incident.

Apostolos Vakalopoulos, the foremost Greek national historian of late Byzantine and post-Byzantine Greece, chose this approach and cited the example of Amiroutzes and his retinue rising to power as the moment when corruption, abuse of power, and cooptation of Greeks by Turks became dominant. The rise of these émigrés from Trebizond seems to have insulted Vakalopoulos' Greek national sensibilities because they represented a faction of Greeks who turned on their fellow co-religionists by using their deep connections to the Ottoman Imperial Court. The faction from Trebizond not only became the object of deep suspicion for being ethnic traitors but it also set a tone for corruption among the rest of the Greek community of Constantinople and throughout the Ottoman lands. Yet, even as Vakalopoulos cast a wider gaze to blame an entire social group rather than a few unsavory individuals as the root cause for corruption, he still focused on individuals behaving poorly having been ensnared by Ottoman malevolence.

According to the chronicles, Ioasaph was apparently a helpless figure, and Amiroutzes was notorious, to be sure. However, this vignette raises precisely the question of what authority the chief bishop of the Church, the patriarch, has among his co-religionists in the Ottoman period. Whether spiritual or temporal, what power, in fact, was at his disposal? As for Amiroutzes, this individual came to represent Greek Orthodox subjects of the Ottoman Empire who were so entwined with the Ottoman ruling class as to wield real coercive power among his co-religionists. Moving beyond the individual stories or personal histories of unscrupulous men to a broader social historical analysis allows us to view the transformations in society itself, from a Byzantine to an Ottoman social and cultural world.

This example of Patriarch Ioasaph raises some important issues for the historian. It is difficult to write the history of the Church in the Ottoman period largely because of its multi-dimensional and dynamic quality. There are many difficulties that the Church, and churchmen face. However, the question for the historian is whether to write a history about men who act poorly because of their bad character, taking the patriarchal chronicles at their word, or to use these and other examples as a window into the nature of Ottoman power and authority dispensed among Ottomans and non-Muslims.

By examining these moments of interaction between the Church and the Ottoman state, one can move beyond the standard motif of seeing the history of the Church in the Ottoman period as the history of a small, conquered, oppressed, insulated Greek community in Ottoman society. The tendency has been to focus on the Church in a vacuum or as an insulated institution, set apart from the rest of Ottoman society. It is abundantly clear that this view limits our understanding of the history of this period. By placing the Church within the broader context of Ottoman society, within the broader context of expansion and the development of state control over local populations and institutions, the seemingly petty conflicts gain significantly more meaning.[10]

Placing the Church in the larger social context raises other important issues as well. The Church played a varied but mostly important social role in the life of the Christian communities from the late Roman, and medieval Byzantine period to the Late Byzantine period, throughout all periods of Ottoman rule and into the modern era. The relationship between the Church and the state goes back to the New Testament itself, where in the Gospel of Matthew certain Pharisees asked Jesus Christ whether it was lawful, according to God, to submit to earthly authority and to pay taxes to Caesar. Christ answered that one must "render unto Caesar that which is Caesar's and unto God that which is God's" (Matthew 22:21). Jesus Christ's answer separated the earthly from the heavenly dominion, and has subsequently set the standard for the way in which Christians are supposed to behave in society, especially in a state governed by those who do not maintain the same beliefs. When standing trial before Pilate, Christ proclaimed, "My Kingdom is not of this world" (John 18:36), signifying the distance between the earthly and the heavenly dominions. The Apostle Paul goes a step further to recognize that it is God who grants power to the state, inasmuch as it serves the good (Romans 13:1–7). Later, the author of the book of Revelation condemns Rome, the political center of the empire, which became the new "Babylon" (Revelations 18) and deserved to be cursed and destroyed.

The dynamic and dialectical approach to power and authority in Church–state relations took a remarkable turn in the fourth century when the Emperor Constantine not only ceased to prosecute the Church but also, in fact, became the protector of the Church.[11] In line with earlier Christian apologists, including Origen, interpreters of the Christianization of empire saw that it was divine providence that created a unity of humanity, "making possible the uniting and universal preaching of the Gospel" within an earthly empire.[12] This understanding was tied to the idea that God granted the king his power.

Within Late Antiquity and all periods of the Byzantine Empire, the relationship between the Church and emperor varied according to the religious and political realities and interests of the day. Twentieth-century Church historian and theologian Georges Florovsky stated the Byzantine system had been "derogatorily labeled as 'Caesaropapism' with the assumption that the Emperor was the actual ruler of the Church, even if he was never formally acknowledged as her head." Emperor Justinian understood the close cooperation between the patriarch and

[10] Among the many reviews praising Runciman's work, historian Cyrial Mango critiqued it for doing precisely this. See Cyril Mango, "Review of *The Great Church in Captivity: A Study of the Patriarchate of Constantinople from the Eve of the Turkish Conquest to the Greek War of Independence* by Steven Runciman," *The American Historical Review* 74/5 (June 1969): 1576–1578.

[11] John Meyendorff, *Imperial Unity and Christian Divisions: The Church, 450-680 AD* (Crestwood, NY: St. Vladimir's Seminary Press, 1989), 29.

[12] Meyendorff, *Imperial Unity*, 29.

the emperor explaining that there were two ministries that derived from God and that served the Christian commonwealth, the priesthood (*hierosyne*) and the imperium (*basileia*). The preface to Justinian's Sixth Novel in AD 535 states, "the former is concerned with things divine; the latter presides over the human affairs and takes care of them. Proceeding from the same source, both adorn human life."[13] The Church is not subjected to the state. Rather, both Church and state are subject to divine will, and because of this, there is a harmonious symbiosis.

A few centuries later, Patriarch Photios the Great (856–867 and 877–886) echoed this ideal in his revision of Emperor Basil I's collection of laws, the *Epanagoge*, that dealt with the emperor and patriarch. He wrote,

> As the constitution of the state consists, like man, of parts and members, the greatest and most necessary parts are the emperor and the patriarch. Wherefore the peace and felicity of subjects in body and soul depend upon the agreement and concord in all things.[14]

Another example is Emperor John Tzimiskes (r. 969–976) who said, "I acknowledge two powers in this life: the priesthood and the empire; the one entrusted by the Creator with the care of souls, and the other with the government of bodies. If neither part is damaged, the well-being of the world is secure."[15] It is safe to say that during most of the Byzantine period there was an idealistic view of the relationship between the emperor and the patriarch, or of state and Church. At times identified as *symphonia,* or harmony, between the state and Church, it was a pattern that was set forth during Constantine's reign, and which became part of the Byzantine political tradition.

According to Orthodox ecclesiological terms, each legitimately elected bishop formed the foundation of the local Church and was, in a sense, its master. The hierarchical structure that developed according to the Byzantine imperial model had raised the Patriarchate of Constantinople to imperial heights. While Byzantine tradition maintained that the Church was under the stewardship of the emperor, it also created significant prestige for the patriarch, who then became a component part of the state structure. In this formulation, Church and state had a synergistic relationship, which means that the Church espoused civil legal principles as well as administrative and judicial duties with the state. The highly centralized Church in Constantinople was mostly supported by the emperors, who realized the advantage of working through this institution.[16]

This Byzantine *symphonia* between Church and state continued in theory as well as in practice until the rise of the Ottomans. This book deals with this

[13] Georges Florovsky, *Christianity and Culture* (Belmont, MA: Nordland, 1974), 77–78.

[14] D. Nicol, "Byzantine Political Thought," in *The Cambridge History of Medieval Political Thought C.350-c.1450,* ed. J. H. Burns (Cambridge: Cambridge University Press, 1991), 69.

[15] Nicol, Byzantine Political Thought, 69.

[16] Speros Vryonis, Jr., *The Decline of Medieval Hellenism in Asia Minor and the Process of Islamization from the Eleventh through the Fifteenth Century* (Los Angeles: University of California Press, 1971), 198. The issue of a centralized Byzantine imperial Church based in Constantinople contrasts with the highly decentralized Church of the late Byzantine and early Ottoman period that Vryonis describes.

Church–state relationship by examining the important period of Ottoman rule (*Tourkokratia*), focusing on the interaction between the Ottoman state and the hierarchy of the Greek Orthodox Church from the fourteenth to the sixteenth centuries. The Church undergoes a transformation from a religious and cultural institution sponsored by Byzantine state to an institution exploited by the Ottoman state primarily for financial gain. This book argues that the fiscal relationships established when the Ottomans first came to power continued well into the sixteenth and seventeenth centuries. These relationships and established patterns of interaction between the Church and the Ottoman state remain the touchstone that gives meaning and significance to many events in the life of the Greek community in Ottoman society until the Tanzimat period (1839–1876).

As society changes over time, so does the role and function of its institutions. In order to understand the importance of an institution such as the Ottoman period Greek Orthodox Church, it is critical to come to terms with its social context. By fighting the tendency to focus on the perspective of the conquered, or the spiritual mission of the Church, and instead observe the Church as the Ottomans saw it, and within the Ottoman social, economic, and political context, one may begin to understand its significance for contemporaries. Seeing the Church through Ottoman eyes also leads to questioning established assumptions, such as the theory of the Ottoman *millet* system, the Ottoman system of governing non-Muslims through their religious leaders and institutions.

Yet, when dealing with the Ecumenical Patriarchate of Constantinople, an institution that champions its continuity to the present day, it is tempting to disregard social change over time and rest upon visions of anachronism. On the east entry wall of the Ecumenical Patriarchate of Constantinople in Istanbul is a modern mosaic featuring the Ottoman Sultan Mehmet II, conqueror of Constantinople, and the Patriarch Gennadios Scholarios, the first patriarch invested following the conquest of the city in 1453. The image shows Sultan Mehmet II offering a document promising Patriarch Gennadios all the privileges of preceding patriarchs. For the patriarchate and historians alike, this moment captured in stone represents the establishment of the *millet* system, a system wherein the Church governed as a state within a state, with the patriarch serving as the communal leader (*millet başı*) or *ethnarch*. The *millet* system became the dominant paradigm employed to describe non-Muslims under Ottomans rule. This powerful mosaic, and its counterpart on the opposite wall depicting the Apostle Andrew and his disciple Stachys, the first bishop of ancient Byzantion, was commissioned in the late 1980s. They dramatically remind those who enter that the Patriarchate of Constantinople possesses ancient authority and prerogatives from Apostolic times, authority that was confirmed by none other than the conquering Sultan Mehmet II. The mosaic announces the patriarchate's authority as the legitimate leader of the Greek *millet* of the Ottoman Empire. The implication is that this authority must continue uncontested to the present.

However, when one considers that the story of Patriarch Ioasaph occurred less than fifteen years after this episode of Sultan Mehmet II and Patriarch

Gennadios, the question that is central of the present work becomes clear: what authority does the chief bishop of the church, the patriarch, have in a society that experienced a dramatic social rupture and whose rulers changed from Byzantine Christian rulers to Ottoman Muslim masters? At a time when the Pope of Rome was commanding armies and inquisitions, and leading massive public works projects, the Patriarch of Constantinople was, perhaps, at his weakest, struggling with lay people making demands, besieged by disobedient priests, and contending with and often resorting to the absolute coercive power of the state.

The dominant paradigm of the *millet* system articulated most fully in Gibb and Bowen's *Islamic Society and the West* has been attacked and partially dismantled by Ottoman historians beginning with Benjamin Braude in his article "Foundation Myths of the *Millet* System."[17] Braude attacked the problem of the *millet* system philologically by arguing that the term *millet* does not appear in administrative contexts until the mid-nineteenth century. He argued that the notion of the *millet* system, in reality, "originated through a combination of myths" that developed well after the Ottoman conquest of Constantinople, and certainly not in the immediate aftermath of 1453. For lack of an alternative, Braude's article has become the standard reference for those historians wishing to jettison the *millet* system. *Render Unto the Sultan* attempts to fill this gap. Not only does it argue against using the concept of the *millet* system to describe the Church's role in early Ottoman society, but also it offers an alternative account of Church–state relations under Ottoman rule.

Based on documents from the Ottoman Archives, the Ecumenical Patriarchate, Greek chronicles, German travelers, and other contemporary sources, this work begins by reconsidering the *millet* system paradigm and identifies the work upon which anachronistic interpretation has depended. Offering an overview of the historiographical issues and the approaches of various scholars working on cross-confessional relations in empire and the *millet* system in particular, the present study may be of use to scholars in the field as well as to newcomers. The reality argued in this book, that the Ottoman state considered the Greek Orthodox ecclesiastical hierarchy primarily as tax farmers (*mültezim*) for cash income derived from the Church's widespread holdings rather than as community leaders, did not emerge in a vacuum. Rather, there is clearly a broad historical context, and long process of historical development that resulted in this state of affairs. The Turkish conquests of Asia Minor from the eleventh to fifteenth centuries contributed to the new realities faced by local churches and bishops. The harsh reaction of the synod of bishops in Constantinople recorded in the Synodal Acta recognize and condemn practices of local negotiation and accommodation by

[17] H. A. R. Gibb and H. Bowen, *Islamic Society and the West: A Study of the Impact of Western Civilization on Moslem Culture in the near East by Sir Hamilton Gibb and Harold Bowen* (London and New York: Oxford University Press, 1967); and Benjamin Braude, "Foundation Myths of the Millet System," in *Christians and Jews in the Ottoman Empire: The Functioning of a Plural Society*, ed. Benjamin Braude and Bernard Lewis (New York: Holmes and Meier, 1982), 69.

local bishops during this period, revealing patterns that continue into sixteenth- and even seventeenth-century Ottoman society.

Through the fascinating and colorful examples taken directly from the Ottoman Archives, one may see how the Ottoman state engaged individuals to take their positions as hierarchs at the cost of yearly payments to the state. The involvement of members of the Greek economic elite in the financial affairs of the Church led to interesting, if not tense, sessions before the Imperial Divan, appealing directly to the sultan's power. The hierarchical positions, like tax farming appointments, became subject to the same forces of financial competition that other Ottoman administrative offices faced. As in the Ottoman Muslim administrative world, Christian hierarchs and laymen alike appealed directly to the sultan for justice. With hierarchs as tax farmers in the throes of competition against other members of the Greek community, it is clear that the *millet* system paradigm does not sufficiently explain the non-Muslim realities in the Ottoman Empire. In this story, patriarchs are challenged by their subordinate bishops, and priests, as well as by lay people, that include wealthy merchants and ordinary villagers. Sometimes bishops happily rub shoulders with Grand Viziers on official business and at other times they frantically try to avoid Ottoman officials and their scrutiny, indicating the complex nature of the relationship of the Greek Orthodox hierarchy and the Ottoman state.

What does this new interpretation—of the Church as an Ottoman tax farm—do to our understanding of how the Ottomans administered the non-Muslim communities and, in particular, the Greek community? What is the origin of this fiscal system, if it was, in fact, a system? Did the Church rule over Christians in any significant way besides fiscally? For instance, what is the relationship of the Patriarch of Constantinople to the local bishops and the members of the local village churches either in the Balkans or in Anatolia? Since the *millet* system has been the standard paradigm describing the Greek community under Ottoman rule, it has been fairly simple to describe the social and political organization of the Greek community in the Ottoman Empire. The typical descriptions of the Greek community shows a relatively uniform, unified community of Greek Orthodox subjects who are governed through the Church. However, this new interpretation presents a more fractured picture of the "*Greek community*" and its leaders. It appears that the Ottoman state is not so concerned with ruling one singular Greek Orthodox *millet* through its leader, but instead is comfortable working through multiple leaders of local Greek Orthodox communities, often in an *ad hoc* manner, and based upon the practices established even before the Ottomans came to power.

The question of the make-up of the Greek community can only be answered after coming to terms, first, with how the Church functioned under Ottoman rule. Complex, multi-faceted dimensions of personal and communal interests emerge from local Greek Orthodox villagers, mid-level clerics, wealthy Greek elites, patriarchs and even sultans. There are also many obstacles to this reconceptualization, ranging from nationalist ideology, orientalist essentialism, religious anachronism, and populist nostalgia. Liberating the past from the concerns of the present is especially challenging because such thick layers of interpretation that must be overcome have colored the history of Greek Orthodox people in Ottoman society. Perhaps the most important of these is Balkan national historiography. Just as the Greek Orthodox church under Ottoman rule is considered a "dark period" marked by capricious rule, and rife with human wickedness inspired by Turkish Muslim oppressors, the *millet* system is raised up as proto-nationalist religio-ethnic organization promoting national independence.[18] This has made the *millet* system a useful tool within a faulty framework. This is true especially in the Greek Orthodox case, because of the prominence in this story of the Greek Orthodox Patriarchate of Constantinople.

In addition to the Balkan nationalist framework, historians, especially of the West, face an additional challenge when considering the Ottoman Empire: *orientalism*. According to Edward Said's formulation, Western historians have interpreted the Ottoman Empire as an "Islamic" state whose social organization, and administrative characteristics were frozen in time. Islamic societies were thus, essentialized as the "other," having been determined by their Islamic religious and legal culture.[19] In response to this challenge, *Render Unto the Sultan* argues against seeing the Ottoman state as a theocratic, Sharia bound "Islamic" state, and instead considers the Ottoman Empire as a pragmatic state that grew in its early centuries by absorbing established local practice into administrative forms even as they contravened Islamic law. By adopting and institutionalizing local (Byzantine) forms, the Ottomans sought to exploit fiscal opportunity with as little disruption to the local administrative mechanisms as possible, regardless of the social, confessional or ethnic background of their subjects.[20]

This tendency to make essentialist assumptions about the Islamic nature of the Ottoman state is sometimes repeated when dealing with the non-Muslim religious institutions. Thus, when considering the Greek Orthodox Church in the Ottoman Empire it is equally important not to make problematic assumptions about a monolithic religiously bound Greek community. Rather, in the case of

[18] Slavica Jakelić, *Collectivistic Religions: Religion, Choice, and Identity in Late Modernity* (Farnham: Ashgate, 2010), 150–151. In the famous 1962 *Slavic Review* debate by Stanford Shaw and Wayne Vucinich, Shaw argued that the *millet* system provided for the non-Muslim communities to maintain their own laws, customs, traditions, and languages, and therefore allowed them to develop national consciousness. See S. Shaw, "The Aims and Achievements of Ottoman Rule in the Balkans," *Slavic Review* 21 (1962): 618. For Vucinich's initial article see W. S. Vucinich, "The Nature of Balkan Society under Ottoman Rule," *Slavic Review* 21/4 (1962): 616–622. He also offers a reply to Shaw, "Reply," *Slavic Review* 21 (1962): 633–638.

[19] E. W. Said, *Orientalism* (New York: Vintage Books, 1978). For the Balkanism which steps beyond orientalism by including not only Muslims, but Orthodox Christians, in the repository of negative characteristics, see M. N. Todorova, *Imagining the Balkans* (New York: Oxford University Press, 1997), 188.

[20] S. Vryonis, "The Byzantine Legacy and Ottoman Forms," in *Byzantina Kai Metabyzantina: Studies on Byzantium, Seljuks, and Ottoman*, ed. S. Vryonis (Malibu: Undina Press, 1982), xiii; J. C. Alexander, *Toward a History of Post-Byzantine Greece: The Ottoman Kanunnames for the Greek Lands, Circa 1500-circa 1600* (Athens, Greece: 1985). Anthony Bryer and Heath W. Lowry, in *Continuity and Change in Late Byzantine and Early Ottoman Society* (Birmingham and Washington D.C.: University of Birmingham and Dumbarton Oaks, 1986).

this book, the confessional communities, with their institutions and constituent members are considered on their own account, and then placed within the broader economic and social context of Ottoman society. This approach moves beyond the traditional historiographical motif of Islamic rule over an oppressed Christian community, and looks at the roles that economics and political interests play in reconstructing the history of Greek Orthodox subjects and their institutions in the Ottoman Empire.[21]

Because modern historians have attempted to identify the post-conquest Greek Orthodox hierarchy as the civil as well as religious leaders of the Greek Orthodox community within the Ottoman system of administration, previous scholarship has focused on the investiture of the Ecumenical Patriarch Gennadios by Sultan Mehmet II the Conqueror in 1454 as the galvanizing moment in the relations between the church and state. This moment is considered the establishment of the patriarch as a civil authority over the Greek Orthodox subjects of the Ottoman Empire. It is important, however, not to place too much emphasis on this one moment as the entire characterization of interaction between the Ottoman state and the Church. This book, therefore, aims to create a more contoured and contextual picture of the established norms of state and church relations beginning in the fourteenth century and extending to the end of the sixteenth century.

Chapter 1 explores the very concept of the *millet* system and demonstrates the manner in which the historiography of non-Muslim confessional groups has been victim to anachronistic analysis. This chapter opens by focusing on the episode of Sultan Mehmet II's installation of George Scholarios as Patriarch Gennadios Scholarios. It considers the alternatives to the traditional narrative, to the Ottoman establishment of Patriarch Gennadios as ethnarch. Additionally, this chapter examines previous conclusions about patriarchal authority and the Greek *millet* system and explains the importance of M. D'Ohsson's introduction of a 1798 document translated and published in his *Tableau Générale de l'Empire Ottoman*. D'Ohsson's presentation became the foundation of historical explanations of the *millet* system, by offering a vision of patriarchal power over the community for all periods. This chapter also examines the new directions in which contemporary historians are moving the discussion of the *millet* system.

Chapter 2, "*İstimâlet*, Ottoman Methods of Conquest, and the Greek Orthodox Church," addresses Ottoman methods of conquest as they relate to the Church in the late Byzantine and early Ottoman period. At the heart of this exploration is the question of cooperation of local bishops with local Turkmen emirs in Anatolia during the period of Turkmen emirates. This chapter concludes that the new rulers based their relationship with local bishops on exploiting local ecclesiastical revenues, and that the bishops demonstrated a practical self-preservation response

[21] P. Wittek, *The Rise of the Ottoman Empire*, (London: The Royal Asiatic Society of Great Britain and Ireland, 1938). Bat Yeor, *The Decline of Eastern Christianity Under Islam: From Jihad to Dhimmitude* (Madison, NJ: Fairleigh Dickinson University Press, 1996); and Anton Minkov, *Conversion to Islam in the Balkans: Kisve Bahas Petitions and Ottoman Social Life, 1670–1730* (Leiden: E. J. Brill, 2004), 20.

in adjusting to the new order, setting a pattern that would continue into the sixteenth century. The chapter opens with a discussion of the testimony of Gregory Palamas, the Archbishop of Thessalonike (1347–60) who provides an important window from which to view the relationship between the early Ottomans and the Greek Orthodox during the mid-fourteenth century.[22] As one of the first written testimonies about the Ottomans by a Byzantine source, Palamas gave important details about Church and society under Ottoman rule.[23] This chapter also reconsiders the complaints against local bishops by the patriarchal synod in light of the new political and social context. A key source for this discussion is the collection of *Patriarchal Synodal Acta*, the minutes of the council of the highest-ranking bishops in the Church, which reveal the resistance of local prelates to the demands of the imperial Church of Constantinople.[24]

Beginning with Chapter 3, Part II of this book examines the economic function of the Greek Orthodox Church hierarchy in the Ottoman imperial system. Ottoman state documents show that the state considered the Greek Orthodox ecclesiastical hierarchs to be not so much leaders of a semi-autonomous community with civil and ecclesiastical authority as tax farmers (*mültezim*) for income derived from ecclesiastical properties and services. As a tax farm (*iltizam*), the terms of office display the general characteristics of other Ottoman tax farms. This examination is conducted *via* a close reading of fourteen documents from *Kepeci Tasnifi Divani Hümayun Ahkâm Defteri* 62 from the Ottoman Archives of the Prime Minister (*Osmanlı Başbakanlık Arşivi)* from the year 1544. This *defter* recorded decrees (*berât*) for the right to collect the tax (*mal-i miri*) for the imperial treasury (*hazine-i 'amir*) issued to bishops upon their petition to the sultan during the reigns of Sultan Süleyman I and Patriarch Jeremias I. This chapter explores the administrative activities of the Imperial Divan and the petitions from the hierarchy for positions, justice, and coercive power. The social dimension of competition among interest groups illuminates the fiscal arrangements by connecting the internal Greek communal context to the broader Ottoman social context.

For a more intensive view into how this relationship between the state and the Church worked, we are able to explore one *defter* over a period of eight months in order to get a sense of the frequency with which the hierarchs approached the Imperial Divan (*Divan-i Hümâyûn*), who some of the figures

22 George Arnakis, "Gregory Palamas among the Turks," in *Speculum* (1952), 104–162. Also see George Arnakis, *Oi Protoi Othomanoi*, ed. Nikos A. Bees, vol. 41, *Texte Und Forschungen zur Byzantinisch-neugriechishen Philologie* (Athens, Greece: 1947).

23 Anna Philippidis-Braat, "La Captivité De Palamas Chez Les Turcs: dossier et commentaire," in *Travaux et Memoires* 7 (1979), 167–185.

24 The *Patriarchal Acta* were preserved by Ogier Ghiselin De Busbeque who was the Imperial Ambassador at Constantinople between 1554 and 1562. For the earliest edition, see F. Miklosich and J. Müller, *Acta et diplomata medii aevi sacra et profana*, 6 vols. Vienna, 1860–90. The latest edition to supercede this covers the years 1315–50 and is accompanied by a German translation: H. Hunger and O. Kresten, eds., *Das Register des Patriarchs von Konstantinopel* (Corpus Fontium Historiae Byzantinae) XIX (Vienna, 1982, 1995). A very useful reference to the Patriarchal Acta for this period is by Jean Darrouzes, ed., *Les Regestes des Actes du Patriarcat de Constantinople*, vol. 1: Les Actes Des Patriarches Fasc. I–VII, *Le Patriarcat Byzantin* (Paris: Institut Francais D'Etudes Byzantines, 1991).

were, and what were their concerns. The *Ahkâm Defteri* 62 covers the year H. 951 (AD 1544–45) and gives copies (sometimes incomplete) of *berâts* and *hüküms* issued to bishops petitioning the Porte. The *Ahkâm defters*, in general, record judicial judgments, including decrees, laws and regulations, issued from the Imperial Divan. In this process, a petition was made to the Divan, and, after a decision was made, a *ferman* or *berât* was issued to an individual, while a copy of the decree was sent out to the administrative unit of the local region informing them of the Imperial decision. These preserved documents offer the opportunity to consider the relationship between the state and church over a significant period of time.

Complementing the Ottoman archival material are chronicles detailing Greek Orthodox patriarchal history. The best-known chronicle that represents the genre is the *Historia Patriarchica Constantinopoleos*, a chronological history of patriarchs from 1453 to 1578, which is found in the form of a text published by Martin Crusius as related to him by Manuel Malaxos.[25] As the scholar of modern Greek literature, Börje Knös, explains in his *L'Histoire de la littérature néo-grecque*, Malaxos was originally from Nauplion and abandoned his hometown after its conquest by the Ottomans in 1540. He undertook notarial duties for the Metropolitan of Thebes. In 1577, Malaxos went to Constantinople, where he became a professor and calligrapher of manuscripts. Most likely, Malaxos used earlier chronicles of Damaskenos the Stoudite to produce this work. He himself wrote a still unedited *Livre Chronologique*, which covers history from the Creation to his own time. As is obvious from reading the *Historia Patriarchica*, the language used is a popular form of Greek, and it is full of colorful anecdotes.[26] The historical importance of this source, however, is that it forms the basis of the

[25] *Historia Patriarchica*, ed. Bekker. The same text is also found in the following editions, M. Crusius, *Turcograecia*, Basiliae, 1584, 107. ff. and C. Sathas, *Mesaionike Vivliotheke*, vol. 3. In the text, the note under the title reads as follows, "Concerning the patriarchs who served in this catholic great Church of Constantine's city after the Sultan Mehmet received it and what things they did in their respective times, and who was the first to give the so-called *peskesion* and the *haratzion* to him, and who increased it, to the point where it exists until today, and in whose sultan's times these things occured. These things were told by me in a common expression by Manuel Malaxos of the Peloponessos to Lord Martin Crusius in the year 1578 in the month of April," 78. The detailed bibliographic note in Theodore H. Papadopoullos, *Studies and Documents Relating to the History of the Greek Church and People Under Turkish Domination*, 2nd edn (London: Variorum, 1990) describes how this text was considered by C. Sathas to be written by Damaskenos the Stoudite and has only been echoed more recently by Marios Philippides in Marios Philippides and Walter K. Hanak, *The Siege and the Fall of Constantinople In 1453* (Farnham: Ashgate, 2011), 55–56. Börje Knös in *L'Histoire de la littérature néo-grecque: La période jusqu'en 1821* (Stockholm: Almqvist & Wiksell, 1962), 407, after describing this controversy, concludes that Malaxos was the copyist of this work who provided it to Crusius. It is likely that he depended on the *Historia* of Damaskenos the Stoudite: see Marios Philippides, "Patriarchal Chronicles of the Sixteenth Century," *Greek, Roman and Byzantine Studies* 25 (1984): 87–94. The most recent discussion of the text is found in Konstantinos Moustakas, "The Logic of Historical Thematology in The Historia Politica Constantinopoleos and the Historia Patriarchica Constantinopoleos," in *Festschrift in Honor of Ioannis P. Theocharides: Studies on the Ottoman Empire and Turkey*, ed. Evangelia Balta, Georgios Salakides, and Theoharis Stavrides (Istanbul: Isis Press, 2014), vol. 2, 363–374.

[26] Knös, *L'histoire de la littérature néo-grecque*, 407–408. For extensive bibliography also Malaxos see G. Moravcsik, *Byzantinoturcica*, 2nd edn (Berlin: Akademie-Verlag, 1958), 414–415,

narrative history of the patriarchate, without which most histories, including the present one, could not be written.

Another essential source for the sixteenth century is Stephan Gerlach's *Tagebuch*.[27] Gerlach was a German chaplain assigned to the Istanbul mission by the Hapsburg Emperor. He was among a small group of scholars whose strong Lutheranism motivated them to approach the Patriarchate of Constantinople in order to seek a religious alliance against the papacy, which they supposed to be their common enemy. He based much of his description upon personal observation, though he also relied heavily on local experts. His chief informant about the inner dynamics of the Greek patriarchate and the life of the Greek community was Ioannes Zygomalas, the Grand Orator of the Patriarchate. Zygomalas had been brought to Istanbul from the Aegean port town of Nauplion with the promise of a steady income. However, he became rather disgruntled because he claimed to have witnessed vast amounts of money changing hands in the patriarchate but none of it sticking to his own. His particular sensitivity to economic matters provides excellent detail concerning various aspects of the ecclesiastical economy.

Chapter 4 is a comparison and contrast of the ecclesiastical tax farm with the principles of an Ottoman tax farm, in general. This chapter depends on Ottoman documents from 1550 to 1580, as well as accounts from Stephan Gerlach and the patriarchal chronicles that were written at approximately this time. The chapter considers why the needs of the Ottoman state made tax farming desirable, and how the church fit into the tax farming administrative model. Aspects of terms of the tax farm, acquiring of tax farms, surety, and coercive power are all part of the inquiry. Original documents from the *Mühimme Defterleri* series of the Ottoman Archives form the foundation for this discussion. The *Mühimme Defterleri*, or "Register of Important Affairs," consists of a combination of documents ranging from formal complaints of provincial subjects, to Sultanic rescripts directed to governors and Islamic judges (*kadis*), to rescripts sent to foreign rulers. Petitions were made to the Imperial Council (*Divan-i Hümayun*), which then ruled on the various aspects of imperial administration in the name of the sultan. The matter could be as important as international diplomacy or as seemingly insignificant as addressing a complaint by a local artisan. There are numerous examples of entries detailing ecclesiastical administrative matters as well. Specific examples from the *Mühimme Defterleri*, from Stephan Gerlach's *Tagebuch*, the patriarchal chronicles, and even a letter by a patriarchal tax collector detailing his journey with population figures and statistics on clergy serve as the basis for this chapter.

The last part and Chapter 5 demonstrates how the Ottoman state, Greek Orthodox prelates, and certain members of the Greek economic elite cooperated with each other in order to exploit the institution of the church and its holdings as an economic resource. Hierarchical positions, as tax farming appointments, were subject to the same forces of competition and corruption that other Ottoman

and Philippides and Hanak, *The Siege and the Fall*, 53, n. 145. On the relationship between Malaxos and Damaskenos the Stoudite see Philippides and Hanak, *The Siege and the Fall*, 55–56.

27 Stephan Gerlach, *Stephan Gerlachs des Aelteren Tagebuch* (Frankfurt-am-Main, 1674).

institutions faced. The Greek elites that supported or vied with the patriarchs were said to be descendants of Byzantine noble families that reconstituted their wealth under Ottoman rule. Ultimately they sought to reconstitute their power over the community and competed for control of its most prominent institution. In addition, this competition for economic control also involved competition between the Church and the lay elites. The most visible and powerful Greek in this period was Michael Kantakouzenos. The impact of Kantakouzenos and others like him influenced the way in which the Church conducted its business within the Greek community and with the Ottoman state. This chapter also considers how "corruption" and "scandal" became a part of the working vocabulary of the Greek community describing the sixteenth-century Church. Finally, the Church will be considered as an Ottoman fiscal institution that existed in an Ottoman social context. The patriarchate, therefore, reflected the trends of Ottoman society where individuals in the Ottoman administration relied on influence peddling and the buying and selling of offices.

When one considers the Greek community squarely within the context of Ottoman society, rather than as an isolated minority community immune from broader social forces, one can begin to understand the complex and interconnected reality of the Greek Orthodox under Ottoman rule. The Greek Orthodox community in Ottoman society, and those individuals who created and worked in the community institutions, were, in fact, constituent elements of Ottoman society. As such, they were faced with the same ebbs and flows, fates and fortunes experienced by Ottoman society as a whole.

1

The *Millet* System Revisited

The Ottoman ruling dynasty validated its right to rule its vast European and Asiatic domains based upon a dream attributed to its founder. At the beginning of the fourteenth century, the Turkmen warrior Osman is said to have related a dream to his future father-in-law, Şeyh Edebali, in which a moon rose from Edebali's breast and descended into Osman's breast. A tree sprouted forth from Osman's navel and grew to encompass the entire world, shading the mountains and streams and all the people. The Şeyh, understanding the auspicious meaning of this dream, shrewdly married his daughter to Osman. As a colorful story found in Ottoman accounts in the late fifteenth century, a couple of decades after the conquest of Constantinople, it became the foundation myth of the Ottoman Empire and circulated at a time when it became necessary to justify the further Ottoman expansion beyond Constantinople, into Europe, Asia, and beyond.

When trying to explain the expansive nature of the Ottoman realm it is tempting to return to such stories that go back to the founder of the empire. After all, the Ottoman state experienced remarkable growth from a small tribe located on the edge of the Sakarya River in the north-west corner of Asia Minor in AD 1299, to a vast empire that controlled the eastern half of the Mediterranean Sea in the sixteenth century and continued more or less in its enlarged state until the twentieth century.

One such founding image called forth to explain Ottoman greatness (and later Ottoman failure for abandoning its principles) is the Ottoman holy warrior, or the *gazi*. Historians, both Ottoman and Western, looked upon the growth of the Ottoman state as an Islamic movement that emerged and drew its strength from championing Islamic holy war. From its earliest moments, the Ottoman emirate was made up primarily of Muslim tribesmen who came to rule over a majority Christian population through lightening fast conquest in the Balkans. Later, after Sultan Selim I's (r. 1512–20) armies conquered the Mamlukes in Egypt in 1516–17, the Ottoman rulers took the title of Servant and Protector of the Holy Cities of Mecca and Medina and later the title of Caliph, successor to the Prophet Muhammad. This title remained in place until the last sultan, Sultan Abdülmecid II, abdicated his throne and the caliphate was abolished in 1924. The *gazi* thesis continues as the prevailing narrative for the rise of the Ottoman Empire even though there has been robust historical debate as to whether the

Ottoman *gaza* (holy war) against the Christian Byzantine state was the raison d'être and source of power of the emerging Anatolian emirate.[1]

Accepting or rejecting the theory that the early Ottomans were *gazi* warriors, however, impacts the general interpretation of Ottoman history, of whether or not the Ottoman Empire was a truly Islamic state. The treatment of non-Muslims and their institutions, including the Church, remained the focal point of this interpretation. Even when accounting for accommodationist practices of the Turkmen warriors described by historians such as Heath Lowry, who argues against the *gazi* thesis in his book *The Nature of the Early Ottoman State*, or Cemal Kafadar, who, in *Between Two Worlds*, defines those impulses as *latitudinarianism*,[2] other historians routinely interpret the relations between non-Muslim and the emerging Ottoman state within the framework of Islamic law (*Sharia*), and its classical Islamic formulations in Hanafi law, in a religious-legal approach to Ottoman history. The majority of historians considering the emerging Ottoman emirate interpret a theocratic Islamic state, in which Sharia forms the foundation of administration and jurisprudence. Thus, one need only understand the legal status and function of the non-Muslims (*zimmi*) established in their early Islamic context and transpose those "realities" onto the seven centuries long Ottoman experience. Noted Islamic historian C. E. Bosworth in fact says as much in the opening essay of the notable volume *Christians and Jews in the Ottoman Empire: the Functioning of a Plural Society*, that was based on the 1978 Princeton University conference "The Millet System: History and Legacy." In his essay "The concept of Dhimma in Early Islam," Bosworth explains that the Ottoman system for ruling non-Muslims, the *millet* system,

> Owed its specifically Islamic bases to the very beginnings of Islam, to the events of Muhammad's Medinan years (622–632), when the Prophet and his followers had achieved majority power in one town at least of Arabia, and were therefore forced to consider the question of the Muslim community's relationship to minorities, in the case of Medina specifically, a Jewish minority.[3]

The seventh-century Muslims, forced to address the administrative challenges posed by a non-Muslim minority living within the physical bounds of the new community, formulated a subordinate status that ensured protection for "people of the book" (*ahl-i kitab*). For the Ottomans, separated from early

[1] For a comprehensive description of the debate over the *gazi* thesis and its systematic refutation, especially of Paul Wittek's *Rise of the Ottoman Empire*, see Heath W. Lowry, *The Nature of the Early Ottoman State* (Albany: State University of New York, 2003), 5–13. Linda Darling argues for "an ebb and flow of religious antagonism in the history of Ottoman conquest" that depends on political circumstances. See Linda T. Darling, "Christian-Muslim Interaction on the Ottoman Frontier: Gaza and Accomodation in Early Ottoman History," in *The Ottoman Mosaic: Exploring Models for Peace by Re-exploring the Past*, ed. Kemal Karpat, 1st ed. (Seattle: Cune Press, 2009), 103–104.

[2] C. Kafadar, *Between Two Worlds: The Construction of the Ottoman State* (Berkeley: University of California Press, 1995).

[3] C. E. Bosworth, "The Concept of Dhimma in Early Islam," in *Christians and Jews in the Ottoman Empire: The Functioning of a Plural Society*, ed. Benjamin Braude and Bernard Lewis (New York: Holmes and Meier, 1982), 37.

Islamic realities both by distance (at their origin) and by time (over six centuries), the simple interpretation based on classical Islamic formulation is problematic. Making this type of postulation limits our ability to see the reality of non-Muslim experience regionally and over centuries as well as myriad other factors that make up the totality of non-Muslim experience within Ottoman society. Yet this is what modern historians have done, especially in the case of interpreting non-Muslim communities in Ottoman society. Interpreters of Ottoman Muslim and non-Muslim relations base their findings on classical Islamic theory of interfaith relations and focus on episodes where Ottoman rulers interacted directly with the non-Muslim religious leadership, specifically the Church hierarchy. Ironically, historians looking for monumental examples ignored the period of the Anatolian emirates, wherein the patterns of relations between emirs and bishops were first formed. However, since historians chose to highlight the most dramatic episode of the meeting of Sultan Mehmet II and the Patriarch Gennadios Scholarios, this chapter will, therefore, reconsider this event first.

According to many modern historians, Fatih Sultan Mehmet II's investiture of Patriarch Gennadios in 1454 became the founding moment of the Ottoman *millet* system. This meeting, accordingly, is said to have defined relations between the Church and state, and established the patriarch as a religious and civil authority over the Greek Orthodox subjects of the Ottoman Empire. Historically, however, characterizing Ottoman–Church relations for all periods by this meeting between Sultan Mehmet II and Patriarch Gennadios is problematic, as this event itself deserves to be placed in its appropriate historical context. This chapter, therefore, will consider whether or not this episode reflects the claims of the *millet* system, after which it will focus on how historians have dealt with this moment of investiture and the *millet* system. While some historians have begun to question the traditional paradigm, few attempts have been made to problematize the *millet* system historically or even historiographically.

SULTAN MEHMET II AND PATRIARCH GENNADIOS SCHOLARIOS

Even though the post-conquest re-establishment of the Patriarchate of Constantinople was a momentous occasion that is revisited time and again by historians, the only contemporary account of the actual event is that of Kritovoulos of Imvros, a Greek who worked in Sultan Mehmet's administration, whose description of the sultan showed a benevolent Ottoman sultan, every bit the successor to the Byzantine emperors.

According to Kritovoulos, Mehmet II had released Gennadios who had been captured and held in Adrianople. Gennadios was renowned for his virtue, and after "various talks with him, and his replies, he [Mehmet] loaded him with noble and costly gifts."

Kritovoulos then goes on to say:

> In the end, he made him patriarch and High Priest of the Christians, and gave him among many other rights and privileges the rule of the church and all its power and authority, no less than that enjoyed previously under the emperors. He also granted him the privilege of delivering before him fearlessly and freely many good disquisitions concerning the Christian faith and doctrine. And he himself went to his residence, taking with him the dignitaries and wise men of his court, and thus paid him great honor.
>
> Thus, the sultan showed that he knew how to respect the true worth of any man, not only of military men but of every class, kings, and tyrants, and emperors. Furthermore, the Sultan gave back the church to the Christians, by the will of God, together with a large portion of its properties.[4]

Kritovoulos presented a positive picture of the relationship between the sultan and the patriarch prior to the investiture, though little more can be gleaned from his description. Gennadios was to be held in honor, both by the Christian community and the sultan, himself, as he granted Gennadios the right to speak about Christian theology "fearlessly and freely." The sultan knew how to "respect the true worth of any man," and Kritovoulos was able to show that only a man of true worth such as Sultan Mehmet II could recognize true virtue in another, as opposed to the countless military men who were only military conquerors.

While the major focus of the passage was the virtues of Sultan Mehmet II and Patriarch Gennadios and their close relationship, Kritovoulos makes it clear that Gennadios was made "Patriarch and High Priest of the Christians," in a formulaic and titular manner. Thus, it was the institution of the patriarchate that was re-established and not simply a favor to the individual man, Gennadios. Furthermore, when Kritovoulos says the sultan bestowed upon Gennadios "among other rights and privileges, the rule of the church and all of the power and authority ... enjoyed previously under the emperors," this raises the question of what "rights, and privileges," "rule of the church," "power and authority" really mean. The reason "rights, and privileges" remain such a question is that there is no extant investiture document for Patriarch Gennadios that outlines the nature of rights, privileges, rule, power, or authority. Even if contemporaries were not troubled by what power and authority meant, the day would come when this investiture and bestowal of power and authority on Patriarch Gennadios might be challenged and would need to be recognized officially by the Ottoman administration and the Christian community. The prestige and friendship and visible gifts might have been enough for 1454, but it is also likely, considering Ottoman

[4] Kritovoulos, *History of Mehmed the Conqueror*, trans. Charles T Riggs (Princeton: Princeton University Press, 1954), 94–95. The exact time of investiture is not entirely certain, although it has been argued convincingly that it was in January 1454. The election of the Patriarch was an important policy that was established to show stability and to hasten the repopulation of Istanbul with Greeks. Halil Inalcik, "The Policy of Mehmet II toward the Greek Population of Istanbul and the Byzantine Buildings of the City," *Dumbarton Oaks Papers* 23–24 (1969–70): 231–249; Gunnar Hering, "Das Islamische Recht und die Investitur des Gennadios Scholarios (1454)," *Balkan Studies* 2/2 (1961): 231–256.

administrative practice, that a document was issued to confirm whatever prerogatives were offered. Such a document is not indicated by Kritovoulos, nor has one survived.

In the final remark in this passage, Sultan Mehmet returns the Church to the Christians along with many properties. The implication is that Sultan Mehmet had captured and controlled the Church, which meant all the local parishes and church buildings and associated land and commercial holdings. There is no indication how these were held or how the Ottomans administered them. Sultan Mehmet returned them to the "Christians" rather than to the more specific "patriarch" or "Patriarch Gennadios," even though the point of Kritovoulos' passage was to highlight the relationship between the sultan and Gennadios. While the implication may be that it was returned to Gennadios, it could also show that the Christian community was vast, and widespread, and that local parishes, church buildings, church holdings, and clergy were administered locally.

In spite of the fact that Kritovoulos, as a Greek serving in Sultan Mehmet's court, pays attention to the events of the investiture of the patriarch and records them, there are many things about this investiture that remain unclear. As subsequent chronicles and histories begin to recount this same investiture story, however, more details are offered and the story about the meeting between the sultan and patriarch appears to become clearer—and the historical narrative begins to take on other characteristics. These subsequent accounts begin to reflect the concerns of their own period as well as the political aspirations of their authors.

The first of these was attributed to the Byzantine author, courtier, and diplomat who served the last Emperor Constantine XI, George Sphrantzes. Sphrantzes, the Emperor's Grand Chancellor (*Megas Logothetes*), was an eyewitness to the conquest of Constantinople who composed a work known as the *Chronicon Minus*. This work gave many observations leading up to and following the conquest of Constantinople, yet Sphrantzes did not actually report on the investiture, more than likely because Gennadios had opposed the imperial policy of union with the Western Church. Interestingly, until the 1930s Sphrantzes was attributed with writing about the investiture in great detail. The work, now known as *Chronicon Maius*, has been shown by scholars to be a *c*.1580 composition of Makarios Melissourgos-Melessinos, a historian and bishop of Monemvasia, now considered Pseudo-Sphrantzes, and a continuator or elaborator of Sphrantzes' history, who completed his work in Naples, Italy.[5] Marios Philippides has argued persuasively that Melissourgos-Melessinos derived his information detailing the investiture from the *Historia Patriarchica*, if not from the *Historia*'s source, which might have been an earlier work by Damaskenos the Stoudite.[6]

[5] Marios Philippides and Walter K. Hanak, *The Siege and the Fall of Constantinople In 1453* (Farnham: Ashgate, 2011), 50. For the pertinent section on the investiture as presented by Pseudo-Sphrantzes, see George Sphrantzes, *The Fall of the Byzantine Empire: A Chronicle by George Sphrantzes 1401–1477*, 1st ed. (Amhesrt, MA: University of Massachusetts Press, 1980), 134–136.

[6] Philippides and Hanak, *The Siege and the Fall of Constantinople In 1453*, 56. On Melissourgos-Melissenos, see Marios Philippides, "Makarios Melissourgos-Melissenos," in *Historians of the Ottoman Empire*, ed. Cemal Kafadar, Hakan Karateke, and Cornell Fleischer, 2008, <http://www.ottomanhistorians.com>.

The *Historia Patriarchica*, written in the mid-sixteenth century by members of the patriarchal court, therefore still stands as a leading source for the events that took place one hundred years earlier.[7] As a source, it emphasized Sultan Mehmet II's relationship with Patriarch Gennadios, though in even more glowing and admiring terms than recounted by Kritovoulos. In this account, the patriarch, hierarchs, clerics, and notables all went to see the sultan, who granted to the patriarch rights and prerogatives according to the custom of those granted by the Byzantine emperors. Sultan Mehmet asked about the specific process by which a patriarch should be installed and followed closely the details that he was told, including granting the patriarch a rich outfit and cloak, and placing him on a white horse to be taken around the city. The sultan personally handed Gennadios the patriarchal office. In addition, they apparently had a very close relationship:

> The sultan greatly loved the patriarch, going to learn that he was a most wise man, worthy of reverence. And he gave to him the famous church of the Holy Apostles and he (Gennadios) made it a patriarchate. . . . Then this sultan went in person to the patriarchate, to the church of the Pammakaristos, and he went into the chapel (where today there is a treasury) and he spoke and discussed with him, the patriarch, Lord Gennadios. And the patriarch demonstrated to him the entire truth of our faith, without a single fear, and wrote down for him according to his questions, twenty chapters which appear below, one at a time, what it says, and gave these to the same sultan.[8]

The re-establishment of the Greek Orthodox Patriarchate has been hailed as a watershed moment for establishing the power and prerogatives of the Church to govern the Greek community. The patriarchal chronicles, in particular, assert that immediately following the conquest of Constantinople in 1453, when Sultan Mehmet II and the monk Gennadios met, Gennadios was made patriarch and leader of the Greek community. Just as with the Armenian and Jewish communities, the Greek community provided accounts that bore what historian Benjamin Braude has termed a "patina of self-serving tradition."[9] Accordingly, Sultan Mehmet II granted authority to the Greek, Armenian, and Jewish communities and made the religious leader their civil leader. In the sixteenth century,

[7] Immanuel Bekker, ed., *Historia politica et patriarchica Constantinopoleos: Epirotica*, Corpus Scriptorum Historiae Byzantinae (Bonn: Impensis Ed. Weberi, 1849), 81–83. Steven Runciman relies heavily on the *Historia Patriarchica*, as does Philippides and Hanak, *The Siege and the Fall*, 53, n. 145.

[8] *Historia Patriarchica*, ed. Bekker, 83–84. The irony of this position is that even in Byzantine times, there were many occasions when the Emperor totally disregarded the Patriarch and denied him the opportunity to be received. For instance, Patriarch Athanasios recounts his frustrations in attempting to arrange an Imperial audience with the Emperor. He complains of having gone to the Chora Monastery (before it was restored by Metochites) in order to be close to the imperial palace. Access to the emperor was not always easy, even for the Ecumenical Patriarch in Constantinople, Alice-Mary Talbot, ed. and trans., *The Correspondence of Athanasius I, Patriarch of Constantinople: Letters to the Emperor Andronicus II, Members of the Imperial Family, and Officials, Corpus Fontium Historiae Byzantinae. v. 7, Dumbarton Oaks Texts 3* (Washington, D.C.: Dumbarton Oaks Center for Byzantine Studies, Trustees for Harvard University, 1975).

[9] Benjamin Braude, "Foundation Myths of the Millet System," in *Christians and Jews in the Ottoman Empire: The Functioning of a Plural Society*, ed. Bernard Lewis and Benjamin Braude (New York: Holmes & Meier, 1982), 74.

Fig. 1.1. Contemporary mosaic of Sultan Mehmet II and the investiture of Patriarch Gennadios on display at the Ecumenical Patriarchate of Constantinople, Fener, Istanbul, Turkey. (Photograph by the author)

the authors of the patriarchal chronicle had an interest in promoting this vision. What might the alternative vision be?

If we examine the *Historia Patriarchica* account more closely, we begin to see there is more to the story. After the description of the patriarchal investiture of Gennadios Scholarios the Most Wise (*ho Sophotatos*) by Sultan Mehmet II, the *Historia Patriarchica* describes the close relationship between Sultan Mehmet II and Patriarch Gennadios that culminated in the patriarch hosting the sultan for friendly conversation and composing a twenty-chapter statement of Christian belief specifically for the sultan. The *Historia Patriarchica* intended to clearly demonstrate that patriarchs subsequent to Gennadios could not match his illustriousness or his virtue. Their comparative lack of virtue and faith engulfed them in the mire of material and economic concerns.[10]

The mire of these concerns, in fact, overwhelmed Patriarch Gennadios himself. The pressure mounted to the point where, on account of the "many and great scandals," Patriarch Gennadios "called for a synod of hierarchs, priests and archons, and all Christians, and he resigned his patriarchal throne." All those attending the synod begged him to remain, but he refused. He, therefore, signed his resignation in the codex of the Great Church, and went into retirement at the monastery of Prodromos on Mount Menoikion near Serres where he lived his remaining days peacefully.[11] The many and great scandals are what did in Patriarch Gennadios, three times in all. It is most likely these scandals were connected with the nature of the office of the patriarchate within the Ottoman administration. Because the office of the bishop, especially the chief bishop in Istanbul, was considered a tax farm, it became the object of financial competition, which in the Church is considered simony, and likely was the scandal implied in the text. Therefore, it is unlikely that Mehmet II's investiture of Gennadios actually intended to transform Patriarch Gennadios into a communal leader of the Greek community.

Sultan Mehmet II had waited nearly eight months after the conquest before he appointed Gennadios as patriarch. Following the conquest, Mehmet II had considered placing Lucas Notaras, the former Byzantine Grand Duke, in charge of the city.[12] Kritovoulos wrote, "He contemplated making Notaras the commandant of the City, and putting him in charge of its repopulation, and he advised him previously regarding this."[13] Notaras was the ranking Byzantine nobleman who survived the conquest and he was a layman. Kritovoulos was in a good position to make these observations since he, himself, was formerly a minor Byzantine official from the island of Imvros. Even as his eyes were on the sultan, he would have been paying attention to the fate of the surviving Byzantine nobility.

[10] *Historia Patriarchica*, ed. Bekker, 83–93. For the confession of faith see also Tibor Halasi-Kun, "Gennadios' Turkish Confession of Faith," *Archivum Ottomanicum* 12 (1992, 1987): 5–103. For Benjamin Braude's assessment of the political agenda of the chronicles see, Braude, "Foundation Myths," 76–77.

[11] *Historia Patriarchica*, ed. Bekker, 94. Nicholas Bakirtzis, "Hagios Ioannis Prodromos Monastery on Mount Menoikeion: Byzantine Monastic Practice, Sacred Topography, and Architecture" (Ph.D. Dissertation, Princeton University, 2005).

[12] Doukas, *Decline and Fall of Byzantium to the Ottoman Turks*, ed. and trans. Harry J. Magoulias (Detroit: Wayne State University Press, 1975), Laonikos Chalkokondylas, *Historiarum Demonstrationes*, ed. E. Darkó (Budapest: 1922–27), Theodoros Spandouginos, *Discorso di Teodoro Spandugino Cantacusino Gentil'homo Constantinopolitano Dall'origine de'principi Turchi. Theodore Spandounes: On the Origins of the Ottoman Emperors*, trans. Donald M. Nicol (Cambridge: Cambridge University Press, 1997), Spyridon Paulou Lampros, *Ecthesis chronica and Chronicon Athenarum* (London: Methuen & Co., 1902). Notaras has been credited with the phrase, "Better the turban of the Turk than the Latin mitre," expressing the bitter rivalry taking place in pre-1453 Constantinople. See Elizabeth A. Zachariadou, "Ta Logia kai o Thanatos tou Louka Notara," in *Rodonia time ston M. I. Manousaka* (1995), 135–146.

[13] Kritovoulos, *The History of Mehmet the Conqueror*, 83. Braude makes this a fundamental point in his argument. He argued that little consideration had been given to Mehmet II's intention of establishing a former elite in a position of power.

This seemingly minor detail preserved by Kritovoulos offers an alternative possibility concerning the reorganization of the Greek community in Istanbul. Why was Notaras considered to play a leadership role in post-conquest Istanbul? Kritovoulos explained that it was part of Mehmet II's plan to repopulate Istanbul quickly, and to allow the nobles to pay their ransoms and re-establish themselves in Istanbul. This policy followed the standard Ottoman practice of absorbing experienced individuals to help rule conquered territories. Notaras was an experienced leader with considerable sway among the Greek community.

In a surprise move, however, the sultan changed his mind about Notaras and ordered his execution. To explain the sultan's quick about-face, Kritovoulos cited the envy of some of Sultan Mehmet II's counselors, "men of great influence," who persuaded the sultan to eliminate the Greeks of prominent positions. Their reasoning was that "after recuperating a little and having become free from slavery, those men would no longer hesitate to plot in their own interests and seek to get back what they formerly had, and especially their freedom."[14] Kritovoulos implied that Notaras was part of a larger group of notable Byzantines who were captured and sought to remain in the city, looking for a place for themselves within the new system. With Notaras, it was more likely that he was executed because his family had strong ties with the Genoese, who were far too closely allied with Western interests. He likely was more of a liability and threat to Ottoman power than originally considered.[15] Two of the "men of great influence" who opposed Notaras were the heroes of the conquest of Constantinople, Zaganos Pasha, and Shihabeddin Pasha, who, perhaps, feared his ability to call upon the Venetian fleet that still lingered in the Aegean Sea to come retake Constantinople.[16] More importantly, they certainly resented Notaras' strong relations with Çandarlı Halil Pasha, Sultan Mehmet II's Grand Vizier who had counseled against laying siege to Constantinople and was executed shortly after the conquest. Both Zaganos Pasha and Shihabbedin Pasha were responsible for going after Çandarlı Pasha and causing his execution. While Sphrantzes records that the janissaries and *ulema* were upset by Çandarlı Halil Pasha's execution, the Ottoman chronicler Aşıkpashazade harshly criticized him for being in the service of the Byzantines.[17] Notaras could not escape this connection.

[14] Kritovoulos, *The History of Mehmet the Conqueror*, 84–85. Inalcik, "The Policy of Mehmet II Toward the Greek Population of Istanbul," 240.

[15] Zachariadou, "Ta Logia kai o Thanatos tou Louka Notara," 144–146. This is a good review of the various versions of the death of Notaras. Kritovoulos' description is preferred, however. Zachariadou accepts Notaras' legacy of facing death heroically, and creating him as an ethnomartyr.

[16] Inalcik, "The Policy of Mehmet II toward the Greek Population of Istanbul," 240.

[17] Asiq-Pasha-zade, *Vom Hirtenzelt Zur Hohen Pforte*, trans. Richard F. Kreutel, *Osmanische Geschichtsschreiber* (Graz, Austria: Verlag Styria, 1959), 198; Inalcik, "The Policy of Mehmet II toward the Greek Population of Istanbul," 232. Also see Stephen Runciman, "Lucas Notaras, 'GAMBROS TOU BASILEVS'," in *Polychronion: Festschrift Franz Dölger zum 75. Geburstag*, ed. Peter Wirth, Corpus Der greiechischen Urkunden des Mittlealters und der neuern Zeit (Heidelberg: Carl Winter-Universitätsverlag, 1966), and Halil Inalcik, *Fatih devri üzerinde tetkikler ve vesikalar* (Ankara: Türk Tarih Kurumu Basimevi, 1954), 55–136.

While Sultan Mehmet II would have wished to establish stability as soon as possible after the conquest of Constantinople, it became necessary to execute Notaras along with his sons because his connections with opposition groups were too many and too messy. Kritovoulos revealed that nine other *archons*, all laymen, were also executed. However, even with these early executions, the *archons* were certainly not eliminated from Ottoman society, nor from their activities within the Greek Church.

The episode of Notaras in the post-conquest reality helps shed light on the role of the Church in the same period. In considering this same event, Benjamin Braude concluded that the Ottomans were not predisposed to use ecclesiastical authority to control non-Muslim groups. During and immediately following the messy business of conquest, the Ottoman leadership was preoccupied with the practical details of cleaning up the city and establishing order. Thus, they likely considered the Greek Orthodox Church an afterthought since it took a full eight months for them to turn their attention upon the Church, and call upon the Church to fill the position of patriarch.

Sultan Mehmet II envisioned the rebuilding of the sacked and broken city to create a capital worthy of his burgeoning empire. To do this, he realized it was imperative to repopulate the city quickly. Certain rebuilding projects he prioritized, such as the building of a citadel, *Yediküle*, and his own palace, *Tahtakale*, in the city center. Paying Greek slaves wages high enough to buy their own freedom, he encouraged craftsmen and builders to return to the city. He used his prerogative as supreme ruler to command thousands of Christians, Muslims, and Jews forcibly resettled in Istanbul to assist in the project. According to Halil Inalcik, Mehmet II called for the re-establishment of the patriarchate to encourage those Christians who had fled "to return and settle in Istanbul."[18] The goal of repopulating the City was accomplished in fits and starts in that first decade after the conquest, and there is no doubt that having a functioning patriarchate went a long way to encourage Greek Orthodox Christians to settle in the new Ottoman capital.

The occasion of Patriarch Gennadios' installation in January 1454 was so celebrated that it became the prevailing narrative of the post-conquest history in the patriarchal chronicles. Both the Ottoman concerns for rebuilding an imperial city and the memory of Notaras' role in the governance of Istanbul after the conquest faded. The alternate story of Notaras' role in the post-1453 is also absent from the secondary literature.[19] Historian Benjamin Braude

[18] Inalcik, "The Policy of Mehmet II toward the Greek Population of Istanbul," 236. For Sultan Mehmed II's imperial building program see Heath W. Lowry, "From Lesser Wars to the Mightiest War. The Ottoman Conquest and Transformation of Byzantine Urban Centers in the Fifteenth Century," in *Continuity and Change in Late Byzantine and Early Ottoman Society*, ed. Anthony Bryer and Heath W. Lowry (Birmingham and Washington DC: University of Birmingham and Dumbarton Oaks, 1986), 323–338.

[19] Braude, "Foundation Myths," 77. Historians that rely heavily on the Patriarchal Histories include Athanasios Komnēnos Hypsēlantēs, *Athanasiou Komnēnou Hypsēlantou Ekklēsiastikōn kai politikōn tōn eis dōdeka vivlion Ē', Th' kai I': ētoi Ta meta tēn halōsin (1453–1789.) (Ek cheirographou anekdotou tēs hieras monēs tou Sina.)* (Typogr. I. A. Vretou, 1870), 3–6. Manuel Gedeon, and

explains that Notaras' disappearance from the historical record was the result of a lay-clerical rivalry in which the Church sought to gain the upper hand. In the sixteenth-century contests for leadership in the Greek community between laymen and clerics Notaras would surely have represented the Byzantine lay nobility. Braude argues,

> As a martyr to the cause of Byzantine lay authority, he could have been a rallying point against both the Church and the sultan in the sixteenth century. Clearly it was in the interests of both [the sultan and the Church] to have him denigrated or ignored.[20]

As a lay leader, Notaras had the potential to muster significant opposition to both. Notaras' perceived opposition was rewarded with execution by Sultan Mehmet II. Yet the Church benefited from Notaras' execution because it left it a window of opportunity to step in to play a significant leadership role in the community. The Ottomans did not automatically choose bishops to be community leaders, perhaps because they were used to dealing with strong Byzantine imperial nobility. In addition, they recognized the bishops first as religious men, and from their pervasive and practical approach to the world, as fiscal opportunities to be exploited. Church leaders, therefore, were unable to appropriate the leadership role immediately following the conquest. Clearly, leadership in the sixteenth-century Istanbul Greek Orthodox community did not go unchallenged by laymen or by clerics.

The contests for leadership in the sixteenth century that Braude refers to are, in fact, for the episcopal positions that became objects of competition. These positions became vehicles by which individuals from the Greek elite could demonstrate their wealth and power. The Greek Orthodox community, in particular, the lay community, was in the process of rising in prominence in Ottoman society because of its wealth. The attendant increase in confidence led the lay Greek community to impose itself on the Church perhaps as a proxy for its real aspiration, namely, dominance in Ottoman society. Thus, episcopal seats became symbolic objects of great value to be contested in their own right.

Lucas Notaras, as an *archon*, was a member of this Byzantine Greek elite who was selected by the sultan and positioned to attain real political authority over the Greek community, though it was ultimately taken from him. The patriarchal chronicles argue that his replacement as the prominent leader was Patriarch Gennadios and his successors. Yet the struggles for the ecclesiastical positions that took place throughout the sixteenth century between influential lay people and

other historians including Vacalopulos, Paparighopoulos, and Vasileios Stephanides, *Ekklesiastike Historia: Ap'Arches Mechri Semeron* (Athena: "Aster" A. & E. Papademetriou, 1948), 632–636. On Patriarch Gennadios see M. Gedeon, *Patriarchikoi Pinakes* (Konstantinoupolis, 1885), 471–479; Kōnstantinos Paparrēgopoulos, *Historia Tou Hellēnikou Ethnous Apo Tōn Archaiotatōn Chronōn Mechri Tōn Neōterōn*, vol. 5, pt. 2, 6th ed. (En Athenais: Ekdotikos Oikos Eleutheroudakēs, 1932) 44–50. Paparrēgopoulos even discusses the idea of the Patriarch as "ethnarchēs," 48.

[20] Braude, "Foundation Myths," 77–78. Kritovoulos has the interests of the Sultan in mind, and also completely ignores this incident, as do the later patriarchal narratives.

ecclesiastical hierarchs belie this reality. With such evident power struggles, the plausibility of the *millet* system is on shaky ground.

The paucity of direct sources for the re-establishment of the patriarchate in the post-Conquest era has allowed the patriarchal chronicles, including the *Chronicon Maius*, to dominate the historical narrative. This means that the investiture episode appears as the most significant moment and a touchstone from which to interpret Ottoman treatment of the Church particularly among the patriarchal chroniclers observing from within the Ottoman Empire. Subsequent writers, mostly from the West, however, also spent a good deal of time thinking and writing about non-Muslims in the Ottoman Empire. While the immediate aftermath of the 1453 conquest of Constantinople and investiture of the patriarch were important, contemporary Western observers interpreted events according to a broader view of Ottoman expansion and conquest. This had a significant influence on how Western obervers viewed the history of non-Muslims in the Ottoman realm.

Beginning with the earliest interaction of Westerners with the Ottoman Empire, and continuing to the end of the empire in 1923, the status of Christians and Jews under Ottoman rule has been an important subject for intellectuals, historians, and travelers to the Ottoman Empire. In *Creating East and West*, intellectual historian Nancy Bisaha accepts the view that Renaissance humanists perpetuated the ancient and medieval formulations of West versus East and Christian versus Infidel. This rhetorical construction continues to form the foundation for the "clash of civilizations" interpretations that abound into the present century. However, Bisaha advances her argument by explaining that the Italian humanists, heavily influenced by Byzantine scholar émigrés to Italy around 1453, revolutionized the Western views of Islam. Rather than simply being the old enemy of the faith, Renaissance humanists wrote extensively about the Ottoman Turks in contemporary political and cultural terms as a "threat to their growing sense of 'Europe.'"[21] Scholars such as Petrarch, Aeneus Silveas Piccolomini (Pope Pius II, 1458–64), Francesco Filelfo, Cardinal Bessarion, and Lauro Quirini made the savagery of the Ottoman conquests of Constantinople the basis for their critique of the "uncivilized" Turk.[22] Some scholars, such as Erasmus, attempted to avoid the biases of their fellow humanists and sought to be more dispassionate and critical with regard to European assessments of the Ottomans. This was also true of travelers and diplomats to the Ottoman Empire who had highly practical concerns, such as Ogier Ghiselin De Busbecq, the ambassador of the Holy Roman Emperor to Istanbul from 1554 to 1562. Busbecq wrote his famous *Turkish Letters* in which he commended principles of "Turkish justice, moral virtues, and military excellence." Yet, even Busbecq had harsh judgments against the Ottomans, the embodiment of "savage barbarism."[23] Other travelers, such as Nicolas de

[21] Nancy Bisaha, *Creating East and West: Renaissance Humanists and the Ottoman Turks* (Philadelphia: University of Pennsylvania Press, 2004), 7.

[22] Bisaha, *Creating East and West*, 50–87.

[23] Bisaha, *Creating East and West*, 180–181. E. S. Forster, *The Turkish Letters of Ogier Ghiselin De Busbecq Imperial Ambassador at Constantinople 1554–1562* (Oxford: Oxford University Press,

Nicolay, continued to use the term "barbarian" throughout his descriptions, and concluded the Ottomans were brutish and barbarous.[24] Nicolay had an immense impact on the European popular imagination, the result both of his travel descriptions and, more importantly, of the illustrations. His influence could be felt late into the nineteenth century in European artistic depictions of the Turks by artists such as Eugène Delacroix and Jean-August-Dominique Ingres.[25]

Yet even among myriad travelers to the Ottoman Empire who made observations about non-Muslims in Ottoman society, coverage of the early post-conquest period is limited.[26] Mostly, they do not comment on the post-conquest meeting of Sultan Mehmet and Patriarch Gennadios, or they depend on the patriarchal histories for information if they in fact do comment on it.

Sir Paul Rycaut, the English Consul at Smyrna from 1667 to 1678, was one of the important traveler/diplomats in the Ottoman Empire who focused his attention in one of his treatises exclusively on the state of the Greek and Armenian Churches. In his 1678 work *The Present State of the Greek and Armenian Churches*, Rycaut attempted to describe the condition of the Greek Orthodox and Armenian churches under "Turkish Tyranny."[27] Rycaut was less concerned with history than contemporary administration, and gave an account of the general administrative structure of the Church, including a discussion of jurisdictions of the various Eastern patriarchates, the primacy of the Patriarch of Constantinople, as well as a description of the financial obligations of the bishops towards the Porte. Additional descriptions covered issues of theology, including the sacraments of Eucharist, chrismation, baptism, and ordination, as well as descriptions of the monasteries of Mt. Athos. Rycaut, however, does not describe the post-1453 era and he omitted the reconstitution of the Church by Sultan Mehmet II and Patriarch Gennadios. Perhaps as his title suggests, he was intent only on offering a view of the Church during his time period and it remains important for its view of the late seventeenth-century experience of the Church under Ottoman rule.

An additional source that was to remain the principal source on the history of the Ottoman Empire in a Western language is Demetrie Cantemir's *The History of the Growth and Decay of the Othman Empire*. Written in Latin and published first in 1717, it was translated into English in London in 1734–35

1927), 40. Also see Zweder von Martels, "Impressions of the Ottoman Empire in the Writings of Augerius Busbequius (1520/2–1591)," *Journal of Mediterranean Studies* 5/2 (1995): 209–221.

[24] Bisaha, *Creating East and West*, 181.

[25] David Brafman, "Facing East: The Western View of Islam in Nicolas De Nicolay's 'Travels in Turkey'," *Getty Research Journal* 1 (2009): 154.

[26] For example see Franz Babinger, *Hans Dernschwam's Tagebuch Einer Reise Nach Konstantinopel und Kleinasien (1551/55): Nach der Urschrift im Fugger Archiv Herausgegeben und Erläutert* (Berlin: Duncker and Humblot, 1923, 1986); and P. Rycaut, *The Present State of the Ottoman Empire* (London, 1668). For a more detailed list of travellers in the sixteenth century see Stefanos Yerasimos, *Les voyageurs dans l'Empire Ottoman, XIVe-XVIe siècles: bibliografie, itinéraires et inventaire des lieux habités* (Ankara: Société turque d'histoire, Atatürk Kültür Merkezi, Türk Tarih Kurumu, 1991).

[27] Paul Rycaut, *Present State of the Greek & Armenian Churches* (London, 1679; AMS Press, 1970), 1.

by Nicolas Tindal. In his work, Cantemir outlined the reigns of the Ottoman sultans up to the year 1711.[28] Cantemir's treatment of the post-conquest era is curious because he, too, did not specifically describe the investiture of Patriarch Gennadios. Apparently, he used a limited number of written sources, even attributing faulty citations to those. Cantemir, however, described the aftermath of the conquest with Sultan Mehmet II saying to the anxious Greeks of conquered Constantinople,

> I promised you in our agreement, that if you chose to remain here, all the Churches and Monasteries should be untouch'd, and your religion suffer no damage. But since I have receiv'd half the City by force of arms, and half by surrender, I think it just, and accordingly order, that the religious Houses and Churches which stand in that part I have conquer'd, be converted into Jami, and the rest left entire to the Christians.[29]

Cantemir was undoubtedly referring to the principle behind Sultan Süleyman's attempt in 1521 to confiscate the Churches of Istanbul from the Greek Orthodox community (to be discussed below in Chapter 3). Cantemir takes liberties in his telling of the early Ottoman history, but he made the Greek community's right to the churches the focal point of his post-conquest account. Clearly, Cantemir is extrapolating from the written sources. It seems clear that the source was, the *Historia Patriarchica,* a detail that Hammer notes in his own historical assessment. This dependence on Malaxos' patriarchal chronicle is evident from Cantemir's extensive Annotations that detail the confiscation episode.[30] Yet, for some reason, he still does not mention the meeting of Sultan Mehmet II and Patriarch Gennadios.

The next major historian who attempted to piece together the post-conquest era is the famous English historian Edward Gibbon (1737–1794). By the time Enlightenment historians such as Gibbon made their historical assessments of the conquest of Constantinople and its aftermath, the sources for the reconstitution of the Church were well established. Gibbon, in his majestic work *The History of the Decline and Fall of the Roman Empire*, described the investiture of Gennadios in the following terms:

> In the election and investiture of a patriarch, the ceremonial of the Byzantine court was revived and imitated. With a mixture of satisfaction and horror, they beheld the sultan on his throne, who delivered into the hands of Gennadius the crosier or pastoral staff, the symbol of his ecclesiastical office; who conducted the patriarch to the gate of the seraglio, presented him with a horse richly caparisoned, and directed

[28] Dimitrie Cantemir (Voivode of Moldavia), *The History of the Growth and Decay of the Othman Empire*, trans. Nicolas Tindal, John James and Paul Knapton (London, 1734), 102–5. For problems with Tindal's translation, see Mihai Maxim, "Demetrie Cantemir (1673–1723)," ed. Cemal Kafadar, Hakan Karateke, and Cornell Fleischer, *Historians of the Ottoman Empire*, 2006, <http://www.ottomanhistorians.com>. Also, Cristina Bîrsan, *Dimitrie Cantemir and the Islamic World*, 1st ed. (Istanbul: The Isis Press, 2004).

[29] Dimitrie Cantemir, *The History of the Growth and Decay of the Othman Empire*, 101.

[30] Joseph Hammer-Purgstall, *Histoire de l'Empire ottoman : depuis son origine jusqu'a nos jours* (Paris: Impr. de Béthune et Plon, 1844), 247, n. 2.

the vizirs and bashaws to lead him to the palace which had been allotted for his residence.[31]

The problem with Gibbon's account is that when it came to the post-Byzantine period it relies on the spurious source by Melissourgos-Melessinos, the *Chronicon Maius*, as its main source for Gennadios' investiture. However, it was not established until the 1930s that the *Chronicon Maius* relied exclusively on Malaxos' account. Ironically, Gibbon used Malaxos' *Historia Patriarchica* to corroborate the *Chronicon Maius*. Compounding matters, the renowned historian J. B. Bury, in his 1900 edition of Gibbon, affirms this corroboration as validity of the *Chronicon Maius*.[32] Gibbon then utilizes the *Historia Patriarchica* to trace the remnant of the Byzantine imperial figures after the Ottomans conquered the empire.

Until Edward Gibbon, Western descriptions of the Church under Ottoman rule were dependent on sources that were not sufficiently sound. Even when used with care, they posed serious problems for historians. The trend continued into the nineteenth century as well. Among the first and most important modern critical general histories of the Ottoman Empire was that completed by an Austrian scholar who studied Ottoman and Arabic, Joseph von Hammer's *Geschichte des osmanischen Reiches* (History of the Ottoman Empire), a ten-volume history written between 1827 and 1835 that was based heavily on Ottoman sources. This comprehensive general history covers the early Ottomans up to the 1774 Treaty of Küçük Kaynarca. Even in this major modern work, the main sources for describing the history and status of Christians and Jews in Ottoman society and history are the *Historia Patriarchica*, and the *Chronicon Maius* of Melissourgos-Melessinos.[33] In Book XIII, Hammer gave an extensive treatment of the investiture of Patriarch Gennadios. He follows very closely the *Chronicon Maius*, including the pronouncement that Sultan Mehmet was to have said"The Holy Trinity has granted the empire to me and the patriarchate of New Rome to you."[34] Hammer includes the important detail of the rights that Sultan Mehmet II granted the patriarch by describing a diploma issued by him to Gennadios. Interestingly, these rights were listed in the last paragraph of the *Chronicon Maius*, stating that no one was to hinder or annoy the patriarch, that the patriarch was protected against all adversaries, and that he remained forever free from all taxation, which was the right of all the hierarchs. Interestingly, Hammer then describes a series of other rights given to the Greek community as reported in Cantemir's account and, following Cantemir, states that the three "liberties" granted to the Greeks include 1) their churches ought no longer be turned into mosques, 2) their marriages and funerals and other religious

[31] Edward Gibbon, *The History of the Decline and Fall of the Roman Empire*, ed. J. B. Bury, vol. 7 (London: Methuen & Co., 1900), 202.

[32] Gibbon, *Decline and Fall,* 202, n. 112.

[33] Joseph Hammer-Purgstall, *Histoire de l'Empire ottoman: depuis son origine jusqu'ànos jours* (Paris: Impr. de Béthune et Plon, 1844), 246–247, n. 1.

[34] Hammer-Purgstall, *Histoire de l'Empire ottoman*, 246. For the *Chronicon Maius*, see Sphrantzes, *The Fall of the Byzantine Empire*, 134.

ceremonies ought not be hindered, and 3) Easter should be celebrated with all the pomp associated, and the gates of the Phanar left open for the Christians to attend the ceremonies.[35]

Among the historians writing in the late Ottoman period that departed from the narrative of the investiture is Ignatius Moradgea d'Ohsson (Muradcan Tosunyan) (1740–1807), an Ottoman Armenian who worked as a translator (*dragoman*) for the Swedish embassy to the Ottoman Empire. D'Ohsson published his multivolume work *Tableau general de l'Empire Othoman* in 1824, with the stated purpose of offering a serious attempt to codify the administrative structure of the Ottoman Empire. He also sought to offer a historical survey of the Ottoman Empire, though this was never fully realized. Historian Christoph Neumann explains that D'Ohsson joined Paul Rycaut, Demetrie Cantemir, and even Joseph von Hammer as historians and commentators on the Ottoman Empire; all three saw their work as describing the "contemporary polity with a meaningful and functioning administrative structure."[36] Each sought to present the contemporary political, military, and social structures of the Ottoman state for the practical purpose of diplomatic, military, and political relations with European states.

As D'Ohsson systematically described each of the features of the Ottoman administrative structure, he spent a considerable amount of time surveying the status of non-Muslims in the Ottoman Empire.[37] By avoiding the story of Sultan Mehmet II's investiture of Patriarch Gennadios, he avoided presenting a narrative that was, perhaps, based on questionable sources. Furthermore, he sought to ground his own presentation in as much detail as possible coming from his contemporary context. For D'Ohsson, it was important to examine administrative documents as well, and it is for this reason he published a French translation of a *berât* granted to a patriarch in 1789. As innovative as his approach was, however, he began with an anachronistic understanding of the status of non-Muslims in Ottoman society.

Part of the problem was that D'Ohsson focused on the legal status of non-Muslims by first dealing with the terms of their tributary obligations to the state.[38] He observed their status as having the same "spirit of humiliation and inferiority" (*esprit d'humilité et d'infériorité*) found in early Islamic traditions based on Koranic injunctions, as well on the traditions of the sayings of the Prophet (*hadith*).[39] His descriptions of non-Muslim status, however, gave little indication of or reference to a historical or contemporary Ottoman context because D'Ohsson offered a summary based on Hanafi law, and in particular, based on a

35 Hammer-Purgstall, *Histoire de l'Empire ottoman*, 247. See also Cantemir, *The History of the Growth and Decay of the Othman Empire*, 104.

36 Christoph K. Neumann, "Political and Diplomatic Developments," in *The Cambridge History of Turkey*, ed. Suraiya N. Faroqhi (Cambridge: Cambridge University Press, 2006), 44.

37 Paparrēgopoulos, *Historia Tou Hellēnikou Ethnous Apo Tōn Archaiotatōn Chronōn Mechri Tōn Neōterōn*.

38 Ignatius M. D'Ohsson, *Tableau general de l'Empire Othoman*, vol. 5 (Paris, 1824), 104–139.

39 D'Ohsson, *Tableau general*, 104–106.

sixteenth-century commentator named Ibrahim al-Halabi, although it included many other commentators as well.[40]

D'Ohsson explained that early Islamic practice prescribed that those who refused to embrace Islam were to pay tribute to the Muslim overlords as well as have other obligations and prohibitions.[41] Only in the chapter observing these obligations and prohibitions did D'Ohsson begin to consider Ottoman historical reality. He referred to the non-Muslim population as divided into three nations whose spiritual leader had spiritual and temporal authority over the community. He explains:

> The tributary subjects are divided into three peoples: The Greeks (Roum), the Armenians (Ermeni) and the Israelites (Yahudi). They are different in all things, culture, language, usage, and character. Each has its own spiritual leader. Those of the first two have the title patriarch, Patrik. The Jews call theirs Grand Rabi, Khakham Baschy. The primates are elected from among the notables of their people, lay and clergy. But, they need to be confirmed by the sultan. Their jurisdiction is at the same time spiritual and temporal. Whenever there is a need to punish an individual of their religion, they have the right to imprison him, without any other formality but to report it to the state. It is through this body that these primates shall publish all ordinances relating to their respective nations.[42]

According to D'Ohsson, the religious leader was elected by the ecclesiastical and lay notables of the "nation" and was confirmed by the sultan. He was both spiritual and temporal leader with authority to issue ecclesiastical punishments, and also to imprison people with little obligation except to report such actions to the state. Thus, through the office of the religious leader, the Ottoman government ruled non-Muslim populations.

D'Ohsson sought to be thorough in his presentation by attempting to give documentary evidence as well. He was one of the first modern historians to publish a document issued by the Ottoman state to a Greek Patriarch. In doing so, however, he was not able to avoid overgeneralizing his conclusions to apply to the whole of Ottoman history. D'Ohsson's document, thus, became the sole primary source used by subsequent writers to describe the rights and role of the patriarchate and non-Muslims in the Ottoman period.

[40] Suraiya Faroqhi, *Approaching Ottoman History: An Introduction to the Sources* (Cambridge: Cambridge University Press, 1999), 156, n. 2. J. Schacht, "Al-Halabi, Burhan Al-din Ibrahim B. Muhammad B. Ibrahim," *Encyclopedia of Islam*, 2nd ed., III (1990): 90.

[41] D'Ohsson, *Tableau general*, 104.

[42] D'Ohsson, *Tableau general*, 111–112. Les sujets tributaires se partagent principalement 'en trois nations: les Grecs, Roum, les Arméniens, Ermény, et les Israélites, Jahoudj. Elles diffèrent en tout, culte, langue, usages, et caractère. Chacune a son chef spirituel; ceux des deux premières prennent le titre de Patriarche, Patrik; celui des Juifs est appelé Grand-Rabin, Khakhan Baschy. Ces primats sont élus par les notables de leur nation, laïcs et clercs; mais ils doivent être confirmés par le Sultan. Leur juridiction est à-la-fois spirituelle et temporelle. Outre le pouvoir de soumettre à des peines ecclésiastiques les individus de leur religion, ils ont le droit dé les faire emprisonner, sans autre formalité que celle d'en instruire le Gouvernement par un rapport, où ils ne sont pas même tenus de motiver leur arrêt. C'est par l'organe de ces primats que la Porte fait publier toutes les ordonnances qui concernent leurs nations respectives.

The document D'Ohsson used to explain the rights and prerogatives of the Patriarch of Constantinople under Ottoman rule was a 1789 Ottoman investiture *berât* granted to the Patriarch Neophytos VII (1789–94, 1798–1801). Outlining the rights and status of Patriarch Neophytos VII, the document granted the patriarch broad religious and civil authority. It stated that it was necessary to name Neophytos VII in Patriarch Prokopios' (1785–89) place because Patriarch Prokopios had acted reprehensibly by neglecting the responsibilities of his office, accruing debts, and not exercising his functions properly. The negative effects on the Greek Christian population and their certain outcry caused a successor patriarch to be installed in his place.[43] This document described, in great detail, the obligations and rights of the new patriarch as well as his jurisdictions. It survived, however, only in French translation in the edition published by D'Ohsson and presented the legal aspects of Ottoman rule without much context or historical analysis.

The problem with D'Ohsson's presentation, however, arises partly from the very late date of this document. This 1789 document is valuable to describe the status of the patriarch only in a late eighteenth-century Ottoman social milieu. D'Ohsson, and historians who came after him, however, assumed that the document's form had not changed substantially over time. The assumption was that based on this legal document, Ottoman legal practice toward the Church could be projected backwards in time to cover all periods of Ottoman rule. As a result, the imprecise use of this document has distorted subsequent presentations by historians discussing non-Muslim communities in the Ottoman Empire.

Due to a lack of available Ottoman documents in translation, Western historians who came after D'Ohsson used the information from this published account to expound upon the privileges and rights of the *millets* and of the non-Muslim communities. In this way the document became the basis for at least two other significant works on the Greek Church under Ottoman rule. Theodore Papadopoullos made extensive use of it in the main section of his book *Studies and Documents Relating to the History of the Greek Church and People under Turkish Domination*, in which he offered a general description of the organization and administration of the Greek Orthodox Patriarchate under Ottoman rule.[44]

Papadopoullos divides his work into three parts, the first of which deals with the Church from 1453 to 1800. Relying heavily on the patriarchal chronicles, as well as the document by D'Ohsson, Papadopoullos is deliberate in building an image of patriarchal authority. He begins his chapter by introducing the re-establishment of the Church under Ottoman rule, specifically focusing on the events related to Patriarch Gennadios. In attempting to offer definitions and descriptions of administrative posts, Papadopoullos gives the impression of reaching for any

[43] D'Ohsson, *Tableau general*, 121.

[44] Theodoros Papadopoullos, *Studies and Documents Relating to the History of the Greek Church and People under Turkish Domination*, 2nd ed. with supplementary material (Aldershot, Hampshire, Great Britain; Brookfield, VT: Variorum; Gower Pub. Co., 1990). First published in Brussels, 1952.

available source to back up his argument. Therefore, Papadopoullos compiled some interesting information and primary source material, but when it was time to discuss the rights and legal status of the patriarchal institution, he exclusively relied on this late eighteenth-century document. He treated this subject by giving a point-by-point paraphrase of the document for ten pages. Had he been less ambitious in his conclusions, he might have offered a reasonable service to the field by placing this document into its historical context. Instead, he presented the document as proof of a fully functioning *millet* system, in which the patriarch was the community leader (*millet başı*). The patriarch, thus, possessed the rights of both religious and civil leadership of the community. Unfortunately, Papadopoullos was interpreting the document from his own historical context and perspective, which, although extremely interesting, distorted the historicity of his claim. Papadopoullos was attracted to the image of the religious leader as *millet başı* because his perspective was informed more by the 1960s political reality in Cyprus than by Ottoman historical development.[45] Papadopoullos wrote at the time when Archbishop Makarios served as both religious leader of the Greek Orthodox Church of Cyprus and as political leader and president of the island republic.

To justify his use of the document to support his conclusion, Papadopoullos stated:

> The date of the *berât* (30 June 1789) is not without interest, since we expect to find in this document the crystallization of previous experience in policy followed with regard to ecclesiastical rights; at the same time, the uniformity, at their basic principles, that characterizes the *berâts* issued during the period, ensures that the data contained in the one under consideration, are fairly representative of the whole field, with the exception of a few non-essential particularities.[46]

The reasoning for this, however, is as faulty as considering contemporary US legislation to be the "crystallization of previous experience in policy" from the writing of the US Constitution to the present, because it does not account for historical development and change. Papadopoullos presented the categories that he took from the document: election, financial obligations, authority and civil status, exercise of authority, ecclesiastical rights, civil rights, protection of worship, property and revenue, civil rights of the subjects entailed by the patriarchal jurisdiction, and fiscal exemptions.

He followed D'Ohsson's published *berât* very closely and, in his turn, made broad generalizations about the status of the patriarch in the Ottoman Empire and his authority over the Greek *millet*.[47] For historical accuracy, however, each

[45] Papadopoullos' perspective is further limited by his observations of the leadership of Cyprus in the 1960s. The last of the articles reprinted in *Studies and Documents* is an analysis of the position of the Archbishop of Cyprus in an attempt to legitimize his civil role as president by looking at the long-standing tradition in the Ottoman period of political authority among the hierarchy; see Theodore Papadopoullos, "Orthodox Church and Civil Authority," *Journal of Contemporary History* 2/4 (1967): 201–209.

[46] Papadopoullos, *Studies*, 29.

[47] Papadopoullos, *Studies*, 29–39.

of the categories Papadopoullos proposed should have been understood in the context of 1789. Also, had he been more interested in diachronic development, he should have produced other examples of investiture *berâts* that were in fact available by the time he wrote his study. In 1943, H. Scheel had already made a great contribution to the discussion of non-Muslims and Ottoman legal practice by publishing a number of similar *berâts* predating the D'Ohsson document by fifty years.[48]

In the same year that Papadopoullos published his study on the Church under Ottoman rule, Ottoman historian, George Arnakis also published the article "The Greek Church of Constantinople and the Ottoman Empire" in the *Journal of Modern History*.[49] Arnakis focused on the investiture of Patriarch Gennadios Scholarios, mistaking the account of *Chronicon Maius* as an eyewitness account, and concluding that Sultan Mehmet II must have issued a *berât* to Patriarch Gennadios safeguarding the position of the patriarch. Arnakis, concluded that additional *berâts* continued this practice, and that, "in the course of time the Greek patriarch of Constantinople came to be regarded as the leader of the *Rum millet*—i.e. of the Orthodox Christians who were under the authority of the sultan."[50] Arnakis then proceeded to offer an anachronistic explanation about treatment of Christians based on the historical experience from the early Islamic period, and the medieval era, examining the cases of St. Catherine Monastery on Mount Sinai and the Patriarchate of Jerusalem under various Islamic dynasties.

Only when Arnakis focused on the *berât* issued by Sultan Ahmed I (1603–17) to Leontios, the Metropolitan of Larissa, in February 1604, did he begin to offer a more substantial explanation. Unfortunately, he based his conclusion on a spurious document. Manuel Gedeon had published the 1604 *berât* that Arnakis referred to in 1909.[51] Referring to the 1604 *berât*, Arnakis described the Ottoman government's stance vis-à-vis the Church of Constantinople according to five general principles. First, Christians were free to practice their faith and execute their religious duties without interference from Muslims. Second, the administration of the Church and Church discipline were not to be hindered, and the patriarch and Holy Synod were free to appoint their clergy. Third, the church properties, including monasteries were to be administered by the patriarch and bishops. Additionally, the patriarch and bishops were charged with the collection of taxes for the yearly dues owed to the

[48] H. Scheel, *Die Staatsrechtliche Stellung der Ökumenischen Kirchenfürsten in der alten Türkei* (Berlin: Berlag der Akademie der Wissenschaften, 1943).

[49] G. Arnakis, "The Greek Church of Constantinople and the Ottoman Empire," *The Journal of Modern History* 23/3 (1952): 235–250.

[50] Arnakis, *Greek Church*, 237–238.

[51] Arnakis, *Greek Church*, 242. Manouel Io Gedeon, *Vracheia semeiosis peri ton ekklesiastikon hemon dikaion [Brief Note Concerning Our Ecclesiastical Rights.]* (En Konstantinoupolei: Ek tou Patriarchikou Typographeiou, 1909), 62–72. Paraskevas Konortas later revisits this *berât* in his study P. Konortas, "He Exelixe Ton 'Ekklesiastikon' Beration Kai to 'Pronomiakon Zetema'," *Historia* 9 (1988): 42–51.

imperial fisc. Fourth, the church was responsible for family and inheritance issues, and the Church was to adjudicate such matters. Finally, the bishops had certain privileges to carry a staff, ride a horse, and have bodyguards and attendants.

Unfortunately for Arnakis, Paraskevas Konortas convincingly argued that Manuel Gedeon mistakenly attributed the *berât* to that issued to Metropolitan Leontios of Larissa in 1604. One of the important reasons this may have happened was that it was published in reaction to a debate wherein the rights of the Patriarchate of Constantinople were being challenged. In the middle of the nineteenth century, when the Tanzimat reforms realigned non-Muslim subjects as Ottoman citizens, the authority of the patriarch was directly challenged. The patriarchate was challenged further in the aftermath of the Young Turk Revolution of 1908, and under duress, it sought to demonstrate the centuries-long existence of administrative rights. Konortas showed that the *berât* in question could not have been from 1604 as it had little in common with *berâts* from the seventeenth century, but rather, it likely was a *berât* issued to the patriarchate in the mid-1880s, as it resembles almost verbatim a 1885 document.[52] Thus, even though Arnakis' approach was thoughtful, he based his own conclusions on a faulty document.

Fortunately for Papadopoullos, he did not focus on the same spurious 1604 *berât*. The D'Ohsson document of 1789 is, in fact, correctly identified. Yet, even with this knowledge, it is possible to see a distortion grow larger as Papadopoullos' analysis became the basis for other subsequent accounts of the "Greek *millet*." The most notable use of the D'Ohsson document via Papadopoullos is that of Steven Runciman in his book *The Great Church in Captivity*. This work became the standard description of the Ottoman period patriarchate, and is frequently cited.[53] Runciman used many Greek and Western language primary sources in addition to the secondary sources he cited when referring to specific Ottoman state practices toward the Greek Orthodox Church. In this way, Runciman further paraphrased the D'Ohsson 1789 *berât* through Papadopoullos's own paraphrase of the document. Based on this third-hand information, Runciman proposed a concise description of the rights and privileges of the patriarchate under Ottoman rule, as follows:[54]

- The patriarch in conjunction with the Holy Synod had complete control over the entire ecclesiastical organization, the bishops and all churches and monasteries and their possessions.
- Though the sultan's government had to confirm episcopal appointments, no bishop could be appointed or dismissed except on the recommendation of the patriarch and the Holy Synod.

[52] Konortas, "He Exelixe Ton 'Ekklesiastikon' Beration Kai to 'Pronomiakon Zetema'," 52.

[53] Steven Runciman, *The Great Church in Captivity* (Cambridge: Cambridge University Press, 1968).

[54] This almost verbatim list was made from Runciman, *Great Church*, 171–172. For this listing, Runciman relies on Papadopoullos, who relies almost exclusively on D'Ohsson, *Tableau general*.

- The patriarchal law courts alone had penal jurisdiction over the clergy; the Ottoman authorities could not arrest or judge anyone of episcopal rank without the permission of the patriarch.
- The patriarch in conjunction with the Holy Synod, had control over all matters of dogma.
- The patriarchal courts had full jurisdiction over all affairs concerning the Orthodox subjects that had a religious connotation i.e., matters of marriage, divorce, the guardianship of minors, and inheritance and successions.
- The patriarchal courts were entitled to try any commercial case if both disputants were Orthodox.
- Although the Christian laity was heavily taxed, the clergy was free from paying taxes, though on occasions they might of their own consent agree to pay special taxes.
- The patriarch could tax the Orthodox on his own authority to raise money for the needs of the Church.
- Complaints against the patriarch could only be heard by the Holy Synod, and only if it agreed unanimously to listen to them.
- The patriarch could call in the Ottoman authorities to see that his flock carried out his commands.
- The patriarch was responsible for the orderly and loyal behavior of his flock towards the ruling authorities, and for ensuring that the taxes were paid. He did not collect the taxes himself, which was the duty of the headman of the local community, who was responsible for keeping the registers.
- If there was any difficulty over the collection, the Ottoman state could ask the Church to punish recalcitrants with a sentence of excommunication.

According to Runciman and Papadopoullos, both of whom depended on D'Ohsson, the patriarch had complete control over the entire ecclesiastical organization, the bishops, and all churches and monasteries in their possessions. Furthermore, the rights and responsibilities of the patriarch's authority extended over the Greek Orthodox population. From this description, Runciman concluded that "he was the Ethnarch, the ruler of the *millet*."[55]

Because of Runciman's repute as a Byzantine historian, his conclusion ultimately became the standard interpretation of the Greek Orthodox Church in the Ottoman Empire. Additionally, Runciman's book became the foundation for subsequent presentations by historians wishing to discuss Ottoman administration of non-Muslims and the history of the Greek community. Specialists and non-specialists writing general histories of the late Byzantine Empire or about

[55] Runciman, *Great Church*, 171. This same explanation is even more concise in his most recent article on the *millet* system called, "Rum Milleti: The Orthodox Communities under the Ottoman Sultans," in *The Byzantine Tradition after the Fall of Constantinople*, ed. John J. Yiannias (Charlottesville: University Press of Virginia, 1992): 1–15.

the Greeks in the Tourkokratia period cite this work.[56] However, because of the dearth of material on this topic, more serious Ottoman history scholars have also cited this work. Halil Inalcik, Yavuz Ercan, and Kemal H. Karpat based a number of their observations on Runciman's conclusions.[57] For these scholars, as well as many other scholars who have worked on different aspects of the Greek community, the conception of the *Rum millet-i*, set forth so vividly by D'Ohsson and articulately by Papadopoulos and Runciman, continues to inform their understanding of the Greek community for all periods of the Ottoman Empire. The danger comes from an uncritical reading of secondary sources, which leads to a distorted understanding of the Ottoman treatment of non-Muslims. The matter is complicated when theoretical descriptions of the treatment of *zimmi* rooted in an early Islamic experience also accompany such analysis. This is a recipe for an anachronistic understanding of the experience of non-Muslims in the Ottoman Empire.

ARCHIVAL RESEARCH AND NEW DIRECTIONS

Recently, historical writing about Ottoman administration of non-Muslims has been moving away from anachronistic analyses based either on chronicles or on singular documents that were once the basis for general conclusions. This change is owed to the open access to the Ottoman archives and to the mining of ecclesiastical or monastic archives and sources. Until this point, there were few opportunities to corroborate historical evidence and even fewer vantage points from which to view non-Muslims interacting in their communities and with the state. A good step towards greater understanding the status and history of non-Muslims is to examine these peoples in their social context and to see them as the multidimensional historical people they once were and not as a one-dimensional cultural monument.

In 1931, the German scholar Frederich Giese was one of the first modern Ottoman historians to examine the multiple dimensions of the Greek community under Ottoman rule. He sought to explore the broader historical background and

[56] For some of the more significant adoptions of Runciman's *millet* system, see T. Ware, *The Orthodox Church*, 3rd ed. (London and New York: Penguin, 1993) 87–93; D. A. Zakythenos, *The Making of Modern Greece: From Byzantium to Independence* (Oxford: Basil Blackwell, 1976), 43–45; R. Clogg, "The Greek Millet in the Ottoman Empire," in *Christians and Jews in the Ottoman Empire: The Functioning of a Plural Society*, ed. Bernard Lewis and Benjamin Braude (New York: Holmes & Meier, 1982), 185–207. D. Obolensky, *The Byzantine Commonwealth: Eastern Europe 500–1453* (London: Weidenfeld and Nicolson, 1971), 368. For the most recent discussion of Orthodox Christianity and Islam that perpetuates the *millet* system, basing the description on Steven Runciman, see Andrew Sharp, *Orthodox Christians and Islam in the Postmodern Age* (Leiden and Boston: E. J. Brill, 2012), 12–19.

[57] Halil Inalcik, "The Status of the Greek Orthodox Patriarchate under the Ottomans," *Turcica* 21–23 (1991): 407–436; Yavuz Ercan, "Türkiye'de XV. ve XVI. Yüzyillarda Gayrimüslimlerin Hukuki, içtimai ve iktisadi Durumu," *Belleten* 47/188 (1983): 1119–1149; Kemal H. Karpat, "Millets and Nationality: The Roots of the Incongruity of Nation and State in the Post-Ottoman Era," in *Christians and Jews in the Ottoman Empire*, 141–169.

legal issues specific to Christian subjects in the period leading up to and including the conquest of Constantinople. Even though he revisited the traditional chronicle sources for the investiture of Patriarch Gennadios by Sultan Mehmet II, Giese approached the question in a new way, picking up on a strand suggesting an alternate possibility and allowing the legal questions to set his focus.

Giese re-examined the Ottoman grant of privileges to the patriarch and concluded that the received wisdom about this was a legacy from long-standing Islamic conventions. He examined the various historical descriptions of the conquest of Constantinople, and highlighted the interaction between Mehmet II and the Greek Orthodox population with particular attention to the institution of the Greek Orthodox Patriarchate. Reviewing the Greek accounts of George Sphrantzes and the *Historia Patriarchica*, and the Ottoman accounts by Aşıkpashazade, Tursun Bey, Ebu's-su'ud Efendi, and Lütfi Pasha, he concluded that the underlying question was whether the Ottomans conquered Constantinople or it had capitulated. Giese, thus, focused on the relevance of Islamic theory and Ottoman innovation. According to Islamic legal theory, capitulation of a city ensures that the general population, in Constantinople primarily a non-Muslim population, was granted privileges and free passage. When Sultan Mehmet II took over Constantinople, he had clearly conquered it. Sultan Mehmet II, however, acted contrary to Sharia law by granting the population and Greek Orthodox hierarchy privileges that belonged to a city that capitulated.[58] Giese identified the arrangement between the patriarch and the Ottoman state as representing an attempt to secure the rights of the patriarch when the state might not have had any obligation to do so under Islamic law. The Ottomans chose to deal with the reality of conquest and ruling a large non-Muslim city in the most practical of ways rather than to adhere to Islamic legal theory. This was clearly a trend that had been followed for a long time. Giese categorically denied the statement of another historian, Sesostris Sidarouss, who wrote about non-Muslims at the beginning of the century. Sidarouss stated that the relationship of the Ottoman state with the Christians was that of a bilateral contract.[59] Sidarouss' approach was typical of the non-Muslim historians who were attempting to establish a status quo after the Tanzimat reforms up to the breakup of the Ottoman Empire. Giese disputed this notion.

Giese concluded by stating that the tendency in the modern period was to stress the moment when Sultan Mehmet II granted privileges to Patriarch Gennadios

[58] The question of the conquest or capitulation became the subject of historical debate precisely because of Ottoman policies towards the subject population post-1453.

[59] F. Giese, "Die Geschichtlichen Grundlagen für die Stellung der christlichen Untertanen im osmanischen Reich (The Historical Background of the Position of Christian Subjects in the Ottoman Empire)," *Der Islam* 19 (1931): 264–277. "In any case, the claim that Sidarouss made, that it was a 'bilateral contract between the Christians and the Muslim government' is a distorition of the worst kind." Giese, "Die Geschichtlichen Grundlagen," 277. See also Sésostris Sidarouss Bey, *Les Patriarcats Dans l'Empire Ottoman Et Particulièrement En Egypte* (Paris: Rousseau, 1907) 273–274, and Y. Linant de Bellefonds, "La Suppression Des Juridictions De Statut Personnel En Egypte," *Revue Internationale De Droit Comparé* 8/3 (1956): 416–417.

and by extension to the Church and Greek community as a whole. This was an outgrowth of the experience of the pre-Tanzimat system, which was threatened by the nationalism of the nineteenth century. Tanzimat reforms attempted to replace the old idea of the *millet* with the new idea of the modern nation-state. It was surprising to Giese how historians, especially from Turkey, transposed the granting of privileges from the later centuries to earlier centuries. He reasoned that this was due to the lack of knowledge of their own history as well as the acceptance of false ideas emanating from Europe.[60] Giese's explanation and approach do not make the task of unraveling the relationship of the Church and Ottoman state any easier, but they do point out the problem of anachronism, and challenge historians to come up with alternative approaches to answering the lingering questions about the role of the Church in Ottoman society.

A few short years later in the aforementioned German Orientalist historian, Helmuth Scheel, did in fact move the discussion away from the sticky question of the nature of the Ottoman rule and conquest to focus on the specific legal aspects of Ottoman administration.[61] Therefore, he approached Ottoman administration of non-Muslims through an examination of the legal status and position of the Ecumenical Patriarchate in the Ottoman Empire. His research moved the discussion towards a new, more productive direction, basing it on documentary evidence from the Ottoman Archives.

Scheel published five documents from 1732 to 1830, offering facsimiles and producing transcriptions and translations. Each document was a *berât* granting the right to an individual to assume the bishopric of the Metropolis of Trabzon 1) 1732 *berât* awarded to "monk" Ananias by Sultan Mahmud I on the occasion of his accession, 2) 1736 *berât* awarded to Ananias II by Sultan Mahmud I on the occasion of the death of his predecessor Ananias, 3) 1798 *berât* awarded to Parthenios by Sultan Selim III on the occasion of the death of his predecessor Dorotheos, 4) 1814 *berât* awarded to Parthenios by Sultan Mahmud II on the occasion of his accession to the throne, and finally, 5) 1830 *berât* awarded to Constantios by Sultan Mahmud II on the occasion of the death of his predecessor Parthenios.

Scheel's documents were localized in the Metropolis of Trebizond, and follow a clear pattern of granting a *berât* either upon the accession of the bishop, himself, or upon the accession of a new sultan to the Ottoman throne. The first of the documents which forms a model for the succeeding documents opens with the statement that upon Sultan Mahmud I's auspicious enthronement, the Greek Patriarch of Istanbul sent a sealed request to the Ottoman Imperial Council, the Divan, to renew to the Metropolitan of Trebizond's authority over the church. Upon examining the previous taxation records, it was concluded that the Monk Ananias would pay the investiture fee of 8,000 *akçe*. Therefore, upon payment in cash, a *berât* was awarded and commanded the following: that the said monk, Ananias, was to take his position according to law and custom as Metropolitan of

[60] Giese, "Die Geschichtlichen Grundlagen," 277.

[61] Helmuth Scheel, *Die Staatsrechtliche Stellung der Ökumenischen Kirchenfürsten in der alten Türkei* (Berlin: Berlag der Akademie der Wissenschaften, 1943).

Trebizond. The churches and monasteries of the region were to be in his possession, and no one was to interfere with his administration of them. Furthermore, no marriages of believers to unbelievers were permitted as they are forbidden, and if a non-Muslim (*zimmi*) wishes to divorce, or reconcile disputes with other *zimmi*, they can adjudicate disputes by swearing according to the rites of his church. The Metropolitan Ananias was to collect the imperial taxes from within the cities, towns, and villages, and could carry a weapon for protection contrary to the ancient custom. If priests of the Metropolis died without a will, all the cash, horses, movable property, or anything else that belonged to the church, was to be collected by the aforementioned monks and delivered to the state. No *zimmi* was to be converted to a Muslim by coercion. The state officials were not to meddle in the administration of the bishop's office, and neither could monks and priests travel about to cause trouble. The tax for alms that the *zimmi* were required to give should be promoted and could be collected in cash, but also in oil, honey, and other goods, though not if in kind items were for the *zimmi's* own sustenance. Neither military men, nor government officials ought to impair the administration of the Metropolis. Each non-Muslim male would be taxed 12 *akçe*, while priests would owe a gold coin to the patriarch. The *berât* finished by describing how Ananias would take control of the rights of donated items, including vineyards, gardens, mill, fields, sacred spring monasteries, and all similar church property. The formula for the 1732 *berât* is followed in general terms by the subsequent *berâts*.

Scheel's work was one of the first modern studies that collected, published and analyzed documents of investiture granted to a metropolitan. Historians have not properly recognized Helmuth Scheel's contribution because he published his article in Berlin during the height of World War II. He admitted that legal research in Ottoman Turkish sources was still a subsidiary science in 1943, and one that had been developing slowly.[62] It was of great value because it helps determine the eighteenth- and nineteenth-century legal status of bishops of the Greek Orthodox Church. More importantly, however, Scheel pointed out how important it is to use archival material to understand how the Church functioned in Ottoman times. The sources existed, but often had to be brought together piecemeal.

A Czech scholar, Josef Kabrda, continued similar research in 1969 when he focused on the fiscal system of the Orthodox Church in the Ottoman period.[63]

[62] H. Scheel, *Die Staatsrechtliche Stellung*, 1.

[63] Josef Kabrda, *Le Système Fiscal de l'église Orthodoxe dans l'empire Ottoman (d'Aprés les documents turcs)* (Brno: Universita J. E. Purkyné, 1969). Others whose work suggest the prominence of the fiscal relationship are part of a new generation of economic and social historians from Greece include Paraskevas Konortas, and Demetris Apostolopoulos. See Paraskevas Konortas, '*Les rapports juridiques et politiques entre le patriarcat orthodoxe de Constantinople et l'Administration ottomane de 1453 à 1600 (d'après les documents grecs et ottomans)*' (Doctoral thesis, Universite de Paris I, 1985) ; and P. Konortas, "Les Contributions Ecclésiastiques: Patriarchikè Zèteia' et 'Basilikon Charatzion" Contribution À l'Histoire Économique Du Patriarcat Oecuménique Aux XVe et XVIe Siècles," in *Actes Du IIe Colloque International d'Histoire: Économies Méditerranéenes Équilibres et Intercommunications XIIIe-XIXe Siecles,* vol. III (Athens: Center de Recherches Néohelléniques de la Fondation Nationale de la Rechereche Scientifique, 1986), 217–255.; and Dimitris Apostolopoulos, "Les Mécanismes d'Une Conquête: Adaptations Politiques et Statut Économique des Conquis dans le Cadre De L'Empire

Kabrda used documentation similar to Scheel's. He examined ecclesiastical investiture *berâts* to explain the ecclesiastical fiscal system that existed in the eparchies in the Balkans for the period after 1635 to the first half of the nineteenth century for the territory of present-day Bulgaria. His chronology was limited to the documents that were available to him and he commented that practically no such documents were known to exist for periods before the seventeenth century. The following chapters will show that earlier documents do exist.

Kabrda went a step beyond Scheel by offering a more in-depth analysis of the specific requirements stipulated in the *berâts* and terms used in the ecclesiastical documents, including the patriarchal tax (*patriklik rüsûmu*), as well as various other taxes that required the hierarchy to act as collectors. In fact, Kabrda rightly argued that the *patriklik rüsûmu* was the tax owed to the imperial fisc (*miri rüsûmu*) that came from the total of all ecclesiastical taxes collected by bishops and priests. Local metropolitans levied these taxes on their congregations to cover their own expenses as well as the yearly assessment they owed to the patriarch in Istanbul.[64] These included all taxes levied, such as holy water taxes (*hagiasmoz*) on the fees given by those who visited the sacred holy water springs for cures to ailments, for fees that were collected during fairs (*panayir*), as well as taxes that were collected that went directly to the patriarch's annual *patriklik rüsûmu*.

Kabrda tackled the important issue of privileges and rights of the higher clergy by basing his statements about the ecclesiastical institution, not on the investiture episode, but on documentary evidence of *berâts* issued to bishops. He argued vigorously that ecclesiastical taxation resembled Byzantine ecclesiastical practice. For instance, he argued that the marriage tax, was a direct continuity from Byzantine times, as was the *kanonikon,* the tax made up of various church-related collections to meet the expenditures of the local church, which in the Ottoman period was identified as the *zitiye.* Through the structure of ecclesiastical taxation, Kabrda showed how the revenue became an institutionalized tax upon the Orthodox clergy and ultimately upon the Greek Orthodox population.[65]

Kabrda made a great contribution to understanding the reality of the legal status of the Church in the seventeenth century. Because he was limited to seventeenth-century documents for Bulgaria, he was unable to place the trends he found in the seventeenth century to earlier periods of Ottoman rule. Like Scheel, Kabrda's great contribution was to show that one could understand the role and function of the Greek Orthodox Church in the Ottoman Empire by looking at the specific terms of their responsibilities during a particular period.

Kabrda's very influential work attempted for the first time to discuss the possibilities of specific fiscal policies aimed at the Church. In many ways, his approach and execution have influenced the present work in terms of methods and

Ottoman," in *Actes Du IIe Colloque International d'Histoire: Économies Méditerranéenes Équilibres et Intercommunications XIIIe-XIXe Siecles*, vol. III (Athens: Center de Recherches Néohelléniques de la Fondation Nationale de la Rechereche Scientifique, 1986), 191–204.

[64] J. Kabrda, *Le Système Fiscal*, 62. [65] Kabrda, *Le Système Fiscal*, 8.

conclusions. His work, however, does not place the Church's fiscal administration into the larger Ottoman context nor tie it to the development and continuity of the treatment of non-Muslims from late Byzantine and early Ottoman times.

While the work of Scheel and Kabrda were real departures from the conventional way in which to explain the status of Christians under Ottoman rule, it was not until a research seminar and conference on the *millet* system held at Princeton University in 1978 that the subject received focused attention. The conference "*The Millet System: History and Legacy*" resulted in two volumes edited by Benjamin Braude and Bernard Lewis with the title *Christians and Jews in the Ottoman Empire: The Functioning of a Plural Society*.[66] These two important volumes contained multiple papers addressing the subject of the *millet* system, beginning with examinations of treatment of non-Muslims in early Islam,[67] to discussions of the meaning of the *Rum Millet* or "Greek Millet,"[68] the establishment of the Jewish community,[69] and of Armenian Patriarchate in Constantinople.[70]

The one paper that has repeatedly challenged the traditional idea of *millet* system is the aforementioned article by Benjamin Braude, "Foundation Myths of the Millet System."[71] This study has caught the imagination of historians working on non-Muslim communities in the Ottoman Empire. Braude intended to undermine what he called the "foundation myths" of the Greek, Jewish, and Armenian *millets* by using the Ottoman archival record to show how the Ottoman state conceived of and referred to members of the non-Muslim communities.[72]

[66] Benjamin Braude and Bernard Lewis, eds., *Christians and Jews in the Ottoman Empire: The Functioning of a Plural Society*, 2 vols. (New York: Holmes & Meier, 1982).

[67] C. E. Bosworth, "The Concept of Dhimma in Early Islam," in *Christians and Jews in the Ottoman Empire*, 37–51.

[68] Clogg, "The Greek Millet in the Ottoman Empire," in *Christians and Jews in the Ottoman Empire*, 185–207.

[69] M. A. Epstein, "The Leadership of the Ottoman Jews in the Fifteenth and Sixteenth Centuries," in *Christians and Jews in the Ottoman Empire*, 101–115; A. Cohen, "On the Realities of the Millet System: Jerusalem in the Sixteenth Century," in *Christians and Jews in the Ottoman Empire*, 7–18; J. R. Hacker, "Ottoman Policy Toward the Jews and Jewish Attitudes Toward the Ottomans During the Fifteenth Century," in *Christians and Jews in the Ottoman Empire*, 117–126.

[70] Kevork B. Bardakjian, "The Rise of the Armenian Patriarchate of Constantinople," in *Christians and Jews in the Ottoman Empire*, 89–100.

[71] Benjamin Braude, "Foundation Myths of the Millet System," in *Christians and Jews in the Ottoman Empire*, 69–88.

[72] Benjamin Braude, "Foundation Myths," 449. See also Benjamin Braude, "Venture and Faith in Commercial Life of the Ottoman Balkans, 1500–1600," *International History Review* 7/4 (1985): 519–542. For a comprehensive disussion on the Jewish community see Aryeh Shmuelevitz, *The Jews of the Ottoman Empire in the Late Fifteenth and the Sixteenth Centuries: Administrative, Legal, and Social Relations as Reflected in the Responsa* (Leiden: E. J. Brill, 1984), Mark Alan Epstein, *The Ottoman Jewish Communities and Their Role in the Fifteenth and Sixteenth Centuries* (Frieburg: Klaus Schwarz, 1980), and "The Leadership of the Ottoman Jews in the Fifteenth and Sixteenth Centuries," in *Christians and Jews in the Ottoman Empire*, 101–115. Stanford Shaw also has produced a volume on the Jews in the Ottoman Empire which demonstrates the justice of the Ottoman state in dealing with the Jewish community; see Stanford J. Shaw, *The Jews of the Ottoman Empire and the Turkish Republic* (New York: New York University Press, 1991). Also see Amnon Cohen, *Jewish Life Under Islam: Jerusalem in the Sixteenth Century* (Cambridge, MA: Harvard University Press, 1984). A. Levy, *The Sephardim in the Ottoman Empire* (Princeton, NJ: The Darwin Press, 1992); Avgidor Levy, ed., *The Jews of the Ottoman Empire* (Princeton, NJ: Darwin Press and the Institute of Turkish Studies, 1994).

Braude's article set out to criticize the established wisdom of Gibb and Bowen's formulation of the *millet system* that had become the normative view of the Ottoman administration of non-Muslims.[73] Braude was able to show that the notion of the *millet system* "originated through a combination of myths" that developed after the period of Ottoman conquest of Constantinople.[74] He focused on the term *millet* to show that this term practically never appeared until the late Ottoman period. Rather, the more common term to denote the non-Muslim (*zimmi)* community was *tâ'ife*, meaning a group, people, class, body of men, or tribe and the less common term, *cema'at*, which means congregation, or religious community.

Millet-i Rum is a term that was used primarily in the late Ottoman period to denote the Greek Orthodox community. While individuals like Roderic Davison wrote about the *millet* reforms in the nineteenth century,[75] Braude argued that the term gained prominence among historians when Gibb and Bowen first used it in their description. Braude suggested that historians relied on nineteenth-century Ottoman legal and diplomatic sources that had little bearing on the earlier Ottoman periods to formulate descriptions of the treatment of non-Muslims in the Ottoman Empire. He described how the term "*millet"* was used extensively during the Tanzimat reforms in the mid-nineteenth century to describe the rights and legal status of confessional minority groups. Also during this period, the diplomatic corps exchanged correspondence with European governments, and frequently used the term *millet* in its external communications to describe the non-Muslim Christian communities. As a result, the term *millet* entered the historical terminology that was applied as if it were used by all segments of the Ottoman government and for all periods. Braude explained that the usage of this term reached such a high level of circulation among historians that it had become an "anachronizing influence of nineteenth-century practice."[76] However, the term for the Greek *millet* that applies to the Ottoman period Greek Orthodox Patriarchate, "*rum milleti,*" did not actually appear in any lexicon until 1899.[77]

Braude criticized the work of Gibb and Bowen saying that although their work on the eighteenth-century Ottoman Empire had become an influential secondary source, especially concerning non-Muslims, they were using sources anachronistically to describe fundamental issues about Ottoman state and society, and that, therefore, their presentation was flawed. In attempting to deal with the issue of non-Muslims in the Ottoman Empire, Gibb and Bowen began with the assumption that the Ottoman state was an exclusively Islamic state governed

[73] H. A. R. Gibb and Harold Bowen, *Islamic Society and the West: A Study of the Impact of Western Civilization on Moslem Culture in the Near East*, 2 vols. (London: Oxford University Press, 1957), vol. 1.

[74] Braude, "Foundation Myths," 69.

[75] R. Davison, *Reform in the Ottoman Empire* (Princeton, NJ: Princeton University Press, 1963), 132.

[76] Braude, "Foundation Myths," 72.

[77] Braude, "Foundation Myths," 73.

by Islamic law. Therefore, in the chapter entitled "The Dimmis" they wrote the following:

> Like everything else in the Sacred Law, the principles upon which non-Muslims are to be dealt with by Moslem rulers were evolved in the early centuries of Islam, and are variously defined by the four orthodox schools. But they have their roots in the attitude of the Prophet to the other religions with which he was acquainted, and to the problem of opposition to his mission.[78]

The authors observed that the expansion of the Ottoman state resembled early Islamic expansion that led to the establishment of the Caliphate and the first Islamic state. Both the early Islamic and Ottoman conquests brought "large territories hitherto Christian into the Domain of Islam and so of presenting the Moslem rulers with vast numbers of Christian dhimmi subjects."[79]

The implication of this approach led to faulty conclusions: 1) the processes of the early Islamic conquests and the Ottoman conquests were identical, as both the early Muslims, and early Ottomans conquered vast *zimmi* areas; 2) that the general organization of Ottoman society was essentially "corporate"; and 3) under Sharia law, *zimmis* were viewed as members of their respective confessional community, and not as individuals,[80] that Sharia law regulated the relationship of the *zimmis* with the state and with individual Muslims because it is easy to draw a religious distinction between people. Yet, according to this interpretation, the same Sharia law did little to regulate *zimmis* as they related to each other. "The status of the individual *zimmi*, in short, derived exclusively from his membership to a protected community."[81] For Gibb and Bowen, the idea of community or *millet*, and the Ottoman administration of the *millet* have its root in early Islamic practice and, perhaps, in earlier Roman practices allowing groups to maintain their own set of internal laws and regulations.[82]

Second, Braude criticized Gibb and Bowen for projecting nineteenth-century Ottoman realities onto the fifteenth century. Braude criticized their use of nineteenth-century Ottoman legal historians who had been preoccupied with untangling the issues raised by the Tanzimat reforms, to make statements about the issue of the "*millet* system." Braude convincingly argued that the late Ottoman conception of *millet* was not in circulation during the fifteenth and sixteenth centuries.

Historian Michael Ursinus, in his article "*Millet*" in the *Encyclopedia of Islam*, addressed usage of the term *millet* to denote various non-Muslim populations. He corrects Braude's assertion that this was exclusively a nineteenth-century term by showing sporadic usage in the *Mühimme Defterleri*. There is evidence for its usage as early as 1591 for the Armenian *millet* (*millet-i Ermeniyan*), and in 1757 for the Greek *millet* (*millet-i Rum*), though the Jewish *millet* (*Yahud milleti*) and Roman Catholic *millet* (*Katolik millet*) are not mentioned until as late as 1839.[83]

[78] Gibb and Bowen, *Islamic Society*, vol. 2, 209.
[79] Gibb and Bowen, *Islamic Society*, vol. 2, 209.
[80] Gibb and Bowen, *Islamic Society*, vol. 2, 211.
[81] Gibb and Bowen, *Islamic Society*, vol. 2, 212.
[82] Gibb and Bowen, *Islamic Society*, vol. 2, 212.
[83] M. Ursinus, "Millet," *Encyclopedia of Islam (2nd Edition)* VII (1990): 62.

Daniel Goffman also pushes the usage back in time adding that usage of the term *millet* was discovered as early as the first half of the seventeenth century, though it was used to describe a general Christian community, rather than a community from a specific religious-ethnic group. In the earliest instance, the Ottomans used *millet* in conjunction with the term *tâ'ife* in 1614 to deal with the community of Franks in Jerusalem. The Ottoman decree from the Divan to the *kadi* of Jerusalem referred to this Frankish "*tâ'ife*" as a "unique *millet*."[84] Goffman adds that the understanding of *millet* may have been impacted when the Ottomans came into contact with Catholics and Protestants, who needed to be distinct from the Ottoman non-Muslim communities. He concludes by describing a term that in "the early-modern Ottoman polity was a disparate and evolving entity ..."[85]

The problem with concrete formulations that do not take into account either the lack of usage, or the fluidity of meaning of such a term, is that historians uncritically accept such descriptions and perpetuate anachronistic views based on the easy explanations. To avoid this pitfall, it is important to examine society directly and begin to see how it functioned "on the ground," to focus on non-Muslims in their social context, and to examine their role as active agents in society. Subjects of the Ottoman Empire ought to be seen as real, living people who did what they could to survive, to achieve security and to advance themselves and their community.[86]

Following Braude's lead, the Ottoman historian Paraskevas Konortas investigated Ottoman terminology specifically for the Greek Orthodox community in the Ottoman Empire.[87] Konortas, relying on his own examination of documentary evidence for his independent conclusions, agreed with Braude that the Ottomans did not use the term *millet* to describe the social organization of the Greek community in the period immediately following the conquest of Constantinople by Mehmet II. Similarly, Konortas identified the term "*tâ'ife*," which refers to members from this community in the sense of a group. Also, he argued that the Ottomans used the term *millet* to refer to non-Muslim communities only after the eighteenth century.[88]

Konortas showed that the Ottomans did not consider the ecclesiastical and administrative claim of patriarchal primacy to be the exclusive right of the

[84] D. Goffman, "Ottoman Millets in the Early Seventeenth Century," *New Perspectives on Turkey* 11 (1994): 139, n. 10.

[85] Goffman, "Ottoman Millets" 154.

[86] Christopher R. Friedrichs, *The Early Modern City, 1450–1750* (London: Longman, 1995), 15.

[87] Paraskevas Konortas, "From tâ'ife to Millet: Ottoman Terms Concerning the Ottoman Greek Orthodox Community," in *Ottoman Greeks in the Age of Nationalism: Politics, Economy, and Society in the Nineteenth Century*, ed. Dimitri Gondicas and Charles Issawi (Princeton, NJ: Darwin Press, 1999), 169–180.

[88] Konortas, *From tâ'ife to Millet*, 169. According to Socrates Petmezas, in his essay entitled "L'Organisation Ecclésiastiques sous les Ottomans," in *Conseils et Mémoires de Synadinos Prête de Serrès en Macédoine (XVIIe siècle)*, ed. S. Asdrachas Paolo Odorico, T. Karanastassis, K. Kostis, and S. Petmezas (Editions de l'Association "Pierre Belon," 1997), 487–569, Konortas was the first to pose the question of whether or not the dignity of the patriarch had been granted by the sultan. "Il a souligné que le concessionaire á ferme (amil) d'une source de revenus (moukata recevait ...)," 508 note. 41.

Patriarchate of Constantinople. According to Byzantine imperial tradition, the hierarchical structure of the Orthodox Church placed the Patriarch of Constantinople at the top of the ecclesiastical administrative structure. However, after 1453 and before the seventeenth century, the Patriarch of Constantinople was considered by the state to be on an equal level with other archbishops in the Ottoman Empire. By citing the independent status of the independent archbishops of Ohrid and Peç, and the example of the Ottomans calling the former, the bishop of Ohrid, "Patriarch" (Ohri Patriği), "suggests that the Ecumenical Patriarch was not yet *millet başı*, that is, leader of the whole Orthodox community of the empire."[89] Konortas reasoned that the patriarchate took on the position of primacy among other jurisdictions, and the power of the *Ethnarch* (leader of the ethnos or nation), only after the decline of centralized Ottoman state authority, from the beginning of the seventeenth century to the eighteenth century. To what extent was the decline of the central Ottoman authority connected to the rise of patriarchal authority? Konortas indicated that this was an important part of the process of consolidation of patriarchal power. He argues that the decline "gave the opportunity to the Orthodox high clergy to acquire more political, administrative, judicial, and economic privilege" a process that was not accomplished until the late eighteenth and nineteenth century.[90]

Both Braude and Konortas philologically problematized the anachronistic usage of the terms *millet, millet başı*, and *Rum millet-i*. This approach of examining Ottoman terminology has moved the discussion of communal organization and leadership down an important path, to question the established wisdom and even the existence of the *millet* system prior to the nineteenth century. In some respects, however, this approach is limited, and has produced meager results in comparison with other possibilities since it does not examine how non-Muslims actually functioned within their own spheres or points of their intersection with the broader aspects of Ottoman society. Braude admitted this shortcoming by stating, "No philological exercise can answer that question completely, but it can help form the outline in which such questions can be posed."[91] By raising the question of whether there was such a thing as a *millet* system, these authors alerted historians to a major problem for those investigating how non-Muslim communities functioned.[92]

A major contribution to tackling this problem appeared in the form of another important international colloquium that produced an edited volume. In particular, the panels sought to clarify some of the broader issues that clouded the

[89] Konortas, *From tâ'ife to Millet*, 174. The details of the conflict between the Patriarchate of Constantinople and the Patriarch of Ohrid are discussed in Chapter 3.

[90] Konortas, *From tâ'ife to Millet*, 173. Konortas is representative of a new generation of Greek historians who have been trained in Europe to use Ottoman sources, and, therefore, look critically upon the historiographic tradition.

[91] Braude, "Foundation Myths," 74.

[92] See also Michael Ursinus, "Zur Diskussion um 'millet' im Osmanischen Reich," *Südost-Forschungen* 48 (1989): 195–207; Michael Ursinus, "Millet", 61–64.

history of the Greek community in the Ottoman Empire.[93] The most important of these articles, by Dimitris Apostolopoulos, dealt with the political and, especially, economic mechanisms of conquest.[94] Apostolopoulos pointed out a new direction in which research about non-Muslims should proceed. He argued that historians should examine the political and economic dimensions of the Ottoman subject population.[95] He sought to explain the impetus for Ottoman conquest by asking what factors contributed to Ottoman willingness to conquer. He argued that Ottoman conquests took place with one basic premise: all territory, goods, and people were economically exploitable. To realize a profit from their efforts, therefore, the conquerors needed to determine a way to blend the interests of the conquered with the interests of the conquerors.[96]

During the long period of Ottoman conquest in the fourteenth and fifteenth centuries, Greek society was partly under Byzantine and partly under Ottoman rule. Apostolopoulos observed a willingness on the part of members of Greek society to submit to the Ottomans. This willingness was due to members of the "Greco-byzantine society" who looked for new ways to survive and thrive in a new system. This was especially true of the Byzantine aristocracy.[97] While it was necessary for the Ottomans to exert a certain amount of violence to gain control of territory, it became more important for the Ottomans to establish legitimate control by incorporating existing political and economic structures into their growing state.

How did the Ottoman conquerors integrate large segments of non-Muslim society into the Ottoman Empire? The key, according to Apostolopoulos, was the integration of important institutions into their own administration. On the imperial level, the Ottomans transferred aspects of Byzantine imperial ideology to their own purposes. Thus, the "well loved of God" (*theophilestatos*) was an idea transferred from the Byzantine emperors to the sultan.[98] This absorption of imperial ideology was also a catalyst for Sultan Mehmet II to reconstitute the patriarchate. Not only did he want to inspire confidence among his Greek subjects to attract them to rebuild the imperial city of Istanbul, but, also, this action

[93] Dimitris Apostolopoulos, "Les Mécanismes d'Une Conquête," 191–204. Among the important contributions are articles by Marina Maropoulou, Paraskevas Konortas, Dimitris Apostolopoulos, as well as a very interesting roundtable discussion whose additional participants were T. Dimaras, Spyros Troïanos, John Alexander, and Robert Mantran.

[94] Dimitris Apostolopoulos, *Ho "hieros kodix" tou Patreiarcheiou Konstantinoupoleos sto B' miso tou IE aiona. Ta mona gnosta sparagmata* (Athens: Ethniko Hydryma Ereunon/Kentron Neoellenikon Ereunon, 1992); Dimitris Apostolopoulos, *To Mega Nomimon: Symvole sten ereuna tou metavyzantinou demosiou dikaiou* (Athens: D. Apostolopoulos, 1978).

[95] Apostolopoulos, "Les Mécanismes d'Une Conquête," 202.

[96] Apostolopoulos, "Les Mécanismes d'une Conquête," 193.

[97] Apostolopoulos, "Les Mécanismes d'une Conquête," 195.

[98] Apostolopoulos, "Les Mécanismes d'une Conquête," 198. Also see Speros Vryonis, Jr., "Byzantine Constantinople and Ottoman Istanbul: Evolution in a Millenial Imperial Iconography," in *The Ottoman City and Its Parts*, ed. Irene A. Bierman, Donald Preziosi, and Rifa'at A. Abou-El-Haj (New York: Aristide C. Caratzas, 1991), 13–52, where he describes in detail the imperial conciousness with which Mehmet II approached the rebuilding of Istanbul after the conquest.

legitimized the sultan by sending the message that he was willing to take on the important roles of the Byzantine emperor by calling forth a monk to become Patriarch of Constantinople.

In addition, the *archons,* the leading economic and social elites of Byzantine society, sought to play a political role in the new state and helped accelerate the mechanisms of conquest. Many *archons* were integrated into the Ottoman system and economy well before the conquest of Constantinople.[99] In numerous cases, *archons* sought to promote their own political aims by attempting to gain control of the post-Byzantine Patriarchate, and, therefore, remained active in community developments after 1453.[100]

When the Ottomans re-established the Patriarchate of Constantinople in 1454, the Ottomans tied it to the fiscal mechanisms of the new state so as to control it. The state had enjoyed a twofold benefit from the Church. First, it reaped profits from tax revenues that the Church was responsible for collecting. Second, it was able to control a major non-Muslim institution, just as it might control any other institution designed to submit revenue to the central treasury.[101] Because the Ottoman state was experienced in appropriating indigenous institutions, they were also able to incorporate the large Orthodox Christian population of the Balkans into their state despite such a decentralized administration. The integration of indigenous institutions and structures into the fiscal system made the difference. These newly adapted structures eventually consolidated their own local power and authority.[102]

During the colloquium mentioned above, Paraskevas Konortas asserted that it was possible that the Church might have functioned as a tax farm because the patriarch submitted a portion of his collected taxes to the state and withheld a portion. He stated that the sources are not clear enough to substantiate this claim, at least until the second half of the sixteenth century. Konortas' work on the Orthodox Church in the Ottoman period has been extensive.[103] He attempted to

[99] Halil Inalcik, "Greeks in the Ottoman Economy and Finances, 1453–1500," in *TO ELLHNIKON: Studies in Honor of Speros Vryonis, Jr.*, ed. John S. Langdon; Stephen W. Reinert; Jelisaveta Stanojevich Allen, (New Rochelle, NY: Aristide D. Caratzas, 1993), 289–365.

[100] Apostolopoulos, "Les Mécanismes d'une Conquête," 201.

[101] Apostolopoulos, "Les Mécanismes d'une Conquête," 203. Also see the article by Marina Maropoulou, "L'Économie: Moyen de Transgression ou d'Adaptation Sociale? Le Témoinage de Gennadios Scholarios,"in in *Économies mediterranéennes équilibres et intercommunications XIIIe-XIXe siècles,* Vol. 3. (Athens: Fondation Nationale de la Recherche Scientifique, 1986), 257–268, wherein the same issue of economy is again stressed. Using the testimony of Gennadios Scholarios, the author tried to show how Gennadios was trying to adapt to the new social and economic situation. Gennadios claimed that he put up with many disappointments and suffered greatly in striving to keep the Christian body united. He did not condemn acts of simony by figures such as the Patriarch of Jerusalem, as this was not the politically expedient thing to do, though he was fully conscious of the fiscalization of the ecclesiastical institution. He used the principle of accommodation (*ekonomia*) to deal with the new social and political factors until the time came when he could no longer take the situation and attempted to retire from the office.

[102] For the issue of consolidation of Patriarchal power also see Socrates Petmezas, "L'Organisation Ecclésiastiques sous les Ottomans," 487–569. Petmezas, however, takes the Bourdieu approach that the Patriarchate increased its symbolic power in the process of consolidating its communal control.

[103] Paraskevas Konortas, "Les Contributions Ecclésiastiques: Patriarchikè Zèteia" et 'Basilikon Charatzion' Contribution à l'Histoire Économique du Patriarcat Oecuménique aux XVe et XVIe

clarify the economic history of the Ottoman period patriarchate when he investigated the subject of patriarchal alms (*patriarchal zitiye*). His goal was to investigate the type of tax imposed upon local metropolitans and archbishops by the patriarchate. He was able to conclude that the *patriarchal zitiye* was the same thing as the *patriklik rüsûmü,* also an imperial tax.[104] He attempted to correlate the terminology of the Greek and Ottoman records dealing with the Church in order to determine if they represent the same type of tax. He hoped the data could be used in the broader analysis of Ottoman taxation.

Konortas made large strides to place the financial situation of the Ecumenical Patriarchate directly into the context of the 1590s Ottoman financial crisis, observing a steadily growing imperial need for revenue reflected in the increase in late sixteenth-century hierarchical payments. Using data from the Greek sources detailing the amounts given for *pişkeş*, Konortas' approach was quite productive because he tied developments in the local non-Muslim community to the broader Ottoman system. Thus, he showed that local communities were not entirely isolated from Ottoman society, and that even the smaller subgroups reflected trends in the larger society.

Most recently in his book *Ottoman Considerations on the Ecumenical Patriarchate: Berâts of the Primates of the Great Church (Seventeenth to Early Twentieth Centuries)*, Konortas compiled previously published Ottoman documents to determine Ottoman perspectives on the legal status of the patriarchate.[105] In his extensive study, he listed each extant Ottoman *berât* granted to the Ecumenical Patriarchs, to the Metropolitans, and bishops. He then listed terms of the various *berâts* in an attempt to create a categorization of the classic Ottoman *berât* while attempting to show the diachronic development of the *berâts*. Curiously, he began his comparative discussion of the articles of a typical Ottoman *berât* by setting forth a *berât* issued in 1835 to Patriarch Gregory VI (1835–40, 1867–71). The reasoning for this selection was to offer a document with an expansive enough range of issues, it demonstrated continuity of form from earlier periods, and finally it was issued just prior to the Tanzimat. Konortas was particularly interested in this last issue, as he later discussed the changes to the legal status of the Church under Ottoman administration during and after the Tanzimat.[106]

Konortas dealt with the question of the *millet* system only insofar as he tried to historicize the nineteenth-century Bulgarian schism and the establishment of the

Siècles," in *Économies mediterranéennes équilibres et intercommunications XIIIe-XIXe siècles,* Vol. 3 (Athens: Fondation Nationale de la Recherche Scientifique, 1986), 217–255. Konortas' dissertation at the University of Paris, 'Les rapports juridiques et politiques entre le Patriarchat Orthodoxe de Constantinople et l'Administration ottomane de 1453–1600 (d'après les documents grecs et ottomans)' (Universite de Paris I Pantheon Sorbonne, Paris, 1985). This dissertation was unavailable to me. Konortas has produced numerous articles about the Ecumenical Patriarchate.

104 Konortas, "Les Contributions Ecclésiastiques," 219 n. 2 and 220, n. 8.

105 Paraskevas Konortas, *Othomanikes Theoreseis gia to Oikoumeniko Patriarcheio: Beratia gia tous prokathemenous tes Megales Ekklesias (17os-arches 20ou aiona)* (Athens: Ekdoseis Alexandreia, 1998).

106 Konortas, *Othomanikes Theoreseis*, 73–93.

Bulgarian Exarchate in 1872. In this example, he described the standard beliefs about the *millet* system and how only in the late Ottoman period it represented a religious-ethnic community. The patriarch, in the face of nationalist challenges, such as that from the Bulgarian Church which sought its independence from Constantinople, was understood as the *ethnarch* or leader of the Greek community or *Rum millet-i*.[107]

Another historian who helped fundamentally change the way we see Ottoman rule over non-Muslims is the don of Ottoman historical studies, Halil Inalcik, who presented groundbreaking analysis and defined the fundamental concepts that continue to stand their ground. According to Inalcik, the Ottoman *modus operandi* for ruling non-Muslims was established in the early years of Ottoman conquests and lasted into the sixteenth century. In the early Ottoman period, conquest was connected with the strategy of accommodation.[108] Inalcik introduced this idea in terms of the broader "Ottoman Methods of Conquest," as well by a specific term, "*istimâlet,*" meaning "a trying to persuade; a gaining goodwill, a coaxing," to signify the early phase of accommodation of non-Muslim populations, thereby, assisting and facilitating Ottoman conquest.[109]

Halil Inalcik came upon this productive explanation of *istimâlet* early in his career, in 1954, with his groundbreaking article "Ottoman Methods of Conquest," which drew on his examination of tax registers in the Balkan territories.[110] How the Ottomans came to control such a large multi-ethnic, multi-religious, multi-racial empire can only be understood within the context of how the state was successful in its early years. Whether termed *istimâlet* or "Ottoman Methods of Conquest" as in Inalcik's 1954 article, this policy contributed to the successful conquest of the Balkans despite the difficult geographic obstacle and majority population that was Christian, albeit governed by fragmented Balkan regimes.[111] The largest and last of these regimes to be of any real significance was Serbian King, Stephen Uroš IV Duşan's kingdom. Stephen Duşan himself became an Ottoman vassal. After his death, local lords and families immediately moved to ally with the Ottomans as vassals. When the Ottomans moved into a new territory, they subdued it quickly and established direct control over it. They reduced the local rulers

[107] Konortas, *Othomanikes Theoreseis*, 303–315.

[108] This is in sharp contrast to the argument advanced by Speros Vryonis, *The Decline of Medieval Hellenism in Asia Minor and the Process of Islamization from the Eleventh through the Fifteenth Century* (Los Angeles: University of California Press, 1971), 498–501. He summarizes his positions concerning the massive violence and deliberate destruction of the Byzantine institutional structures as a step in the process of Islamization of Anatolia.

[109] *"İstimâlet," Redhouse Yeni Türkçe İngilizce Sözlüğü* (İstanbul: Redhouse Yayinevi, 1968), 557. It was not, however, found in Mehmet Zeki Pakalin, *Osmanlı tarih deyimleri ve terimleri sözlüğü* (Istanbul: Milli Eğitim Basimevi, 1946). For an extended discussion of *İstimâlet* see also, Muhammed Aruçi, "Islamic Authority and Its Attitude Towards Non-Muslim Groups and Minorities in Muslim Society," in *Authority, Privacy and Public Order in Islam: Proceedings of the 22nd Congress of L'Union Européenne Des Arabisants Et Islamisants*, ed. Barbara Michalak-Pikulski and Andrzej Pikulski (Louvain:Peeters, 2006), 254–258.

[110] H. Inalcik, "Ottoman Methods of Conquest," *Studia Islamica* II (1954): 104–129.

[111] Inalcik, "Ottoman Methods of Conquest," 104–129.

to tributary vassals who, in the process, were able to preserve a semblance of their former autonomy and political identity.[112]

During the second stage of conquest the Ottomans established direct control and annexation of the territories, often relying on the territory's former ruler. During this stage the institution of the *timar* became the chief fiscal and administrative mechanism. The conquered lands were inspected, and all sources of revenue were recorded. Supporters of the sultan were allowed the right to share in the taxation of local revenues. In summary, during the first of these stages, local rulers were given the opportunity to rule as Ottoman vassals over territory previously under their control. In the second of these stages, direct control was given to *timariots*, who were also members of the previous aristocracy, and continued even as Christians for generations beyond the initial conquests.

Inalcik argued against the idea that the Ottoman conquest in the Balkans deprived the area of its indigenous aristocracy through forceful measures and replaced it with a feudatory class of Turks and local Christians. Using data from the *timar* and *tahrir defters* of Rumeli that can be dated to the period of Murat II (1421–51) and Mehmet II (1451–81), Inalcik demonstrated that many of the *timar* holders could be identified as members of the Christian aristocracy who were offered the same *timar* rights as their Muslim Turkish counterparts. Converting to Islam was not a requirement for receiving a *timar* or becoming a member of the Ottoman provincial elite. Over time the local ruling class became Ottomanized, Islamicized, and Turkified during the second, third or later generations after the conquest. However, in the early period of Ottoman expansion, the Ottomans relied upon the local Christian ruling aristocracy to assist in their conquests.[113]

What has been described as the holy war character of the early Ottoman frontier state (*üç gâzi devleti*) does not explain examples from a Tırhala register showing 36 out of 182 *sipahis* as being Christians with notations like "*Timâr-i Dimitri veled-i Mihal, kadîmî sipâhi oğluymuş*" (The *timar* of Dimitri the son of Mihal, the son of an ancient *sipahi*).[114] Additional evidence appears in Inalcik's published *Tahrir Defteri* of 1435 for the Sancak of Arvanid. With timar's granted to individuals like Andranikos (*timar* n. 242), Dimitri Prespe (*timar* n. 257), Petros Agramatikos (*timar* n. 258), and Konstantin (*timar* n. 264).[115] Evidence of Christian timariots does not exactly support the arguments for purely Turkish origins of the Ottoman state. Rather, the state was primarily interested in expanding its geographic control and its influence and used the available local military resources, Christian irregulars such as the *voynuks, martolos,* and *eflâks,* who served as auxiliaries

[112] H. Inalcik, "Stefan Duşan'dan Osmanlı Imparatorluğuna: Asırda Rumeli'de Hrlstlyan Sipahiler ve Menşeleri," in *60. Doğum Yılı Münasebetiyle Fuad Köprülü Armağanı* (Istanbul: Dil ve Tarih Coğrafya Fakültesi Yayını, 1953), 207–248.

[113] Inalcik, *Fatih devri üzerinde tetkikler ve vesikalar,* 141. For a more recent discussion of Christian timariots, see Linda T. Darling, "Nasihatnameler, Icmal Defterleri, and the Timar-Holding Ottoman Elite in the Late Sixteenth Century," *Osmanli Arastirmalari (The Journal of Ottoman Studies)* XLIII (2014): 193–226.

[114] Inalcik, "Stefan Dushan'dan Osmanli Imparatorluğuna," 215.

[115] H. Inalcik, *Suret-i Defter-i Sancak-i Arvanid* (Ankara: Türk Tarih Kurumu Basimevi, 1954).

receiving and maintaining special privileges due to their specialized services to the Ottoman state.

Finally, as a class, Christian *timariot* families were not tied to the land in one particular region for generations. The *timar* administration functioned as in most areas and was granted to non-related individuals over time. The exception was an interesting case of Bosnia and Trabzon. Bosnia had an indigenous land tenure system based on *bashtinas. Bashtinas* were *timars*, or fiefs that acted as transferable and inheritable property. Neither *timars* nor the Byzantine versions of the *pronoia* were transferable. This *bashtina* was granted to local elites who could then transfer them to whom they chose. This was a further Ottoman accommodation to rule the region of Bosnia that was so distant from the Ottoman center. This process was interestingly transferred to Trabzon as a result of Ottoman policy of forced population movement (*sürgün*) and can be seen in the *Tahrir Defters.* The Ottomans preserved these local practices for centuries.[116] It is fascinating to note that even after establishing his groundbreaking historical conclusions, Halil Inalcik backed away from his impressive assertion about the accommodationist practices of the early Ottoman emirate. Rather, he dramatically returned to the standard paradigm of the *gazi* thesis where the Ottomans sought to spread their rule and Islam by the sword. This change of heart had not gone unnoticed by other Ottoman historians attempting to deconstruct the *gazi* thesis, among whom is Heath W. Lowry, one of the historians who early on built upon Inalcik's conclusions through his own work in the *Tahrir Defters.*[117]

The *Tahrir Defter* registers recorded for the region of Trabzon corroborate the preservation of local practices. The Ottomans conquered Trabzon (Byzantine Trebizond) in 1461. Lowry demonstrated that the Ottoman conquest of Trabzon was accompanied by little disruption to the Christian, predominately Greek-speaking population. If one examines the series of registers up to the ending point of Lowry's study in 1583, which includes entries extending 100 years beyond the initial conquest, one can conclude that there was an increase in Islamization, though the process of Turkification was still at a very early stage.[118]

[116] Inalcik, "Stefan Dushan'dan Osmanli Imparatorluğuna," 207–248. Other studies confirming Ottoman continuity of Byzantine forms are: Halil Inalcik, "The Problem of the Relationship between Byzantine and Ottoman Taxation," in *Akten des XI internationalen Byzantinisten Kongresses Munich 1958*, ed. F. Dölger and H. G. Beck (Munich:C.H. Beck, 1960), 237–42; Speros Vryonis, Jr., "The Byzantine Legacy and Ottoman Forms," in *Byzantina Kai Metabyzantina: Studies on Byzantium, Seljuks, and Ottoman*, ed. Speros Vryonis, Jr. (Malibu: Undina Press, 1982), XIII; Heath Lowry, *The Ottoman "Tahrir Defters" as a Source for Urban Demographic History: The Case Study of Trabzon (c.1486–1583)* (Ann Arbor: University Microfilms International, 1984) developed and published in 1981 as *Trabzon Şehrinin İslamlaşma ve Türkleşmesi, 1481–1583* (Istanbul: Bosphorus University Press, 1981). The recently translated English edition is *The Islamization & Turkification of Trabzon (Trebizond), 1461–1583* (Istanbul: The Isis Press, 2009); John Christos Alexander, *Toward a History of Post-Byzantine Greece: The Ottoman Kanunnames for the Greek Lands, circa 1500–circa 1600* (Athens: J.C. Alexander, 1985); A. Bryer and H. Lowry, ed., *Continuity and Change in Late Byzantine and Early Ottoman Society* (Birmingham and Washington DC: University of Birmingham and Dumbarton Oaks, 1986).

[117] Heath Lowry observed the Inalcik's use of the term H. W. Lowry, *The Nature of the Early Ottoman State* (Albany: State University of New York Press, 2003), 91–92.

[118] Lowry, *The Ottoman "Tahrir Defters,"* xvii.

Lowry's study confirmed the interpretation that the process of the Ottoman conquest was marked by institutional and social accommodation in their effort to control vast territory in the Balkans and Anatolia.

In his important study, Lowry offered a quantitative case study to examine the way in which "Christians were first Islamicized and then gradually Turkified."[119] He agreed with Speros Vryonis as to the small ethnic Turkish input into the process, while the factor responsible for the growth of the city's Muslim community was Christian apostasy.[120] However, by showing the process of Islamization of Trabzon that took place after the reconstitution of the church hierarchy, Lowry was able to prove that, despite this reconstituted institution, there was little to prevent these conversions. He offers the economic incentives as a primary factor contributing to facilitate and encourage the process.[121] In the case of Trabzon, the reconstitution of the patriarchate did little to stop the conversions and to strengthen the hold of the Church over its members. The ramifications of this conclusion are far-reaching. It shows the limited importance of the patriarchal hierarchy in maintaining religion and ethnicity in the early Ottoman period. If, in Asia Minor, a portion of the majority non-Muslim Greek population eventually converted to Islam and was Turkified, this was in spite of an established patriarchate and ecclesiastical hierarchy. Perhaps the importance of this institution for preserving the community intact has been overestimated.

By *istimâlet*, Inalcik meant a policy of granting concessions to the local population, the peasantry, townspeople, soldiery, and to clerics by going beyond the limits of Islamic law in order to incorporate them into the administrative system. During the early years of the Ottoman state, this policy kept local laws and customs intact and allowed the Ottomans to incorporate both military and clerical groups into its administrative system.[122]

Part of the aim of this chapter has been to reconsider the periodization regarding the *millet* system that Inalcik puts forth in his article "The Status of the Greek Orthodox Patriarchate." *İstimâlet* makes up the first period.[123] The second period is the period of the "so-called *millet* system" which began with the conquest of 1453. In this period, Sultan Mehmet II's imperial designs and plans for universal empire led to a stronger conception of sultanic authority and law. Sultan Mehmet II's reign ushered in a new age for non-Muslims who were organized into formal, semi-autonomous communal structures under the leadership of their religious leaders. The imperial structure continued until the period of decentralization in the eighteenth century and the rise of the *a'yan*.[124] In this, the third period, the Church also underwent similar tensions, including the dominance by a new

[119] Lowry, *The Ottoman "Tahrir Defters,"* 241.

[120] Lowry, *The Ottoman "Tahrir Defters,"* 243.

[121] Lowry, *The Ottoman* "Tahrir Defters," 244.

[122] Halil Inalcik, "The Status of the Greek Orthodox Patriarchate under the Ottomans," *Turcica* 21–23 (1991): 409.

[123] Inalcik, "The Status of the Greek Orthodox Patriarchate," 409.

[124] See Deena Sadat, "Rumeli Ayanlari: 18th Century," *Journal of Modern History* 44/3 (1972): 346–363.

bourgeois class, as well as an increased level of autonomy both in the capital and in the provinces. Finally, the fourth period is that of the Tanzimat reforms, which reorganized non-Muslim communities along entirely new legal conceptions when non-Muslims were considered as citizens, thus decreasing the strength and centralized power accumulated by the Church. While Inalcik believes these periodizations are convenient and often productive for the study of non-Muslims in the Ottoman Empire, our task is to show that the treatment of non-Muslims was, in fact, part of a continuous process that began in the early years and extended into the sixteenth century.[125]

Three of Inalcik's studies, in particular, present a range of possibilities open to the study of the Greek Orthodox community in the Ottoman period.[126] The first, Inalcik's description of bishops in Ottoman archival sources, presented a very detailed listing of specific payments by bishops to the Ottoman Porte from 1641 to 1651, as listed in the *Piskopos Mukata'asi* register. He demonstrated the potential that Ottoman archives had to illuminate the relationship between the hierarchy and the state in the mid-seventeenth century. Inalcik's second important study concerning the Greek community is one that has been discussed previously. His third article, "The Status of the Greek Orthodox Patriarchate under the Ottomans," offered a broader perspective of the Greek Orthodox Patriarchate under Ottoman rule. Inalcik began his discussion by explaining that it was the common belief among historians that Sultan Mehmet II granted a "charter" of rights to the newly invested Patriarch Gennadios Scholarios, offering him privileges and guarantees for himself and the Church. These rights included "politico-religious jurisdiction" over all the Orthodox subjects *(reaya)*. He pointed out that the Ottomans followed the *Hanafi* Islamic legal tradition according to the *Sharia*, which was often offset by the rules and regulations based on the sultan's independent judgment (*kanun*). Inalcik differentiated the development of *kanun* and sultanic innovations from the legal prescripts of the Sharia, making room for a less anachronistic approach to the study of non-Muslims.[127]

In dealing with the issue of conquests, Inalcik stressed the special treatment *zimmi* received when submitting to the Ottomans voluntarily. Inalcik described the relationship as a pledge or contract for security characterized by the term *ahdname*. This pledge, at times, granted to individuals or collectively, insured a level of security for the subject people. This is similar to the relationship that Sultan Mehmet II had with the Genoese of Galata when he conquered the city of Constantinople in 1453.[128]

[125] Inalcik, "The Status of the Greek Orthodox Patriarchate," 411.

[126] Halil Inalcik, "Ottoman Archival Materials on Millets," 437–449; "Greeks in the Ottoman Economy and Finances, 1453–1500," in *TO ELLHNIKON: Studies in Honor of Speros Vryonis, Jr.* (New Rochelle, NY: Aristide D. Caratzas, 1993), 289–365.

[127] Inalcik, "The Status of the Greek Orthodox Patriarchate," 407–408.

[128] Halil Inalcik, "Ottoman Galata, 1453–1553," in *Première rencontre internationale sur l'empire Ottoman et la Turquie moderne*, ed. E. Eldem (Istanbul: Isis Press, 1991). Also see H. Inalcik, "Galata: Osmanli Dönemi," *Dünden Bugüne Istanbul Ansiklopedisi* (Istanbul: Türkiye Ekonomik ve Toplumsal Tarih Vakfi, 1994) 349-54.; Halil Inalcik, "Istanbul," *Encyclopedia of Islam* 2 (1956–): 224–48; and Halil Inalcik, "Istanbul: An Islamic City," *Journal of Islamic Studies* 1 (1990): 1–23.

Inalcik argued that the organization of the Orthodox Church was similar to the professional organization of the guild, and the practice of granting a *berât* of investiture to a guild warden (*kethüda*) is similar to the investiture of Orthodox prelates. This argument revolves around the question that is central to the *millet* system: when the Ottomans dealt with subject populations, did they consider them to be individuals or members of a larger "corporate" body? Inalcik offered the following lengthy analysis:

> The question of why the Ottoman Empire maintained the Churches, each to represent its own community, in a manner similar to that of other organized bodies, must be examined within the context of the peculiar social system of the Islamic empires, in which socio-economic and religious organizations were the units through which the authority of the state was often mediated to the individual. . . . But it is an undeniable fact that in these vast empires the central government had to operate, for practical reasons, through such already established social organizations, religious or professional, in which communal identity was essential. That is, in these medieval empires, individuals were not considered citizens in the modern sense of the word; rather they were perceived as members of a community, which was the only type of entity officially recognized within the larger political framework of the Empire. This system was based on the sultan's recognition, through a diploma, of the existence and limited authority of such communities.[129]

The question of whether the Ottomans considered non-Muslims as a corporate body or as individuals is a crucial one. Inalcik relied on secondary sources that discuss the nature of the Ottoman period Church in terms of the *millet* system.[130] According to the Ottoman rulers, was the corporate body of the Church, led by the hierarch, responsible for the governance of the Greek Orthodox populations throughout the Empire, or at the very least, in the Balkans? This is a question that will be revisited below in Chapter Three. The indication of Inalcik's argument is that the Ottomans were following an administrative strategy based on Islamic tradition. He argued that the Ottomans displayed a typically medieval notion of seeing corporate bodies and not individuals. This position, however, is incongruous with the other evidence that points to the opposite picture. Villages were held accountable for their assessments, yet each subject was assessed for taxes on an individual basis. Inalcik's position that the role of the patriarch was similar to the *kethüda* should be reconsidered. The similarities are not very deep, and the office of the patriarch as well as of the other Orthodox prelates is most similar to a tax farmer. Therefore, the view that the Ottomans considered the Church simply as a revenue source to be exploited seems more reasonable. Ultimately, the ecclesiastical organization was too loose to function like a guild. Hierarchs had little control over members of the community. Local priests were responsible for collecting taxes on the local level, while bishops were often more concerned about their own financial circumstances to consider the demands of their superiors.

Inalcik did say, however, that,

[129] Inalcik, "The Status of the Greek Orthodox Patriarchate," 407–408 and 420.
[130] Inalcik, "The Status of the Greek Orthodox Patriarchate," 420.

Emphasis upon the autonomy of the Greek "nation" under the Ottoman sultans or upon the sovereign rights of the patriarchs allegedly agreed to by Mehmet II, merely shows a distorted interpretation of Islamic and Ottoman legal concepts as well as of historical reality.[131]

Inalcik discussed the fiscal status of the Greek Orthodox Church mostly by reviewing the published work of Joseph Kabrda, referring to Kabrda's own work point by point. In one important respect, however, Inalcik diverged from Kabrda. Inalcik considered the patriarchal tax, *Patriklik rüsûmu,* as the institutionalization of the *pişkeş,* while Kabrda saw it as a continuation of regular taxes from the Byzantine period, such as the *kanonikon.* In this article Inalcik tackled broad historiographical issues as well as taking some very detailed and technical questions.[132]

Among the most important works on the subject of the Church under early Ottoman rule is Elizabeth Zachariadou's book *Ten Turkish Documents Concerning the Great Church (1483-1567),* valuable because it offers for consideration ten of the oldest Ottoman documents concerning the Patriarchate of Constantinople.[133] Granted to individual hierarchs by the Porte, these documents were later deposited into monastic archives,[134] and published in facsimile, with transcription into Ottoman (Arabic) script and with a translation.[135]

1. A *berât* issued by Sultan Bayezid II to Patriarch Symeon I, April 9–18, 1483.
2. A receipt document of Bayezid II to the patriarch showing the taxes owed to the sultan were paid by the Metropolitan of Thessalonike, January 8, 1489.
3. A *berât* of Sultan Bayezid II in response to Patriarch Maximos's request for assistance to collect ecclesiastical taxes from uncooperative clergy, August 31 1494.
4. A *berât* of Sultan Selim I Yavuz in response to charges that the patriarch's tax collectors had converted to Islam causing them to lose their legitimacy to collect taxes, February 13, 1516.
5. A judicial decision recording a resignation of a priest from the island of Patmos, July 7–15, 1550.

131 Inalcik, "The Status of the Greek Orthodox Patriarchate," 421.

132 Inalcik, "The Status of the Greek Orthodox Patriarchate," 421–428.

133 Elisabeth A. Zachariadou, *Deka Tourkika engrapha gia ten Megale Ekklesia: 1483–1567* (Athens: Ethniko Hidryma Ereunon, Institouto Byzantinon Ereunon, 1996).

134 Researchers are realizing the value of the monastic archives, and it is certain there will be still more discoveries of documents shedding more light on the subject. Among these is the published Master's thesis by Georgios Salakides, *Sultansurkunden des Athos-Klosters Vatopedi aus der Zeit Bayezid II. und Selim I* (Thessalonike: Institute for Balkan Studies, 1995). Salakides contributed a number of unpublished documents that were discovered in the monastic archives of the Monastery of Vatopedi on Mt. Athos. He gave photocopies, a German translation, and a very light commentary about them. Phokion Kotzageorgiou reviewed the archives and history of the Monastery of St. Paul on Mt. Athos, in P. Kotzageorgiou *He Athonike mone Aghiou Paulou kata ten Othomanike periodo (tele 14ou ai.-1830),* (Thessalonike: University Studio Press, 2002).

135 E. A. Zachariadou, *Deka Tourkika engrapha*, 157–187, with fascimiles in plates.

6. A command of Sultan Süleyman to Ottoman authorities ordering cooperation during Patriarch Jeremiah I's journey to collect the patriarchal taxes, January 10, 1525.
7. A *berât* of Sultan Süleyman commanding the dismissal of Patriarch Ioannikios and the elevation of Patriarch Jeremiah, October 17, 1525.
8. A *berât* of Sultan Süleyman elevating a priest to bishop on the island of Karpathos, June 30, 1551.
9. A *berât* of Sultan Süleyman elevating a monk Pachomios to bishop, March 26, 1564.
10. A *berât* of Sultan Selim II confirming a *berât* issued previously to a Bishop Kallistos concerning the *pişkeş*.

Before introducing these documents, Zachariadou offered general considerations concerning the Greek Orthodox Patriarchate as she described the status of Ottoman rule over the Balkans and the fate of Byzantine Greek society. She argued that, after the conquest of Constantinople, the survival of Greek society and Hellenism depended on the institution of the patriarchate. At the same time, the patriarchate depended on stronger members of the Greek community, the wealthy *archons* to prop it up. Zachariadou used the Ottoman documents to focus on historical issues related to the Church such as the origins of the social class that supported the institution of the patriarchate after the conquest of Constantinople, the usage of the *haraç* and its meaning for ecclesiastical taxation, the rights granted by the Ottomans to the patriarchate, the income of the patriarchate, and the significance of the listed sees and jurisdictions of bishops and metropolitans. Both the documents Zachariadou published and a considerable portion of her historical discussion have been useful in the present analysis, offering additional examples and evidence with which to make fresh conclusions.

Finally, among the most recent scholarship related to the *millet* system is Macit Kenanoğlu's *Ottoman Millet System: Myth or Reality* (2004) which follows the arguments set forth by Braude, that there is little evidence of an actual *millet* system in the early period of Ottoman rule.[136] Kenanoğlu compiled dozens of individual documents from the Ottoman archives dealing with non-Muslims. Approaching the subject from a legal background and perspective rather than a social or cultural historical perspective, Kenanoğlu focused on the legal implications of the individual documents. While this was useful to examine specific administrative concerns of the state towards the non-Muslims and their institutions, it prevented a fuller historical context with which to offer a more contoured interpretation. Among Kenanoğlu's conclusions is the position that the Ottoman state had full authority over all of their population, including the non-Muslims, and did not rule by any sort of proxy or through the service of the Church. The Patriarchate of Constantinople maintained its prerogatives as a religious institution, even though it did not represent civil authority. Kenanoğlu had a very positive

[136] M. Macit Kenanoğlu, *Osmanli millet sistemi: mit ve gerçek* (Aksaray Istanbul: Klasik, 2004).

view of the relationship between the Ottomans and the non-Muslims, focusing on the toleration granted by the rulers. Kenanoğlu argued that the Church functioned as a tax farm, an assertion that the present book makes, though it does not offer historical context as to how this occurred in an Ottoman system, and among a subject population. His book does focus on the legal ramifications of each of the documents.[137]

Kenanoğlu makes a valuable contribution to the discussion of the myth of the *millet* system. Yet, rather than fully historicizing or contextualizing the information he collects and the documents he presents, he focuses on the legal prescriptions and their implications to the legal status of non-Muslims under Ottoman law. By this method, he was able to offer examples of Ottoman administration of non-Muslims, but little by way of social or cultural framework of the non-Muslim communities under Ottoman rule.

While the present work follows on from Kenanoğlu's contribution (both works attempt to move beyond the traditional paradigm of *millet* system), it attempts to offer a more representative explanation for how the Ottomans ruled the Greek Orthodox Church. Central to both works is the focus on the ecclesiastical tax farm. However, this book seeks to place the fiscal relationship in a historical context, examining continuity of administrative practice from the earliest interactions of the Church with Turkmen nomads, to the period following the conquest of Constantinople in 1453, through to the end of the sixteenth century. Bridging Ottoman and Byzantine/Greek perspectives allows the legal issues to be placed in their proper historical context, and strengthens the ability to approach the realities and concerns of non-Muslims in the early Ottoman centuries.

Clearly, investigating non-Muslims in the Ottoman Empire is not a new enterprise. This chapter attempts to acknowledge various contributions and developments as well as to raise some of the questions still left unanswered. The scholars mentioned above have contributed in one way or another to discussion of non-Muslims in Ottoman society or, at the very least, are representative of certain perspectives held by historians in the field. This presentation demonstrates the importance of archival documentation and the need to assess the actual economic motivations in terms of the relationship between the state and the Greek community and the institution of the Church. This type of analysis will allow us to re-evaluate the ways in which we perceive other aspects of non-Muslims in Ottoman society. From this perspective, we may conclude that the history of non-Muslims in the Ottoman Empire is not as black and white as either the anachronistic or nationalist historians wish it to be, nor as harmonious and cheery as the imperial ideologues project.

137 Kenanoğlu, *Osmanli millet sistemi*, 59–69.

2
İstimâlet, Ottoman Methods of Conquest, and the Greek Orthodox Church

Had we all been able to agree in debate, we might as well have been of one faith.
St. Gregory Palamas, *Archbishop of Thessalonike in Conversation with an Imam*

GREGORY PALAMAS AND THE OTTOMANS

One of the earliest descriptions of the Ottomans comes from the pen of Archbishop Gregory Palamas, Archbishop of Thessalonike (1347–60) and champion of the spiritual discipline of silent meditation (*hesychasm*) in the mid-fourteenth century. Palamas was traveling off the coast of Gallipoli when a violent storm forced his ship to land on the European shore. He and his retinue of monks with the rest of the passengers were surprised by Turkmen warriors, members of the Osmanlı tribe, who had captured them and took them to Lapseki (Lampsakos) in the northern Troad on the Asiatic shore. Upon his arrival, the local Greek population became excited, raising awareness of his importance and unwittingly increasing the amount considered for his ransom. Palamas received many locals who wished to understand "the cause of the abandonment of our nation by God." After seven days in Lapseki, Palamas was taken to Biga (Pegai), to the main church of the town. Christians who lived in the neighborhood surrounding the church offered Palamas hospitality, and a prominent man named Mavrozoumis hosted him and his entourage. Mavrozoumis offered lodging and provisions and invited Palamas to preach in the church without fear of Turkish retribution.

Next, Palamas was taken to İznik (Nicaea) where he stayed at the Monastery of St. Hyakinthos in the center of the Christian quarter. Palamas described the monastery as containing a beautiful church within its walls. There was no mention of clergy, so perhaps the properties remained in the hands of the local population. Palamas continued to preach, and to receive and counsel visitors. Surprisingly, he does not mention the Church of St. Sophia of Nicaea, the site of the ancient Ecumenical Councils, nor does he observe local clergy or bishops who would by tradition come to greet him, and conduct liturgical service in the church with him; he remains ambiguous as to whether local priests could continue in their pastoral duties under the Ottoman regime.

In reporting on the condition of the cities to which he was taken, İznik, Bursa, and Biga, Palamas commented that İznik appeared to be a decayed city, having suffered from a long gradual change in reduced productivity and loss of trade, rather than from ravages of recent Ottoman conquests. As for Bursa, the Ottoman capital at the time, Palamas noted a Greek community whose vitality and Greek Orthodox consciousness was still intact. At Biga, Palamas also encountered a visible Greek community, of which the leader, Mavrozoumis, had considerable prestige among the Ottomans. This may have been due to his active collaboration with them. Perhaps Mavrozoumis was a military leader who maintained his position because he accompanied the Ottomans on campaign. That he was able to host Palamas personally without fear of discrimination or being accosted shows that he may have functioned as a local authority (*subaşı*). Mavrozoumis was clearly a member of the local Byzantines elite living on the frontiers who cooperated with the Ottomans. Others were the famous Beardless (*Köse*) Mihal, Evrenos Bey, and Markos, all of whom joined the Ottomans early on, and maintained their elite status, their leadership positions, and remained Christian well after joining forces with them.[1]

Palamas personally met the "Great Emir," Orhan. The only other Byzantine figure to meet and write about Orhan was John VI Kantakouzenos, who married his daughter, Theodora, to him.[2] Excited by the prospect having captured such a noted theologian, Orhan set up a theological debate between Gregory Palamas and his Ottoman subjects whom Palamas refers to as Chiones.[3] Palamas had to address issues of compatibility of Christianity with Islam, beginning with an explanation of the Holy Trinity. Palamas freely answered formulaic questions that included questions about the divinity of Christ, the use of images in church, and circumcision. The more challenging question was put to him, "We believe in your prophet, why don't you believe in ours?" Palamas responded with reference to biblical passages about the role of Jesus Christ in the revelation (John 5:43–44 and Galatians 1: 8–9). While the discussion itself was very cordial, at the very end, when they were about to depart, Palamas was punched in the eye by one of the Chiones in the only violent act mentioned in his description. The attacker, however, was severely reprimanded by his colleagues for his disgraceful behavior towards Palamas. A man named Taronites, a Greek physician who also served Orhan personally, recorded this dialogue.[4]

[1] G. Arnakis, "Gregory Palamas Among the Turks And Documents of His Captivity As Historical Sources," *Speculum* 26 (1951): 115.

[2] Stephen W. Reinert, "Orhan," *The Oxford Dictionary of Byzantium (New York: Oxford University Press, 1991)* III, 1533.

[3] For the debate on whether the Chiones were from the Ahi brotherhood, or were Jews who converted to Islam, see George Arnakis, "Gregory Palamas, the Chiones and the Fall of Gallipoli," in *Byzantion* 22 (1952): 305–312. Also see J. Meyendorff, "Grecs, Turcs et Juifs en Asie Mineure au XIVe siècle," *Polychordia. Festschrift F. Dolger (Byzantinische Forschungen)* I (1966): 211–217.

[4] George Arnakis, "Gregory Palamas Among the Turks," 108. Arnakis discusses the manuscript tradition of the dialogue which was published from a seventeenth-century manuscript by A. J. Sakellion in *Soter*, XV (1892): 240–246. George Arnakis, "Gregory Palamas among the Turks," 104–105.

As one of the first written testimonies about the Ottomans by a Byzantine source, the testimony of Gregory Palamas' debate provides important details about Church and society under Ottoman rule with a unique view of ecclesiastical life under Ottoman rule.[5] Palamas' position as Archbishop of Thessalonike and involvement in the leading ecclesiastical controversy of the day, the Hesychasm controversy, meant that he was clearly a member of the Byzantine imperial elite. Therefore, after he was captured and it became known how important a Byzantine figure he was, the Ottomans sought to increase the amount of his ransom. However, even in captivity, the Ottomans allowed him to function as a clergyman, and to conduct his pastoral duties with dignity. He preached in the local Greek Orthodox Church, counseled Greek Orthodox individuals, and even became the central figure in an inter-religious dialogue. He also was accorded respect by the young grandson of the Great Emir Orhan, Ismail, known as "one of the most merciless enemies of the Christians," with whom he had conversed peacefully and at length.[6]

Palamas noticed that in Lapseki, Bursa, and Iznik the members of the Greek community were accustomed to life under Ottoman rule, and in a sense became part of the fabric of Ottoman society, both as a subject population, and as the human resource contributing to the growth of the state.[7] The local Greeks were still cautious about the acceptable limits of behavior because they were subjects in close proximity to the ruling regime. Local leaders such as Mavrozoumis, who most likely gained their status in the Byzantine period, were eager and clever enough to align with the new regime.

What this episode meant for the Byzantines, however, was another story, since they could no longer secure the safety of their own subjects in areas where, for hundreds of years, Byzantine imperial authority had previously been unchallenged. Competing political pressures and internal conflicts led to a loss of territorial control and contraction. The blows to imperial authority and prestige ran deep. By the fourteenth century, the process of decentralization had left the provinces completely vulnerable to external invaders and conquests, and internal political conflicts and civil war prevented any resolute action. The strong bond between Church and state that had been the hallmark of Byzantine imperial reality also dissolved in the face of the same pressures. The Church was left to fend for itself in the new political landscape. Local ecclesiastical institutions were forced to negotiate their own existence among the new rulers, often against the wishes of the Synod in Constantinople.

[5] Arnakis, "Gregory Palamas, the Chiones and the Fall of Gallipoli," 305–312. Arnakis was one of the first historians to use Ottoman and Byzantine sources to investigate this early period, combining these sources to lay a foundation for his argument that Bithynian society was made up of Greeks and Turks collaborating to create the genius and impetus for Ottoman growth. See George Arnakis, *Oi Protoi Othomanoi*, ed. Nikos A. Bees, vol. 41, *Texte Und Forshungen zur Byzantinisch-Neugriechischen Philologie (Athens: Byzantinisch-Neugriechischen Jahrbüchern*, 1947). Anna Philippidis-Braat, "La Captivité De Palamas Chez Les Turcs: dossier et commentaire," in *Travaux et Memoires* 7 (1979).

[6] George Arnakis, "Gregory Palamas among the Turks," 107.

[7] Philippidis-Braat, "La Captivité De Palamas Chez Les Turcs," 188–189.

Palamas' experience also raises the broader question of how the Ottomans treated ecclesiastical figures in this period. What were Ottoman attitudes toward clergy they encountered during their dynamic expansion? What were the factors that determined the specific interactions between the Ottomans and the Church when the Ottomans dominated Byzantine territory? The Ottomans in this early period did not have a standard or structured way to manage their relationships with the clergy of the Greek Orthodox Church. It is true that the Islamic milieu that the Ottomans shared had many examples for how Christians and Muslims ought to relate, going back several centuries. The Ottomans, however, were more practical in their interactions with the populations they conquered. Therefore, Palamas was not treated according to a prescribed Islamic policy for Greek Orthodox bishops, nor was he considered by the Ottomans to be an imperial Byzantine agent tied to the Byzantine political and military system. The long-standing Ottoman practice was to exploit prisoners to gain ransom, rather than seek to strike a blow at the Byzantine Church. The Ottomans were not concerned with the political implications or the strategic military advantage of capturing even such a famous and important individual as the Archbishop of Thessalonike. Thus, they approached this capture more as a successful raid than as a component of conquest and imposed rule. The Ottomans could have taken a more hostile attitude towards Palamas, but, rather, once the ransom was raised they allowed Palamas to depart.

The nature of the relationship between the Church and the Ottoman state was basically ad hoc, though its financial value was very clear. This ad hoc treatment was largely based on the process of exploitation of the Church for financial profit, which eventually became institutionalized. As they came increasingly into contact with Byzantine ecclesiastical leaders in the cities of Asia Minor, the Ottomans came to view individual hierarchs as financial opportunities. What began as a simple act of payment as ransom, as in the case of Palamas, ultimately became a fairly developed program of ecclesiastical tax farming by the sixteenth century.

The resources of the Church not only included personal fortunes of individual bishops, but the vast fortune that belonged to the Orthodox Church commanded by the hierarchs. The noted Byzantine historian Joan Hussey explained that while the donations of the faithful made up a large part of the Church's income, "the vast bulk of ecclesiastical revenue came from property which steadily accumulated over the centuries. This was inalienable, though the Church sometimes had to struggle to preserve its rights . . .".[8]

By the middle of the sixteenth century, the ecclesiastical hierarchy of the Greek Orthodox Church in the Ottoman Empire became integrated into the fiscal administration of the Ottoman state. Beginning with the Patriarch and extending to local bishops, the hierarchy was considered by the Ottoman state

[8] J. M. Hussey, *The Orthodox Church in the Byzantine Empire* (Oxford: Clarendon Press, 1986), 332.

to be tax farmers, submitting yearly tax payments for revenues produced by their ecclesiastical properties as well as for revenues collected from the Orthodox faithful. This situation, however, was not the result of an imperial fiat or a deliberate decision by the state. Rather, this tax farming reality was the result of a longer historical process tied to the decline of one empire and the rise of another.

As part of their conquest of Christian-ruled territories and populations, the Ottomans had to take into consideration the widespread institution of the Church for three important reasons: 1) the Byzantine state was collapsing and vulnerable and could no longer serve the administrative needs of the people, and 2) local bishops had gained considerable political strength at the provincial level, often becoming the only local authority, and certainly the local manifestation of Byzantine imperial authority, and 3) faced with this grim reality, the bishops sought recourse in cooperation with emirs, rather than in simply running away. Since the Ottomans exploit the wealth of the Church, they understood the most effective and efficient way to do so was with the cooperation of the local hierarch. In response to this practical reality, the Ottomans dealt pragmatically with the hierarchs of the Church.

A DECLINING BYZANTINE STATE

To put the relationship of the Church hierarchy with the Ottomans in proper context, it is necessary first to understand the status of the Church in the late Byzantine period. Under the Palaiologoi in the fourteenth century, the Byzantine emperor was reduced from his towering position as emperor of the *oikoumene* to the head of the most powerful clan.[9] This was due, according to Byzantine historian Ihor Ševčenko, to the "weakening of imperial prestige, and the desacralization of the imperial office." In the late Byzantine period, there was a deep conflict between Byzantine urban populations and the land owning nobility, identified most clearly in a rivalry between two court factions. The long-standing struggle between the bureaucratic and the feudal factions had existed since the eleventh century when the Komnenian Dynasty came to power as the champions of the feudal faction. This rivalry came to a head in the mid-fourteenth century during the civil war between John VI Kantakouzenos and John V Palaiologos (1341–47). Each faction vied at all costs for control of the Imperial throne, and each had his own supporting constituency. John VI Kantakouzenos was strongly identified with the feudal land-owning aristocratic class. Byzantine society had become strained from the many political pressures, and the same types of imperial power struggles meant a continued disregard for the needs of the common people. Kantakouzenos eventually was crowned legitimate emperor in conjunction with

[9] Ihor Ševčenko, "Society and Intellectual Life in the Fourteenth Century," in *Actes Du XIVe Congrès International Des Études Byzantines, Bucarest, 6-12 Septembre 1971,* ed. M. Berza and E. Stănescu (Bucharest: Editura Academiei Republicii Socialiste România, 1976), vol. 1, 80–81.

John V Palaiologos, but the trauma of these political conflicts on society had severely undermined the state's effective control. Because of this internal political struggle, the state was unable to withstand external challenges.

During the Second Palaiologan Civil War (1341–47), and in an attempt to gain the upper hand, John VI Kantakouzenos had called upon Umur Pasha, the emir of Aydin, to assist him in quelling a rebellion incited by Alexios Apokaukos, a loyal follower of his opponent, John V Palaiologos. In his letter to Umur Pasha, Kantakouzenos wrote that since the death of Andronikos II, Umur Pasha had become "the sultan of the earth," and that all lands belonged to him. He asked Umur Pasha for help as the overlord of two quarreling vassals. According to his duty as an overlord, Umur Pasha offered to assist John VI Kantakouzenos, but also called for the land tax (*haraç*) tax from the latter. The payment of the *haraç* was a sign of submission to Umur Pasha's rule.[10]

Dependence upon Umur Pasha showed the degree to which Byzantine strength had fallen. The complex relationships between the Anatolian emirates (*beyliks*) and the Byzantine state, however, revealed that the imperial actors had their own interest at heart, and did not always act to preserve the strength and prestige of the Byzantine state.[11]

The Byzantine economy was on the verge of a general collapse, again because of the discontent of large segments of society. The aftermath of the eleventh-century clash between the civil bureaucracy and the military feudal magnates moved the state administration increasingly towards a feudal system of administration.[12] This was a result of the latter's landed wealth and military prominence combining to destroy the centralized Byzantine administration.[13] Large landholders had already made agreements for immunity from taxation while common people suffered greatly because they were continually taxed by a state overburdened

[10] E. A. Zachariadou, "Holy War in the Aegean," in *Latins and Greeks in the Eastern Mediterranean after 1204,* ed. Bernard Hamilton, Benjamin Arbel, and David Jacoby (London: Frank Cass, 1989), 220–222. For another example of Christian-Muslim interaction as described by Neshri see K. Hopwood, "Low-Level Diplomacy between Byzantines and Ottoman Turks: The Case of Bythinia," in *Byzantine Diplomacy*, eds. J. Shepherd and S. Franklin (London: Variorum, 1992), 151–155.

[11] The low level to which the Byzantine imperial prestige fell is visible in the example recorded by Enveri in the *Düstûrnâme.* Although Enveri composed his work in the second half of the fifteenth century, he wrote about the emirate of Aydin and about Umur Pasha, the emir of Aydin, which followed an anonymous contemporary source of the mid-fourteenth century. See Paul Lemerle,*L'emirat d'Aydin, Byzance et l'Occident; Recherches Sur La Geste d'Umur Pacha,* vol. 1. (Paris: Presses universitaires de France, 1957). E. Zachariadou, "Holy War in the Aegean," 215. Zachariadou notes that Inalcik used this same chapter to stress the religious context of the Turkish naval struggle. Umur Pasha's father had concluded a treaty with the Byzantine emperor and attempted to stop his son Umur from raiding Byzantine territory in agreement with the treaty. The son's reply was, "*It is a sin to forbid the holy war; father should favor our campaign; Mohammed the Prophet carried out the Holy War to punish the infidels.*" Enveri's account carefully told how the Byzantine emperor Andronikos II granted to Umur Pasha overlordship over the land and movable property. Zachariadou, "Holy War in the Aegean," 220.

[12] Speros Vryonis, Jr., *The Decline of Medieval Hellenism in Asia Minor and the Process of Islamization from the Eleventh through the Fifteenth Century* (Los Angeles: University of California Press, 1971), 71.

[13] Vryonis, *The Decline of Medieval Hellenism*, 72.

with warfare that could scarcely protect them nor offer any positive benefits. Because of the violence and movements towards a more feudal economy, the free peasantry—which formed the backbone of the Byzantine economy and was the basic source of revenue for the state—also experienced a sharp decline. The loss of a substantial tax base had devastating effects on the essential state bureaucracy and military structure.[14]

Territorial losses in Anatolia and in the Balkans also meant a decrease in the taxable population and productive revenue sources. The Byzantine loss at Manzikert in 1071 opened the way for Turkic raids, which hobbled Byzantine provincial administration in the Anatolian countryside and culminated in the establishment of the Seljuk Kingdom, which undermined imperial control. The Seljuks took over large areas of Byzantine territory and established their capital in the famed Byzantine city of Iconium (Konya). Losses in Anatolia seemed to have leveled off during the period 1204–1261, when the Latin imperial administration was established in Constantinople, and the Byzantines founded their own exile governments in Nicaea, Trebizond (Trabzon), and Epirus. The equilibrium created between the Kingdom of Nicaea and the Seljuk Kingdom even resulted in stability and cultural bloom, though this did not last long. When Michael VIII Palaiologos regained Constantinople in 1261, however, the Byzantines shifted their focus away from Anatolia and became preoccupied with Constantinople and the Balkans. Thus, their neglect of Anatolia allowed the remaining institutional and administrative infrastructure to collapse. At roughly the same time, however, Seljuk control also began to decline due to pressure coming from the East, from the Ilkhanid dynasty, the Mongol dynasty of Iran. What remained in Anatolia was a power vacuum, out of which emerged small Turkish emirates (*beyliks*). Turkmen groups continued to move westward into Asia Minor under continual Mongol pressure from the east. Among the independent emirates throughout Anatolia were the dynasties of Osman, Saruhan, Karaman, Menteşe, Aydin, and Karesi.[15] Ultimately, the dynasty of Osman, known as the Ottoman dynasty, grew to dominate the others.

In the late Byzantine period, Anatolian territories became the scene of military expenditure rather than a source of strength. The Ottoman emirate was geographically well positioned because its origin and power base was Bithynia, south

[14] Vryonis, *The Decline of Medieval Hellenism*, 77–78. "The crucial phase of this decline was the appearance of the powerful landowner (both ecclesiastical and lay) in the communities during the tenth and eleventh centuries. The peasants sold or gave their land to the magnates, sometimes willingly in order to escape burdens imposed by taxation, inclement weather, famine; at other times unwillingly, having been the victims of coercion by the powerful. ... the free peasantry declined in a process that did not provide the state with sufficient recompense for its loss of revenues and soldiery. Simultaneously, the magnates became more powerful and thus a greater menace to centralized authority. Byzantium was in the process of an evolution that for want of a better word, must be described as '*feudalization*.' "

[15] H. Inalcik, *The Ottoman Empire: The Classical Age 1300–1600,* trans. N. Itzkowitz, and C. Imber, 2nd ed. (New Rochelle, NY: Aristide D. Caratzas, Orpheus Publishing, 1973), 9–16. Also see Colin Imber, *The Ottoman Empire 1300–1481* (Istanbul: Isis Press, 1990), and Donald M. Nicol, *The Last Centuries of Byzantium: 1261–1453* (Cambridge: Cambridge University Press, 1993).

of Byzantine controlled territory. The Ottoman's advanced at the expense of their weaker Byzantine neighbor to the north and west. Compounding the failings of Byzantine sovereignty, John VI Kantakouzenos enlisted the Ottomans to fight against Stephen Uroš IV Duşan in 1348, and later in 1350 to help quell a rebellion in Thessalonike. In both cases, the Ottomans fought in Thrace and later deserted the campaign to pillage surrounding areas, further degrading Byzantine imperial authority.[16] Palamas' encounter with the Ottomans took place during this period, and his account even helped mark the chronology of the Ottoman advance into Europe. Palamas reported on the earthquake in early March 1355 that destroyed the Byzantine fortress at Gallipoli. This earthquake spurred the Ottomans to attack to take it over, giving them their first stronghold in Europe.[17]

The Byzantine state tried to fight off the Turkmen emirates at various times, and at one point sought assistance from Catalan mercenaries who, earlier in the fourteenth century had wreaked violent havoc and economic instability on the state that they were intending to serve. Other attempts to enlist aid from the West took the form of religious reconciliation with the Church of Rome. Top-level Byzantine imperial factions hoped to reunite with Rome and sent formal delegations to Rome to iron out the conditions of Church union. For their commitment to union, the Byzantine delegation sought tangible aid from the West, ideally in the form of military campaigns against the encroaching Turkmen emirates. Since they were negotiating from a position of weakness, The Byzantines made concessions for union. The reaction in Constantinople, however, was complete opposition, due partly to the still bitter memory of the Latin occupation of Constantinople in 1204. Popular rejection of the Union of the Council of Florence-Ferrara (1439), however, signaled a watershed moment for Byzantine society, where the common people consciously rejected what they felt would change their identity as a society, the Roman Catholic faith.

Political and military alliances as well as trade concessions had also weakened the Byzantine state. In the eleventh century, in exchange for direct support against the Norman invaders and also Pecheneg raiders from the north, Alexios Komnenos (1081–1118) had made major maritime trade concessions with the Venetians that later came back to haunt the state. These concessions struck a major blow to Byzantine maritime trade, as well as to any semblance of a standing naval force, leaving the empire even more vulnerable by sea. The lack of control of this important component of the Byzantine economy further weakened the state. Furthermore, the Venetians led direct violence against Constantinople in 1204 during the Fourth Crusade.

A general depreciation of gold currency in this period also helped deplete the finances of the state. The disastrous Black Death of 1348–49, that caused a large number of deaths and vast depopulation of Constantinople and areas of the Balkans, further aggravated the financial weakness. This epidemic caused a

[16] Imber, *The Ottoman Empire*, 23.
[17] Arnakis, "Gregory Palamas Among the Turks," 111.

shortage of labor and forced the state to put salary caps on wage laborers, further aggravating the economic situation.[18]

While the dramatic mark of late Byzantine decline was the loss of Byzantine territory to the advancing Ottomans, numerous other internal factors led to a real loss of Byzantine imperial power and prestige. When the Byzantine state could no longer offer stability and authority to the populace, the Church attempted to step in to offer continuity of administrative function.

BYZANTINE BISHOPS

The tradition of authority of Christian bishops extends to early Christianity. In earliest Christian times local Christian communities were quite small, and their internal organization varied. Until the second century they often functioned without the formal office of bishop. However, as divisions and alternate theologies threatened the unity of the Christian community, there was a need for the Christian community to establish a theology, and to manage the beliefs of the community. The New Testament identifies three offices: deacon (*diakonos*), the servant or minister, presbyter (*presbyteros*), the elder or "priest," and the bishop (*episkopos*), the overseer or supervisor. The function of the *episkopos* was to oversee the community and ensure that they followed the correct doctrine. In the second and third centuries, and with the theological developments of Ignatius of Antioch, and later Ireneus of Lyons, the episcopal office became more formalized as a "monarchical episcopacy," which means that each Church community has one bishop who leads the community. The bishop took on the role of standing in the place of Christ with full religious authority over the community.

With the exponential growth of Christianity in the first three centuries, the office of bishop became increasingly important. Historian Peter Brown describes the office of bishop emerging from "oblivion" to take on the role of teacher, formerly held by the sophists and learned men, eventually becoming part of the intelligentsia of Greek cities. In addition, their ability to rise in power as patrons of the poor of Mediterranean cities made them formidable political brokers even before the imperial patronage of Emperor Constantine. With the financial resources they could marshal and the social services they could provide, especially to the poor, the local bishop became a political force within the Late Antique cities with which local governors had to contend. With the Emperor Constantine in the fourth century, Christians bishops came onto the political scene with amazing force, becoming powerful patrons of the poor as well as members of elite society.[19]

18 Alexander Kahzdan, "Plague," *The Oxford Dictionary of Byzantium*, III, 1681.

19 Peter Robert Lamont Brown, *Power and Persuasion in Late Antiquity: Towards a Christian Empire* (Wisconsin: University of Wisconsin Press, 1992). Portions of the following are reprinted from Tom Papademetriou, "The Turkish Conquests and Decline of the Church Reconsidered," in *Church and Society in Late Byzantium*, ed. Dimiter G. Angelov, *Studies in Medieval Culture* 49 (Kalamazoo:MI: Medieval Institute Publications, 2009) 183-200, by permission of the publisher.

The convergence of secular law and ecclesiastical function culminated in Justinianic legislation that offered the bishop supervisory functions among the state bureaucracy. Both the wealth of the Church and the bishop's status in imperial circles gave the bishop a powerful role and ability to report abuse of secular power to the emperor. It has been suggested that the Church functioned as an organization parallel to the state administration. The geographic range, the hierarchical order, and the close connections to the state made the Church a shadow administration when local government existed, and a fail safe for the Byzantine state when state authority lagged or was extinguished.[20]

It was clear, however, that members of the Church were not directly permitted to take on secular state roles, being considered incompatible with ecclesial function. According to Orthodox ecclesiology, each legitimately elected bishop formed the foundation of the local church and was, in a sense, its master. The hierarchical structure that developed according to the Justinianic Byzantine imperial model had raised the Patriarchate of Constantinople to imperial heights. While Byzantine tradition maintained that the church was under the stewardship and ultimate control of the emperor, it also created significant prestige for the patriarch, who then became a component part of the state structure. In this formulation, Church and state had a synergistic relationship, which means that the Church shared civil legal principles as well as administrative and judicial duties with the state. The highly centralized Church in Constantinople was at times supported by the emperors, who more often than not realized the advantage of working through this institution.[21] From the eleventh to the fourteenth centuries, the Greek Orthodox Church gained significant political power in inverse proportion to the real decline in Byzantine imperial power.[22] The centralized Church, whose power was based in Constantinople, contrasts with the more decentralized Church with local hierarchs increasing their authority; a picture that emerges in the Ottoman territories.

According to historian Michael Angold, the positions of the bishops and metropolitans became increasingly more important to imperial administration during the twelfth century. Relevant developments included the legal reorganization by the twelfth-century canon lawyer Theodore Balsamon, who effectively "enriched [canon law] by annexing much of [civil law]."[23] The jurisdiction of the bishop pertained not only to spiritual matters but also to civil and judicial matters, particularly in regions outside of the immediate administrative control of Constantinople. For this reason, Byzantine state administration raised the level of the bishop to an important civil post, often determining the election of bishops according to political rather than religious priorities.[24]

[20] Vera von Falkenhausen, "Bishops," in *The Byzantines,* ed. Guglielmo Cavallo (Chicago: University of Chicago Press, 1997), 175.

[21] Vryonis, *The Decline of Medieval Hellenism*, 198.

[22] For a comprehensive discussion of this development see Michael Angold, *Church and Society in Byzantium under the Comneni, 1081–1261* (Cambridge: Cambridge University Press, 1995).

[23] Angold, *Church and Society*, 8.

[24] Helen Saradi, "Imperial Jurisdiction over Ecclesiastical Provinces: The Ranking of New Cities as Seats of Bishops or Metropolitans," in *Byzantium in the 12th Century*, ed. Nicholas Oikonomides (Athens: Hetaireia Byzantinon kai Metabyzantinon Meleton, 1991), 150–151, nn. 6, 8.

This interdependence of Church and state determined the fate of the Church, since the state was contracting. A weakened and decentralized state had grafted much of its civil powers onto the Church hierarchy, especially in Anatolia. However, ecclesiastical administration was not immune to the same process of decline the state was experiencing. There is a continued assumption by modern historians that the Church as an institution should have remained hierarchical and centralized while resisting the overall political decentralization and contraction taking place in this later period.[25] In the late Byzantine period, the Patriarchate of Constantinople remained the focal point of the Orthodox world, perhaps more in theory than in fact. Subordinate clergy, including metropolitans and provincial bishops, continued under the ecclesiastical jurisdiction of the Patriarchate of Constantinople even while their civil authority changed hands. This situation proved difficult for the central authority in Constantinople to accept, and, as a result, it resented the activities of accommodation by local hierarchs. It also proved difficult for local hierarchs who were caught between the demands of the synod in Constantinople and the reality they faced in their own areas on the ground.

In spite of the conflict and difficult balancing act that the provincial clergy faced, the Church remained the most widespread and stable Byzantine institution in the Asia Minor provinces.[26] Not only were they responsible for the maintenance of the spiritual life of the empire, they also were charged with specific administrative judicial functions as well, the mark of a rapidly decentralizing state structure. One example of the Church's function in the face of overall Byzantine decline is the prominent role it continued to play in the judicial system, particularly at the beginning of the fourteenth century, when there was a general attempt at imperial Byzantine judicial reform. We have the example of the judicial council of "Supreme Justices of the Romans" established in Constantinople, that was made up of four judges, two of whom were ecclesiastics, and two laymen.

This judicial model spawned the proliferation of such courts throughout the provinces of the empire, with clergy taking on the prominent role of judges. Thus, in the late Byzantine period, the clergy played an increasingly important role as judges in the imperial law courts. In addition, an ecclesiastical law court could, when necessary, even replace the imperial courts and authority.[27]

[25] Vryonis, *The Decline of Medieval Hellenism*, 76–77.

[26] George Ostrogorsky, *History of the Byzantine State*, trans. Joan Hussey (Oxford: Blackwell, 1956), 487.

[27] Ostrogorsky, *History of the Byzantine State*, 504. For more on the General Judges see Paul E. Lemerle, "Documents et Problèmes Nouveaux Concernant Les Juges Généraux," *Deltion Tes Hristianikes Archaiologikes Hetaireias*, 4 (1966): 29–44; P. E. Lemerle, "Le Juge Généneral des Grecset la Réforme Judiciare d'Andronic III," in Institut français d'études byzantines, *Mémorial Louis Petit; mélanges d'histoire et d'archéologie byzantines,* Archives de l'Orient chrétien, 1 (Bucharest: Institut français d'études byzantines, 1948), 292–316.; Paul Lemerle, "Recherches sur les institutions judiciares à l'époque des Paléologues," I: le tribunal impérial, *Mélanges Henri Grégoire* (*Annuaire de l'institut de philologie et d'histoire orientales et slaves*, 9), (Brussels : Secrétariat des Éditions de l'Institut, 1949), 369–384; Paul Lemerle, "Recherches sur les institutions judiciares à l'époque des Paléologues, II: le tribunal du patriarcat ou tribunal synodal," *Mélanges Paul Peeters*, (*Analecta bollandiana*, 68) (Brussels: Société des Bollandistes, 1950), 318–333.

Balkan legal historian Nicholas Pantazopoulos likewise agrees that the dispensation of justice fell into the hands of the church during the late Byzantine period. This occurred, in particular, because the hierarchs became the leaders in each of the judicial councils. More importantly, he argued that because the military and political authorities fell under the court's judicial jurisdiction, the Church became the real head of the court and was the ultimate authority in charge. In a heavily declining Byzantine state where decentralization had occurred, the bishop clearly grew in responsibility and prominence.[28]

CASES OF EMIRS AND BISHOPS

When imperial control over Anatolia waned and religious policies of the state weakened, local hierarchs gained independent authority, and began to disregard the wishes of the central ecclesiastical administration in Constantinople. This was exacerbated under the rule of foreign Turkmen masters. According to the imperial Byzantine Church, any adjustments and accommodations made by local bishops towards competing political and military power was perceived by the synod of Constantinople as disobedience to the traditional hierarchical order of the Holy Synod and rebelliousness against the empire. As Balsamon's balance of power between Church and state had tended towards a type of "Caesaropapism," rebellion against the empire and breaking civil law implied breaking canon law as well.[29] With the decline of the state administrative structure in the provinces, however, local hierarchs were left with little choice but to face reality. Contrary to the theoretical role the hierarchy was supposed to play as representatives of the Byzantine imperial Church, individual hierarchs exercised their privilege of self-determination by making administrative compromises with the new rulers.[30]

Because the ecclesiastical administrative authority of the Patriarchate of Constantinople was in the capital city, the Turkic emirates, which later included the Ottomans, considered local bishops who were elected from the Byzantine center and who received their episcopal authority from the Byzantine institutional Church as agents of the enemy state. The result was that the bishops often felt forced to flee the provinces to settle in Constantinople, or venture to another Byzantine controlled territory. As individuals, they received stipends for sustenance either from the patriarchal Church or from another revenue producing bishopric assigned by the Patriarchal Holy Synod. However, some of these local

[28] Nikolaos Pantazopoulos, *Church and Law in the Balkan Peninsula during the Ottoman Rule* (Thessaloniki: Institute for Balkans Studies, 1967), 39–43.

[29] Angold, *Church and Society*, 102–103.

[30] Speros Vryonis argued that the dissolution of state control, and the subsequent weakening of the official church hierarchy in Asia Minor by the repeated and violent Turkish invasions, led to the large-scale conversions and Turkification of Asia Minor, see Vryonis, *The Decline of Medieval Hellenism*, 500. Vryonis attempted to show both the Byzantine and Turko-Islamic factors producing the vast cultural transformation in Asia Minor. In doing so, he focused extensively on Byzantine political and cultural decline, and Turko-Islamic political and cultural ascendance.

bishops did not feel the compulsion to flee and chose to remain in their sees within the boundaries of a Turkish domain, and as such arranged to coexist with the local emir. After the fourteenth century in Ottoman controlled territory, this was possible largely due to the practice of accommodation (*istimâlet*) that was the first step in incorporating the entity of the Church into the state structure. Going beyond the limits of Islamic law, the Ottomans integrated the Church into their administrative system.[31] The nature of Ottoman conquests meant that former administrative practices were preserved and absorbed for practical reasons, and thus local populations were subdued more easily.

The ecclesiastical hierarchy was such an institution that was absorbed by the new masters. Examples of this absorption of local hierarchy by Turkic emirs are evident in the *Patriarchal Synodal Acta*.[32] The entries in the *Acta* are important because members of the Patriarchal court who were sensitive to encroachments on their ecclesiastical authority wrote them in Constantinople. The *Acta* also offer the cases of the local prelates of the provinces who were busy trying to preserve their existence by negotiating and even collaborating with their new masters. The local responses recorded in the *Patriarchal Acta* are mainly attempts to preserve local episcopal autonomy and are part of the process of incorporating the Greek Orthodox hierarchy and church into the administrative structure of the new regimes that ultimately became the Ottoman Empire. It is clear the church hierarchy and monastic institutions based their relations with Turkish emirs upon shared fiscal interests. Understandably, the relations between local emirs and bishops deeply troubled the standing synod in Constantinople. Yet, in their own areas, local bishops faced a completely alien ruling regime, and had two choices: either to flee or to capitulate.

It has been argued that the Byzantine ecclesiastical hierarchy was "decapitated" because hierarchs were forced to flee their sees for safety.[33] However, evidence from the *Acta* also shows that some bishops chose to stay in their sees and created for themselves a new *modus vivendi*. This new situation spurred cries of indignation from the synod of Constantinople, bemoaning its lack of authority over bishops who chose to capitulate. The Acta offer multiple examples of hierarchy and clergy engaged in disputes among themselves with much of the debate dealing with ecclesiastical jurisdiction and church property. When the debates became particularly heated, some among them chose to solve these disputes by seeking recourse from Turkish authorities, a clear violation of ecclesiastical order. This

[31] Halil Inalcik, "The Status of the Greek Orthodox Patriarchate," *Turcica* 21–23 (1991): 409.

[32] Franz Miklosich and Joseph Müller, eds., *Acta et diplomata medii aevi sacra et profana*, vol. 1 and vol. 2 (Vienna: C. Gerold, 1860–62). Some of the documents of the patriarchal register have been re-edited by Herbert Hunger and Otto Kresten, eds., *Das Register des Patriarchats von Konstantinopel (Corpus Fontium Historiae Byzantinae,* 19), 3 vols. (Vienna: Österreichische Akademie der Wissenschaften, 1981–2001). See also Jean Darrouzès, *Les regestes des actes du patriarcat de Constantinople,* vol. 1, *Les actes des patriarches*, fasc. 5–7 (Paris: Institut Français d'Etudes Byzantines, 1977–91).

[33] S. Vryonis, "Decisions of the Patriarchal Synod in Constantinople as a Source for Ottoman Religious Policy in the Balkans prior to 1402," in *Byzantina Kai Metabyzantina: Studies on Byzantium, Seljuks, and Ottoman*, ed. S. Vryonis (Malibu: Undina Press, 1982), XVI.

phenomenon must be understood as part of the broader conflict between the centralized, imperial, ecclesiastical bureaucracy and the peripheral tendencies of the provinces. Whether conscious or unconscious, the local hierarchy was competing with the central Byzantine administration to see who would play a more significant role in ruling the Church. The change in political rule, thus, could be used as an advantage for the local bishop to gain local power.

In contrast to the Greek Orthodox ecclesiastical structure that had an official political affiliation with the Greek Orthodox Patriarchate of Constantinople, the non-politically allied Armenian and Syrian patriarchs did not face the same "either/or" choice. Vryonis offers a lengthy example of the Armenian patriarch Basil (*c.*1090–91) who appealed to the sultan Malik Shah for lenient treatment. After offering many gifts of gold, silver, and cloths, he received exemption for payments for the churches, monasteries, and priests, and also received honors as well. By their lack of identification with an enemy state, they were free to pledge loyalty and offer gifts to the new rulers as a matter of course. As a result, they often gained charters of immunity that protected their rights and privileges over their communities.[34] Capitulation was clearly part of their agenda.

The impact of the Turkish advances into Byzantine territory was, in fact, devastating; many bishops could not reach their assigned bishopric and others were forced to flee their posts because they were violently threatened by the assaults. In his attempt to assess the declining number of bishoprics, historian Speros Vryonis relied on the *Notitiae Episcopatuum*, which are lists of the hierarchical sees used by the synods and courts to define seniority and rank that reflected the formal status of the episcopacy.[35] From these lists, he argued, it was possible to measure the contraction of the hierarchy in Asia Minor from the eleventh to the fifteenth centuries. The presence of a metropolitan see on one list and its disappearance in a subsequent list indicated that there was some type of disruption, namely, either a bishop fled, or was not able to take up his proper appointment. Vryonis argued that one could measure the contraction of ecclesiastical administration by examining them serially, and identifying which of the bishoprics disappeared from the roles over time.[36]

To judge by these criteria, disruption occurred when the metropolitans, archbishops and bishops were not able to take their places at their own bishoprics and they were unable to benefit financially from their episcopal fiscal holdings. The seizure of their episcopal property and associated income prevented them from

[34] Vryonis, *The Decline of Medieval Hellenism*, 199.

[35] Vryonis, *The Decline of Medieval Hellenism*, 302. See Jean Darrouzès, ed., *Notitiae Episcopatuum Ecclesiae Constantinopolitanae (Géographie ecclésiastique de l'Empire byzantin,* 1) (Paris: Institut Français d'Etudes Byzantines, 1981). Also see Joan M. Hussey, *The Orthodox Church in the Byzantine Empire, Oxford History of the Christian Church* (Oxford: Clarendon Press, 1986), who echoes this.

[36] Vryonis, *The Decline of Medieval Hellenism*, 302–310, esp. 311, where he explains: "The *Patriarchal Acta* therefore furnish further striking confirmation of the highly disruptive character of the Turkish conquest, a characteristic already established from chroniclers and other contemporary literature."

fulfilling important societal duties and functions. Used in this way, the *Notitiae Episcopatuum* present a case for massive impoverishment of the Church. As historians Michael Hendy and Michael Angold would argue, these lists, are problematic because they require corroborating evidence from other sources to make them convincing.[37] The lists of bishops are known to represent ecclesiastical protocol rather than the actual situation. Even if in one location the ecclesiastical hierarchy is subverted by Turkmen conquest, the title still could be used to signify rank. For example, a metropolitan found on the lists might continue to use the metropolitan see to identify himself even if he had not been functioning as actual bishop in that location, or even if it had become defunct. The corroborating source that assists in determining whether contraction occurred is the collection of synodal decrees from the *Patriarchal Acta*. Relying on these *Acta*, however, leads to uneven results because they record very specific ecclesiastical affairs and issues facing the synod of the Patriarchate of Constantinople, and they do not reveal the situation in the entire church. The *Patriarchal Acta* show metropolitans who were granted the right to the incomes of other dioceses, as Vryonis says, "for reasons of sustenance" (*kata logon epidoseon*).[38] A region that could not sustain a metropolitan or bishop would either be absorbed or absorb another bishopric to make it financially viable. Upheavals caused the widespread phenomenon of absentee metropolitans and bishops. In Vryonis' words, "the victorious *emirs* and *beys* often expelled the hierarchs for extensive periods of time, for as long as 30 years in some cases."[39] Thus, a large number of hierarchs fled their own sees, gathered in Constantinople for safety's sake, and were placed in charge of vacant but still accessible bishoprics. But what were the alternatives to flight?

A careful examination of *Patriarchal Acta* reveals that there are twenty-six *Acta* that mention Turks in their text. Often the cases have to do with the local bishop interacting with the local Turkish ruler. These examples reveal discord and oppressive violence, yet they also raise important questions about diverging interests between the hierarchy in the capital and the prelates in the hinterland: Did local bishops resort to accepting the political will of local Turkish emirs because they were forced to, or because they were seeking to escape the centralized control of the Byzantine state? Or were they simply attempting to adjust to the new local reality? If it was an issue of competition of the central authority with the periphery, or even an urban versus rural divide, at the very least, the bishops acted very shrewdly with a sense of *Realpolitik*.

If we consider the social transformation taking place in the Byzantine Empire, we may be able to reassess the documents in a slightly different light and offer

37 Michael Hendy warns against the unreliable nature of the *notitiae* and argues that, because of their deceptive nature, they require corroborating evidence, which is almost impossible to come by. See Michael Hendy, *Studies in the Byzantine Monetary Economy, c.300–1450* (Cambridge: Cambridge University Press, 1985) 68–145. Also see Michael Angold, *Church and Society*, 140. n. 4.

38 Vryonis, *The Decline of Medieval Hellenism*, 288–302, offers analysis of this phenomenon when he examines 140 *Acta*.

39 Speros Vryonis, Jr., "The Byzantine Patriarchate and Turkish Islam," *Byzantinslavica* 57 (1996): 75.

another dimension to the story of upheaval, impoverishment, lack of discipline among the hierarchy and clergy, and recourse to the Turks. Rather than take at face value and sympathize with the testimony of the petitioners and writers of the *Patriarchal Acta*, whose interests were centered in Constantinople, we can come to a different conclusion.

RE-EXAMINING THE CASE STUDY OF MATTHEW, THE METROPOLITAN OF EPHESUS

Turning to some examples, we begin with a re-examination of the famous case of Metropolitan Matthew of Ephesus, a classic example used by Vryonis for his argument about the Turkish decapitation of the ecclesiastical hierarchy.

In the fourteenth century, the city of Ephesus prospered under the rule of the emirate of Aydin (*Aydınoğulları*) due to good trade relations with the Italian maritime states.[40] General prosperity and thriving city economies in western Asia Minor during the period of the emirates meant that there was a sense of stability with a certain amount of flexibility that led to commercial cooperation. However, this prosperity contradicts the sorry condition projected by Metropolitan Matthew of Ephesus in his correspondence and in the *Patriarchal Acta*.

As Metropolitan of Ephesus, Matthew first appeared in the synodal document of December 2, 1329, and we can trace him in synodal documents at least until June 1339.[41] His main complaint was that he was not allowed to enter into the geographical area in which his see was located. The aforementioned Umur Pasha, the *Aydınoğulları* ruler of Smyrna, was in control of the territory. As a result of his inability to report to his rightful see, Matthew was granted another bishopric's revenue from the area of Thrace, which provided his economic needs. Sometime between June 1339 and February 1340 Matthew attempted again to go to Ephesus. He was obliged to offer bribes to be allowed into his bishopric. Although he attempted to gain back the properties and holdings of the Church, he was completely unsuccessful in negotiating with Umur Pasha's brother, Khidir. The local church was economically deprived. It depended on six priests alone to support the work of the entire local community.[42] Matthew says they were not killed or abused because this would have angered the emir, but at the same time, he complains bitterly about the difficulties, being deprived of his throne and revenues, and about the continued oppression at the hands of the Turkish overlords.

[40] Clive Foss, *Ephesus after Antiquity: A Late Antique, Byzantine and Turkish City* (Cambridge: Cambridge University Press, 1979), 158; Paul Lemerle, ed., *L'émirat d'Aydin, Byzance et l'Occident: Recherches sur la Geste d'Umur Pacha (Bibliothèque byzantine. Etudes*, 2) (Paris: Presses universitaires de France, 1957).

[41] MM, vol. 1, 149–151; Hunger and Kresten, *Das Register*, vol. 1, no. 100; Darrouzès. *Les regestes des actes*, no. 2153 (December 1329).

[42] Max Treu, *Matthaios Metropolit von Ephesus: Über sein Leben und seine Schriften* (Potsdam: Programm des Victoria-Gymnasiums zu Potsdam, 1901); for extensive excerpts of Matthew of Ephesus' correspondence see Vryonis, *The Decline of Medieval Hellenism*, 345–346.

The basic assertions concerning the number of years he was prevented from entering his see, the economic shape of the bishopric, and the small number of priests show that the situation was, in fact, difficult. However, looking at the situation from a different angle suggests a more complex reading.

The first interesting issue is the relationship of the hierarch with the emir of Aydin, Umur Pasha. As mentioned above, many scholars stress the ideological framework of the *gazi* that would explain an antagonism of the Muslims toward the Christian hierarchs. The *Düstûrnâme* certainly projects Umur Pasha as a *gazi* even though, clearly, he cooperated fully with both sides of the Byzantine civil conflict.[43] It is, therefore, more useful to frame the question of their relationship in a different way. Moving away from religious or ideological motivations to political and fiscal interests changes the image of their relationship. What reason did Umur Pasha have for allowing the hierarchy of the Orthodox Church to re-enter into his territory? Why should a Turkish emir allow a metropolitan, who, in theory, was clearly aligned with the enemy state, to take his place within his own *beylik*? What conditions would the hierarch need to accept to live under Turkish rule? Umur Pasha did not need assistance to subdue the Orthodox population. He was clearly in control of the area. From Matthew's perspective, this meant that most of the Greek Christians were "enslaved."[44] Umur Pasha did not need to elevate or co-opt the local bishop either to claim legitimacy in the eyes of the Orthodox subjects or to gain control of the Church's institutional wealth.

The turning point in Matthew's career came when he decided to follow the advice of an advisor, a man from Chios, who instructed him to offer Umur Pasha money; in other words, to offer a bribe. Metropolitan Matthew was allowed to take his place in Ephesus only after bribing the emir and giving gifts to the emir's brother. This critical detail is crucial for understanding the relationship of the Turkish *beylik* vis-à-vis the Church hierarchy. In this situation, giving of gifts would be understood as a sign of loyalty and obeisance. In other contexts this may even be a form of *pişkeş*, an investiture gift that marks the loyalty of subject to the ruler. There is not much in the account that can be said concerning the specific gifts to the emir and his brother except that they were very expensive.[45]

In his correspondence Matthew continued to describe himself nobly as one of the Apostles among the non-Greek and non-Orthodox people.[46] Another critical detail for understanding Matthew's position, however, is that he was also planning to take over a neighboring metropolis. In this, he opposed the Patriarchate of Constantinople. Furthermore, he even became one of the undisciplined

[43] M.H. Enverî, *Le Destan d'Umur Pacha (Düstûrnâme-i Enveri).*, ed. Irene Melikoff-Sayar, Bibliothèque Byzantine. Documents, 2. (Paris: Presses universitaires de France, 1954), 72; Elizabeth Zachariadou, "Holy War in the Aegean," in *Latins and Greeks in the Eastern Mediterranean after 1204,* ed. Bernard Hamilton, Benjamin Arbel, and David Jacoby, (London: Frank Cass, 1989), 212–225.

[44] Vryonis, *The Decline of Medieval Hellenism*, 348.

[45] Vryonis, *The Decline of Medieval Hellenism*, 347.

[46] Vryonis, *The Decline of Medieval Hellenism*, 345.

metropolitans recorded in a later document because he petitioned the Turkish authorities to support him.

Elizabeth Zachariadou has pointed out the complication in Metropolitan Matthew's case.[47] In 1342, after Metropolitan Matthew was firmly enthroned in his see in Ephesus, he sought, independently, to ordain one of his own people as Metropolitan of Pyrgion, a nearby city west of Ephesus, and to bring the Metropolis of Pyrgion under his direct influence. In the process, he had accused the sitting metropolitan of Pyrgion of being a murderer and a perjurer. The Holy Synod investigated Metropolitan Matthew's charges and found that he had manufactured charges. In the process of illegally subordinating the see of Pyrgion to his control, Metropolitan Matthew went so far as to slander the Metropolitan of Pyrgion to Umur Pasha, while addressing Umur Pasha as "good son" and calling himself "father."[48] By these terms, Metropolitan Matthew wanted to show his loyalty and endear himself to the Turkmen *emir*. This conflict between Metropolitan Matthew of Ephesus and the sitting Metropolitan of Pyrgion, played itself out in similar ways multiple times during Ottoman rule as well.[49]

This early conflict during the period of the Turkmen emirates is also an example of conflicts that arise in the Ottoman period. In later years, conflicts involving one or both ecclesiastical parties are motivated to go to the Ottoman authorities to dispute the rights to a bishopric's property. As long as Metropolitan Matthew was identified with the Byzantine state, he could not enter the territory where his episcopal see was located. Yet when he bribed the emir to pass through his area, and gave gifts to the emir's brother to enter Ephesus, the relationship between the two changed. Moving from an antagonistic relationship to a clientalist relationship on the emir's terms, Matthew negotiated with the emir to regain his episcopal possession, though with real limits to former possessions.[50] When historians attempt to make the case of Metropolitan Matthew of Ephesus a case study of Turkish oppression of the hierarchy, it raises more questions about the relationship between rulers and ruled than it answers. From the perspective of Constantinople, it was an example of a bishop who lacked ecclesiastical discipline. In the eyes of the Patriarchate and the Byzantine Emperor, it is clearly treasonous. However, from the perspective of a local hierarch under the control and power of foreign local rulers, it was expedient, and represented the new *modus vivendi*. Only by accepting and pledging loyalty to the emirs could the local bishops take their proper places. From the perspective of the emirs, these incidents were not calculated or premeditated, but came out of local ad hoc concerns.

[47] Elisabeth Zachariadou, *Deka Tourkika Engrapha gia ten Megale Ekklesia:1483–1567* (Athens: Ethniko Hidryma Ereunon, Institouto Byzantinon Ereunon, 1996), 96, n. 21, suggests that Vryonis took only Matthew's side and did not consider that Matthew was also in conflict with the patriarchate over the metropolis of Pyrgion.

[48] MM, vol. 1, 237. Also see Vryonis, *The Decline of Medieval Hellenism*, 328 and 332, n. 220.

[49] MM, vol. 1, 236. Also see Vryonis, *The Decline of Medieval Hellenism*, 326–327, and 332. See also Zachariadou, *Deka Tourkika Engrapha*, 96, n. 21.

[50] MM, vol. 1, 235–237.

Another important pre-Ottoman example was recorded in 1361. The synod complained about having suffered greatly from hierarchs from other jurisdictions encroaching on Constantinopolitan territory. They found the Metropolitan of Tyre, who was a suffragan bishop of the Patriarchate of Antioch, guilty of encroachment. The complaint was that the metropolitan entered the jurisdiction (*enoria*) of Constantinople, performed priestly functions, ordained clergy, and collected money. These actions were contrary to the canonical order, according to which a clergyman from outside his jurisdiction must seek permission to enter and act officially. In another case, the Metropolitan of Germanoupolis took over two of Constantinople's churches, in Attaleia and Syllaion on the Mediterranean coast near modern-day Antalya. The synod reported that he was able to do this through the authority of the emir in the area. As a result of Germanoupolis' negotiations with the Turkish emir, he held these as his possession. Constantinople reacted as if it was a case of rebellion. However, the synod could do little more than register the complaint, as they had no real coercive power beyond their verbal condemnation.[51]

Dorotheos, the Metropolitan of Peritheorion, a region in Thrace near Xanthi, also sought recourse from the Turks in 1381. According to the *Acta*, Dorotheos had been in prison in Constantinople for an unknown reason. After he escaped, he sought aid from the Turks and with their backing ruled the Church of Peritheorion. Dorotheos refused to return to Constantinople to be judged by the Synod. He had made an agreement with the Turks to turn over any Christian prisoners who fled to Peritheorion. The Holy Synod was angry that he had honored a dishonorable agreement, and utilized secular authority, in this case the Turkmen emir, to take control of the Church. The synodal document specifically makes mention of the Holy Canons, and quotes them as saying 'if it happens that any bishop uses lay authority in order to gain control of churches, let him be deposed." The synod recommended that he be removed and exiled not because he "was led astray by the Turks" which they did remark upon, but more so because he had "rejected the authority of this Holy Synod."[52] As a result the synod deemed that Metropolitan Dorotheos openly rejected Constantinople's imperial and ecclesiastical leadership when, in the words of the synodal decree, Dorotheos considered the Turks his "emperors, patriarchs, and protectors."[53]

The most infamous villain to appear in the *Patriarchal Acta* is Paul Tagaris. The account of Tagaris was recorded in 1384, in his confession before the Synod as he sought to be received back by the Constantinople Church. Tagaris was a bishop who wreaked havoc on the ecclesiastical administration from the 1370s to 1390s, according to the synodal documents. He ordained individuals to vacant sees without the legitimate right to do so. The synodal minutes of 1370 and 1384 both complained of his illegal actions and called in the individuals to be examined by legitimate metropolitans to consider whether they were worthy to be ordained.[54] In 1391, he later decided to return to the Patriarchate and confess his sins. He admits,

[51] MM, vol. 1, 412, 511–512.
[52] MM, vol. 2, 38. Also see Vryonis, *The Decline of Medieval Hellenism*, 332.
[53] MM, vol. 2, 38. Also see Vryonis, *The Decline of Medieval Hellenism*, 332.
[54] MM, vol. 1, 537 and vol. 2, 64–65. Also see Vryonis, *The Decline of Medieval Hellenism*, 336

> Satan entered into me again and there was nothing illegal or unlawful which he did not force me to carry out for shameful gain. I trampled under foot the jurisdiction (*enoria)* of the Ecumenical Patriarch; bishops who had no evil were thrust out of their own bishoprics, and in their places were brought in other dissolute men ... [who] gave money and received bishoprics from a presbyter.[55]

Tagaris clearly was making money from people who sought ordination and used this opportunity to create a profitable concession that was granted through support of the local emir. Even after he had falsely taken over the office of Patriarch of Jerusalem, he continued this practice of bestowing offices and ordinations on those who paid the most money. Then he slandered these men to the local emir to get his way, and also to avoid the pressure from legitimate bishops. He exclaimed in his confession, "For the love of money which had seized my soul and the desire for wealth moved me to work every evil ..."[56] It is hard to say what the emir's interest was in cooperating with Tagaris. The two possibilities are that either he was eager to flout the legitimate metropolitan who was in a sense a Byzantine agent, or he gained a portion of Tagaris's earnings. The emir could very well have been motivated by both of these aspects.

At one point, Tagaris wished to go to the Persian borders and to Georgia because he was not satisfied with the office of Patriarch of Jerusalem and its financial benefits. Acting as mediator to resolve a royal dispute in Georgia, he gained even greater fame and wealth. The Patriarchate in Constantinople, however, tried to thwart further abuses and circulated a letter describing how evil Tagaris and his partner, the Metropolitan of Tyre, were. As a result of the increased pressure, Tagaris went to Rome. After making a confession of faith to the Pope, the Pope named him Patriarch of Constantinople, further alienating himself from the authority in Istanbul.[57] The example of Tagaris illustrates the disarray in Anatolia about which the Synod in Constantinople bitterly complained. Certainly Tagaris' personal confession offers interesting insight into the greedy exploits of one man. Tagaris was brash in his approach, traveling broadly and exploiting opportunities with local rulers. Tagaris showed there were many ways that individual hierarchs could exploit imperial weakness, the ecclesiastical institution, and the interests of the local authority.

In another case from 1387, the synod reacted to another situation of direct collaboration between (another) Matthew, the Metropolitan of Myra, and an emir who was most likely the Turkish ruler of the Hamid emirate on the Mediterranean coast.[58] The decree claimed that the Metropolitan and the emir were both enjoying the spoliation of a metropolitan seat belonging to another, namely, Theophilos, Metropolitan of Attaleia-Perge. The emir, by his own authority, granted these extra-jurisdictional ecclesiastical properties that were within his own territory to the Metropolitan of Myra.[59] The patriarchal synod concluded that Metropolitan

[55] MM, vol. 2, 226. Also see Vryonis, *The Decline of Medieval Hellenism*, 336. Vryonis'translation.

[56] MM, vol. 2, 227. [57] MM, vol. 2, 238.

[58] This named Metropolitan Matthew of Myra is not to be confused with the aforementioned Matthew, Metropolitan of Ephesus.

[59] MM, vol. 2, 92–95. Also see Vryonis, *The Decline of Medieval Hellenism*, 333.

Matthew of Myra had no right to intervene and take over the rightful prerogatives of Theophilos. According to the reasoning used by the Holy Synod, it was not necessarily unacceptable to receive properties from lay people or from lay authority, as there was ample precedence for receiving properties from lay benefactors, but rather it was unacceptable because it was a Turkish emir who had made the decision of what should occur with the properties of the Church.

The main issue, therefore, was that one metropolitan took over the jurisdiction of the other through the agency of the Turkish emir. Taking over abandoned episcopal sees was clearly familiar to the Holy Synod, as it was becoming standard practice among provincial bishops. In this case, a standard solution to this problem would have been for the Holy Synod to assign the jurisdiction of the Metropolis of Attaleia-Perge to Metropolitan Matthew of Myra for "reasons of sustenance" (*kata logon epidoseos*). It would have been practical for Attaleia-Perge to be given over to the needy Metropolis of Myra. Metropolitan Theophilos could then have been assigned a bishopric in friendlier territory. The Holy Synod of Constantinople, however, did not want to take this approach because this would appear as if it were condoning the Turkish emir's intervention.

The second important consideration gleaned from this example is that the Turkish emir distributed ecclesiastical jurisdictions and properties to the metropolitan who was cooperative and was willing to remain under Turkish rule. As a reward for agreeing to stay in his episcopal see, he was granted jurisdiction by the emir that went beyond his enlarged territorial boundaries. There was a common interest, which was to use the diocese as a source of economic revenue to be exploited jointly. Metropolitan Matthew of Myra was simply shrewd enough to reap the material benefits for having stayed in a new regime, at the expense, however, of alienating himself from Constantinople. He appeared willing to take the criticism.

Another example from the *Patriarchal Acta* of Constantinople concerns the Metropolitan of Chalcedon (Kadiköy) in 1394. This incident struck much closer to home, in the environs of Constantinople. When conquering the regions in Asia Minor across from Constantinople, the Ottomans had taken over the Monastery of Akapnios and its estates, and had granted what would otherwise be an independent monastery and its properties to the neighboring Metropolitan of Chalcedon. Upon learning of this, the patriarchal synod condemned this transfer.[60] It condemned the Metropolitan of Chalcedon for acting "like an Ottoman." The Ottoman intervention irritated the synod because it was not only a lay authority, but also an enemy regime intervening into ecclesiastical administration. Charging that the metropolitan had violated the holy canons, the synod characterized his sin as greed and admonished him to read from the work of the third-century writer from the Pontos, St. Gregory the Wonderworker, on the subject of "greediness." The original context for this "Canonical Epistle" was an

60 MM, vol. 2, 200–201. Also see Vryonis, *The Decline of Medieval Hellenism*, 333.

unusual incursion by Goths into Asia Minor to Pontos in AD 257.[61] It is significant that the synod in 1394 chose this short treatise that details and condemns the sins of the third-century Christian community of Pontos, which collaborated with Gothic invaders. At the heart of both condemnations were admonishments of the individuals who, out of greed, stole their colleagues' properties with the support of foreign powers.

By focusing on the corrupt and greedy action of the individual bishop, the Holy Synod was responding to a dramatic transition that was taking place threatening the very institution of the Church. In this time period, all sorts of anomalous arrangements were being made that were contrary to the canonical principle of attaching a single bishop to a single see. This certainly caused anxiety among the bishops of the Holy Synod of Constantinople, but rather than critique the now accepted practice of granting sees for "reasons of sustenance" (*kata logon epidoseon*) and, as a result, risk critiquing the irregular but contemporary routine of episcopal appointments, it was easier for the Holy Synod to focus on individuals who clearly relied on lay Turkish authorities for their gain. Passing judgment on greedy individuals avoided criticizing the faltering institution. The canonical order and structure of the Church were not corrupt. Rather it was evil individuals who deserved condemnation. This process of condemning greedy individuals strengthened the symbolic power of the Holy Synod, which retained the moral authority and power to condemn. In 1394, when the Ottomans and the Metropolitan of Chalcedon had formed a collaborationist and symbiotic relationship to collect revenues and administrate property, the Holy Synod condemned the Metropolitan in a letter warning against becoming a "publican" and a "foreigner." While the Holy Synod focused their condemnation on the human failings of one man, it avoided the larger and more important question the legitimacy of episcopal appointments during this period, thus ensuring that the numerous bishoprics could continue to function, even in their anomalous fashion.

Another extremely important example is the accusation levied by the Holy Synod against Patriarch Matthew I (1397–1410), who was thought to have made secret negotiations with the Ottoman ruler Bayezid in order to preserve his position under the Ottoman regime. At the time of this incident, Bayezid was laying siege to Constantinople, and things looked rather ominous for the city's inhabitants. While it is unlikely that the Patriarch of Constantinople would have collaborated with the Ottomans, the fact that Patriarch Matthew felt compelled to respond to this charge in a well publicized general letter to the faithful in 1401 means that the charge might easily have been believed by his contemporaries. Even if this was a false charge that was motivated by personal envy or political expedience, the fact that his contemporaries were familiar with numerous examples of such collaboration meant that they were conditioned to believe such

[61] M. Slusser, ed., *St. Gregory Thaumaturgus Life and Works, The Fathers of the Church* (Washington, DC: Catholic University of America Press, 1998) 2, n. 8, and 147–151.

a charge, even of a patriarch. At any rate, Patriarch Matthew I, obliged to dispel any such notions, wrote in his defense:

> The claim is that I, having sent a certain person to the emir, arranged for myself to have security from him on my own account in the great city, should indeed it ever be taken. Which act I judge as nothing other than open betrayal of Christ himself.[62]

As patriarch and head of the Holy Synod, he, of course, denied and condemned this practice of negotiation with the Ottoman emir, Bayezid.

ECCLESIASTICAL TIMARS

Financial considerations were often at the heart of many of the conflicts between the local bishops and the Synod at Constantinople. What were the fiscal considerations that concerned them, and how did they play out strictly under Ottoman rule? What were the sources of revenue that a local bishop depended upon and that the local emir desired? Revenues from the landholdings are surely a major part of the answer.

Land tenure appears to be a common link between Ottoman rule and ecclesiastical administration. The intention to incorporate the Greek Orthodox hierarchy into the Ottoman administrative structure was part of a deliberate policy intended to assist the conquest of largely Christian populations and territory. However, the process by which this was to take place was not as systematic as previously thought, a conclusion demonstrated by the previous examples showing the ad hoc nature of relations between bishops and emirs.

Territory conquered by the Ottomans came under the eminent domain (*dominium eminens*) of the state, which had proprietary rights on the land. The state could choose to abrogate its proprietary rights in cases where it granted land as freehold property (*mülk*) or individuals formed pious endowments (*vakıf/evkaf*) to manage estates. With its imperial holdings (*miri*) the state had to distinguish between lands leased to the peasantry, who had to pay all taxes and provide services to the state and the local Ottoman cavalry (*sipahi*), and lands that were freely rented (*mukata'asi*) to individuals with a promise of a lump-sum payment for the tithes (*mâktu'*). Monasteries attempted to transform their holdings from *miri*, as conquered lands, to *mülk* and ultimately to *vakıf*, to preserve their resources.

During the period of the early Ottoman conquests, *timariots* were responsible for supervising and acting as state agents overseeing land possession and use. The sultan granted fiefs (*timars*) to individuals on the basis of meritorious service, and these individuals had the responsibility to maintain productivity as well as the imperial status of these lands. In the process of incorporating conquered

[62] MM, vol. 2, 626. For Barker's translation see John W. Barker, *Manuel II Palaeologus (1391–1425): A Study in Late Byzantine Statesmanship* (New Brunswick: Rutgers University Press, 1969), 207–211.

ecclesiastical lands into their administrative system, the Ottomans considered ecclesiastical estates as eminent domain of the state. As a result, in the second quarter of the fifteenth century, there are important examples where the local clergy are considered *timariots*.

The important 1431–32 *tahrir defter* for the Sancak of Arvanid published by Halil Inalcik in 1954 was recorded just prior to the Albanian revolt of 1432, and perhaps even precipitated this revolt with a show of state power looking to exploit fiscally the local population. Throughout this register, Christians held timars as *sipahi*. Among them were immigrants who had been transplanted according to the Ottoman policy of *sürgün* to the region from places that had experienced political opposition to Ottoman rule. According to the theory of the timar system, timars were temporary possessions that were well regulated by the state. They were to be held by individuals and then upon the *sipahi's* death, to be distributed to another eligible sipahi. This *defter* shows, however, that about half of the timars in the region were held as uninterrupted family possessions. The end result of this development is the formation of a family-based land-tenure system that was contrary to the well-defined Ottoman principles. This, perhaps, was the result of efforts by settled and conservative rural gentry who pushed for administrative continuity. This *defter* provides useful statistics which suggest trends and patterns of official land-tenure and composition of the Ottoman army.

In one of the important examples from this register, there is a clear policy by those who were registering the *vilayet* of Belgrade that the metropolitan was considered as a *timariot*, and in the most abstract sense would be on an equal level with the military (*Askeri*) class of Ottoman subjects. The differentiation between *askeri* and *reaya* was important in Ottoman administration. The *askeri* were in the service of the sultan, traditionally in a military capacity, while the *reaya* were the peasantry, agriculturalists, and laborers.[63] Item no. 200 lists the metropolitan's *Timar* (*Timâr-i Medrepolid*), which in Sultan Murat II's time (1421–51) was the region of the Bey Ibrahim. The *timar* was made up of two villages, *Karye-i Apanohore*, which had fourteen households, and *Karye-i Vloş*, which had four households. The total combined revenue was 1,424 akçe, making them both reasonably sized *timars*.[64] This example, however, raises significant questions concerning the Ottoman administrative intentions towards the Church. There are three other cases of this type of arrangement. Rather than a metropolitan's timar, they are bishops' timars, (*Timâr-i Peskopos,* No.270 and with slight spelling variation *Timâr-i Peskopoz*, No. 100 and No. 299).[65] It is logical that the existence of a metropolitan's *timar* would be in the *Sancak* of Albania and in the *vilayet* of Belgrade where there would be a large Christian population and the Church had a prominent place in the region. Naming the timar as the metropolitan's timar is significant especially if it was indeed

[63] Inalcik, "The Status of the Greek Orthodox Patriarchate," 409.
[64] H. Inalcik, *Suret-i Defter-i Sancak-i Arvanid* (Ankara: Türk Tarih Kurumu Basimevi, 1954), 73.
[65] Inalcik, *Suret-i Defter-i Sancak-i Arvanid*, 43, 99, and 110.

assigned to a sitting metropolitan. Yet, even if this was not the case, simply the preservation of the term "Medropolid" is still significant in terms of the Ottomans confronting an ecclesiastical administration. The same follows for the term *Peskopos(z).*

If an actual metropolitan or bishop were assigned a *timar*, it follows the sequence of Inalcik's "Ottoman Methods of Conquest" wherein local administrative forms were adopted until the Ottomans established more direct control over the territory.[66] In this case, the metropolitan after whom the timar was named became a *timariot* and was directly brought into Ottoman administration as an agent of the sultan. In the traditional relationship, the *sipahi* was required to report for military service and field his own retinue. There is no indication that a metropolitan in this case had any military or even administrative function. However, he was granted a source of revenue from two villages for an unspecified reason.

These instances of a metropolitan or bishop's "*timar*" also fits within the guiding principle of *istimâlet,* in which certain accommodations are granted to the subject populations in order to win them over. A *timar* concession granted to a Greek Orthodox hierarch would certainly go a long way to convince him as well as other clerics and local leaders that it is a wise thing to submit to Ottoman rule. Thus, this grant would have helped the Ottomans more easily gain basic political control of the Christian population. Additionally in this case, Church properties and ecclesiastical incomes were not mentioned. Presumably, the local metropolitan would still be responsible for ecclesiastical incomes. The designation of *timar* was likely the easiest and most readily available solution for the *sancak bey* to assign to a metropolitan in the *vilayet.* Surely his ecclesiastical authority would have extended beyond the assigned timar boundaries of two villages, but his incorporation into the timar structure would ensure the loyalty of the region's Christian villagers.

If the title was more of an honorific descriptive term of a region, and did not indicate an actual metropolitan serving as a *timariot,* it still is significant because it signifies the importance of the role of the metropolitan for the local people. The Ottomans must have thought it important enough to preserve, perhaps, to encourage local Christian loyalty. Another explanation is that by the time this particular *timar* was assigned, "metropolitan" was not a threatening title, and the Ottomans simply maintained it.

Adding to the complexity of the 1435 *defter,* there are a couple of curious examples wherein churches were granted to *timariots* as income-producing sources. This occurs in No. 267, *Timâr-i Andranikos,* which was granted not only the town of Ayos Aleksandros, but the Church of Aleksandros. The actual value of this grant was the in kind production of the attached property that produced fifteen bushels from a vineyard with ten laborers, three olive trees, seven cherry trees, nine fig trees, and six pear trees.[67] The other

66 H. Inalcik, "Ottoman Methods of Conquest," *Studia Islamica* II (1954): 104–129.
67 Inalcik, *Suret-i Defter-i Sancak-i Arvanid,* 99.

was No. 254 *Timâr-i Tudular,* which was granted the churches Ayos Nikola (a vineyard with twenty laborers, twenty apple trees and twenty-one pears), Ayos Todoros (a vineyard with twenty-five laborers, ten apple trees and twenty pear trees), and Ayos Martin (a vineyard with seventeen laborers, twenty-one apple trees and twenty pear trees).[68] In the *Timâr-i Peskopoz* (No. 100) the *Peskopiye* church property was granted to the *Piskopos timar*, which was made up of a vineyard in the hamlet of the *Piskopiye* made up of a vineyard with ten laborers, a second vineyard in the area of Kanina, with five laborers, and six walnut trees.[69] Halil Inalcik, in his introduction to the *defter*, explained that timars granted to bishops were rarely seen, as was the assignment of Churches and church property to timars.[70] However, these examples are still instructive.

One other such example of an ecclesiastical *timar* comes from the famous monastery in the Balkans. In her work on the Monastery of Saint John of Serres, Evangelia Balta offers the example of the Ottomans assigning the Monastery itself as a *timariot* with the monastery property and holdings as the *timar.* Balta argues that the monastery was not a traditional *timar* wherein the monks would be expected to perform military duties. Rather, it was a way for the Ottomans to administer the monastic community, rather than coming up with a new and original administrative form. In fact, it turns out that the monastic timar was granted as a type of preferment to the monks. Clearly not reflecting Islamic legal practice, it was a practical approach to dealing with the monastery. As late as 1460, Sultan Mehmet II sent a firman to the monastery confirming the monastery and attached villages, gardens, orchards, and mills as belonging to the *timar.* By the time of the next registration in *Tapu Tahrir Defteri* 3 in 1478, the monastery was assigned as a timar to other *sipahis.* By the beginning of the sixteenth century, it became normalized as a religious endowment (*vakıf*).[71] Thus, even in time of relative stability, it took some time for the monastic timar to be normalized as religious endowment.

For the purposes of this discussion, the fact that these types of examples exist shows that even in the fifteenth century, there was still some ambiguity surrounding what to do with monasteries, churches and their bishops. While the Ottomans, in fact, entertained the possibility of offering Church hierarchs *timars*, and Church properties as income for *timars*, they chose not to make this a common practice.

CHURCH AND OTTOMANS: THE MONASTERIES

Monasteries posed a different challenge to the Ottomans. In Greek Orthodox ecclesiastical administration, there is a great distinction between the administration of a monastery and the secular ecclesiastical administration of a regional

[68] Inalcik, *Suret-i Defter-i Sancak-i Arvanid*, 94.
[69] Inalcik, *Suret-i Defter-i Sancak-i Arvanid*, 43.
[70] Inalcik, *Suret-i Defter-i Sancak-i Arvanid*, XXX–XXXI.
[71] E. Balta, *Les Vakifs De Serrès Et De Sa Région (XVe Et XVIe S.)* (Athènes: Centre De Rechereches Néo-Helléniques, 1995), 42–43.

Church community by the bishop. Just as the local bishop and metropolitan were components of imperial Byzantine administration, so too was the monastery. In early Christian times, monasteries were founded by individuals who fled society, with its material concerns, for the desert with the goal of living an ascetic life and finding spiritual enlightenment. However, the historical development of Byzantine monasticism ensured that monasticism would become high profile, with monks taking clear positions in religious, political, and cultural battles. Monasteries were especially important for their contributions to the theological debates in the early centuries of the Church. In the later centuries they were important for their wealth that they acquired through donations and bequests by aristocratic and imperial patrons.

Historically, the monastery was a religious foundation where individual monks came under the supervision of an abbot (*hegoumenos*) for the purpose of continual prayer, meditation, and work. It had real and movable property and sought to sustain itself by means of its own production. As an ecclesiastical institution, it could either come under the authority of a local bishop, or it could come directly under the Patriarchate of Constantinople, a status called *stavropegion*.[72] A local bishop's authority would defer to the patriarchal status of *stavropegion*. This meant that a monastery's jurisdiction was legally independent from a local bishop's control, and it reported, instead directly to the Patriarchate of Constantinople.[73]

The struggle between monasteries and local bishops over *stavropegion* status was common. Local monasteries often preferred this status because it meant increased prestige due to being associated with the Patriarchate of Constantinople and thus, an imperial institution. It also meant practical benefits and relief from local intervention. Monasteries that were wealthy and receiving imperial and aristocratic patronage naturally wished to become *stavropegeaic*. With a vibrant economy on Mt. Athos in the late Byzantine period due to the numerous bequests and donations that it received, it comes as no surprise that the Athonite monasteries became largely *stavropegeaic* and under the direct jurisdiction of the Patriarchate of Constantinople. However, the road to achieve this status was not an easy one.

Both the Emperor at Constantinople and the patriarch sought at different times to maintain sole control over Mt. Athos. In fact, Mt. Athos had come under Patriarchal authority as late as November 1312 as instituted in a chrysobul of Andronikos II Palaiologos.[74] In the late fourteenth century, there was a movement to abandon the cenobitic (communal) monastic life in favor of the idiorythmic (individualistic) monastic life. The impetus for this movement was

[72] Alice Mary Talbot and Alexander P. Kazhdan, "Stauropegion," ed. Alexander P. Kazhdan, *The Oxford Dictionary of Byzantium*, III, 1946–7.

[73] Michael Angold, *Church and Society*, 149; Alan Harvey, "The Monastic Economy and Imperial Patronage From the Tenth to the Twelfth Century," in *Mount Athos and Byzantine Monasticism: Papers from the Twenty-eighth Spring Symposium of Byzantine Studies, Birmingham, March 1994*, ed. Anthony Bryer and Mary Cunningham (Birmingham: Variorum, 1996).

[74] Emmanuel Amand De Mendieta, *Mount Athos: The Garden of the Panaghia*, trans. Michael R. Bruce (Amsterdam: Adolf M. Hakkert, 1972), 93. See Denise Papachryssanthou, ed., *Actes Du Protaton*, VII (Paris, 1975), no. 12.

chiefly a financial one.[75] In the idiorythmic system, monks possessed more personal autonomy than those living in cenobitic communities. The relaxation of the traditional Orthodox monastic austerity stemmed from the political uncertainty of the period. Wealthy individuals increased the enrollment of the Athonite monasteries. Many of these people sought to preserve their wealth by placing it in the monastic foundation that was typically exempt from Ottoman taxation. The move towards monastic idiorythmy was, therefore, partly the result of a desire to shelter personal financial resources. Patriarch Anthony IV's letter to the monks of Pantocrator monastery in June 1394, identifies this trend toward idiorythmy when he exhorts the monks to maintain their cenobitic rule. In 1400, the patriarchal synod in Constantinople issued a *Typikon* (regulation establishing order) which freed Mount Athos from the claims of the local bishop at Ierissos whom the monks were continually resisting, and also tried to increase the powers of the local leader (*protos*) who was the main arbiter of authority for Mount Athos chosen directly by the patriarchal synod.[76] Emperor Manuel II made a statement to the same effect concerning the order of Mount Athos and the spread of idiorhythmy when he attempted to institute direct rule over the monasteries. He attempted to establish greater order and control through a Chrysobul of June 1406 (No. 13, *Actes du Protaton*). This document shows idiorhythmy's wider and deeper implications on the social and political situation. At first sight, this chrysobul is simply a letter enjoining the monks to follow the Typikon and to live a cenobitic monastic life. Manuel II says that any monk has come to the monastery and feigns to practice hesychasm, but really is a devotee of idiorythmy, then he shall not receive any *hyperpera* from the monastery. Manuel II showed a keen interest in the inner workings of specific monasteries, and how they were run. He also sought to reign in those wealthy men who became monks in order to protect their personal fortune, and who were promoters of the more individualistic idiorythmy. What was at stake for Manuel II was his control over a large group of income producing men, and his ability to collect taxes as well as to keep the general order.[77]

The wealth of Mt. Athos can be likened to the modern Swiss banking system in which individuals can deposit their wealth into an institution that possessed the greatest possible security. Mt. Athos vigorously maintained a protected status under the various Byzantine, Serbian, and Ottoman rulers. The lands belonging to the monasteries were fertile and productive enough to provide surpluses to be commercialized for the benefit of the monasteries, or could be given as pensions (*adelphata*) to those patrons making donations. It is no surprise, therefore, that

[75] A. E. Vakalopoulos, *History of Macedonia: 1354–1833*, trans. Peter Megann (Thessalonike: Institute for Balkan Studies, 1973), 176.

[76] De Mendieta, *Mount Athos*, 101. De Mendieta dates this at April 1396 rather than as above. See Denise Papachryssanthou, ed., *Actes Du Pantocrator*, VII (Paris, 1991), no. 17 and De Mendieta, *Mount Athos*, 94.

[77] Papachryssanthou, ed., *Actes Du Protaton*, no. 13, and no. 109.

seven monasteries were established or rebuilt after the middle of fourteenth century and into the fifteenth century.[78]

What was the fate of the Byzantine monasteries under Ottoman rule?[79] Monasteries were very practical in their negotiations with whichever state exercised rule over them. In the late Byzantine period, and especially in the Balkans in the fourteenth century when larger amounts of territory came under Serbian rule, monastic foundations increased in importance. Perhaps there was a sense of competition between Greek and Serbian nobility supporting their respective monastic communities.[80] Regardless of the reason, under Ottoman rule, the Athonite institutions were able to preserve large portions of their widespread holdings and to continue to survive as important monastic centers throughout the following centuries. Monastic cooperation also directly benefited the Ottomans, who gained prestige among Christian subjects by being protectors of the monasteries. Keeping these issues in mind, the experience of the monastery can help us understand better how the rest of the ecclesiastical hierarchy related to Ottoman rulers.[81]

Mount Athos and the Monastery of St. John Prodromos in Serres, another monastic institution facing similar circumstances, provide the most prominent examples of relations between the monastic communities and the Ottomans.

[78] Nicholas Oikonomides, "Patronage in Palaiologan Mt. Athos," in *Mount Athos and Byzantine Monasticism: Papers from the Twenty-eigth Spring Symposium of Byzantine Studies, Birmingham, March 1994*, ed. Anthony Bryer and Mary Cunningham (Birmingham: Variorum, 1996), 99–100. In the same volume see Elizabeth A. Zachariadou, "A Safe and Holy Mountain: Early Ottoman Athos," 127–132; Also see Elizabeth A. Zachariadou, "The Worrisome Wealth of the Çelnik Radic," in *Studies in Ottoman History in Honour of Professor V. L. Menage*, ed. C. Heywood and C. Imber (Istanbul: Isis Press, 1994), 383–397.

[79] P. Lemerle and P. Wittek, "Recherches sur l'histoire et le status des monasteres Athonites sous la domination turque," *Archives d'Histoire du Droit Oriental* 3 (1947): 411–471; Heath W. Lowry, "The Fate of Monastic Properties under the Ottomans: Examples from Mount Athos, Limnos and Trabzon," *Byzantinische Forschungen* 16 (1991): 275–311; Heath W. Lowry, "A Note on the Population and Status of the Athonite Monasteries Under Ottoman Rule (c.1520)," *Wiener Zeitschrift fur die Kunde des Morgenlandes* 73 (1981): 229–246; E. A. Zachariadou, "Ottoman Documents from the Archives of Dyonisiou (Mt. Athos) 1495–1520," *Sudost-Forschungen* 30 (1971): 1–36; E. A. Zachariadou, "Early Ottoman Documents of the Prodromos Monastery (Serres)," *Sudost-Forschungen* 28 (1969): 1–12; N. Beldiceanu, "A propos de deux registres ottomans de recensement des monastères du Mont Athos," *Byzation* 52 (1982): 496–499; Heath W. Lowry, "Polemique à propos d'un compte rendu paru dans Byzantion LII," *Byzantion* 55 (1982): 403–414; Most recently published is the volume, K. Chrisochoides, ed., *Mount Athos in the 14th–16th Centuries*, vol. 4, *Athonika Symmeikta* (Athens: The National Hellenic Research Foundation Institute for Byzatine Research, 1997). N. Oikonomides, "Le Haradj Dans L'empire Byzantine Du XVe Siecle," in *Actes Du Premier Congrès International Des Études Balkaniques et Sudest Europeénes*, ed. Association internationale d'études du Sud-Est européen (Sofia: Académie bulgare des sciences, 1966), 681–688.; N. Oikonomides, "Monasteres et moines lors de la conquete ottomane," *Südost Forschungen* (1976): 1–10.

[80] Oikonomides, "Patronage in Palaiologan Mt. Athos," 99.

[81] For early attempts to publish the various monastic documents, see L. Petit, W. Regel, E. Kurtz, and B. Korablev in an older series, *Vizantijskij Veremennik* beginning in 1903. These first published archives were incorporated into what became the main initiative in editing and publishing the various archives, namely the *Archives de l'Athos* series that was founded by Gabriel Millet and Paul Lemerle. These earlier publications were incorporated into the present series, which until 1991, exist for seventeen of the twenty-one established monasteries. While the main emphasis of the *Archives de l'Athos* is to publish documents from 932 to 1500 written in Greek, the monastic

Mt. Athos was established as a peninsula dedicated to the monastic life where the monasteries were under the direct care and stewardship of Byzantine imperial patrons. Caught in the struggle between Byzantium and the Serbian kingdom, and suffering numerous invasions by Turkic raiders from among the various Anatolian emirates, the monasteries of Mt. Athos, and Serres sought to preserve their existence by engaging with the local authorities. They wanted not only to protect themselves but also to protect their smaller dependent monastic communities (*metochia)* in Thrace and Macedonia in the face of an unstable political and military landscape, because the *metochia* were essential to the economic maintenance of the actual monasteries.

In the first half of the fourteenth century, Turkish pirates and brigands continually invaded the coasts of the Chalkidike region and especially Mt. Athos. The emirate of Aydin (*beylik)*, for instance, directed numerous raids against settlements in the Aegean islands, the coastal mainland of Greece, and the monasteries of Mt. Athos. This emirate on the western coast of Asia Minor had developed a sophisticated naval force and used its fleet to target vulnerable coastal towns.[82] Attacks leveled against the monasteries of Mt. Athos from Turkmen pirates threatened the property and possessions of the monastic institutions. These attacks continued until tribute agreements were drawn up between the monasteries and the raiding pirates.[83] These raids, accordingly, decreased in number from the mid-fourteenth century onward to such an extent that there are very few recorded instances of new attacks in the Byzantine sources.[84] After 1350, there was a renewed feeling of general safety on Mt. Athos that encouraged increased patronage, restoration, and repopulation. The change in climate from being under siege to being stable and prosperous was connected to the Ottoman recognition of the status of the monasteries on Mt. Athos. During his reign from 1326–62, the Sultan Orhan

archives themselves are more expansive and include Serbian, Georgian, Bulgarian, Latin, Turkish and Italian acts that exist. Those non-Greek acts that manage to be included in the archives, though not necessarily with edited texts, are usually the acts written in Slavic languages having to do with the Slavic administration, monastic centers and population that was always an important part of life on Mount Athos. The character of the documents vary in scope and authorship ranging from acts of individual monks to imperial chrysobuls in tact with their seals. Mostly, however, they are documentation of donations of land and *paroikoi* of various types of properties including fields, pastures, and mills. See Nicholas Oikonomides, "Les Archives medievales du Mont Athos," XVI, 489. The acts of monasteries published thus far are: Chilander, Docheriariou, Dionysiou, Esphigmenou, Iveron, Kastamonitou, Kutlumus, Lavra, Panteleimon, Philotheou, Prodrome, Protaton, Xenophon, Xeropotamou, Zographou. Those not published are Gregoriou, which burnt in 1761 and no longer possesses medieval documents, nor does Stavronikita. Simonopetra's archive was also burnt in 1891. Vatopedi still has not been published in the series though 80 documents have been edited and published; see Oikonomides, "Les Archives," 492.

82 Zachariadou, "Holy War in the Aegean," 212–225.

83 See Elizabeth A. Zachariadou, "Early Ottoman Documents of the Prodromos Monastery (Serres)," and Vassilis Demetriades, "Athonite Documents and the Ottoman Occupation," in *Mount Athos in the 14–16th Centuries*, ed. K. Chrisochoides, vol. 4, *Athonika Symmeikta* (Athens: The National Hellenic Research Foundation, 1997), 41–67.

84 Elizabeth A. Zachariadou, "Some Remarks About Dedications to Monasteries in the Late 14th Century," in *Athos in the 14–16th Centuries*, 28.

was recognized for establishing the precedent of respecting the independent status of the Athonite monasteries.[85]

In the 1370s, however, Mt. Athos again suffered when it was caught in the crossfire between the Byzantines and the Ottomans. When the Byzantines faced a major blow, losing to the Ottomans at Maritza in 1371, Mt. Athos suffered severe consequences, but from the hands of the Byzantines. In order to maintain military strength and to preserve the holdings in the Balkans, the Emperor John V Palaiologos, decided to alienate half of the monastic estates and turn them into fiefs similar to *timars*, known by the Byzantines as *pronoia,* in order to strengthen the defenses of the empire. The Byzantine soldiery received their pay at the expense of the monastic properties.[86] Obviously, these policies were unpopular with the monasteries in the regions near Thessalonike, where many of the estates were located.

After the Battle of Maritza in 1371, Mount Athos underwent one final siege by the Ottomans, who were encouraged by their latest victory. In 1372 or 1373, the Ottomans directed a flotilla against Mount Athos to conquer the fortified monasteries. They were prevented from invading the peninsula, because at the last moment, a combined Venetian and Byzantine flotilla intercepted them and defended it. This was the last major attack against Mount Athos by the Ottomans and, although Mount Athos was rich and prosperous, it managed to avoid further raids.

Not surprisingly, lasting stability came to Mt. Athos when the monasteries definitively capitulated to the Ottomans in the late fourteenth century. The monasteries managed to continue their prosperity and maintain their possessions under Ottoman rule. The vast monastic estates produced vibrant revenue that included agricultural production from grains, vineyards, and livestock. Managing and controling this aspect of the ecclesiastical economy was an important step for the Ottomans not only to gain control of a large indigenous institution, but also to reap the benefits from such a large economic resource.

The oldest surviving document issued by an Ottoman Sultan to a monastic institution is a tax exemption granted to the Monastery of St. John Prodromos (Margarites) in Serres. Murat I issued a *hüküm* that survives in Greek only, dated December 27, 1372–January 5, 1373. Murat I ordered the monks of the monastery of "Margarites" set free (meaning exempt from imposts) with their villages, lands and mills. None of Murat I's successors nor their dependents were to ever cause the monastery trouble, and, if anyone chose to denounce the monks in court, that person must, himself, be dismissed.[87] Although this document is brief and extremely vague, it does show how a relationship was established between the Ottomans and a monastic complex in the countryside. The monastery was free to exist without harassment from the Ottomans.

This monastery was established as a quasi freeholding, with certain exemptions from *ispence* and the tax on sheep, indicating that the monastery functioned

[85] Zachariadou, "Some Remarks About Dedications to Monasteries," 28.

[86] Peter Charanis, "The Monastic Properties and the State in the Byzantine Empire," *Dumbarton Oaks Papers* IV (1948): 119.

[87] Zachariadou, "Early Ottoman Documents of the Prodromos Monastery," 3.

like a *vakıf*, with the exemptions of a pious foundation. Monastic institutions desired to receive full exemptions from taxation, and ultimately gain the status as *vakıf*, and to receive treatment equal to that of a Muslim pious foundation. That a Christian monastic institution would be considered a *vakıf* surprised researchers including Lemerle, Wittek, and Balta, each of whom explored the meaning of this classification in real terms.[88] About 140 years later, the same monastery was considered as a freeholding (*mülk*) with certain *vakıf* privileges in the late fourteenth century. Some 200 years later, in the 1454–1455 period, it received the status of a *timar*, meaning that the monastery was considered a *timar* and the monks *timariots*. Finally, it was considered a *vakıf* by the sixteenth century. The Ottomans attempted to deal with the institution of the monasteries and their properties in practical terms.[89] The monasteries did not pose any threat to the Ottoman status quo, and the *timar* was offered as a form of reward for their open acceptance and tacit approval of Ottoman rule. The application of the *timar* system both to the church and monasteries appears to have been an innovation that was attempted in some instances in the fourteenth century. By the time Sultan Mehmet II came to power for the second time in 1451, the Ottomans were trying to determine the best way to govern over this unconventional ecclesiastical institution. The ambivalence with which they began to incorporate monasteries into the Ottoman system, that is, the ad hoc manner, demonstrates that the Ottomans were still not fully certain as to the most advantageous practices to deal with the monasteries. Well after the Ottomans had successfully conquered large parts of the Balkans, there was no longer a need to reward local ecclesiastical figures and institutions for their cooperation. Therefore, the status of the monasteries moved more steadily towards that of formal pious foundations, and the hierarchs were transformed into *mültezims*.[90] The Ottomans had hoped to extend rapprochement to the monasteries as part of the policy of *istimâlet*. In addition, there were perhaps many Christian wives and mothers of former Christians in Ottoman service who would have been concerned about the preservation of the monasteries.[91]

88 Paul Lemerle and Paul Wittek, "Recherches Sur L'histoire Et Le Status Des Monasterès Athonites Sous La Domination Turque," *Archives d'Histoire Du Droit Oriental* 3 (1947): 411–471. See also G. Salakides, *Sultansurkunden Des Athos-Klosters Vatopedi Aus Der Zeit Bayezid II. Und Selim I* (Thessalonike: Institute for Balkan Studies, 1995).

89 Evangelia Balta, *Les Vakifs De Serrès et de sa Région (XVe et XVIe s.)*, trans. Edith Karagiannis (Athènes: Centre de Rechereches Néo-Helléniques, 1995), 42–43.

90 "The status of timar of the monastery of St. John Prodromos did not last long. In a *firman* sent by Mehmet II in 1460, the goods of this monastery are described in the Tapu *Tahrir Defteri 3* as a reserve timar. The *timar* of the monks is thus removed and, as seen in the census of 1478–78 [*sic*], the villages are recorded as a *timars* of other *sipahis*. The monastery will only preserve the property of what was constituted as "*mülk*," Balta, *Les Vakifs De Serrès*, 43. During the confiscation crisis of 1568, however, the state chose to wipe out the previously granted privileges in order to alienate revenue from the monastic communities. See John C. Alexander, "The Lord Giveth and the Lord Taketh Away: Athos and the Confiscation Affair of 1568–1569," in *Athos in the 14th–16th Centuries*, 149–200; and Aleksandar Fotic, "The Official Explanation for the Confiscation and Sale of Monasteries (Churches) and Their Estates at the Time of Selim II," *Turcica* 26 (1994): 33–54.

91 Vassilis Demetriades, "Athonite Documents and the Ottoman Occupation," in *Mount Athos in the 14th–16th Centuries*, 43.

Mt. Athos came under direct Ottoman rule in 1383, and this lasted uninterrupted until 1402, when Sultan Bayezid was captured during the Battle of Ankara against Timur.[92] Bayezid's famous defeat and capture led to the period of Ottoman Interregnum and civil war when each of Bayezid's sons attempted to reconsolidate some semblance of their father's former authority.[93] The three sons vying to succeed Bayezid were Süleyman Çelebi of Rumeli, Isa Çelebi of Anadolu, and Mehmet Çelebi, the governor of Anatolia. After establishing control over his territory in Rumeli, Süleyman Çelebi turned his focus on Asia Minor and marched against his brother Isa, defeating him.[94] As he was trying to maximize his control and power, Süleyman followed traditional Ottoman policy. When he focused on Asia Minor, he made peace in Rumeli. During the period in which he was vying for the control of Anatolia between 1403 and 1410, there were few conflicts in Rumeli between the Christians and the Ottomans.[95] As part of his peacemaking, Süleyman had to address not only Manuel II, but also the issue of the monastic communities. He concluded a treaty with the Byzantines, dealing with the regions surrounding Mt. Athos, conceding lands that were previously ruled by the Ottomans. Süleyman referred to Manuel II saying, "To my father, the Emperor of the Greeks, I have given Thessalonike and Kalamaria, Chalkidike and the littoral of the Thermaic Gulf."[96] This territory included the districts from the Galikos River to the Vardares region (*Parardaron*). These regions remained under Byzantine rule until the last years of the empire.[97] The peninsula of Chalkidike passed into Byzantine control because it was included in Kalamaria's administrative sphere. Generally, east, and north of the Strymnon River remained under Süleyman's control. The areas southwest of Thessalonike within Vardares once again passed under Byzantine control. In addition, the Byzantines were not required to pay taxes or tributes on their newly reacquired areas, and all Byzantine prisoners were to be released.[98] Süleyman Çelebi made a number of other concessions to the other treaty signers, ranging from free movement of grain, to staying clear of the Dardenelles, to giving Athens

[92] Demetriades, "Athonite Documents and the Ottoman Occupation," 42.

[93] Imber, *The Ottoman Empire*, 63.

[94] N. Oikonomides, "Le Haradj Dans L'empire Byzantine Du XVe Siecle," in *Actes Du Premier Congrès International Des Études Balkaniques et Sudest Europeénes,* ed. Association internationale d'études du Sud-Est européen (Sofia: Académie bulgare des sciences, 1966), 681–688. On the Interregnum, see Dimitris J. Kastritsis, *The Ottoman Interregnum (1402–1413): Politics and Narratives of Dynastic Succession* (Cambridge, MA: Harvard University Press, 2005).

[95] Zachariadou, "Süleyman Çelebi," 291. Yet, Doukas writes that Musa, who had been freed from his captivity by Timurlane, said about Süleyman, that " he did not show proper regard for our paternal faith, but- it must be said- he also became half an infidel."(D. Doukas, *Decline and Fall of Byzantium to the Ottoman Turks*, trans. Harry J Magoulias (Detroit: Wayne State University Press, 1975), 108.) Whether he was or was not an infidel is open for debate, but what Süleyman's political and military aims were can be seen through the record of his diplomacy. Reliable information about this civil war rarely comes to us from the Ottoman historians such as Neshri, simply because the histories favored Mehmet Çelebi who was, after all, victorious. (Zachariadou, "Süleyman Çelebi," 268.)

[96] G. Dennis, "The Byzantine-Turkish Treaty of 1403," *Byzantium and the Franks, 1350-1420* (London:Variorum Reprints, 33, 1967), 80.

[97] Zachariadou, "Süleyman Çelebi," 277.

[98] Zachariadou, "Süleyman Çelebi," 278.

to the Venetians.[99] There is also an interesting addition in the terminology beyond the basic, primarily Islamic protocol. In addition to "granting" these things to the Christians in the name of Muhammad, it also states they were granted in the name of "another great prophet," implying Jesus Christ.[100] The treaty also indicates that there was still a fear of Timur crossing the Dardanelles into Europe, because it included concessions made by Süleyman to assist in fighting against him if he ever did invade again.[101]

After his journey to Europe for Western aid, Manuel II returned to Constantinople on June 9, 1403, almost a year after the Battle of Ankara. Manuel II's nephew, John VII, who remained as the legitimate ruler in Constantinople, had just contracted a treaty with Süleyman in 1403. However, Manuel II made his intentions clear in a separate decree stating that Mount Athos was to be under the direct jurisdiction of the Emperor of Constantinople, though there still seemed to be some question as to who was actually in control there.[102] Taking the reins from his nephew, John VII, Manuel II sought to show that he was the ruler of Thessalonike and Chalkidike by issuing the *Prostagma* of 1404 detailing the administrative policy he wished to institute for Mt. Athos.[103] This important source gives information about the administration of Mt. Athos before and after 1402,[104] and dramatically marks the continuity and change in administrative policies (specifically tax policies) of the Byzantine and Ottoman rulers of this important monastic entity. Manuel II decided, very practically, to maintain the tax policies laid down by the previous Ottoman regime, even using the previous tax with its Ottoman name, *haraç*.

Emperor Manuel II commanded Demetrios Bouliotes, the imperial official governing Mt. Athos, to go to "his son, the *emir*" and request easement on the taxes, and to seek the sum from the *metochia* from Ali Pasha who appeared to be in direct control. Manuel II was more willing than his father, John V, had been

99 Dennis, "The Byzantine-Turkish Treaty of 1403," 81. The treaty between Süleyman and the Byzantines is quite important to help piece together the actual events and chronology as well as the agreements that would determine each party's behavior as they honored the treaty. The Prostagma helps us to see how Manuel II was dealing with administering the empire in the aftermath of the treaty and the Prostagma offers a good vantage point and enough perspective from which to see continuity and developments in political and economic policies. Arkadios ho Vatopedinos, "Agioreitika Analekta 15. Basilike diatage pros Demetrion ton Boulioten peri Agion Oros," *Gregorios ho Palamas* 2 (1918): 452.

100 Thus, as Zachariadou says, Doukas is perhaps justified in having Musa call him half an infidel. Zachariadou, "Süleyman Çelebi," 275.

101 Zachariadou, "Süleyman Çelebi," 276.

102 During the period in which Manuel II was in Europe, John VII had ruled legitimately, and he even contracted and signed the treaty with Süleyman. John Barker says that though he reigned by Manuel II's authority, he was a *Basileus* and even commissioned his own coinage; John Barker, *Manuel II Paleologus: 1391–1425, A Study in Late Byzantine Statesmanship* (New Brunswick, NJ: Rutgers University Press, 1969), 238.

103 Arkadios ho Vatopedinos, "Basilike diatage pros Demetrion ton Boulioten," 449–452. I thank Professor Steve Reinert for pointing this document out to me.

104 G. Ostrogorsky, *History of the Byzantine State*, 557, n. 4, identifies the Byzantine resurgence in Thessalonike and Chalkidike.

to exercise direct control. In addition, Manuel II was willing to let subordinates know that he had given them favors or positions.[105] The monks there hurried to be autonomous and sought the restitution of their rights even seeking to restore property from before the alienation of their properties after Maritza in 1371.[106] Manuel II made the distinction between the property of Mount Athos proper, whose *haraç* belongs to him, and the *metochia* property of Athos in the region of Thessalonike: two-thirds of the *haraç* should be given to the monasteries and the other one-third Manuel II granted to John VII, keeping none for himself.

The significant feature of this document is that the emperor in Constantinople recognized the previous Ottoman administrative transactions as useful after he became the ruler of the territory abandoned by them. This, essentially, gave him the right to collect the taxes for those properties.[107] In the case of this *Prostagma* of 1404, this term *haraç* was an Ottoman holdover used by the Byzantine state. The word *haraç* appears in this and other Byzantine documents, maintaining its Ottoman usage.[108] The *haraç* of the villages belonging to Mt. Athos was divided between the monasteries of Athos, who took two-thirds of the collected total, while the emperor took the remaining one-third of the *haraç*. Thus, the monasteries had to pay one-third of the *haraç* and other applicable taxes to the imperial fisc. The exception to this were those taxes that were very inconvenient to collect by the agents, and the *pronoiars* who themselves collected taxes as their own revenue, which would not be transferred to the imperial fisc. This also was valid for Thessalonike, which was controlled by John VII, to whom Manuel II relinquished his due of the imperial one-third of the *haraç*. Yet, the intent was to levy the tax according to the old custom, as it was under the Ottoman emir Sultan Bayezid, in a way that would profit both the monasteries and the imperial fisc. There was also continuity with the other taxes that the monasteries had paid to the Ottomans.

Perhaps the most interesting thing about the document is that it offers us a look at the relationship of the reigning regimes, Byzantine and Ottoman, with Mount Athos, and more generally, Chalkidike and Thessalonike. Moreover, one can also see a surprising continuity between the Ottoman and the Byzantine administration of this region. The historical circumstances for issuing this *Prostagma of 1404* are in themselves interesting. Manuel II had responded to a request by certain

105 Donald M. Nicol, *The Last Centuries of Byzantium: 1261–1453* (Cambridge: Cambridge University Press, 1993), 323.

106 Nicholas Oikonomides, "Le haradj," 682. This is seen in this *Prostagma* as well as in later appeals to Manuel II for the restitution of previously held properties.

107 The following observations concerning taxes are largely observations of Oikonomides, Oikonomides, "Le haradj," 682.

108 Oikonomides, "Le haradj," 684. He cites Schwarz's etymological study proposing that the "*choreigeion*" is closely related to "*haratzion*." Acknowledging its validity as a scholarly exercise, he admits that there is no positive proof that might connect these words. Claude Cahen, however, in the *Encyclopedia of Islam* article on the *haraç* argues in favor of this connection. See Claude Cahen, "Kharadj," *Encyclopedia of Islam*, 2nd ed., IV (1997), 1030–33.

Also see Nicholas Oikonomides, "Ottoman Influence on Late Byzantine Fiscal Practice," *Südost-Forschungen* 45 (1986).

monks who had appealed to him to lessen their tax burden by granting certain tax breaks, as well as sending a representative to Mount Athos to settle any difficulties that might arise from Athos and the Turks, or even Athos and John VII. He gave them the option to settle things themselves, and, if that did not work, "my imperial person intends to force this correction [of peace and justice] by ourselves."[109] It appears that Demetrios Bouliotes was sent to address whatever difficult affair might arise which the parties might not have been able to settle. Since these affairs could not be settled without intervention, Manuel II needed both to confirm the earlier rulings, and to establish order as he desired.[110]

In 1408, John VII died after being governor of Thessalonike for only five years. Manuel II, who had been in the Morea, went to Thessalonike to establish direct control over the city. The Athonite monks met with him and requested him to lighten their tax burden. Manuel II responded by issuing another *Prostagma* in December 1408, which recalled the history of the monastic properties and allowed them to regain the properties that had been appropriated after 1403/4. In addition, they made an agreement to rescind the taxes on wine, pasturage rights, and other secondary taxes. In this *prostagma*, Manuel describes granting the two-thirds of the "*choregeion*" to the monks for the property that the emir (Süleyman) had given to him. For those monasteries that in certain cases were paying up to one-half of the "*choregeion*," they would again pay one-third as in the beginning.[111] Byzantine economic historian Nikos Oikonomides concluded that this decree could only be referring to the *haraç* and the terms established in 1404.

Other decrees and imperial acts contain instances of the term *haraç*. One interesting example that also appears in the *Actes de Lavra* is the *praktikon* of Paul Gazes and George Prinkips. It was compiled in April 1409 and shows how the system actually worked. Gazes and Prinkips, residents of Thessalonike before 1402, and thus would certainly have been familiar with the Ottoman system of taxation, were called to compile, in essence, a tax register and to oversee and record negotiations. This document in particular marks the transaction of Lavra, which, in order to maintain a better position vis-à-vis taxation, gave two dependency Church properties (*metochia* of Siderokapsia and Karvea) to the state in order to keep three others (Drimosyrta, Pinsson, and Loroton) free of financial obligation. This was actually done in order to avoid the protests of the local peasant residents (*paroikoi*) who were responsible for the taxes, and this would alleviate their burden. The *paroikoi* in this document are listed according to household and according to the taxes that each was to pay.[112] There is direct reference to the *haraç*

[109] Arkadios ho Vatopedinos, "Basilike diatage pros Demetrion ton Boulioten," 452.

[110] Papachryssanthou, ed., *Actes Du Protaton*, no. 13, 257 The text also includes in lines 81–83 direct reference to the earlier Prostagma, and the "merikoteron kefalaion" is a reference to the impost mentioned in that Prostagma.

[111] Oikonomides, "Le haradj," 684. See P. Lemerle, A. Guillou, D. Papachryssanthou, and N. Svoronos, eds, *Actes De Lavra, III De 1329 A 1500*, X (Paris: P. Lethielleux, 1979), no. 161.

[112] Oikonomides, "Le haradj," 685–686.

"*to triton haratzion ton famelion*" (a third of the *haraç* from among the families).[113] There is also a similar reference to "*to triteuma tōn choreiōn.*"

A year after Manuel II died there was another important document that tried to bring control of Mount Athos under the central government and under the Patriarchate. It is an act of the monastery of Kastamonitou, No. 6 written by Patriarch Joseph II in 1426. Three years earlier, Manuel II's son Andronikos, despot of Thessalonike, withdrew from the starving city and handed it over the city to the Venetians. The Ottomans, however, had taken control of the surrounding regions, including Mount Athos, and had laid siege to Thessalonike. With the Act of 1426, Patriarch Joseph II made it quite clear under whose jurisdiction Mount Athos should be. He stated that any conflicts needing arbitration should be brought to himself or the emperor in Constantinople, and taken to the Turkish tribunal.[114]

In 1423 and 1424, the Ottomans again reoccupied Mt. Athos, and continued recognizing the status of the properties belonging to the monasteries. The monks continued to petition the sultan to preserve the monastic properties, in particular the *metochia* of Thrace and Macedonia that proved to be major sources of sustenance. When the Ottomans advanced towards an area where *metochia* existed, the monks would approach the sultan and request that the monastic property be recognized as it was in the past, even if their rights were obtained during the political rule of the enemy state.[115] Until the late fifteenth century, individual documents were issued both by the sultans and by local Ottoman *sancak-beys* who functioned independently from the sultan, confirming tax exemptions and the integrity of properties from alienation, thus preventing their properties from becoming part of *timars*, or from having *Yürüks* settle on their lands.[116]

113 P. Lemerle, A. Guillou, D. Papachryssanthou, and N. Svoronos, eds., *Actes De Lavra*, 156. It is extremely interesting to note that two conflicts in which the monastery of Pantocrator was involved. The first occurred in 1491/2 (Papachryssanthou, ed., *Actes du Pantocrator*, No. 28) and reported that there was a quarrel between the monks of Pantocrator and the Russian monks at Panteleimon over rights to the property at Loggos. Not being able to resolve it on their own, they sought assistance from the civil authorities. The act says that Mehmet Tzelepis (Çelebi), the envoy of Bayezid II made the judgment in favor of the Pantocrator monastery. Almost ten years later however, Pantocrator is in another land dispute over a sheep run (*mandra*) with the monks of Dionysiou, this time on the island of Lemnos. The record of this dispute comes to us from a letter from the Metropolitan of Lemnos who writes to the Council at Karyes informing them of the decision in favor of Dionysiou. Here, rather than suffer the "scandal" of going before a foreign court, the established custom of going to the council of the island for arbitration was maintained. Their decision was in favor of Dionysiou. Perhaps Pantocrator should have insisted on the foreign court, given that they were successful before Mehmet Çelebi not ten years earlier concerning Loggos.

114 Nicholas Oikonomides, ed., *Actes De Kastamonitou*,, IX (Paris, P. Lethielleux, 1978), no. 6. Also see H. Lowry, "The Island of Limnos: A Case Study on the Continuity of Byzantine Forms Under Ottoman Rule," in *Studies in Defterology: Ottoman Society in the Fifteenth Cenuturies* (Istanbul: The Isis Press, 1992), 165–180.

115 Vassilis Demetriades, "Athonite Documents and the Ottoman Occupation," in *Mount Athos in the 14–16th Centuries*, 50–51.

116 For a later example of the independence of sancak beys, especially in relation to the Ragusans in sixteenth century Herzegovina, see Salakides, *Sultansurkunden Des Athos-Klosters Vatopedi*, 89–92.

The Ottomans continued their recognition of monastic rights and privileges. The documentary record, therefore, concerning monastic taxation of dependent houses survived in the form of *tahrir defters* from the late fifteenth and sixteenth centuries. However, the monks were not as successful in maintaining their properties intact as they had been during the more turbulent early period. Previously, the resident monks received a special tax-status, which allowed them to be taxed not on a per-capita basis but in a lump sum. They were therefore assessed a "yearly sum without regard to the number of its inhabitants." In addition, they had long held Ottoman imperial exemptions, which meant they were not subject as individuals to the *cizye* tax. The agricultural production of produce from the peninsula was not subject to the tithe (*öşr*). However, the *metochia* properties outside of the confines of the peninsula most likely were subject to the more traditional *haraç* tithe. This is true among the monasteries of Mt. Athos as well as for the monasteries of Trabzon.[117]

The increasing Ottoman pressure in the late fourteenth and fifteenth centuries to tax the *metochia* properties, however, shows that the Ottomans were also interested in the value of the land itself. Examples from Athonite holdings on the island of Limnos demonstrate that over the period of many years in the sixteenth century the tax base was steadily decreasing. The implication of these observations is that the *metochia* were no longer part of the taxable land base. The possibility is great that they were alienated by the state. The Ottomans would want to exploit the productive agricultural land outside the general vicinity of the main houses of the monasteries. The *metochia* closest to the main house of the monastery were preserved, while the fate of *metochia* outside of the general areas were subject to alienation to the Ottoman state.[118]

The monastic community fared well during most periods of Ottoman rule. In 1568, however, the Ottoman state attempted directly to confiscate Athonite properties.[119] The question surrounding this "confiscation crisis" is whether this event was the result of an urgent need for immediate cash, or part of the broader changes in society that sought to establish Islamic legal codes (Sharia) in place of the previously established sultanic laws (*kanun*.) In either case, the monasteries faced a major dilemma. Sultan Selim II had commanded that all monastic

[117] Heath Lowry, "The Fate of Monastic Properties Under the Ottomans: Examples from Mount Athos, Limnos and Trabzon," 249.

[118] For more on Athonite monasteries and Ottoman rule see H. W. Lowry, "A Note on the Population and Status of the Athonite Monasteries Under Ottoman Rule (c.1520)," *Wiener Zeitschrift Fur Die Kunde Des Morgenlandes* 73 (1981): 229–246. N. Beldiceanu, "A Propos De Deux Registres Ottomans De Recensement Des Monastères Du Mont Athos," *Byzantion* 52 (1982): 496–499. J. C. Alexander, "The Lord Giveth and the Lord Taketh Away: Athos and the Confiscation Affair of 1568–1569," in *Athos in the 14th–16th Centuries*, 149–200.

[119] For literature see A. Fotic, "The Official Explanation for the Confiscation and Sale of Monasteries (Churches) and Their Estates at the Time of Selim II," *Turcica* 26 (1994): 33–54. Alexander, "The Lord Giveth and the Lord Taketh Away," 151–159, n. 4–21. Elias Kolovos, "Christian Influence and the Advent of the Europeans: Negotiating for State Protection: Çiftlik-holding by the Athonite Monasteries (Xeropotamou Monastery, Fifteenth-Sixteenth C.," in *Frontiers of Ottoman Studies*, ed. Colin Imber, Keiko Kiyotaki, and Rhoads Murphey (London: I.B.Tauris, 2005), 197–210.

properties that did not pay tithes and that had supposedly purchased their properties illegally with falsely acquired documents were to revert to the Ottoman imperial treasury. A *fetva* by the *sheyh-ül-islam* Ebu's-su'ud Efendi justified the ruling according to Sharia. The monasteries would be alienated, and then the monks would have the right of first refusal to repurchase the properities, though under a different code. The monks in their fervent attempt to secure their holdings exploited the newly emphasized Sharia to establish their monasteris as *vakıf*, thus averting a major financial catastrophe.[120] Thus, a greater degree of Islamization benefitted the monks.

Examining the issue of ecclesiastical administration requires that one consider both its religious and fiscal aspects. The Ottoman approach to the local hierarchs and the church developed in an ad hoc manner according to specific needs of the state. The ambiguity of the state with regard to the bishops and the monasteries led to bishops at one point becoming *timariots*, and monasteries eventually becoming *vakıf*. Under the Turkmen emirates, religious cultural questions and Church administration were of minimal concern. The signal that the Turkmen emirs received from bishops was that those who hoped to stay on in territory of the emirates, had to pay in cash. This process of paying to stay on as bishop eventually led to the prominence of the fiscal concerns when the Ottomans finally take over. This holds true for the monastic institutions as well as for the secular clergy and local bishops.

CONCLUSION

This chapter has described the process by which the Church was absorbed into the Ottoman fiscal administration. The Church underwent its own process of decentralization with local hierarchs proving to acting independently of the Synod in Constantinople by establishing relations with the new regimes. At the heart of the negotiations were financial considerations and promises of payment to the emir of revenues from ecclesiastical properties. The same aspect is true of monastic institutions, which sought to preserve their properties by negotiating agreements with the Ottomans.

The principle of *istimâlet* governed relations between the Ottoman state and the Church from the early fourteenth century well into the sixteenth century. Since fiscal concerns were at the heart of the relationship between the Ottoman state and the Church, the state continued its policy of accommodating the wealthy ecclesiastical institution to exact revenues. Examples of this include monks and metropolitans who were considered feudal lords (*timariots*) and later were transformed into ecclesiastical tax farmers (*mültezim*). While some historians propose that the relationship between state and Church was established when Sultan Mehmet II elevated Gennadios Scholarios to the office of Patriarch of Constantinople, it is

[120] Alexander, "The Lord Giveth and the Lord Taketh Away," 174–179.

Fig. 2.1. Ottoman Sultan Selim II (r.1566–1574) in procession. (Source: Lambert de Vos, *Kostümbuch* (Codex Ms. Or. 9, Bremen: Staats- und Universitätsbibliothek Bremen, fol. 36))

more fitting to see continuity in their relations. However, a careful examination of Ottoman documents and Greek chronicles reveals that the only difference between the pre-1453 period and the following periods had to do with the standardization of the fiscal practices into an actual ecclesiastical tax farming system. This precludes the idea that a *millet* system determined the relations between the Ottomans and the Church. The Patriarch and metropolitans were considered by the Ottoman state primarily for their cash, and thought of them more as tax farmers rather than leaders of the community. The establishment of the ecclesiastical *iltizam* administration will be examined in the following chapter.

PART II

THE PATRIARCHAL TAX FARM

3

The All-Holy Tax Farmer

The *İstanbul Rum Patriği* as *Mültezim*

IN SEARCH OF A DOCUMENT

In the year 1521, Patriarch Theoleptos frantically searched his archives for a special document that was supposed to prove to Sultan Süleyman that the Greek Orthodox community and Patriarchate did indeed have special privileges and rights to their Church properties. The document was purported to be an imperial sultanic edict (*berât*) issued by Sultan Mehmet II soon after the conquest of Constantinople that gave the right of possession of property and authority over the Church to Patriarch Gennadios. Theoleptos' search was in response to Süleyman's attempt to reconcile Sharia law and sultanic law (*kanun*). This reconsideration meant that the Ottoman state ought to demand that the Christian churches be turned over to the state because Constantinople had been conquered and had not capitulated. According to Islamic law, the conquered city ought to have been completely overcome by the conquerors, including its churches. The question asked in the sultan's court was why Christians still maintained control of Church properties when the Muslim ruler Sultan Mehmet II clearly had conquered Constantinople?

To his dismay, Patriarch Theoleptos was not able to locate the document. The community went into a panic but responded through the assistance and intervention of the benevolent pasha, described as Tulphi Pasha. The patriarch, through the assistance of the Greek community, was able to produce three aged janissaries who testified that they had witnessed Sultan Mehmet II grant privileges and protection to the Greeks and to the Church.

> The sultan asked them, How did the sultan take this city? by war, or by capitulation? And they answered that it was by capitulation. And listen, my sultan, how it happened so that you can learn the details of the situation. After we came with the army here with the sultan, we set up camp outside and remained there.

The janissaries then proceed to describe how the sultan had offered peace, but was rejected by the Constantine Palaiologos, until many all around him had died.

He then prostrated himself to Sultan Mehmet, who accepted his request with the following words,

> I, the emperor, Sultan Mehmet, through this written command wish, whole heartedly, to give to the king of the City, Constantine Paleologos and to his *archons*, whatever they wish according to a just manner, in order they might have the comforts and slaves (male and female) in order to live life well as *archons*. For the rest of the people I wish them to be free from all compulsion or oppression. And that neither I nor my descendants never to take their children as janissaries.

The janissaries then related to the Pasha that the Byzantine Emperor with the *archons* offered Sultan Mehmet the keys to the city. In turn, the sultan who commanded him to sit at his right hand embraced him. The pasha, on hearing this story from the janissaries,

> Went to the sultan and described all these things, and he told about the aged and old witnesses. And having heard these things, the sultan marveled greatly, and immediately commanded, and gave the decree for the patriarch not to have any more any detractors or interference concerning this situation of the churches for as long as the world exists.[1]

Whether this tale told by the ancient janissaries confirmed the privileges of the Patriarch and secured the rights of the Church, or whether there was an actual Ottoman edict of investiture granted to Patriarch Gennadios remains unknown. Considering Ottoman practice, Patriarch Gennadios should have received an investiture document from the sultan that would, at the very least, have resembled the other documents dealing with the particulars of patriarchal taxation and payments owed to the imperial treasury. The fact that no such document survived leaves open the question of what exactly took place not only between Sultan Mehmet II and Patriarch Gennadios in 1453, but also between Sultan Süleyman and Patriarch Theoleptos in 1520, as well as in 1578 when the *Historia Patriarchica* was composed. The problem of the lack of historical sources for the post-conquest period is compounded by the composition of chronicles and tales about the relationship between Patriarch Gennadios and Sultan Mehmet II. These accounts written in Greek for a Greek audience may reflect the sixteenth century justification for why the Christian community was so closely associated with the Ottoman administration.

The context of Patriarch Theoleptos' challenge offers us some additional insight into how the Ottomans dealt with the Church over time. What was going on in the Ottoman Empire at the time that would have forced the Ottoman sultan to issue such a decree? Was there a change taking place in Ottoman society that incited the state to revisit the status and privileges accorded to the Greek

[1] *Historia Patriarchica*, ed. Bekker, 157–69. For additional legends see Dean Sakel, "Three Tales for a Sultan? Three Tales on Mehmet the Conqueror and Patriarch Gennadius," *British Journal of Middle Eastern Studies* 35/2 (2008): 227–238. Sakel rightly concludes the lack of sources about Patriarch Gennadios and Sultan Mehmet II leaves open the door to the sixteenth-century authors to offer their own historical distortion in order to promote their interests. Sakel, "Three Tales," 229.

Orthodox Church? According to the *Historia Patriarchica,* this event took place in 1537, in the middle of Sultan Süleyman's reign. However, historian Christos Patrinelis convincingly dated it to February or March of 1521, the second year of Süleyman's reign.[2] The chronicle states that a judicial decree issued by the leading Islamic authority (*sheyh-ül-islam),* along with a sultanic edict, called for all the Christian churches to be torn down or made into mosques.[3] The timing of this incident is significant as it took place only a few years after Süleyman's father, Sultan Selim I, conquered the Mamlukes of Egypt in 1517, and brought the Islamic holy cities of Mecca and Medina under Ottoman control. With his father's accomplishment staring at him upon his enthronement, Sultan Süleyman was forced to confront this legacy, and consider directly the ideological (i.e. religious) underpinning of the Ottoman Empire. Some historians may argue that it was at the beginning of Süleyman's reign that Ottoman administrative culture began to transform to reflect more of an Islamic and Arab culture.[4] In this period, the Ottoman state was more intent than ever to establish its Islamic orthodox *bona fides* because of their pronounced efforts to consolidate political control over eastern Anatolia and the Arab lands. Under Yavuz Sultan Selim I, who expanded Ottoman control against the Mamluke dynasty over the majority of the Middle East, opposition arose from Sufi-oriented *kizilbaş,* the numerous eastern Anatolian tribesmen the Ottomans encountered on their journey to the southeast. The *kizilbaş* were not only considered at worst adherents to extremist Shia sects, or at best heretical sufis, but they were also charged with being traitors because of their sympathy for Shah Ismail, the Safavid ruler.[5] The Ottoman struggle was political, and ideological, and moves against the *kizilbaş* forced the state to assert its Sunni "orthodoxy." Back in the Ottoman capital of Istanbul, the complicated series of political and ideological factors taking place in Anatolia and the Arab lands signaled the move towards a more traditional Islamic approach to Ottoman state administration, especially when dealing with non-Muslims and their Church. This historical context heightened the great challenges Patriarch Theoleptos faced. He had no choice but to cope as best as he could with the effect of these empire wide transformations.

The events of 1521 posed an actual threat to the Church, since this new antagonism of the state appeared to be out of line with established Ottoman practice. The relationship between Church and state established in the early Ottoman period was one of cooperation, or *istimâlet.* Aside from the churches that were taken over during the period of conquest, the only real transformation that took place during the early Ottoman period regarding the Church was the fiscalization

[2] Christos Patrinelis, "The Exact Time of the First Attempt of the Turks to Seize the Churches and Convert the Christian People of Constantinople to Islam," *Actes du 1er Congrès International des Etudes Balkaniques et Sud-Est Europe'ens* III (1969): 567–574.

[3] Immanuel Bekker, ed., *Historia politica et patriarchica Constantinopoleos: Epirotica*, Corpus Scriptorum Historiae Byzantinae (Bonn: Impensis Ed. Weberi, 1849), 158–169.

[4] Heath W. Lowry, "Early Ottoman Period," in *The Routledge Handbook of Modern Turkey,* ed. Metin Heper and Sabri Sayari (New York: Routledge, 2012), 12.

[5] R. M. Savory, "Kīzīl-Bāsh," *Encyclopedia of Islam*, 2nd ed., V (1990), 243.

of the ecclesiastical administration. The hierarchs were understood as tax farmers for a rich and widespread tax farm, in line with early Ottoman practices and concerns.

Ottoman documents describing the mechanics of the ecclesiastical tax structure are scattered among various monastic archives where prelates deposited their personal papers upon retirement from active ecclesiastical duty.[6] Many sultanic decrees issued upon an individual's episcopal investiture survive intact. Some documents outline the fiscal responsibilities of individual bishops, while others detail conflicts and problems that had arisen in the administration of ecclesiastical holdings. Among decrees recorded in the Ottoman archives are decisions of the Imperial Council (*Divan-i Hümayûn*) ruling on ecclesiastical administrative matters in the name of the sultan. Prelates went personally before the Divan to complain about anything that might have impeded their ecclesiastical administration, which meant mostly tax collecting. In the main, these documents attempt to establish and clarify jurisdictional rights by resolving conflicts between high-ranking and low-ranking clergy, as well as conflicts with the common tax paying subjects.

The Greek Patriarchal chronicles can corroborate some of the Ottoman archival documents because the Patriarchal chronicles diligently listed amounts paid to the Porte for investiture fees (*pişkeş*) as well as for taxes.[7] However, the terminology of the chronicles also caused some confusion about what types of taxes were collected. Examining the sources and putting them into historical context enable us to understand more fully the concept of the Patriarchal tax farm, or "Patriarchal *iltizam*."

POST-CONQUEST PERIOD

Early on, when the Ottomans conquered territory, their primary concern was to divide the spoils according to a system of meritocracy. However, extending this practice to the Church was problematic. Creating ecclesiastical fiefs (*timars*), a possible option, did not seem to solve the problem for the Ottomans. Instead of turning the ecclesiastical properties into a fief, the Ottoman state transformed them into a taxable concession.

[6] Elisabeth A. Zachariadou, *Deka Tourkika engrapha gia ten Megale Ekklesia:1483–1567* (Athens: Ethniko Hidryma Ereunon, Institouto Byzantinon Ereunon, 1996). Georgios Salakides, *Sultansurkunden des Athos-Klosters Vatopedi aus der Zeit Bayezid II. und Selim I* (Thessalonike: Institute for Balkan Studies, 1995). In general, monastic archives have very valuable information from the Ottoman period because the monks preserved whatever documents outlined their rights and properties. In addition to keeping documents detailing their holdings, they act as depositories for Patriarchs, who would bring their personal and ecclesiastic papers to the monastery as their collection of personal papers.

[7] For the literature see Marios Philippides, "Patriarchal Chronicles of the Sixteenth Century," *Greek, Roman and Byzantine Studies* 25 (1984): 87–94.

This trend is visible in one of the earliest documents that survive directed to a church hierarch. This earliest extant Ottoman document addressed to a high-ranking bishop is an edict (*berât*) issued probably prior to 1453 to a metropolitan who is not named. The document was, therefore, directed not to an individual, but to the office of the metropolitan. It likely was as the template for the appointment of any metropolitans and bishops since no specific name of a reigning Patriarch, metropolis or bishopric was given either. While there is some question of its dating, this *berât* is clearly one of the earliest Ottoman documents to a high-level hierarch dealing directly with ecclesiastical affairs. It is assumed to be similar to that which would have been issued to the Patriarch Gennadios.[8]

An examination of the terms reveals that it was given to a monk who paid the *pişkeş*, or fee of investiture, to the imperial treasury whereupon he was granted the metropolitan see. This investiture fee, distinctive to Ottoman administrative practice, will be discussed in the following chapter. Secondly, the document asserts that the metropolitan had administrative control over his clerics and other Orthodox Christians in his district, and that he was to take possession of churches, vineyards, orchards, and plots of land that had been in the control of his predecessor metropolitan. The nature of this jurisdiction over Orthodox Christians was not made clear. However, considering the issue of administrative jurisdiction in the context of the material and real possessions of the Church, the Orthodox Christians referred to in the document were likely individuals who lived on and worked the specific ecclesiastical properties in the unspecified region, not the wider Greek Orthodox community. Thirdly, the document granted the metropolitan exemption from the non-Muslim capitation tax (*cizye*) and extraordinary levies, a fairly standard exemption granted to Christian and Muslim clerics alike. Finally, the clergy and Orthodox Christians of the region were to bring to the metropolitan whatever litigation fell under his jurisdiction. This implies the ecclesiastical affairs of the clergy were under his direct jurisdiction. This included matters related to family law for which Christians could request adjudication within an ecclesiastical judicial system. The judicial and administrative boundaries of the metropolitan's jurisdiction, however, were not specified in this document.[9]

Halil Inalcik has argued that there is evidence of broad rights and jurisdiction to govern the Greek Orthodox community granted to the Church hierarchy.[10] However, this raises the question as to whether the ecclesiastical hierarchy

[8] Zachariadou, *Deka Tourkika engrapha*, 150.

[9] See Pantazopoulos for his discussion of Church and law in the Balkans, and a more in-depth discussion of the legal issues that an ecclesiastical court would have judged. Analysis of the Patriarchal Codices of the sixteenth and seventeenth centuries shows the matters coming before the Patriarchal Synod were almost exclusively ecclesiastical or family related. N. Pantazopoulos, *Church and Law in the Balkan Peninsula during the Ottoman Rule* (Thessaloniki: Institute for Balkan Studies, 1967). Evgenia Kermeli, "The Right to Choice: Ottoman Justice vis-à-vis Ecclesiastical and Communal Justice in the Balkans, Seventeenth-Nineteenth Centuries," in *Studies in Islamic Law: A festschrift for Colin Imber*, ed. Andreas Christmann and R Gleave (Oxford: Oxford University Press on behalf of the University of Manchester, 2007).

[10] Halil Inalcik, "The Status of the Greek Orthodox Patriarchate under the Ottomans," *Turcica* 21–3 (1991): 407–436.

actually had civil authority, and if so, what this authority entailed. In the document, the terms of the exemptions specific to the bishops, the listing of material resources that produce revenue, and the assessment of ecclesiastical taxes appear more prominently in the document than do the terms of judicial jurisdiction. The documents are specific in their assignment of property rights, "possession of churches, vineyards, orchards, and plots of land that had been in the possession of his predecessor." Each of these items was a specific income-producing source that called for taxation. The fact that the document delineates these, as well as exemption from *cizye* and extraordinary levies, it appears that the document had as its main concern a fiscal relationship of the metropolitan and the Ottoman state. No *berât* similar to this granted by Sultan Mehmet II to Patriarch Gennadios exists. However, by using this document as a guide, and by examining other similar cases, it is possible to determine the overall trend of the Ottoman state when dealing with Church appointments. These trends give substance to the testimony of the Patriarchal chronicles that seem to capture controversies surrounding episcopal appointments. There are a series of early episodes that on first glance, appear to be irreconcilable with ecclesiastical order and proper understanding of canon law. The descriptions from the Patriarchal chronicles take on a very bald-faced tone describing a series of early scandals. These episodes must be considered not as indicators of people of bad character behaving poorly, but rather with the focus on Ottoman involvement in the administrative practice of appointing Church officials.

One of the early clues we have about how Patriarchs were elected under Ottoman rule centers around the figure of Maria (Mara) Branković (d.1487) the widow of Sultan Murat II and stepmother of Sultan Mehmet II.[11] During the reign of the Patriarch Markos Xylokaraves (1466), there was a Greek Orthodox faction from Trebizond that had grown strong in Istanbul, and developed strong influence in imperial Ottoman circles. Through their influence with the sultan they pushed to have their own candidate, Symeon, elected and installed as Patriarch. Since more than a few of the sons of Trebizondine families were highly respected servants of the sultan, *devşirme* who rose in administrative ranks as viziers, they felt bold enough to approach the sultan concerning the selection of the patriarch. First, they defamed the sitting patriarch Markos Xylokaraves, saying he was involved in bad practices including paying the *pişkeş* to the Porte in the amount of 1,000 florins. Accusing him of simony, they remarked that none of the Patriarchs before had given the sultan a gift of any amount, and that Markos was the first to do so. In spite of the criticism that was primarily for their own community's consumption, the leadership of the Trebizondine families, the *archons,* with some other cooperating Constantinopolitan *archons* raised 2,000 florins to submit to the sultan to install their candidate Symeon as Patriarch. When Mara-Maria heard about this, she approached her stepson, Sultan Mehmet II, and offered him 2,000 florins on behalf of her own candidate and confessor, the monk, Dionysios of Filibe. In the end, her candidate was successful.

[11] *Historia Patriarchica*, ed. Bekker, 39–42.

Patriarch Dionysios, in fact, reigned two times. In his first reign he ruled for five years and continued to serve as a spiritual father to Mara-Maria. He was severely criticized by his Greek opponents who charged him with becoming like the Turks, saying that he had been circumcised when he had been taken captive in Edirne during the conquest of Constantinople. His only defense was to lift up his robe to demonstrate to the Holy Synod and to all the people who had gathered to judge him that he was not circumcised. After he cleared his name, he resigned from the office of Patriarch and retired to a monastery in Kosinitza near Kavala where he would be close to Mara-Maria's residence. Symeon became Patriarch and ultimately served three terms. Even the sultan's stepmother did not have enough sway over her stepson when it came to administrative appointments.

After Patriarch Symeon's second term (1471–75), Patriarch Raphael the Serb (1475–76) took office. His situation was defined by financial obligation to the Ottomans. Patriarch Raphael was extremely popular with some of the Ottoman pashas and was able to get elected with their support. He managed to pay the *pişkeş,* and receive his *berât* of appointment. The *Historia Politike* mentions that he offered a *pişkeş* of 500 florins, and that he was to give 2,000 florins yearly. His indemnity, however, was not reliable. He had not collected and submitted to the Porte the required amounts, nor could he find a wealthy benefactor to assist him. When the year ended, and he was supposed to hand over the 2,000 florins, the *pashas* called him to the divan to pay the promised yearly amount. He himself could not pay nor did he have financial assistance to pay what he owed from the priests, the *archons,* and the people. When the pashas realized this, they "laughed, and placed him in jail."[12] In each case, the terms of the financial relationship were specified in the Ottoman document of appointment.

Confirming the financial relationship between the Church and the Ottoman state are a series of documents from the Patriarchal Synod following the conquest of Constantinople, documents that survived in a manuscript in the archive the monastery of the Holy Cross on the island of Samos. The documents themselves addressed both the internal dynamics of the Church in the aftermath of the conquest, as well as the obligations that were owed to the state. They are useful because they offer the perspective of the Patriarchate.[13] The first three documents, issued between October 1474 and the beginning of 1475, deal directly with the Patriarchate of Symeon of Trebizond. In the first, Patriarch Symeon's innocence was confirmed by the Synod, and the financial obligations to the Porte were described. Apparently, going back to the time of Patriarch Gennadios, there were individuals who charged the individual in the Patriarchal see had participated in corruption, and even in office buying, or simony. In the case of Symeon, he was recognized by the Synod as innocent of those charges, but the document refers directly to the financial obligation.

[12] *Historia Politike,* ed. Bekker, 43; *Historia Patriarchica*, ed. Bekker, 114.

[13] D. G. Apostolopoulos, *Ho "Hieros Kōdix" Tou Patriarcheiou Kōnstantinoupoleōs: Sto 2΄miso Tou 15΄aiōna: Ta Mona Gnōsta Sparagmata,* Thesmoi Kai Ideologia Stē Neoellēnikē Koinōnia (Athēna: Ethniko Hidryma Ereunōn, 1992).

Apostolopoulos concluded that it was the work of "some Greeks," opponents of Patriarch Symeon, who because of their own designs on the Patriarchate imposed the idea of a yearly payment by the Patriarchate to the Porte.[14] The sultan readily adopted this idea of a yearly payment. The amount was meant to be a personal obligation. Apostolopoulos mentioned that the Church at this time, and according to Muslim custom, was not understood by the Porte to be a legitimate legal body. Therefore, Patriarch Symeon as an individual was responsible for the payment. Furthermore, the Porte did not respond favorably to Patriarch Symeon's opposition, who hoped to disrupt his rule, and were the ones responsible for having him removed from office in the first place. The sultan ensured that Patriarch Symeon was restored to his position. This was partly because the Porte deemed the sycophant opponents incapable of garnering support from the rest of the hierarchs and the people in order to collect the yearly payment. In the document, it describes the required payment of "2,000 gold coins."[15] Furthermore, it uses the term, "aforesaid *haraç*" (*eiremenon haratzion*) to describe the obligation. By calling it "aforesaid" it implies that this was a tax that Patriarch Symeon faced as a "horrible command" of the state. This command insisted he take the position of Patriarch or there would be dire consequences both to him and to the community and churches.[16]

The weight of this responsibility becomes clear in the next document, an encyclal by Patriarch Symeon I to his flock in Constantinople, explaining his need to travel outside into the provinces to collect funds. In this encyclical, Patriarch Symeon explained he was not happy with the heavy obligation set by the Porte upon to the Church to collect funds, especially in winter (prior to Christmas, 1474). Patriarch Symeon was not used to asking for help, and he did not like being absent from the city. He offered the care of the church to the Metropolitans of Ephesus and Tirnovo while he was gone. In order to maintain harmony of the Church it was necessary that he make this journey.[17]

The role of kings, as well as that of the sultan and his servants, in commanding the Patriarch was criticized in Apostolopoulos' next document. As part of a Patriarchal Synodal decree to depose three individuals from their ecclesiastical posts, the former bishop of Herakleia, and two officers of the Patriarchate, the Grand Sacristan (*Mega Skevofylaks*), George Galesiote, and the Grand Ecclesiarch, Manouel Christonymo. These three had received their positions in the days of Patriarch Gennadios, but became enemies of Patriarch Gennadios. Among the charges against them were that they opposed Patriarch Symeon, but, more importantly, they depended on lay authority to interfere with the Church. The deposition opened with numerous examples of how kings ought not to interfere with the proper functioning of the Church. Furthermore, they were largely responsible for instituting the *haraç* of the 2,000 florins that was due to the Porte from the

[14] Apostolopoulos, *Ho "Hieros Kōdix,"* 79.
[15] Apostolopoulos, *Ho "Hieros Kōdix,"* 90.
[16] Apostolopoulos, *Ho "Hieros Kōdix,"* 94–95.
[17] Apostolopoulos, *Ho "Hieros Kōdix,"* 102.

Church. The synod agreed that they were guilty of many other sins and therefore, would be removed from their positions.[18]

The final documents worth noting were in response to the fiscal problems of the hierarchy. In May 1484, a Synodal decision was made to confirm the repudiation of simony. Simony was considered the great scandal that polluted the bishops, and priests. This problem was present in the reign of Maximos III (March 1476–April 1482) and again during Patriarch Symeon's third reign (1482–1486). The Synod acted in concert to condemn the action. The condemnation of simony was again condemned thirteen years later in a much more extensive Synodal pronouncement, which repeated the condemnation of 1484, but added much more force. Produced in June 1497, this document referenced condemnation of simony by the canons of the Apostolic Council, the Fourth Ecumenical Synod, the Sixth Ecumenical Synod, and the writings of the fathers, Basil the Great, John Chrysostom, Tarasios, and Gennadios I. It pronounced against the great sin of simony, initiated by Simon Magus among the apostles. It also stated categorically that the Holy Spirit was a gift that was granted to the clergy, and that it was a sin to receive through money the office of bishop, auxiliary bishop, priest, deacon, sub-deacon, or any other office of the Church, including custodians, readers, chanters, or any other office dedicated to the Church.

Among the issues that were raised was what to do with the *emvatoikion*, which was a traditional sum paid to the bishop upon ordination and appointment. Other associated collections were also deemed unfair, such as any collections that were directed for liturgical acts. Still, the decision was to allow the bishop to collect from the priests of his jurisdiction the customary fee (*kanonikon*) that had been established. If there is no priest to collect this fee, then the bishop may do so, and keep half of it for the first year when a priest is appointed. When a bishop dies, the entire income would go to the metropolitan of that region until a new bishop would be appointed. Additionally, the incomes coming from the fairs would be distributed according to the following manner: for a country church, the income would go to the bishop who appointed the priest to that church. In more populated areas, half the income would go to the priest and half to the bishop.[19]

The Patriarchal Synod condemned the problem of simony on multiple occasions. In fact, within the first fifty years after the conquest of Constantinople the Patriarchal Synod recognized this as a major problem, and this concern echoed loudly in the *Patriarchal Chronicles* of the mid-sixteenth century. By 1531, the situation was seen differently. In fact, in the same manuscript with the previous condemnation, a document recording another Synodal decision canceled the 1497 synodal decree. The very brief note of a single line voided the condemnation of simony. This synodal decision, of course, raises some serious and interesting questions, one of which is, why would a patriarchal synod cancel a condemnation of simony.[20] It is clearly a sin, and one that commanded great attention in the past.

18 Apostolopoulos, *Ho "Hieros Kōdix,"* 112–116.
19 Apostolopoulos, *Ho "Hieros Kōdix,"* 152–162.
20 Apostolopoulos, *Ho "Hieros Kōdix,"* 167–168.

One possible response is that the condemnation of simony hit too close to home and too often. The hierarchy, because of their responsibility to the Porte, was forced to pay the *pişkeş* in order to take their position, and yearly dues thereafter. In a sense, this responsibility to the sultan, which became institutional, forced all bishops to commit simony by virtue of being ordained in the Ottoman Empire. One had to pay the investiture fee in order to take the position. It is for this that Patriarch Raphael was first criticized. It is for this reason that subsequent patriarchs were also condemned. Simony had become the way in which one became a bishop. There was no need, therefore, to be reminded of the moral concern with the system.

The case of Patriarch Raphael was just one of a series of cases that ended poorly because of failing to meet the financial obligations to the Ottoman state. The bishops who faced the scandals and charges of simony faced internal censure and loss of their position as well. There was some indication from the Patriarchal Synodal documents of financial obligations. However, to consider more carefully these obligations to the state, it is helpful to examine what the Ottoman state expected of the bishop. This is seen best from an example of an appointment document of this same period. The earliest contemporary appointment order is an Ottoman document addressed to Patriarch Symeon sometime between April 9 and 18, 1483, during his third term in office. It is a *berât* granted by Bayezid II that was found in the monastic archive of Vatopedi on Mt. Athos. This and nine other early documents were from such monastic archives were published by Elizabeth Zachariadou in 1996.[21]

What follows is a summary of the copy of the *berât* was issued upon the appointment of Symeon as Patriarch for the third time. It recognizes that Symeon was responsible for the yearly payment to the imperial treasury each year that was to be paid upon the feast of the Christians, which the Ottomans considered to be Easter but also was tied to St. George's day. It then listed the multiple places, including the important city names where bishops resided, that were in his power. These places stretched from Anatolia, to Rumeli, as well as to regions beyond the boundaries of the Ottoman Empire that included Russia and Crete. The include [Marmara] Eregli, Tekir-daği, Silivri, Enez, Edirne, Midye, Süzebolu, Ahiyolu, Mesivri, Varna, Filibe, Sofya, Tirnovi, Siroz, Zihne, Dırama, Selânik, Kara-Ferye, Tırhala, Atina, Poros, Koritos, Balya Badra, Arkadya, Misitra, Yanya, Vize, Avlonya, Silisre, Vidin, Trabzon, Istavros, Halkidon, Iznikmid, Iznik, Aydıncik, Bursa, Ankara, Amasya, Sivas, Alaça-hisar, Konya, Atalya, Egridir, Tonguzlu, Balat, Ayasoluk, Izmir, Kengri, Midilli, Molinos, Imros, Limnos, Eğribos, Sakız, Krati, Arodos, Eflâk, Bogdan, Aleksi, Kefe, Kirasuna, and Rizova. The Patriarch was to maintain his position until his death, unless he contravened his own religious practices, upon which his colleague metropolitans could remove and punish him, and replace him with another. Those who become metropolitans and bishops must beforehand offer the traditional gift (*pişkeş*), and no one was to hinder

[21] Zachariadou, *Deka Tourkika engrapha,* 157, plate 1a.

their offering. The *berât* then explains that whatever in the past was authorized to the Patriarchs, was to be confirmed. Beyond those rights, no one was to intervene or mix up the situation concerning the debt of the Church, among the Patriarchs, metropolitans and priests. No one was to hinder their activities. The *berât* continued to explain that authority of the Patriarch extends over the metropolitans, bishops, abbots, and priests, as well as the *vakıfs*, the vineyards, the gardens, the lands, the holy springs, the fairs, the mills, which are attached to the churches. Aside from those commanded, no Muslim of unbeliever regardless of where they are from ought to interfere with him. The above-mentioned names are in his authority in the manner directed. He may dispose (from office) or appoint as he wishes in the churches. If the patriarchs or metropolitans or priests, or monk should die, and if they have a will, it should be recognized. If a clergyman dies without a descendent, and the estate is worth more than 5,000 (akçe), they are directed to the sultan. If they are below 5,000, then the patriarch is to take them. The financial bureaucrat in charge of collation (*mekufci*) is not to interfere.

If a woman leaves her husband secretly, and if a non-believer wants to divorce his wife, or if a non-believer wants to get married, or in the rituals according to their tradition, no one except the patriarch may intercede. Without the patriarch, no non-believer may conduct a wedding according to their religious practices, nor may they divorce, nor should these be recognized in church.

No one besides the aforementioned patriarch ought to be involved in inheritance issues. The patriarch ought to be selected with whatever manner they had previously been selected. Each of the *kadis* ought to make decisions to collect the taxes that are connected to the patriarchate, in each region.

No one may make an unbeliever into a Muslim with force. No one is to get involved with the concerns that are in the patriarch's jurisdiction. The church and surrounding area of the Pammakaristos, along with some other churches ought to be allocated to him, along with the attached vineyards and homes and mills. These ought to be allocated by the patriarchs according to the tradition, and ought to be free of impost. The wheat and grape must (*moustos*) brought to the patriarchate ought not to be taxed.

The patriarch must not face difficulty when giving the 2,000 florins to the Imperial Treasury. Each should assist according to his situation. For this situation, no one ought to get involved or interfere. The above patriarch is the valid patriarch, and the rights are not to be given to another who offers more. These are to be acknowledged according to the laws, which he had prior to the imperial *berât*. He is again made the valid patriarch and he received the imperial *berât*. From this time forward he is ought to give a yearly payment of 2,000 florins to the imperial treasury, and no violation ought to be made to the above commands.

The 1483 *berât* explicitly describes the patriarch as a tax farmer (*mültezim*), and the patriarchate as a tax farming institution (*iltizam*). While the pre-1453 metropolitan *berât* laid out, in very general terms, the metropolitan's jurisdiction and possession of real properties, this document to Patriarch Symeon explicitly describes the latter's responsibilities to the state and describes Patriarch Symeon with specialized Ottoman terminology, "*mültezim*." The sultan granted him the

Fig. 3.1. Courtyard of the Patriarchate of Constantinople at the Monastery of the Pammakaristos. (Source: Martin Crusius, *Turco-Graeciae, Libri Octo* (Basileæ: Per Leonardum Ostenium. Sebastiani Henricpetri impensa, 1584), 190: Rare Books Division, Department of Rare Books and Special Collections, Princeton University Library)

right to travel in person to the sixty-four districts listed in the *berât* to collect taxes in order to submit 2,000 florins to the imperial treasury, and confirmed the patriarch's jurisdiction over all the metropolitans, bishops, priests, monasteries, and their attached properties. Extending beyond the borders of the empire to include Russia, Kafa, and Crete, the Ottoman Sultan recognized the Patriarchate's "extra-territorial" authority.[22] The sultan clearly understood that the jurisdiction of the Patriarchate of Constantinople extended beyond the boundaries of the Ottoman Empire. One might conjecture from this *berât* that the Ottoman state had expansionist goals eventually to encompass the regions under the Church's ecclesiastical jurisdiction within the political boundary of the Ottoman Empire. While not precisely servants of the state, the bishops responsible for collecting the Church taxes within the empire, and beyond the Ottoman realm represented the ambitions of the state. More practically, however, the *berât* recognized the extraterritorial status of the Patriarchate of Constantinople, and extended the financial obligation to include those regions. The local churches in these regions were required to pay the amounts they had collected due to the Patriarchal jurisdiction. The Patriarch, thus, submitted taxes to the imperial treasury for the entire Church.

[22] Zachariadou, *Deka Tourkika engrapha,* 157, plate 1a.

Including territories beyond the Ottoman realm in the Patriarchal *berât*, in fact, does demonstrate an Ottoman desire to expand Ottoman authority. This question of extraterritorial jurisdiction became an important issue five years after the conquest of Constantinople when, in November of 1458, Patriarch Athanasios, the Greek Orthodox Patriarch of Jerusalem and a subject of the Mamluke Sultan *Inal*, came to Istanbul to seek protection from Sultan Mehmet II and to confirm his property rights. It is likely the property rights he was seeking to protect were the ecclesiastical properties in Istanbul that historically belonged to the Jerusalem Patriarchate. However, by granting protection and confirming property rights over the churches that included those in Palestine, Sultan Mehmet II ultimately encroached on the Mamluke sultan's authority. Ralph Hattox argues that Mehmet II sought to make the Patriarch of Constantinople the leading bishop of the entire Orthodox Church, and not simply the Church within in his empire. He argues that, "Mehmet's sultantopapism was just another indication of a heightened sense of authority."[23]

While Mehmet II may have wished to extend the administrative boundaries of the Church beyond the borders of his kingdom, Patriarch Gennadios assumed religious authority over territory outside the Ottoman Empire when in 1455 or 1456, he responded to a series of questions posed by the ruler of Serbia, Kral George. In his letter, Gennadios explains that in the absence of knowledge by the local Metropolitan Theophylaktos, and of translated texts dealing with theological issues, he would address a series of questions set forth by the Kral, and offer answers as a spiritual leader to a communicant of the Orthodox Church. The questions and concerns dealt with religious matters, such as whether a priest can drink water in the evening before conducting a liturgy or if a Patriarch can conduct a service without a deacon. The fact that Patriarch Gennadios felt obliged to address the Serbian Kral on matters of spiritual edification did not necessarily indicate extraterritorial administrative authority. However, it shows that he fulfilled his religious duty as Patriarch of Constantinople and premier bishop of the Orthodox Church to communicate properly the true faith of the Church, especially to an Orthodox prince outside of Ottoman control. According to internal Church tradition, it is the duty of the Patriarch to ensure the Orthodox faith is transmitted properly to all members of the Church, even if this means intervening in another's metropolis. This obligation does not imply administrative authority, but remains within the realm of theology and religious instruction.

Returning to the matter of the *berât*, the information the *berât* offers indicates that the holdings of the Church were widespread. From the Ottoman point of view, it required a special bureaucratic effort to exploit its revenue. Thus, the sultan assigned the patriarch as imperial tax farmer (*mültezim*) over all ecclesiastical holdings and made him responsible for gathering taxes derived from the widely dispersed ecclesiastical revenues. The patriarch administered this responsibility by relying on the Church hierarchy that was in place. The relationships

[23] Ralph S. Hattox, "Mehmet the Conqueror, the Patriarch of Jerusalem, and Mamluk Authority," *Studia Islamica* 90 (2000): 117.

between the Patriarch and the local Church hierarchy were often distressed, and became points of conflict that further demonstrate the importance of the financial obligations.

Another such early example occurs in a *berât* of 23 February 1489 that concerns a metropolitan, not a patriarch. A copy of the *berât* was sent to the military governors and kadis of Rumeli explaining the appointment of the local metropolitan of Serres as imperial tax farmer in order to collect the taxes for the Patriarch Dionysios, who was serving his second term (1489–91). The document gives specific instructions that the representative of the patriarch, whose name is Manyasi, the Metropolitan from Siroz, was to come to collect the amounts owed by the bishops, priests, abbots, and monks according to custom. The military governors and Islamic judges were commanded to ensure that no one withheld any amounts and no excuse was given to withhold "even a single coin." These sums would be submitted to the agent, Manyasi, who would then convey them to Istanbul. In this case, Ottoman officials were enlisted to guarantee the proper collection of the Church dues.[24]

Although there is no similar appointment document for the Patriarch Ioakeim (1498–1502), there is every indication that his election became wrapped up in a controversy surrounding the tax farming administration. Patriarch Ioakeim and some of his non-clerical friends had gathered and agreed to give 3,000 florins yearly to the sultan, and 500 florins for *pişkeş*. Ioakeim may have urged this action, but it was the lay people who actually collaborated to raise the money. After Ioakeim, a monk named Pachomios of Zihnon was elevated to the throne. He, too, had his friends raise the 500 florins for the *pişkeş* to acquire the Patriarchal office.[25]

Other examples from Patriarchal documents demonstrate how the Patriarch, like imperial tax farmers, was responsible for collecting the "patriarchal tax" (*patriklik rüsûmu*). For instance, in the Morea, Father Gabriel and John Argyropoulos were required to collect these taxes for the Patriarch Maximos (1491–97), as recorded on August 31, 1494.[26] In another instance there was a complaint by the aforementioned, Patriarch Theoleptos, who on February 13, 1516 stated that his tax collectors were being harassed by the local Muslims. The sultan ordered this interference to stop. In each of these cases, the issue of tax collecting was at the forefront of Ottoman administrative concern.[27]

MID-SIXTEENTH CENTURY HIERARCHS

Examining episodes up to the year 1520, it has only been possible to examine sources as isolated cases, either from the Patriarchal chronicles, or from the

[24] Salakides, *Sultansurkunden Des Athos-Klosters Vatopedi Aus Der Zeit Bayezid II. Und Selim I.*, No. 7.
[25] *Historia Politike*, ed. Bekker, 70.
[26] Zachariadou, *Deka Tourkika engrapha*, 165–166, and plate 3.
[27] Zachariadou, *Deka Tourkika engrapha*, 167–168, and plate 4.

Ottoman administration. From the year 1522 onward, it is possible to begin corroborating these important sources and start the process of explaining more clearly the role of the Greek Orthodox Patriarch, and by extension, the role of the Greek Orthodox hierarchy, in Ottoman society. One of the interesting episodes that is easily corroborated takes place in the reign of Patriarch Jeremiah I (December 31, 1522–May 1524; September 24, 1525–January 13, 1546).

Patriarch Jeremiah I, was installed in December 1522, about nine months after the confiscation affair with Patriarch Theoleptos was said to have taken place. Early in his Patriarchal episcopacy, he had decided to go on a pilgrimage to Jerusalem, and while he was away, certain hierarchs and *archons* deposed him.

> However, the Lord Jeremiah crossed over by land, therefore over the mainland, with his own synod to Constantinople to see the conclusion. And as he drew near to those places he went to the good Praïpasia (Grand Vizier Ibrahim Pasha) and he paid reverence. And they greeted each other as the pasha loved him greatly. And that pasha went away in order to take care of an important matter, and he said to the patriarch to return to Galata and wait until I come, and I will give you back your place. And thus, he paid respect to him and he went to Galata to the church of Chrysopege and waited. And what a marvel, just as the people heard, it occurred. And so many people were there that for three days they ran and kissed his holy hand. As the pasha had arrived, he sat in the divan, and all the people came forth and shouted with a great voice, "O my sultan, the illegitimate patriarch Ioannikion we do not want in our church. We only want the first, who was properly ordained according to the law and to our faith." And thus the pasha did these things for the basileus. And he commanded that the will of the people happen.[28]

The opponents of Jeremiah had decided to create a new ecclesiastical law, or *canon*, making it illegal for a bishop to remain away from his see for a period of more than six months. Beyond that period, the hierarch would automatically be deposed. The *archons* and clerics agreed to enact this law specifically to depose Patriarch Jeremiah I through the imposed technicalities. The genesis of this opposition is unclear. Perhaps Patriarch Jeremiah I simply was not their choice, or hailed from another interest group, or maybe he was a foppish, illiterate monk who dishonored the patriarchal throne. Another of the patriarchal chronicles, the *Vivlion Historikon*, states that Patriarch Jeremiah I's opposition worked with the Turkish interests to make another cleric, Ioannikios, patriarch. The opponents not only tried to claim that Patriarch Jeremiah was breaking ecclesiastical canons, but at the same time, they tried to cut a financial deal to place their candidate on the patriarchal throne. To accomplish their goal, they needed to raise their *pişkeş* payment to the imperial treasury from 3,500 florins to 4,000 florins. Once they had raised the extra 500 florins, they were permitted to elevate their own candidate, Ioannikios, Metropolitan of Sōzopolis to patriarch.[29] After they placed Ioannikios

[28] *Historia Patriarchia*, ed. Bekker, 155–156.

[29] Constantine Sathas, *Viographikon Schediasma peri Patriarchou Hieremia B' (1572–1592)* (Athens: 1870), 4. See also (Pseudo) Dorotheos, *Vivlion Historikon Periechon en Synopsei Diaphorous kai Exochous Historias* (Venice: Nikolaos Glykeis, 1750)

on the throne, they guarded it by show of force, in case Jeremiah should return. However, the patriarchal chronicle explains that the people of the old city within the Byzantine walls, as well as people from across the Golden Horn in Galata, did not respect Ioannikios as patriarch, and criticized him, anathematizing him, and complaining about the injustice he brought upon them by his manner of deposing Jeremiah.

Meanwhile, Patriarch Jeremiah I, who was in Jerusalem, had heard about how he had been deposed. Staying on there for some time, he gathered the Patriarchs of Jerusalem, Alexandria, and Antioch, and proceeded to call a meeting to excommunicate Patriarch Ioannikios for illegally taking over the Patriarchate of Constantinople. Patriarch Jeremiah I returned overland to Constantinople, and went to see his good friend, Frenk Ibrahim Pasha (according to the chronicle, *Prai pasha*). Ibrahim Pasha had promised that he would take care of the matter after he returned from his campaign to the East. He told the patriarch to return to Galata and wait for his return, which Jeremiah did at the Church of Chrysopege. On his arrival these people thronged to see him. When Ibrahim Pasha returned, both he and Patriarch Jeremiah together approached the Divan, and asked that the illegitimate Patriarch Ioannikios be removed and the rightfully ordained Jeremiah to be restored. The sultan decided to restore Jeremiah I, though Jeremiah I was still expected to match his payment to the extra 500 florins that Ioannikios had promised. The Pasha called both patriarchs to the Divan, and each went accompanied by their own supporters. When the Pasha announced the decision of the Divan, Patriarch Jeremiah I announced that he refused to pay any increase and would resign. However, when the people heard this, they pleaded to the Pasha not to accept his resignation, and promised they would pay the increase even if Jeremiah I would not. They then took Jeremiah I and again placed him on the patriarchal throne, escorted by the sultan's agent. Ultimately, Jeremiah served one of the longest terms as patriarch in the Ottoman period, from 1522 to 1545. He appears to have learned well how his position could be threatened by internal factions, and also understood the type of imperial power and connections needed to maintain control.[30]

This episode of competition between bishops recorded in the Greek patriarchal chronicles is also recorded in the Ottoman state documents. Ottoman documents confirming the appointments of both Ioannikios and later Patriarch Jerermiah I (after his restoration) survive intact from monastic archives.[31] The document concerning the appointment of Patriarch Ioannikios was a decree issued from Sultan Süleyman in 1525 that was copied by the *molla* of Serres, Yusuf Abdulkerim, and posted to the military governors and Islamic judges of Rumeli stating that the Patriarch of Constantinople personally was to make rounds to collect the taxes, and was to receive the full cooperation, according to their religious practice, from the metropolitans, the bishops, the priests, and abbots. The Ottoman

[30] *Historia Patriarchica*, ed. Bekker, 153–157.
[31] Zachariadou, *Deka Tourkika engrapha*, 171–178, no. 6 and no. 7.

administrators were to make sure that the taxes were paid, forcing people to sell their movable property if necessary. Payments that the patriarch gathered were to be sent to the imperial treasury. The decree was meant to protect the bearer from interference or theft while in transit. The military governors and Islamic judges were to ensure that, when the patriarch made his rounds, his people would pay the full amount owed. No amount was to be left uncollected, but no laws were to be broken in the process. The document explained that, although priests might complain saying they had had more time to pay taxes in the past, they were still to pay on demand. Any of the metropolitans, bishops or others who disobeyed were to be deposed by the patriarch.[32] This decree was critical of Ioannikios who, to begin with, came to the patriarchal throne under questionable circumstances.

Subsequently, a surviving Ottoman *berât* of appointment confirms the removal of Patriarch Ioannikios and the appointment of Jeremiah I as patriarch.[33] This document not only offers confirmation of some of the events in the chronicle, but also displays a formula that appears in later documents that survive in 1544–45.

A sultanic *berât* dated October 17, 1525 exists in the archive of the Monastery of St. John the Theologian on Patmos. In the document, Sultan Süleyman confirms Jeremiah I as patriarch and records that Jeremiah I had given the amount of 500 florins as a gift to the fisc, while promising to give 3,500 florins as a yearly payment to replace Ioannikios who was deposed. Thus, there exists a direct corroboration of the patriarchal chronicles with Ottoman documentary sources. This *berât* supports the extraterritorial claims of the patriarchate over areas under Latin rule, as well as over the semi-autonomous Principalities of Wallachia and Moldavia. As in the past, the Patriarch of Constantinople had been appointed in Istanbul with responsibility to oversee and protect the religious practices found in the community of non-believers. The document then mentions Chios (*Sakiz*), Crete (*Kriti*), Rhodes (*Rodos*), and the vilayets of Eflâk and Karaboğdan, and Russia, saying that, if they were to require a bishop or metropolitan, then one was to be given as they would also pay the customary gift (*pişkeş*) demanded by the sultan. The document declared they could receive their office by permission of the patriarch in Istanbul. The extraterritorial jurisdiction of the patriarchate in this case was quite significant. Clearly, the Ottomans realized they might have the opportunity to collect taxes from local churches in foreign lands, such as those as far away as in Russia.

In accordance with the *berât*, Jeremiah I was to pay a sum of 500 florins to receive the *berât* and then yearly, on the feast of St. George in April, give 3,500 *florins*. The patriarch was to oversee the areas throughout Rumeli and Anatolia, and the Aegean islands. Anyone wishing to become a metropolitan or bishop was to give *pişkeş* first. The patriarch was to manage the metropolitans, the bishops, the abbots, the priests, the vineyards, the holy water fountains (*ayasmata*), the fairs (*panayir*), the mills, and the gardens, which were part of the income sources of the churches. Neither Muslims nor Christians were to hinder this collection.

[32] Zachariadou, *Deka Tourkika engrapha*, 171–173, no. 6.
[33] Zachariadou, *Deka Tourkika engrapha*, 174–178, no. 7.

The patriarch was to ensure that marriages in the Greek Orthodox communities were conducted according to their proper religious practice and to oversee issues of inheritance. No one in the Greek Orthodox community but the patriarch had this type of authority. Only if a leading hierarch in an active office died and his family was involved in an inheritance struggle would an Islamic judge step in to make a final determination. Additionally, if the patriarch or any one of the metropolitans, priests or monks died, and if, according to their religious practice he created a will, then the will was to be considered valid. If, however, any of these listed clerics died without a will, and his property was worth 5,000 *aspers* or more, it was to pass the imperial treasury (*beyt ül-mal*). Estates worth less than 5,000 *aspers* reverted to the patriarchate.

The patriarch collected specific amounts from the various communities he visited to assist in paying the investiture gift (*pişkeş)* and the yearly patriarchal tax to the treasury. The *berât* stipulated that the patriarch, personally, was to pay this amount; nothing was to be taken from individuals by force or threat. Finally, the metropolitans (*medrepolidler*), bishops (*piskoposlar*), abbots (*gomonoslar*) and clerics were not to get involved in any activities without the patriarch's knowledge especially any matters out of the ordinary.[34] Islamic judges were to enforce the patriarch's collection of taxes from the various territories in cases of resistance. The document also stated that non-believers (Christians) were not to be forcibly converted to the Muslim religion.

Clearly, the patriarch was responsible for the collection of considerable sums of money, and he was supported in this by the Ottoman administration including in territory outside of Ottoman domains. In the case of Wallachia and Moldavia, these territories were at least tributary vassals paying a yearly assessment to the Porte. Crete and Chios, however, were at this time under Venetian control, Russia was well outside the Ottoman domain, while Rhodes had only been captured in 1522. Although Halil Inalcik argued against this type of extraterritorial authority, explaining that such jurisdiction in an institution was clearly outside the pale for the *zimmi* subjects in an Islamic state, this document shows that patriarchal jurisdiction was well beyond the immediate boundaries of the Ottoman Empire.[35] It was in the fiscal interest of the state to allow the patriarchate this right so the patriarch could exploit the added income from these areas. Naturally, the jurisdiction included traditional Ottoman territory of Rumeli and Anatolia.

Without commenting directly on the competition between the two bishops for the office of Patriarch of Constantinople, the documents confirm the major object of concern for their competition. As far as the Ottomans were concerned, the patriarchs were responsible for collecting ecclesiastical taxes. The decree made sure that Patriarch Ioannikios' authority would not be questioned either by the general Christian population under his authority, nor by the ecclesiastical figures under his control, even promising the state's coercive authority if required. The

[34] Zachariadou, *Deka Tourkika engrapha*, 174–178, no. 7.
[35] Inalcik, "The Status of the Greek Orthodox Patriarchate," 417.

details of the increase of *pişkeş* and yearly payments to the state indicated the fiscal responsibility to the state. The willingness for two sides to compete and to raise the stakes so dramatically, meant there was a real financial gain for the office holders.

Although the *iltizam* profits are not revealed, it is safe to conclude that they existed. One indication of the excess collection of funds is revealed in Patriarch Jeremiah I's expenditures. Patriarch Jeremiah I, founded (or re-established) the monastery of Stavronikita located on the northeast side of the Mt. Athos peninsula. He built a large church and decorated it "brilliantly, offering to the church many beautiful and expensive vessels of gold and silver, and he built the structures and walls to house and protect the monks." The text of the *Historia Patriarchica* also says that he offered, "many lands, that were *mülk*, for the sustenance of the monks." In his attempt to make them into religious foundations (*vakıf*), Jeremiah I's benefaction and building, however, became the object of criticism. As the *Historia Patriarchica* explains,

> Thus, Jeremiah had wished to make a monastery, and he took from the hierarchs, whomever had been made one, gifts, and he opened the door to *simoniacal* practice, in the time of the Turks. And he built the monastery of Stavronikita on Agion Oros, and it is there until today. He went, therefore, to collect funds and he went to Vlachia, and on way, the house where they were staying caught fire, and burnt the building, and the wonderful vestments of the Great Church . . . Jeremiah died on the road beyond, in Frantzan and he was buried respectfully. And he served as hierarch for thirty-eight years and more.

Couched in the narrative about Patriarch Jeremiah I building a monastery is a curious statement, "he took from the hierarchs, whomever had been made one, gifts, and he opened the door to simoniacal practice, in the time of the Turks." The implication that Patriarch Jeremiah I had made his money through selling offices may be a way of criticizing the fiscalization of the Church offices. It is not clear if he actually encouraged simony, or directly benefited from the yearly sums of money that each "simoniacal" bishop paid the imperial treasury. It is possible to conclude that the monastery may also have been built for safekeeping or as a storehouse for his wealth,[36] or as a tax shelter to avoid the inheritance tax that clearly would alienate the excess funds.

Patriarch Jeremiah I died in 1546 at Tirnovo while on a journey to collect funds from the provinces of Wallachia and Moldavia. The *Historia Patriarchica* states that he appointed his own successor, Patriarch Dionysios II, who was from Galata and who was well liked by the majority of the lay people. But Patriarch Dionysios II was strongly disliked by many bishops and many important *archons*. The ecclesiastical situation was still rather unsettled and was subject to destabilizing actions from the state as well as from wealthy and powerful individuals. Only

[36] See N. Oikonomides, "Patronage in Palaiologan Mt. Athos," in *Mount Athos and Byzantine Monasticism: Papers from the Twenty-eighth Spring Symposium of Byzantine Studies, Birmingham, March 1994*, ed. A. Bryer and M. Cunningham (Birmingham: Variorum, 1996), 99–111 on wealthy aristocrats going to Athos in the late Paleologan period as a safeguard for their wealth.

through the inheritance under the will of Demetrios Kantakouzenos *Monoraites*, a wealthy and powerful *archon*, did Dionysios II become patriarch.

Because the state was the strongest and most authoritative institution that existed in Ottoman society, individual bishops, archbishops and patriarchs approached the state to confirm their authority and jurisdictions and to adjudicate their disputes. Shortly before his death, Patriarch Jeremiah I was involved in a series of additional disputes and challenges to his patriarchal authority. These challenges appeared between 1544 and 1545 in a series of Ottoman documents collected in a registry called the *Kâmil Kepeci Tasnifi Ahkâm Defteri* 62.

This series of documents created by the Ottoman state is, perhaps, the first series that deal directly with the patriarchate and the ecclesiastical hierarchy. It is clear the state was vigilant in responding to appeals and requests of ecclesiastical officials. Documents such as those compiled here, that appear serially, are particularly helpful to demonstrate how and why the hierarchs interacted with Ottoman state officials, as well as to observe on what basis the Ottoman state rendered its decisions concerning the Church. In a sense, the series of decrees serves as a microcosm of the relationship of Church and state and of the internal ecclesiastical issues. The numbered list (for purposes of analysis) of documents is as follows:

No. 1 10 June 1544 (19 Rebiülevvel 951) A decree to the Voyvodes of Eflâk and Karaboğdan concerning the Archbishop of Ohrid, Prohor's rights to collect taxes from Eflâk and Karaboğdan.
(Ahkâm Defteri 62, f. 270)

No. 2 16 June 1544 (25 Rebiülevvel 951) A decree to the Voyvodes of Eflâk and Karaboğdan concerning the Archbishop of Ohrid, Prohor's rights to collect taxes from Eflâk and Karaboğdan.
(Ahkâm Defteri 62, f. 289)

No. 3 June 1544 (Rebiülevvel 951) A decree sent to a local Kadi ordering that the Archbishop of Ohrid must submit the 930 akçe he gathered to the imperial slaves sent to gather the amount.
(Ahkâm Defteri 62, f. 378)

No. 4 23 July 1544 (3 Cumadelulâ 951) A decree to a local kadi concerning a dispute between two bishops, Karto and Dionis, over who is the rightful bishop.
(Ahkâm Defteri 62, f. 378)

No. 5 3 August 1544 (14 Cumadelulâ 951) A decree to the kadi of Mihaliç concerning the Patriarch Jeremiah's right to collect taxes. A representative is appointed to collect the amounts and pay them to the imperial treasury.
(Ahkâm Defteri 62, f. 396b)

No. 6 22 September 1544 (5 Receb 951) A decree to the Voyvodes of Eflâk and Karaboğdan stating that the Archbishop of Ohrid no longer had

the rights to collect taxes, but, according to ancient custom, Jeremiah actually has the right.
(Ahkâm Defteri 62, f. 500)

No. 7 25 September 1544 (8 Receb 951) A decree to the Rumeli Sancakbey, and the kadis stating that Patriarch Jeremiah received a *berât* giving him all the rights as patriarch to collect all the taxes due to his office.
(Ahkâm Defteri 62, f. 503)

No. 8 10 October 1544 (28 Receb 951) A decree to the kadis of Sivas and Tokat stating that the local Metropolitan Sodoş was forbidden from withholding payment from Patriarch Jeremiah.
(Ahkâm Defteri 62, f. 549b)

No. 9 10 October 1544 (28 Receb 951) A decree to the Rumeli Sancakbey and kadis stating that Patriarch Jeremiah received a *berât* granting him the right to collect taxes unhindered, and that he is sending a representative in his place.
(Ahkâm Defteri 62, f. 553a)

No. 10 19 October 1544 (2 Şaban 951) A decree to the kadi of Delvine (Epirus) stating that the Biromori monastery was forbidden from withholding taxes from the Patriarch Jeremiah.
(Ahkâm Defteri 62, f. 565a)

No. 11 8 December 1544 (23 Ramazan 951) A decree to the Rumeli Sancakbey and kadis stating that Patriarch Jeremiah received a *berât* granting him the right to collect taxes unhindered.
(Ahkâm Defteri 62, f. 665)

No. 12 28 December 1544 (13 Şevval 951) A decree to the Rumeli Sancakbey and kadis stating that Patriarch Jeremiah received a *berât* granting him the right to collect taxes unhindered, and that he is sending a representative in his place.
(Ahkâm Defteri 62, f. 729)

No. 13 17 January 1545 (4 Zilkade 951) A decree to the kadi of Gördos stating that the local priest Yasef had complained about encroachments on the Church's gardens, fields, and vineyards from members of the sipahis, and this was forbidden as they were rightfully dependencies of the Church.
(Ahkâm Defteri 62, f. 821)

No. 14 24 February 1545 (20 Zilhicce 1554) A decree to the Sancakbey of Köstendil and kadi of Somako concerning the embezzlement of funds by the solak Abdulkerim and yeniçeri Yusuf who had been appointed to collect the taxes locally.
(Ahkâm Defteri 62, f. 884)

These fourteen decrees were created in short succession between June 10, 1544 and February 24, 1545. This was a very busy time for Sultan Süleyman's territorial expansion and legal reform activities.[37] Due to his success in forging the Ottoman Empire as an international power that European states feared, and as a result of his legal reforms, Süleyman gained a reputation within the empire for being a just and intelligent ruler, but a ruler in need of wealth.

From the earliest times of the Ottoman emirate, territorial expansion was tied to the establishment of a profitable reward system for the military. The *timar* system was designed to encourage meritorious service in battle in exchange for the reward of fiefs. This, however, required the constant territorial expansion of the state. According to the Ottoman economic mind in the sixteenth century, military expansion and political power depended on the ability to reward the military class (*askeri*). While *timars* were a chief means of collecting taxes from Ottoman subjects, they generally did not enrich the Ottoman treasury directly. Whatever funds were collected locally went to support the local *timariot*'s household and military retinue, not to the imperial treasury. Additionally, the *timariot* kept putting pressure on the state to keep up the value of the *timars*, as well as to increase the access to them. Thus, it was necessary for the state to keep expanding.

The Ottoman state was also in search of alternative forms of wealth for itself. It was necessary to increase opportunities to collect imperial taxes.[38] The state received almost all of its hard revenue for the imperial treasury from the poll tax for non-Muslims (*cizye*) and from the system of tax farms (*mukata'a*) on various revenue producing enterprises. To support the imperial revenue consumption of the Ottoman administration, which included the sultan's household, the Ottomans targeted tax revenues produced by traditional monopolies in manufacturing and in commodity production.[39] The transformation of the Ottoman state from a small Anatolian *beylik* to an imperial power meant that the fiscal responsibilities also grew in proportion to the state. Further aggravating the need for cash were expenses such as the standing army of janissaries, which put even more pressure on cash resources. It was through the exploitation of tax farms that the state could gain enough cash to run its administration and pay its soldiers.

Sultan Süleyman's campaigns to the West and East also put pressure on the imperial treasury. At the beginning of his reign, Sultan Süleyman's first major conquest was Belgrade (1521). He then set out to take Rhodes (1522), a major step to break the hold of the Knights of St. John over the Mediterranean. Sultan Süleyman continued his westward movement against Hungary, first making it a vassal state after the victory in the Battle of Mohaç in 1526, and later annexing

[37] Ibrahim Metin Kunt, "State and Sultan up to the Age of Süuleyman," in *Süleyman the Magnificent and His Age: The Ottoman Empire in the Early Modern World,* ed. Ibrahim Metin Kunt and Christine Woodhead (London: Longman, 1995), 21–25; Halil Inalcik, "State, Sovereignty and Law During the Reign of Süleyman," in *Suleyman the Second and His Time,* ed. Cemal Kafadar and Halil Inalcik (Istanbul: Isis, 1993), 76–78.

[38] Halil Inalcik, ed., *An Economic and Social History of the Ottoman Empire 1300–1914* (Cambridge: Cambridge University Press, 1994), 49.

[39] Inalcik, *Economic and Social History of the Ottoman Empire,* 44.

it completely in 1541 and turning it into the *sancak* of Buda. In the East against the Safavids of Iran, the Ottomans conquered Tabriz and Baghdad during the eastern campaigns of 1533–35. As a result, the Ottomans dominated the trade routes from the Middle East to India, setting up a governorship (*beylerbeylik*) in Baghdad. It was only in 1555, when the treaty of Amasya was settled, that Tabriz was returned to the Safavids, but the eastern boundary lasted until the end of the century.

By the late 1530s, Holy Roman Emperor Charles V of Vienna joined forces with leaders of Venice and the Pope against the Ottomans. Despite this alliance, Ottoman naval victory at Preveza in 1538 gave the Ottomans dominion in the Mediterranean until their defeat at Lepanto in 1571. Venice finally gave up its right to its holdings in the Morea in 1540. In 1543 and 1544 the Ottomans continued into the Balkans, conquering Peç, Vişegrad, and the areas of Bosnia. This late date for capturing Peç is significant because twenty-five years later it became the seat of an independent patriarchate that governed the Church in Bosnia and Serbia. None other than Sultan Süleyman's famous Grand Vizier who hailed from this region, Mehmet Sokollu Pasha, established this patriarchate.

Vassal princes who pledged loyalty to the Ottomans governed the Danubian provinces of Eflâk (Wallachia) and Karaboğdan (Moldavia), but also were forced at times to make difficult alliances with the Hapsburgs, the Poles, and Moscow. In the 1530s in particular, there was an increase in competition between Moscow, whom the Ottomans previously supported against the Poles, and the Ottomans. As a result, the Ottomans did not trust the Voyvode of Karaboğdan, Petru Rareş. The Ottomans invaded in 1538 and replaced Petru Rareş with his son. Eventually, in 1541, the father made his way back to the throne, but had to accept a janissary guard and pay a heavy tribute of 12,000 *ducats*. This amount paid by Petru Rareş is the first indication of a Romanian version of the *pişkeş*, which was inaugurated when Petru Rareş became Prince of Moldavia. Later, this gift to the sultan would develop into a regular tax.[40] Moldavian voyvodes were particularly prosperous and offered cash as well as payments in kind to Istanbul for the provisioning of the City.[41]

Eflâk was always a much larger and wealthier province than Karaboğdan, and its tribute was significantly higher.[42] The princes were actually responsible for collecting and submitting the taxes to Istanbul. However, they relied upon the local nobles to collect what was required from the peasantry and these nobles eventually grew strong at the expense of the ruling princes.[43]

Within the context of the unsteady relationship between the Ottomans and the Voyvodes of Eflâk and Karaboğdan, there is visible an Ottoman concern

[40] P. F. Sugar, *Southeastern Europe under Ottoman Rule, 1354–1804* (Seattle, University of Washington Press, 1977), 122.

[41] Sugar, *Southeastern Europe*, 118.

[42] Sugar, *Southeastern Europe*, 122. For instance between 1545 and 1559 the yearly tribute of Wallachia was 50,000 ducats, while the tribute of Moldavia in 1552–61 was 30,000.

[43] Sugar, *Southeastern Europe*, 123.

reflected in the 1544 documents that detailed the conflict between the Patriarch of Constantinople, Patriarch Jeremiah I, and the Archbishop of Ohrid, Prohor. Within eight months, there were eight petitions that dealt with ecclesiastical control and authority made by the Patriarch of Constantinople, Jeremiah I (*Istanbul Rum Patriği Yeremiye)*, four petitions made by the Archbishop of Ohrid, Prohor (*Ohri Patriği Prohor*), and two other petitions by a local priest and a bishop. The Divan was open to each individual bishop who wished to appear and to make a request. The Divan made a decision, and issued a *berât* to each bishop either as a document of appointment, or as a decree commanding an audit or some other type of administrative action. This open access allowed the Ottomans to oversee and even manage the fiscal and administrative affairs of the Church. Although, all the petitioners were ecclesiastical officials, their petitions articulated the possession and administration of their offices as ecclesiastical tax farms.

The Divan responded to the petitions by granting decrees according to each situation. Among the fourteen documents listed above, three recorded the granting of general *berât*s of appointment, six appointed representatives other than the patriarchs to collect taxes, while five recorded requests for resolution to various conflicts. From these groupings alone, it is possible to see how the patriarch and other bishops approached the Divan for *berât*s of appointments, to confirm their rights, or to protect their prerogatives.

The evidence from the series of 1544 documents suggests that the institution of the Church was *not* a tightly organized hierarchy, nor governed by the exclusive authority of a single patriarch, including the Patriarch of Constantinople. Rather, there were separate and competing interests, individuals resisting and attempting to bypass the central authority of the patriarch, and attempts to use the Ottoman system of appeal to secure ecclesiastical offices possessing wider jurisdictions.

In some respects, this was the continuation of the ad hoc nature of the relationship established by the Church and the Turkmen emirates in the fourteenth century. In 1544, the major conflict was between the aforementioned Patriarch Jeremiah I, and the Archbishop of Ohrid, Prohor.

The first document in this series is, dated June 10, 1544 (Document No. 1), arises from a petition by Prohor, the Archbishop of Ohrid.[44] The content is reiterated in a second copy dated six days later (Document No. 2).[45] These were addressed to the Voyvode of Eflâk and Karaboğdan. The patriarch (*patrik*) whose name was given as Prohor went to the sultan to request the right to collect the imperial taxes (*miri rüsûmu*) that were in arrears in his territory. Prohor asked to collect those taxes to which he was entitled according to the "age old custom" (*âyın-ı batılalar üzerine kadîmden*). The formula, "age old custom" indicates the longstanding practice of collecting customary ecclesiastical taxes. Prohor asserted this claim in order to bolster his own position. He claimed that the

[44] Başbakanlık Osmanlı Arşivi (BOA), Ahkâm Defteri 62, f. 270. Also see Maxim Mihai, "Les Relations des Pays Roumans avec L'Archevêché D'Ohrid à Lumière de Documents Turcs Inédits," *Revue Études Sud-Est Europeen* XIX, (1981): 653–671.

[45] BOA, Ahkâm Defteri 62, f. 289.

metropolitans were interfering with the collection of taxes and he suffered losses of income that was his due. The decision by the Divan was that the infidels who were in arrears should be summoned together with Prohor, and since Prohor had the right to collect the taxes in arrears, the metropolitans were not to interfere with the process.

The use of the term patriarch (*patriği*) raises an interesting question. The term was used to describe the bishops of the ancient Churches of Jerusalem, Antioch, Alexandria, Rome, and Constantinople, recognized formally in the Novella's of Justinian in the sixth century.[46] Churches that developed as independent self-governing, or autocephalous, were led by archbishops, such as the church of Cyprus, which became formally independent from the Patriarchate of Antioch in AD 431.[47] The term "Patriarch" of Ohrid has a residue of Bulgarian independence that remained Tsar Samuel II (974–1014) who established the residence of the independent patriarchate in Ohrid. The residue of independence survived the suppression of the independent Bulgarian patriarchate by the Emperor Basil II, known as the Bulgar-slayer (*Boulgaroktonos*, 976–1025). Ohrid was the only Bulgarian bishopric to remain autocephalous with its own Archbishop, even amidst various challenges to its authority.[48] When the Ottomans took over the Bulgarian regions, the Patriarchate of Constantinople was able to do what it long sought under the Byzantine Empire, subordinated the archbishops of Serbia and Ohrid.[49]

Under Ottoman control, the Patriarchate of Constantinople was deemed to have jurisdictional authority. Therefore, according to Constantinople, the correct ecclesiastical title for Prohor was Archbishop of Ohrid. However, the title *patriği* must have been advanced somewhere along the line to the Ottoman Divan, perhaps in a bid to place Ohrid semantically on equal status with Constantinople, the location where the petition was made. It is not clear whether the petitioner, the archbishop of Ohrid, created this term or it was adopted by the Divan chancery. In either case, the archbishop of Ohrid understood this to be true, and convinced the Ottoman officials that his claim was legitimate.

We are not told who the metropolitans were. But because they were trying to interfere with the tax collection of Prohor, they might have been acting either on their own behalf, or more likely, on Patriarch Jeremiah I's behalf as he had full claim to this jurisdiction. Prohor, essentially, was exercising his rights to collect taxes in arrears due from Eflâk and Karaboğdan. Infidels (*kefere*) were specifically

[46] A. P. Kazhdan and Aristeidis Papadakis, "Patriarchates," *The Oxford Dictionary of Byzantium* (New York: Oxford University Press, 1991) III, 1599–1600.

[47] Benedict Englezakis, Silouan Ioannou, and Misael Ioannou, *Studies on the History of the Church of Cyprus, 4th–20th Centuries* (Brookfield, Vermont: Variorum, 1995), 29.

[48] Engelzakis, *Church of Cyprus,* 29. In the thirteenth century, there were competing claims on the Archbishopric of Ohrid between the exiled Empire of Nicaea, and the Despotate of Epiros. The Empire of Nicaea counteracted the authority of Ohrid by establishing a new Patriarchate in Trnovo. This ceased to be an issue when Nicaea reclaimed Constantinople and the Epiros faded away after 1261.

[49] A. P. Vlasto, *The Entry of the Slavs into Christendom: An Introduction to the Medieval History of the Slavs* (Cambridge: Cambridge University Press, 1970), 187.

referred to, but it is unclear what their status was and how they might have been attached to ecclesiastical lands. Presumably, they were cultivators working the landholdings or producing some other income attached to the Church from which taxes could be alienated. Also interesting is that the command was sent to the voyvodes of Eflâk and Karaboğdan. One would assume that for whatever tribute the voyvodes were paying they would collect the amount in their own fiscal administrative system. However, in this and many other cases, the Church leaders had the right to collect imperial taxes in provinces independent from direct Ottoman control. Archbishop Prohor chose to appeal to the sultan, although we do not know if he also appealed to the voyvodes or to the Patriarchate of Constantinople.

Shortly after these two commands were sent to the voyvodes of Eflâk and Karaboğdan, another command was sent to a local Islamic judge (*kadi*) concerning the *Ohri Patriği Prohor* who had previously visited the Porte (Document No. 3).[50] The decree stated that the 930 *akçe* Archbishop Prohor collected from monasteries in arrears, and sent to the sultan by means of a slave (*kûl*), was deficient, and it was necessary to submit the balance that was due.

In this series of documents concerning Constantinople and Ohrid, each following closely upon the other, is an intervening document concerning another ecclesiastical conflict over another bishopric in a different place. On August 3, 1544 (Document No. 5), Patriarch Jeremiah appeared before the Divan to request a *berât* granting the right to send a representative (*vekil*) in his place to collect taxes. The responsibility to submit taxes to the Imperial treasury would still be his, but he would be able to delegate the difficult task to another.

When Jeremiah went to the Porte in August asking about requesting to recognize his representative, (*vekil*), perhaps, he was not aware of Prohor's intentions or earlier actions. Had he been aware, he would not have requested a vekil, but would have addressed the far more threatening situation. In other words, he would have requested from the Divan a *berât* confirming his own rights over Eflâk and Karaboğdan since the ecclesiastical jurisdiction had previously belonged to him. This event was recorded in the patriarchal chronicles, too. According to the *Historia Patriarchica* that comments directly on this situation, the "Patriarch, the Archbishop of Ohrid, formerly called Ioustiniannes, by the name of Prohoros, came here to Constantinople and appeared before the Divan and presented the Imperial [Byzantine] chrysobulls stating that his archbishopric included the region of Verroia," which, in fact, is within the Metropolis of Thessalonike. In the chronicle, Prohor then promised to submit 100 more *florins* as *haraç*. The *Historia Patriarchica* makes much more of the issue. It continues,

> The Patriarch [Jeremiah], hearing that he [Prohoros] had offered the *haraç*, came to the *addemonian*, (*müfti üz-zema, şeyh-ül-islâm*), [for advice on] what to do and so that Prohor would take no lands. So, they discussed it [lit. interpreted the prophesy] and went and had a *fetwa* issued. And the *fetwa* stated that if a certain person possesses something and he holds it for 100 years, henceforth another person is not

[50] BOA, Ahkâm Defteri 62, f. 339.

allowed to take it from his hands. And so he appeared before the Divan and presented the *fetwa* and demonstrated that the Church of Constantinople has this for about 300 years. And when the Pashas heard this they judged that he should take possession of it, after realizing the 100 *florins*, the increase of Prohoros. ... And so as not to hinder this, the Patriarch paid this, too. And thusly, they expelled Prohoros from the Divan. The total of the *haraç* of the Great Church of Constantinople was 4,100 *florins*, and these are given each year to the Sublime Porte of the sultan on the day of the Great [St.] George.[51]

The patriarchal chronicle corroborates the concerns that were found within the testimony of the *Ahkâm Defteri*, the only difference being the specific region in question. The document, describes Eflâk and Karaboğdan, while the *Historia Patriarchica* tells about the rights of the Metropolitan of Thessalonike being encroached. The importance of this corroborating evidence should not be underestimated. The information is also significant because it displays many of the same terms and conditions of the documents already discussed. The amount to be submitted to the sultan by both the archbishop of Ohrid and the Greek Orthodox Patriarch was termed "*haraç,*" meaning the yearly payment on the land holdings of the Church, which was extensive. The document insured the recipient the right to collect taxes over the Churches and Christians within the jurisdiction.

We also learn that Patriarch Jeremiah was concerned about the encroachment of another bishop into his jurisdiction. Therefore, according to the Greek sources, he proceeded to get an Islamic legal opinion concerning his rights of ownership according to Islamic law. What is interesting is that the decision addressed the issue of the jurisdictional rights as a property issue. In fact, if it belonged to the patriarch for over 100 hundred years (they were able to show the patriarchate "owned" it for 300 years) and recently it was taken over by Prohor without justification, it should still have remained Constantinople's, or specifically, under Jeremiah's jurisdiction. The third thing we learn from this account is that the *Istanbul Rum Patriği* was responsible to pay the extra 100 *florins* of "*haraç,*" which made its yearly submission to the Porte 4,100 *florins*.

When we continue reading in the *Ahkâm Defteri* we find that, on September 22 (Document No. 6), a decree went out to the Voyvodes of Karaboğdan and Eflâk stating that Prohor had previously been collecting the taxes of these territories, but that according to ancient custom and practice (and according to the same terms maintained by Prohor) Jeremiah and his *vekil* would be taking over. Jeremiah was able in this case to convince the Divan that this had previously been the Patriarch of Constantinople's prerogative. In addition, Jeremiah was to pay the extra 100 *florins* Prohor had previously promised to bring his total amount to 4,100 *florins*. After this episode, one finds Patriarch Jeremiah at the Divan asking for notification of *berât*s to be sent to the Rumeli military governors and Islamic judges to reaffirm his right to collect taxes over those areas and to use surrogates. Interestingly, Prohor does not disappear entirely. He appeared before the Divan at

[51] *Historia Patriarchica*, ed. Bekker, 170.

the end of this series of documents, to request the sultan's support to investigate a conflict in the collection of taxes in Kostendil and Somako, which remained properly under his control.

Immediately following the Divan's reinstatement of Jeremiah's jurisdiction over the territories of Eflâk and Karaboğdan, Patriarch Jeremiah must have requested another *berât* that confirmed his office, rights, and jurisdiction and to inform the Rumeli *sancakbeys* and the *kadis*. He was granted the right to collect the regular and customary taxes from the metropolitans, bishops, abbots, priests, monks and other infidels, (*metropolidlerde ve piskoposlarda ve gomonoslarda ve papaslarda ve keşişlerde ve sair kefere*) from the area of Rumeli and Mt. Athos. He was to collect, unhindered, the taxes for the year, and any taxes that were in arrears, and was granted safe conduct throughout all the roads. No one was to delay in paying, nor to give any excuses for non-payment. It also mentioned the aforementioned policy concerning the inheritance from deceased hierarchs. If a bishop died with a will, then the will should be honored. If he died without a will, and his wealth is more than 5,000 florins, then the amount would go to the sultan. If it were less than 5,000 florins, then it would go to the aforementioned patriarch. The patriarch was permitted the staff, a mule, and the black kaftan, to take place according to the "ancient law" (*kanunu kadim*).[52]

About twenty days later, on October 10 (Document No. 8), Patriarch Jeremiah returned again to the Divan on another mission, this time to complain about a Metropolitan in Anatolia, in the region of Sivas and Tokat who refused to submit (*ta'allul idüp vermez*) the full amount of the tax due. The sultan's decree was sent to the *kadis* of Sivas and Tokat and ordered the local Metropolitan Sodoş to submit the customary tax for the imperial treasury, and that any taxes in arrears should also be submitted. Not one *akçe,* the sultan decreed, should be withheld from the Patriarch Jeremiah.[53]

Then, to confirm Patriarch Jeremiah's position again, the Divan issued another general *berât* to the Rumeli military governors and Islamic judges (Document No. 9), in which all the same terms and conditions concerning the tax collection process were repeated. In this case, however, the patriarch was seeking the rights for his representative rather than his own person.[54]

A few days later, on October 19 (Document No. 10), a document shows that Patriarch Jeremiah's representative had confronted another similar situation of an individual withholding money. This time, it was a monastery that refused to pay its proper dues. Patriarch Jeremiah went to the Divan to report that his representative had gone to the Biromori (*Geromeri*) monastery, and the monks there would not hand over the taxes due. This would have been contrary to practice as this was a *stavropegeaic* monastery that was not dependent on the local metropolitan of Ioannina, but was likely dependent on the Patriarchate of Constantinople as early as the 1330s. The Divan issued a decree directed to the Islamic judge of Delvine (Epirus) that no excuse should be given to withhold any amount from

52 BOA, Ahkâm Defteri 62, f. 503.

53 BOA, Ahkâm Defteri 62, f. 549b.

54 BOA, Ahkâm Defteri 62, f. 553a.

the patriarchal representative, and that they should pay their taxes according to their custom.[55]

Patriarch Jeremiah, on December 8 (Document No. 11), returned to the Divan to request a *berât* granting him the rights to travel through Rumeli and to Mt. Athos to collect the customary taxes. Apparently, during this journey, Patriarch Jeremiah wished to go in person.[56] The next *berât* he requested was on December 28 (Document No. 12), for his representative.[57]

Thus far, a number of things can be said concerning the nature of the visits to the Divan and their frequency. Apparently, the patriarch did not feel entirely secure that he had full authority in his own right even over the ecclesiastical institutions and personalities within his jurisdiction. Withholding of taxes by a metropolitan and by a monastery produced a flurry of activity aimed at the Divan to successfully exact the appropriate dues. After an episode of conflict, the patriarch would go back to request a more general *berât*, granting him the right to travel and collect taxes throughout Rumeli and on Mt. Athos. The fact that all the issues in these documents deal with finances should come as no surprise. There was no concern expressed in the documents for religious practice, or aspects related to the proper functioning of Church canons or beliefs. The main issue with which the state was concerned was whether or not the patriarch could pay the required amount due to the state. Any interference in the process resulted in reprimands and direct intervention by the state to ensure this customary process continued.

There are also cases within this series of documents brought to the Divan by other clerics that make no reference to the patriarch. If the patriarch personally had to run back continually to the Divan to assert jurisdictional authority in tax collecting, one would not expect him to be fully in control as an authority to resolve local jurisdictional problems either. The best case that demonstrates local bishops seeking recourse from the state, without any consideration of the patriarchate, is the case of Dionis and Karto that was recorded on July 23, 1544 (Document No. 4). In this case there was an explosive situation where two competing bishops appeared before the Divan, without any patriarchal representative present. A decree was issued to a local Islamic judge (*kadi*) describing a conflict raging over who had the proper rights to an episcopal see. Karto, the priest, appeared before the Divan, claiming he was appointed with the imperial *berât* as bishop of the "infidels" of the unnamed town. Then Dionis, the *zimmi*, came forth declaring, "I received the bishopric and he [Karto] is committing fraud (*telbis etmek*), and he is coming and gathering for the state treasury the taxes, according to the old custom. He took two years of revenues and devoured it and

[55] BOA, Ahkâm Defteri 62, f. 565a. On the stauropegiac status of the Geromeri Monastery see Donald MacGillivray Nicol, *The Despotate of Epiros, 1267–1479: A Contribution to the History of Greece in the Middle Ages* (Cambridge: Cambridge University Press, 1984), 243; John Thomas and Angela Constantinides Hero, eds., *Byzantine Monastic Foundation Documents: A Complete Translation of the Surviving Founders' Typika and Testaments*, Dumbarton Oaks Studies: 37 (Washington, D.C.: Dumbarton Oaks Research Library and Collection, 2000), 1396.

[56] BOA, Ahkâm Defteri 62, f. 665.

[57] BOA, Ahkâm Defteri 62, f. 729.

there was damage to the region and to the finances of the imperial treasury." The Divan ordered the *berâts* to be examined and the rightful bishop to be restored, and the Porte to be informed.[58]

Certain important elements offer insight into how lower-ranking clerics related to the patriarch and to the Ottoman state. First of all, the two bishops went directly to the Imperial Divan in Istanbul. We do not know if they had attempted to appeal to the Patriarchate of Constantinople first, but we do know the patriarch represented neither individual at the Divan, nor did any other members of the Greek community intervene. These two bishops went directly to the sultan to settle their disagreement. Both of them said they could produce official *berâts*. This might mean that either that Dionis or Karto was a forger, though this is probably not the case as fraud was a serious crime in Ottoman Criminal Code for which the penalty, if done repeatedly, was the cutting off of the hand.[59] The other possibility was they each received a recommendation from the patriarch, and had legitimate *berâts* from the sultan, and this conflict arose from an administrative mistake on the part of the patriarchate. The last possibility is that this is an administrative mistake by a secretary of the Divan. This might be innocent or tied to corruption. Even at the height of Ottoman imperial administration under Sultan Süleyman, this type of inefficiency or corruption could occur. When coming to appeal the case before the Divan, a claimant's right as bishop was identified not in religious terms, but in terms of the right to collect the taxes. Therefore, we can conclude that the bishopric was considered to be a right that could be owned as property by the individual possessing the *berât*. The statement that "I took (*aldim*) the bishopric," again emphasizes that the office of bishop was considered to be a form of property. The other bishop was accused of fraud, trying to steal his property. To be more specific, these bishops were seeking support for their right to collect taxes and, in effect, be the imperial tax farmer (*mültezim*) for the ecclesiastical concession, just as if it were a salt works or a customs port. This is certainly a different view of the role of the high-ranking clergy than traditional historical interpretations determined by Church historians.

Just as in the previous case, on January 17, 1545 (Document No. 13) the patriarch is nowhere present in a petition of a local priest to protect Church properties. The priest Yasef, of the town of St. George (*kaza-i Aya Yorgi*) in the area of Gördos, went to the Divan by himself, and said that as he had been appointed bishop and he complained that certain members of the *sipahi* (*sipahi tâ'ife*) were claiming the vineyards, gardens, and fields for themselves. A *berât* was issued saying that these properties were dependent on the Church and not to be alienated by the *sipahi tâ'ife*. The state lands were to remain in the possession of the non-Muslims (*zimmiyi tasarruf etdiresin*).

[58] BOA, Ahkâm Defteri 62, f. 378.

[59] Uriel Heyd and V. L. Ménage, *Studies in Old Ottoman Criminal Law* (Oxford: Clarendon Press, 1973), 121.

Finally, the last of the series of documents from Ahkâm Defteri 62 shows that the Archbishop of Ohrid, Prohor, returned to the Divan on February 24, 1545 (Document No. 14) to deal with his own problems arising from tax collection. Apparently, Prohor had appointed two Ottoman individuals, military guardsman (*solak*) Abdulkerim and janissary (*yeniçeri*) Yusuf, to collect taxes on his behalf from his territory. This time it was not monasteries or metropolitans refusing to pay, but two representatives serving as tax collectors withholding money from Prohor. Therefore, he went before the Divan, which ordered an audit to take place, and stated that any amount they took beyond what they were allowed, was to be repaid to Prohor. The decree was directed to the military governor of Kostendil and Islamic judge (*kadi*) of Somako. In previous examples appointing a representative to collect taxes, the *vekil* was unnamed and it was unclear whether it was an Ottoman guard or Greek clergy. It is likely that in the former case of Patriarch Jeremiah's representative the individual was a member of the patriarchal staff. This is true for earlier periods, as well as later. In the case of Prohor, however, he relied on the two individuals who were clearly Ottoman and Muslim. Perhaps, this is the reason the guardsman and janissary felt they could take advantage of their position.

CONCLUSION

In a little more than twenty years, during the reign of the Sultan Süleyman, the Patriarchate of Constantinople went from frantically searching for investiture documents proving Patriarch Theoleptos had rights to churches and Church properties, to actively utilizing the Imperial Divan to protect and confirm their administrative rights and authority as in the case of Patriarch Jeremiah I. It makes sense that after 1521 there are more documents related to the Church recorded in the Defters of the Imperial Divan. It may be that the patriarch went from being helpless at the hands of a direct challenge by the Ottoman state that sought to appropriate churches and properties to actively using the Ottoman governing council as an instrument to protect its rights.

While proximity in time is, perhaps, the only evidence to infer that the patriarchate became more proactive and involved at the Imperial Divan after the episode with Patriarch Theoleptos, it is clear that under Patriarch Jeremiah I the Patriarchate of Constantinople was engaged fully in protecting its authority granted according to "age old custom." In the case where the Archbishop Prohor of Ohrid tried to extend his authority and governance, the patriarch was able to return to the Imperial Divan and get the state not only to confirm Constantinople's rights but to police them as well. However, this did not mean that this was a certainty for the Patriarch of Constantinople. The existence not only of these challenges but also of other episodes of conflict among bishops of the Church over ecclesiastical governance and authority indicates that the power of the Patriarch of Constantinople was limited. That the patriarchate needed the state to defend its interest by coercive power is not surprising. At the same time, however, the patriarch became accustomed to assert that the rights granted to him were according to "age old custom." This "age old custom" is exactly what Patriarch Theoleptos sought to establish with the missing document.

4

Ottoman Tax Farming and the Greek Orthodox Church

In the middle of the fourteenth century, the Ottomans directed their military campaigns and raids outside of their home territory of Bithynia in Asia Minor and moved into the Balkans. Rapid expansion in the Balkans resulted in a distinctly small Ottoman minority that conquered and ruled over a substantially larger and primarily Christian population. In order to rule conquered territories with a small number of forces, the Ottomans required an administrative structure that was elastic and mobile enough to easily impose itself on the local population in order to collect taxes from the subject people. The feudal institution of the *timar* system developed to suit the needs of the growing state that expanded by attracting armed warriors through the promise of booty and the rewards of a fief (*timar*). The *timar* system was a particularly effective institution for establishing effective rule over a wide geographic territory. However, the taxes that were collected by the *timariots* and their agents did not directly benefit the Imperial Treasury. These collected payments outfitted and sustained each *timariot* during the campaign season and supported him throughout the year. The state therefore needed to find alternative methods to gather revenue.

One of the primary ways the state directly gained cash was the practice of treating non-agricultural operations as tax farms. Many types of production were exploited through tax farms; these included precious metals, fisheries, salt works, port and custom fees. Each of these was treated as a concession whose rights of possession and profit could be bought and sold. These concessions could not be assigned in the same way as cultivated lands, by assigning them as *timars* to worthy *timariots*. Rather, the specialization in labor that was required to maintain productivity precluded the state from assigning non-trained personnel to oversee these concessions. When, for example, the Ottomans targeted the precious metal mines of Serbia and Bosnia, and were considering how to exploit them, they did not attempt to change the personnel or any of the production methods with the intention of gaining greater control. Instead, they figured out how to graft the tax farming system (*mukata'a*) onto the administrative organization of the mines. Thus, they were able to use local expertise and experience to continue producing the precious commodities and found opportunities to exploit the gold and silver mines for bullion to feed the cash-starved state.[1] An individual tax farmer would pay the state a one-time down payment, and then an agreed upon sum each year. These tax farming concessions could be granted to individuals as privileges and rewards for loyalty or service without harming the central treasury.[2] Frequently, however, tax farms required specialized and experienced agents who knew best how to exploit them. This is precisely the case of the Church, a specialized institution that the Ottomans needed to consider carefully.

THE QUESTION OF A PATRIARCHAL TAX FARM

If we consider the institution of the Greek Orthodox Patriarchate of Constantinople (*İstanbul Rum Patrikliği*) as an Ottoman tax farm similar to any other tax farm in the Ottoman Empire, how does this change the way in which we understand the Church in the Ottoman period? According to the accepted wisdom concerning the *millet* system, the Greek Orthodox subjects of the Ottoman Empire were governed as a state within a state, with the patriarch serving as the chief administrator of the of non-Muslim communities. Although historians have questioned the Ottoman *millet* system paradigm, there have been few attempts to describe the actual dynamics between the Ottoman state, the Greek Orthodox Church, and the Greek Orthodox population.[3] Previous chapters have described the first steps towards the establishment of a fiscal relationship between the Ottoman state and the Church. The present chapter will examine direct evidence from Ottoman documents issued to patriarchs and bishops in the fifteenth and sixteenth centuries that moves the discussion further in this direction.

The Ottomans considered the Church a revenue-producing institution, with incomes not easily regulated by established methods of taxation. The widely dispersed holdings alone made tax farming a practical solution to the problem of exploiting Church revenues for the state. In effect, the Ottomans understood how to graft a tax farming system onto the administrative organization of the Orthodox Church, making the Church a tax farm, an *iltizam,* producing and collecting revenues for the state. Our understanding of the Greek Orthodox hierarchy, the patriarchs, metropolitans, bishops, and priests and monks, shifts from considering them as leaders of the Greek community to seeing them as Ottoman

[1] Halil Inalcik, ed., *An Economic and Social History of the Ottoman Empire 1300–1914* (Cambridge: Cambridge University Press, 1994), 58.

[2] Linda Darling, *Revenue-Raising and Legitimacy: Tax Collection and Finance Administration in the Ottoman Empire 1560–1660*, (Leiden: E. J. Brill, 1996), 121.

[3] Benjamin Braude, "Foundation Myths of the Millet System," in *Christians and Jews in the Ottoman Empire: The Functioning of a Plural Society*, ed. Benjamin Braude and Bernard Lewis (New York: Holmes and Meier, 1982), 69–88; Daniel Goffman, "Ottoman Millets in the Early Seventeenth Century," *New Perspectives on Turkey* 11 (1994): 135–158; Michael Ursinus, "Zur Diskussion um 'millet' im Osmanischen Reich," *Südost-Forschungen* 48 (1989): 195–207; and M. Ursinus, "Millet" *Encyclopedia of Islam*, 2nd ed., VII (1990), 61–64.

fiscal administrators, and more specifically, tax farmers (*mültezim*.) This shift undermines the notion of hierarchs possessing full civil authority and representative power for the Greek Orthodox community at large. Instead, the bishop became a functionary of the state who collected taxes specifically from the ecclesiastical administration, though not the more general taxes paid by non-Muslims, such as the *cizye*.

Since the *cizye* is a tax imposed upon and collected from non-Muslims, its administration is sometimes confused with the taxes collected by bishops. One of the reasons for this confusion is that throughout the sixteenth century, the term *haraç* was used to describe the *cizye*, and the term for *cizye* payers was *haraçgüzar*.[4] The *cizye* had a completely separate administration from the ecclesiastical taxes. Among the sixteenth-century revenues destined for the Imperial Treasury (*havass-i humayun*), taxes on monopolies, urban taxes, and commercial taxes, as well as on unallocated land revenues formed the greatest part. As for other sources directed to the Imperial Treasury, the *cizye*, because it was a flat fee tax paid per non-Muslim household, became the largest revenue source in the sixteenth century. By the seventeenth century, additional taxes, the extraordinary levies (*avariz*), became more important to the overall income.

The *cizye* was assessed on either on a whole community in a lump sum (*mâktu'*) or on individual males aged 15–60. Multiple exemptions were available to non-Muslims providing military service, or to those who were indigent and disabled, and sometimes to monks and clerics. The *cizye* payers were recorded in the *timar tahrir* register, wherein a list of taxable individuals was most often recorded. Local *kadis* also maintained individual *cizye* registers. Every three years those *cizye* payers were reassessed, and recounted by a *kadi* or another official called a *cizyedar* or *haracci*, the agents in charge of *cizye*. The collection of the *cizye* was of such great importance that an accounting bureau for the poll tax (*cizye muhasebesi kalemi*) was created around 1569–70 and was run by dozens of scribes who filed the *cizye* registers from throughout the empire.[5]

Collecting *cizye* was based on the assessments established by the sultanic laws and recorded in the *kanuname*, the code of regulations for each region. The assignment of collectors, usually two men, an *emin* and a *kâtip,* was recorded in the registers of the distribution of the *ciyze* (*tevzi-i cizye defterleri*).[6] A majority of the *emin* and a *kâtip* originated from the Ottoman military regiments, standing cavalry (*sipahi*). This of course, was true of other tax collection revenues as well.[7] According to the numerous examples from the sixteenth and seventeenth centuries presented in historian Linda Darling's study on Ottoman revenue-raising, Greek Orthodox bishops do not appear to have been collection agents of the *cizye*.

[4] Linda T. Darling, *Revenue-raising and Legitimacy* (Leiden: E. J. Brill, 1996), 82–83. See also M. Kiel, "Remarks on the Administration of the Poll Tax (*Cizye*) in the Ottoman Balkans and Value of Poll Tax Registers (*Cizye Defterleri*) for Demographic Research," *Etudes Balkaniques* 4 (1990): 70–99.

[5] Darling, *Revenue-raising and Legitimacy*, 86.

[6] Darling, *Revenue-raising and Legitimacy*, 162–163.

[7] Darling, *Revenue-raising and Legitimacy*, 169.

Although Darling does not offer an exhaustive study of all the *cizye* collectors' registers, if an anomaly appeared, such as a cleric collecting *cizye*, it would have warranted comment.

If Greek Orthodox bishops were responsible for the collection of the non-Muslim poll tax, one might be able to argue that the bishops were a full extension of a vital tax collection process of the Ottoman state. Thus, one might be able to conclude that the Greek Orthodox hierarchy maintained a high level of communal authority because they were responsible for *cizye* collections from the entire Greek Orthodox non-Muslim community. This is not the case.

Greek Orthodox bishops were, in fact, limited in their authority over the non-Muslims community, both economically and socially. Because the revenue they collected originated from ecclesiastical holdings, the payment to the state was limited to the revenues produced by Church holdings, and through ecclesiastical agents, namely the clergy. While the economic impact of this revenue-raising was significant, it was also limited to the ecclesiastical administration.

Concluding that the Greek Orthodox hierarchy had a much more circumscribed authority allows historians to begin to reconsider the relationship between the bishops and the Greek Orthodox community. One of the important relationships was the relationship between the lay financiers who backed a bishop's fiscal enterprise and the bishops themselves. It should come as no surprise that we observe strong parallels between the competitive activity among the group of wealthy Greek economic elites for an ecclesiastical "*iltizam*," and the competitive activity of other economic elites (Muslim and *zimmi*) for profitable tax farming posts. We assume that the underlying social and economic situation motivating the competition was the same. Clearly, the patriarch did not have administrative control over the wider Greek community because he functioned more as a fiscal administrator of a specific tax revenue source. It is because of this situation that the patriarch could not control the metropolitans and bishops who should have been under his jurisdictional control. In the tax farming system, these individuals would have been sub-contractors, and therefore, could act independently to exploit their own property.[8]

Ottoman Tax Farming

What did Ottoman tax farming look like, and what were its advantages? Tax farming was a very convenient tool for a widespread state whose administrative bureaucracy was neither widespread nor efficient enough to gather revenues on its own. The precedents for this form of fiscal administration appear in the earlier

[8] Darling, *Revenue-raising and Legitimacy*, 131–132. Darling addresses the broader issues of selling *iltizam*, and comments that the obvious problem of control has not been covered in detail. The finance department kept separate registers to keep track of the layer of officials that developed over time. No such complete register appears to be available for the church tax farms, but like other *iltizams*, they do appear in the *Mühimme Defterleri*, 134. Nenad Moačanin, in *Frontiers of Ottoman Studies*, ed. Colin Imber, Keiko Kiyotaki, and Rhoads Murphey (London: I. B.Tauris, 2005), 77–89.

empires of Anatolia and especially in the Byzantine administration that had a fundamental impact on Ottoman fiscal practice. However, because the Ottomans began as a small mobile band of warriors, rather than as a fully developed state bureaucracy, it is helpful to examine the fiscal administration of the Ilkhanid Empire that resembled Ottoman practice, and which to some degree influenced Ottoman practice.[9]

In general, Ottoman fiscal administration suffered from the basic limitations and difficulties that Ilkhanid fiscal administration had faced. Both lacked manpower and the availability of liquid funds. Therefore, tax farming became a well-established means of collecting revenue for both states. A tax farmer would contract with the central or provincial government to farm taxes for a region or a specific concession. In a smooth- running administration, the assessment of taxation was usually established by the central administration but that administation would not have to send tax officials or other bureaucrats to the provinces because the funds collected in the periphery could be used locally for government expenses.[10] Contractors could not legally impose any additional taxes beyond these stipulated in the contract. After submitting the obligatory amount to the central administration, the contractor generally was free from government interference. Often, the tax farmer could vary the exaction according to his local power and influence, but in general, he was limited by local custom. In addition, the contractor could subcontract his district to other contractors. The contractors for the Ilkhanids were local rulers, merchants, or landowners and sometimes bureaucrats temporarily residing in the provinces.[11] Their functions were mainly financial, and they were willing to take the risk and danger as well as the considerable profit attached to such contracts.

The difference between the Ilkhanid and the Ottoman tax regimes was that the Ilkhanids were unable to establish an independent fiscal administration that could adapt to new conditions beyond their central power base, while the Ottomans developed a complex and sophisticated financial bureaucracy and administration.[12] Additionally, "the arbitrary nature of the power of the Mongol leader, molded under the influence of conditions of perpetual warfare in the steppe, remained virtually unchanged, and in the new circumstances of government, it manifested itself in intrigue and corruption ..." "unprecedented" in the pre-Ilkhanid period.[13]

[9] Ann Lambton, "Mongol Fiscal Administration in Persia," *Studia Islamica* 64 (1986): 79–99. Because of the dependence on Ilkhanid financial practices, Persian terminology in the financial administration of the Ottoman Empire was prevalent.

[10] Lambton, "Mongol Fiscal Administration," 97.

[11] Lambton, "Mongol Fiscal Administration," 98.

[12] Linda Darling provides a very good summary of the governmental finance bureacracy (*maliye*), Darling, *Revenue-raising and Legitimacy*, 51–57. This department is usually dated as a department distinct from the sultan's household, sometime during the reign of Bayezid I, 51.

[13] Lambton, "Mongol Fiscal Administration," 99. Lambton comments that greed was perhaps the main motive for accepting a *mukata'a*. Interestingly, she also mentions that some people felt that because Mongol rule was an inevitable fact, it was better to preserve local interests by accepting such contracts than to give up this opportunity for some semblance of self-rule.

As the Ottoman state became more centralized and developed an administrative bureaucracy, its dependence on tax farming also increased. Tax farming can be compatible with more developed bureaucracies, because it provides quick and available cash needed to pay salaries of the bureaucrats themselves as well as the soldiers in the standing army. As the state depended less on the feudal military system, and more on the standing army, even during periods of expansion, the Ottoman state became increasingly bureaucratized. This is particularly true for the sixteenth century when the benefits of cash flow from tax farming became so extensive that it developed into an industry in its own right. The mention of Ottoman tax farming generally conjures up negative images of unsupervised and corrupt officials gaining considerable wealth at the expense of an abused populace. However, increasing evidence of a stronger centralized state control and involvement in the tax farm administration undermines this view.[14] Tax farmers were not immune from government control.[15] The *'amil*, or tax farmer, would settle accounts with the government represented by the person of the local *kadi*.

The Ottomans clearly recognized the advantage of tax farming in dealing with the limited supply of cash money, of silver and gold in circulation in a feudal economy. They may even have prevented potentially dire consequences to the local economies as a result of a more centralized tax collection process. Instead, the state had recourse to a more decentralized method to ensure flexibility while ensuring a quick return of money into the local economy, often to pay for local imperial projects and expenditures.[16] Thus, the government was able to keep the currency in circulation and satisfy local expenditure without straining the fiscal administration with higher costs.[17]

Factors that contributed to cash starvation during the sixteenth century are the costs of a standing army, staging many land and sea campaigns towards the West and the East, the decline in gold bullion and high inflation which undermined the effectiveness and popularity of the *timar* system, as well as an increase in the number of state bureaucrats.[18] The Ottomans displayed many of the characteristics of other early modern states in Europe, developing a large bureaucracy that required regular salaries.

Tax farms were very lucrative operations for those who could afford to purchase them. Financiers from the capital often were able to speculate on the profits and exploit the farms to receive their maximum yield. These financiers often formed consortia in order to raise the high amounts required to purchase the tax farms. These consortia, constituted of Turkish, Greek, and Jewish or Armenian financiers, served to provide surety to purchase the concession rights, as well as to manage the tax district.[19] The individual or group that had purchased a tax farming concession could

[14] Darling, *Revenue-raising and Legitimacy*, 119.

[15] Darling, *Revenue-raising and Legitimacy*, 120.

[16] Inalcik, *Economic and Social History of the Ottoman Empire*, 65.

[17] Inalcik, *Economic and Social History of the Ottoman Empire*, 65.

[18] Also see Halil Sahillioglu, "The Role of International Monetary and Metal Movements in Ottoman Monetary History 1300–1750," in *Precious Metals in the Later Medieval and Early Modern Worlds*, ed. J. F. Richards (Durham, NC: Carolina Academic Press, 1983), 269–304.

[19] Inalcik, *Economic and Social History of the Ottoman Empire*, 66, see also Zachariadou's chapter entitled "Hoi Ischyroi Hypodouloi," (The Powerful Servants) in Elizabeth A. Zachariadou, *Deka*

divide the job locally and sublease the right to collect taxes to local agents who would better be able to exploit the revenues from the subjects. However, as Halil Inalcik eloquently explains, "At the top of the tax-farming hierarchy stood rich bankers in the capital."[20] This system extended to over half of the public revenues, including agrarian revenues and, as we shall see, ecclesiastical revenues, too.[21]

What Were the Responsibilities of the Patriarch as Mültezim?

In the *Mühimme Defterleri* there are many examples of Church officials involved in disputes over tax assessment and collection. The grievances mostly concerned properties and duties of collecting taxes and obligations to submit them to the imperial treasury. The explicit mentioning of the patriarchal tax (*patriklik rüsûmu*) or metropolitan tax (*medropolidlik rüsûmu*) is common, as was the sense that the tax collecting matter was well institutionalized. For the purposes of examining the patriarchal *iltizam*, some of its standard characteristics will be considered. This analytical description allows us to understand the mechanisms and functioning of an Ottoman tax farm and to see how the situation of the Church either blends with this idea, or contrasts with it.[22]

Iltizam: A Mandate to Collect Taxes

Iltizam, a term that literally means "an undertaking," is understood as an imperial tax farm.[23] For an *iltizam*, the sultan mandated a third party to collect revenues derived from non-land tenure-based sources, and then submitted the agreed upon amount to the Imperial Treasury.[24] This third party submitted the revenue or rent (*mukata'a*) on Imperial (*miri*) property to imperial agents in the provinces in order to cover military or public works expenses, or submitted it to the sultan's servants (*kûl*) directly to the Imperial Treasury (*Hazine-i 'Amir*).[25] The *iltizam* was auctioned to a tax farmer (*mültezim*) who made payments according to the contractual agreement. Usually, a cash down payment secured the *iltizam*, and subsequent installments were paid monthly, quarterly or semi-annually. The *mültezim*

Tourkika engrapha gia ten Megale Ekklesia: 1483–1567 (Athens: Ethniko Hidryma Ereunon, Institouto Byzantinon Ereunon, 1996), 63–77, where she discusses some of the wealthy families involved in both tax farms and in the Church. This issue will be revisited in the next chapter where one family and a particular individual will be examined in both of these contexts, that of Michael Kantakouzenos.

20 Inalcik, *Economic and Social History of the Ottoman Empire*, 66.

21 Inalcik, *Economic and Social History of the Ottoman Empire*, 66. Inalcik reiterates that the Ottoman state sold tax farming concessions to exploit complex revenue producing enterprises.

22 Halil Inalcik, "Military and Fiscal Transformation in the Ottoman Empire, 1600–1700," *Archivum Ottomanicum* 6 (1980): 327.

23 Darling, *Revenue-raising and Legitimacy*, 123.

24 Halil Inalcik, "Hawala," *Encyclopedia of Islam*, 2nd ed., III (1971), 283–285.

25 Inalcik, "Hawala. *Encyclopedia of Islam*, 2nd ed., III (1971), 283–285. Mukata'a (lit. something divided) "refers to the division of the state revenue sources into portions to be distributed in return for a mutually agreed upon price." Darling, *Revenue-raising and Legitimacy*, 123.

could only take control of an *iltizam* if he could display appropriate sureties for the tax farms.[26] *Mültezim* is a term that specifically refers to the collection of taxes for the imperial domains rather than the rent (*mukata'a)*, which could refer to other more general revenues.[27] As a condition of his office a hierarch was mandated to collect revenues from ecclesiastical revenues, which included production from ecclesiastical landholdings, as well as fees charged for services such as weddings and baptisms and the income from saints' festivals. The tax farmer was required to submit an amount derived from these to the Imperial Treasury.[28] The ecclesiastical *berât* issued to the hierarch stipulated that the prelate was responsible for collecting either the *patriklik rüsûmu, metropolid rüsûmu* or the *mal-i miri rüsûmu* from the metropolitans, bishops, abbots, priests, and monks.

An *emin* was assigned to each *mültezim* in order to check his accounts. The state always had the ability to interfere with an *iltizam* by annulling a contract if the amount agreed upon was deemed insufficient. In addition, the state also was concerned with providing the *mültezim* with coercive pressure in order to assist him in collecting the revenues.[29] Generally, the *iltizam* could be subdivided into smaller units and sold to secondary *mültezim*s, as was usually the case in the extensive *mukata'a* holdings covering large territories.

Examples from the previous chapter, especially dealing with Patriarch Jeremiah I, as well as other examples not yet discussed, demonstrate the explicit use of the term "*mültezim*" to describe the patriarch and other bishops.[30] In the aforementioned 1483 Vatopedi document, the term "*mültezim*" referred to the patriarch's yearly obligation of 2,000 florins to the Imperial Treasury. As "*mültezim*," Patriarch Symeon collected the amount from the metropolitans, bishops, priests, the monasteries, and their holdings. These individuals were required to pay to the patriarch the amounts they had collected from their own jurisdictions. The patriarch, thus, was required to submit taxes to the Imperial Treasury for the entire Church.

The February 23, 1489 document mentioned above concerns a metropolitan, not a patriarch. There was a copy of the *berât* of appointment that was sent to the military governors and Islamic judges of Rumeli appointing the local metropolitan of Serres as "*mültezim*" in order to collect the *mal-i miri* for Patriarch Dionysios in Istanbul.[31] This example shows the local metropolitan from Siroz collecting the amounts owed by the bishops, priests, abbots, and monks according

[26] Inalcik, "Military and Fiscal Transformation," 328.

[27] Göçek, "Mültezim," *Encyclopedia of Islam*, 2nd ed. VII (1990): 550b. Murat Çizakça, *A Comparative Evolution of Business Partnerships: The Islamic World and Europe, With Specific Reference to the Ottoman Archives* (Leiden: E. J. Brill, 1996), 140–168.

[28] On the *iltizam* for religious foundations see John Robert Barnes, *An Introduction to Religious Foundations in the Ottoman Empire* (Leiden: E. J. Brill, 1987), 67 and note 2. Also see Mehmet Genç's description of the importance of non-Muslims as *mültezim* from his article Mehmet Genç and Osman Oykar, "Osmanlı Maliyesinde Malikâne Sistemi," in *Türkiye Iktisati Semineri* (Ankara: Hacettepe Üniversitesi Yayınları, 1975), 234–235.

[29] Inalcik, "Military and Fiscal Transformation," 328.

[30] Zachariadou, *Deka Tourkika engrapha*, 157–162, and plate 1a.

[31] Georgios Salakides, *Sultansurkunden Des Athos-Klosters Vatopedi Aus Der Zeit Bayezid II. Und Selim I.* (Thessalonike: Institute for Balkan Studies, 1995), No. 7.

to custom. The military governors and *kadis* were to see that no one withheld any amounts and no excuse was given for witholding even a single coin. *Mültezims* collected the *patriklik rüsûmu* in the Morea in 1494 and were harassed by the local Muslims in 1516 until the sultan ordered the harassment to stop.[32] However, tax collecting was at the forefront of Ottoman policy toward the Church.[33]

Berâts to patriarchs and metropolitans similar to this do exist, although not in great number for the early period of Ottoman rule. However, there are enough examples that can help us establish this relationship as standard practice of the Ottoman state. Among the documents from the 1544, Patriarch Jeremiah I (1522–45) was required to hand over in the manner of rent (*mukata'a*) on an annual basis were 4,000 florins (*sikke*) as an "*iltizam*."[34] In this manner, he was to receive the imperial *berât*.[35] The term "*mültezim*" and "*iltizam*," and "*mukata'a*" were explicitly used, and, while not every document concerning patriarchs and metropolitans used these terms, the contractual terms of the agreements demonstrated that their offices were considered by the Ottomans to be tax farms. In fact, one should consider the 1544 series of documents as ample evidence to show that the state, and in particular the Imperial Divan, was deliberate in its policy of supporting the tax collection of Patriarch Jeremiah I. At each point of conflict or resistance to payment, the state came out in favor of the Church, affirmed the rights of the patriarch, and condemned those who resisted submitting their dues.

The patriarch and his representative sent to collect taxes in his place was to be granted the appropriate diploma designating him a collector. The amount of investiture fee (*pişkeş*) was specified, as well as directives concerning the more complicated issue of inheritance taxes on the estates of deceased clergy. Among the sub-collectors, there are both Christians and Muslims agents, showing the remarkable flexibility with which the state and the Church approached the subject of harvesting money from the Christians.

Iltizams were obtained via direct bidding but the office of a bishop in the Orthodox Church was elected through the closed structure of the Holy Synod. The sixteenth-century patriarchal chronicles suggest various patriarchs and bishops obtained their positions through "corrupt" or "scandalous" means which, to authors, meant payment to a powerful state official followed by a legitimate ecclesiastical election. This process of attaining offices is also confirmed in the Ottoman administrative context. Those in authority understood their right to material gain and the potential for compensation of their appointments. Bribery, in the form of investiture gifts, became routine and was not considered a form of "corruption" or "scandal." Accepting bribes for major appointments eventually represented standard Ottoman administrative practice.[36]

[32] Zachariadou, *Deka Tourkika engrapha*, 165–166, and plate 3.

[33] Zachariadou, *Deka Tourkika engrapha*, 167–168, and plate 4.

[34] Başbakanlıl Osmanlı Arşivi (BOA), Ahkâm Defteri 62, f. 500.

[35] The interesting point about this document is that it also is important in establishing the relationship between the Istanbul Patriarchate and the see of Ohrid as well as corraborating the same incident in Immanuel Bekker, ed., *Historia politica et patriarchica Constantinopoleos: Epirotica*, Corpus Scriptorum Historiae Byzantinae (Bonn: Impensis Ed. Weberi, 1849).

[36] Inalcik, *Economic and Social History of the Ottoman Empire*, 74–75.

What is often described in the patriarchal chronicles as the ancient right of election of the religious leader is not how the Ottoman system worked. The Ottomans saw the office of the prelate as a tax farmer, and a *berât* for a hierarchical office could be obtained through a down payment and a promise of subsequent yearly payments. Following this transaction, the individual was then to be elected according to canonical ecclesiastical practice. An individual could even request that the sultan establish a brand new tax farm to exploit an unexploited revenue source. This was precisely the situation on the island of Karpathos on June 30, 1551.[37] A Papa Yanis went to the Divan and proposed that, because there was no bishop for the villages of Koraki, Menetes, and Olympos on the Island of Karpathos, he would be their bishop. He gave to the Imperial Treasury six gold florins and became the bishop in the area and received a formal *berât* in the name of Sultan Süleyman. The *berât* commanded that he go to be elected according to the religious practice of the Church, and then all the priests, monks, and abbots would recognize him. He was to be responsible for the taxes derived from the revenues from all of the churches and properties in his newly created diocese. In this case, Papa Yanis basically created this office by offering to purchase the ecclesiastical tax rights. He paid the Ottomans for the *berât*, thereby gaining authority over Church affairs.

This was an extra-ecclesiastical appointment not resembling Byzantine imperial Church order. It is, however, a practical approach for the Ottomans to exploit a revenue source, and a clever way for an individual clergyman to rise in prominence and wealth.[38] The practice of individuals purchasing bishoprics continued to such an extent that, by the beginning of the seventeenth century, the Ottoman financial administration established a bureau of episcopal rents called the *Piskopos Mukata'a Kalemi* to record the various appointments of bishops and the amounts they were responsible to submit to the Imperial Treasury.[39] Inalcik's study of archival material on millets is based on a document from this series. Inalcik's contribution is very valuable because it describes the administrative jurisdiction and obligations towards the state. In addition, he uses this *defter* as the base for his argument that the *pişkeş* became institutionalized and therefore, was the origin of the patriarchal tax.

In trying to make sense of the *mukata'a kalemi* (the Ottoman bureau that oversaw the tax farm rental concession system) and to help clarify the role and function of the hierarchy in the Ottoman state, Halil Inalcik raised the following question: how similar was the role of the leader of the guild (*kethüda*) to the ecclesiastical hierarchy?[40] In terms of the election process and requirements for

[37] Zachariadou, *Deka Tourkika engrapha*, 179–182, and plates 8a and 8b.

[38] Zachariadou, *Deka Tourkika engrapha*, 179–182, and plates 8a and 8b.

[39] Ismet Binark, Yusuf Ihsan Genç, and Turkey Osmanlı Arşivi Daire Başkanlığı, *Başbakanlık Osmanlı Arşivi Rehberi*, (Ankara: Devlet Arşivleri Genel Müdürlüğü, 1992), 294. Also, Inalcik's article, Halil Inalcik, "Ottoman Archival Materials on Millets," in *Christians and Jews in the Ottoman Empire: The Functioning of a Plural Society*, ed. Benjamin Braude and Lewis Bernard, 437–449.

[40] Inalcik brings this question up in his discussion in Inalcik, "The Status of the Greek Orthodox Patriarchate," *Turcica* 21–23 (1991): 407–436.

leadership, there were, in fact, similarities. The leader of the guild was decided from within the guild itself, which was a continuation of their "ancient right." The name of the nominee (*muhtar*) was submitted to the *kadi* in order to register that this election had indeed taken place. In order for this election and the leadership to have meaning for the guild members, the *kethüda* needed to have coercive power. This, however, could only be accomplished by means of a sultanic *berât* that confirmed the election and leadership role of the individual. Therefore, the guild began a process of sending a report and petition to the Divan, which initiated an investigation and discussion by the pertinent bureau in the central administration. Eventually, a decree was promulgated and finally a diploma was issued affirming the election of the individual.[41] Inalcik argues that a similar situation occurred in the case of the election of autonomous groups in the Ottoman Empire, namely non-Muslim communities led by their religious leaders, which he states, functioned as guilds. In theory each was independent of the state authorities and could elect their own officers. The elected officers, however, had to go as a group and register the act of election in the records of the Islamic court. For more significant cases the nominee had to obtain the sultan's diploma.[42]

To some degree, the same situation existed among the Church hierarchy. From this similarity, one is tempted to conclude that the guild and the non-Muslim communities had the same types of administration, since they were both semi-autonomous bodies. It is true that there was a governing body within the Church that was responsible for electing an individual from among their ranks to become patriarch or bishop for any of the lesser hierarchical positions. In the case of the patriarchal office, the Holy Synod in Constantinople made the decision by election. There are, however, a couple of important differences between the election of the patriarch and the *kethüda*, the first difference lies in how the responsibilities of each were laid out.[43] In the case of the *kethüda*, the election took place, it went to the *kadi* for his seal, and then went to the *ru'us kalemi*, whereupon the seal was examined for authenticity, the records were examined in order to clear the title of the incumbent. When the grand vizier gave his order, then the imperial order and *berât* were issued. In the case of the election of the Greek Orthodox hierarchy, the documentation of investiture or *berât*s granted to the individual hierarchs outlines an entire set of terms of financial responsibility. In the latter case, it is clear that the responsibilities of the hierarchy were to collect and pay ecclesiastical taxes.[44] A *berât* was necessary for the very reason that was mentioned by Inalcik, namely to make sure that coercive control over dependants

[41] Halil Inalcik, "The Appointment Procedure of a Guild Warden (Kethüda)," *Wiener Zeitschrift für die Kunde des Morgenlands* 76, Festscrhift Andreas Tietze (1986), 136–137.

[42] Inalcik, "Appointment Procedure,"138–139. "A *berât* was necessary as a pre-requisite for excercising authority over dependents. The *berât* established and guaranteed the authority of the officer over a group of subjects of the sultan, the sole and supreme authority by whom solemn authorization and installation was therefore necessary."

[43] The results of the procedure are written out on the original petition. Darling, *Revenue-raising and Legitimacy*, 137.

[44] Darling, *Revenue-raising and Legitimacy*, 135–139.

was understood and enforceable. Receiving a *berât* was necessary for the more important positions in the guild.

ACQUIRING AN *ILTIZAM*

The bidder for an *iltizam* often competed with other individuals and small consortiums for the right to own a tax farm. Bidding was subject to dispute, which often was brought back to the Divan for resolution. The aforementioned case described a conflict over who had the right to be a bishop over a certain area. The fundamental question became who owned the property rights of the *iltizam*. In a sense, the practice of bidding for ecclesiastical offices began between the Trebizondine community and Maria (Mara) Branković. The competition between the Patriarchs Symeon and Dionysios I was echoed in cases well below the top patriarchal office, including the case between Karto and Dionis, in 1544. While the ecclesiastical offices were not necessarily revolving doors, the turnover due to competition was rather high.

In the account of Kritovoulos, as well as in the patriarchal chronicles, Sultan Mehmet II is reported to have given generous and costly gifts to the newly installed patriarch.[45] The custom changed quickly from the sultan giving gifts to the patriarchs, to the sultan receiving gifts from the patriarchs. The *Historia Patriarchica* described that the first four patriarchs after the conquest of Constantinople were installed as patriarchs but did not give any gifts to the sultan. During the reign of the fourth, Markos Xylokaraves, Mehmet II conquered Trebizond. The large Trebizondine refugee population came to Constantinople and disrupted life there, and one of the monks who had great influence, Symeon, was in fact the first to give a yearly payment of 1,000 florins (*sikke*) and the *pişkeş* (*peskesion*) to the sultan to receive the patriarchal throne and to depose the former patriarch.[46] The *pişkeş* was increased to 2,000 florins by Symeon's successors. Interestingly, the historian Apostolos Vakalopoulos cites this incident as the first moment that the *pişkeş* was instituted and blames the "corrupt Trebizondine nobles" for having begun this corruption of the ecclesiastical offices. He characterizes the satisfaction of the sultan, upon receiving the gift, as pleasure because of income and also that the "satisfaction from contemplating the adversity of these successors of the Byzantine Empire and the Orthodox hierarchy."[47]

Pişkeş usually was considered a present given from an inferior to a superior. In some instances it also referred to a regular tax or ad hoc tax levied by the ruler. Under Ilkhanid rule, gift giving by the officers to the ruler was common practice. It appears that "the practice of giving gifts to the ruler and his officers

[45] Kritovoulos, *History of Mehmed the Conqueror*, trans. Charles T. Riggs (Princeton: Princeton University Press, 1954), 94.

[46] *Historia Patriarchica*, ed. Bekker, 102

[47] Apostolos Vakalopoulos, *The Greek Nation: 1453–1669*, trans. Ian and Phania Moles (New Brunswick, NJ: Rutgers University Press, 1976), 118.

became, 'institutionalized', such gifts being transformed into taxes or dues."[48] Ann Lambton described the significance of gift giving for medieval Persian society by explaining that in medieval Ilkhanid society there was an absence of impartial justice, and power was personal and at times arbitrary. Lambton argues that as a result,

> protection must be sought on a personal basis. Further, it was generally understood that 'protection' and leadership, whether by a government official or a private individual could not be given or exercised without material support. Hence, the all pervasive nature of the *pishkash*. Almost inevitably it was associated with extortion on the part of those to whom it was given and subjection on the part of the givers and with the spread of bribery throughout society. This cannot but have had a harmful effect on the general tone of society. *Pishkash* has long since lost its meaning of tribute or tax but it survives in the sense of gift or present.[49]

Her basic argument is that gifts are deemed protection money to ensure that the giver has the goodwill of the ruler. One cannot have protection in society, not to mention communal authority, without paying for it. Later, subsequent dynasties such as the Safavids had provincial governors paying the *pişkeş* upon their appointment and then every year at Nevruz."[50] In addition, major officials of the bureaucracy were expected to offer the same present of *pişkeş* to the ruler upon appointment and on special arrangement. The term *pişkeş* covered much ground and described many forms of tributes and taxes. Ultimately, it was a mark of the loyalty and subordination of the giver and an agreement to protect on the part of the ruler.

An example of this type of protection payment can be seen from a much earlier period, as described in a seventh-century west Syrian chronicle: "In the same month (June AD 659) the bishops of the Jacobites, Theodore and Sabukt came to Damascus and held an inquiry into the Faith of the Maronites in the presence of Muawiya. When the Jacobites were defeated, Muawiya ordered them to pay 20,000 denarii and commanded them to be silent. Thus there arose the custom that the Jacobite bishops should pay that sum of gold every year to Muawiya, so that he would not withdraw his protection and let them be persecuted by the members of the (Orthodox) Church."[51] The person called 'patriarch' by the Jacobites fixed the financial burden that all the convents of monks and nuns should contribute each year towards the payment in gold and he did the same with all the adherents of his faith. He bequeathed his estate to Muawiya so that out of fear of that man all the Jacobites would be obedient to him.

[48] Ann Lambton, "Pishkash: Present or Tribute," *Bulletin of the School of Oriental and African Studies* 57 (1994): 147.
[49] Lambton, "Pishkash: Present or Tribute," 158.
[50] A. Lambton, "Pishkash," *Encyclopedia of Islam*, 2nd ed., VIII, 312–313. In one case, the Armenian Catholicos, in 1060/1650 sent his *pişkeş* to Shah Abbas and in return received a grant of splendid robes of honor (*khil'as*). A. Lambton, "Pishkash: Present or Tribute," 150.
[51] Andrew Palmer, Sebastian Brock, and Robert Hoyland, eds., *The Seventh Century in West-Syrian Chronicles*, vol. 15, *Translated Texts for Historians* (Liverpool: Liverpool University Press, 1993), 29–30.

Even with the institutionalization of the *pişkeş*, the ecclesiastical tax farmer differs in two ways from any other tax farmer. First, he was always a cleric. Secondly, according to canon law, a bishop was to be elected by a synod made up of legitimately elected bishops. As described above, Inalcik considered this election process the basis for his argument that the religious leader was similar to a guild warden (*kethüda*) and that the community functioned like the semi-autonomous community. However, as a broader cross-section of documents dealing with the Church suggest, that semi-autonomy was illusory. The Church was governed by the state like any other fiscal institution, which meant state control of purchasing, process, and auditing.

Frequently, the "ancient right of election" of religious leaders was not in effect within the community. In the example discussed above of Papa Yanis, who became bishop of Karpathos by proposing to pay *pişkeş* and an annual sum of six florins, it is clear that the major responsibility of the bishop according to the Ottomans was to supply the Imperial Treasury with tax money. The issue of correct autonomous elections and legitimacy was of secondary importance to them especially with regard to the main transaction taking place, which was to establish the person responsible for the revenue stream. The Porte treated the office as an administrative one and controlled the process through the granting of imperial *berâts*. It is, therefore, clear that the offices of the prelates were closer to tax farms than to *kethüdaliks*, though perhaps on the surface there may be some general similarities.

Further insight into this process comes from the *Tagebüch* of the German traveler Stephan Gerlach that records the events of the early 1570s. Gerlach records the account of John Zygomalas, and his son Theodosios Zygomalas, who were both lay officials working in the patriarchate. Their testimony concerning the collection of taxes is valuable because Theodosios Zygomalas actually worked as a tax collector for the patriarch, while John, his father, was an often frustrated official who constantly complained of his own poverty. As a result, he had an acute awareness of the financial transactions taking place at the time.

Gerlach reported that, indeed, individuals purchased their bishoprics. To his horror, Gerlach noticed that the offices of the Greek clergy were constantly up for bidding. Each individual would give to the overseeing *kadi, sipahi*, or whoever else was in charge several *ducats*. The bidding was also often rigged, with Ottoman officials demanding and often placing their preferred candidates in ecclesiastical positions. According to Gerlach,

> If somebody desires to become bishop in a town, he makes a gift of some *ducats* to the Turk who is in charge there. Then the Turk will order the metropolitan that he should make the other a bishop. The election of the sultan proceeds in the same way. Those who have money will make gifts to the *Bassas* [Pasha] and to Kantakouzenos of several hundred *ducats*, then this or that one will write to the patriarch: "Give this one there the office of metropolitan; then the patriarch has to obey without speaking a word against it."[52]

[52] Stephan Gerlach, *Stephan Gerlachs des Aelteren Tagebuch* (Frankfurt-am-Main: 1674), 52–53.

Whoever wished to become a metropolitan had to be ready to offer to the patriarch 500 or 1000 ducats to be elected. In addition to offering gifts to the local Ottoman *pasha* or, for greater positions, to the appropriate officials in Istanbul, an individual might even be able to go straight to the Ottoman pashas and directly buy the positions and remove others from their posts. Gerlach saw the system as corrupt as the papist system. From his perspective, clerical offices were simply a means for individuals to collect money. It boiled down to the general population having to pay for each and every liturgical service, which was completely the opposite of what a Protestant Reformer like Gerlach considered to be correct.[53]

Who were the men who wished to acquire the episcopal sees? In the 1570s John Zygomalas informed Gerlach of the numerous monks who served the patriarch's court. They would arrive at the patriarchate and serve the patriarch in either administrative or domestic capacities for seven or eight years, without receiving any formal salary except their room and board. Their aim was ultimately to become metropolitans, an office which in the end they needed to purchase from their superiors. In the estimation of Gerlach and Zygomalas, these monks were a constant source of trouble for the patriarch. They would often go to the pasha promising to pay him a certain amount if the pasha would see to it they would be appointed bishop or metropolitan in the place where they desired. In response, the pasha might send a message to the patriarch demanding that the office be given to a certain monk. Other times, he might go to the extremely wealthy and well connected merchant, Michael Kantakouzenos, and offer to pay him as well. Kantakouzenos would then order the patriarch to satisfy the monk's request. Even when disregarding patriarchal protests that he broke ecclesiastical laws forbidding the removal of sitting bishops, Kantakouzenos would marshal his influence with the Ottoman officials, and would essentially force his preferred appointment. Thus, because many of the monks had the goal of acquiring higher offices, they were all the time short of money. This created a very poor atmosphere in the patriarchate, where according to Zygomalas, the servants became "disloyal and cheating and lying."[54]

TERM OF TAX FARM

Most kinds of tax farms (*iltizam*) were farmed out for periods of three years. However, in the Church, a bishop is technically appointed to an office for life. It rarely happened, however, that one individual would remain in office for life. At times there was a rapid succession of hierarchs to the same see, with some individuals being granted, losing, and reacquiring the same hierarchical office multiple times.

Competition to acquire these offices was extremely fierce and created conditions that led to a high turnover rate for the patriarchal office. From 1453 to 1600

[53] Gerlach, *Tagebuch*, 323. [54] Gerlach, *Tagebuch*, 209.

the office of the Greek Orthodox Patriarch of Constantinople changed hands an average of once every 2.3 years. The rapid succession should be seen within the context of the Ottoman tax farm, whose term in general was three years, but because of competition often was much shorter.

The possibility to remain in office over a long period of time did exist. With the right formation of factors, meaning cooperative financial backers, good connections within the state administration, trustworthy metropolitans as subcontractors, and the ability to steer clear of major ecclesiastical dangers, a patriarch could remain in office even until his natural death. Three years was the norm for Ottoman tax farmers until the end of the seventeenth century, when the tenure of Ottoman tax farms increased to life terms. This development later became known as the *malikâne* system, and had its roots in later Ottoman decentralization. It is likely that there is some connection of the *malikâne* to the ecclesiastical tax farmer. Official historiography states that the *malikâne* system, which in essence was a life term tax farm, was established at the end of the seventeenth century and was a strategy for the Ottoman budget to become balanced which succeeded only in times of peace.[55] The *malikâne* system, however, is very similar to the ecclesiastical *iltizams* because in both cases, the terms of the *mültezim* were for life.[56] It remains unclear as to what extent in the development of the *malikâne* system relied upon the experience of the ecclesiastical tax farms. For the hierarchy, of course, there were other stipulations to be elected, such as, one had to be celibate and be ordained to the episcopacy. Nevertheless, the term itself lasted as long as the prelate lived or could keep up the payments.

There is one possibility to explain the direct correlation of a three-year term to the ecclesiastical tax farm. In each instance, the patriarch was granted the right to travel throughout his jurisdiction every three years to collect all of the taxes that might be in arrears. To do so, the patriarch needed a *berât* granting permission to him or to his representative. The three-year tax farm term, therefore, most reasonably corresponds to this continuing function. While this rule is technically true, it is also true that Church officials get *berâts* any time they feel it could help them and it seems desirable to the Ottoman officials, as in the cases when the authority of the patriarchate was challenged.

SURETY FOR AN *ILTIZAM*

A *mültezim* could only take control of an *iltizam* if he could display appropriate surety for the tax farms.[57] The issue of surety, or guaranteed payment to the

[55] Inalcik, "The Appointment Procedure," 239.

[56] Darling, *Revenue-raising and Legitimacy*, 239. On the *malikâne* see Çizakça, *A Comparative Evolution of Business Partnerships*, 159–178.; Barnes, *An Introduction to Religious Foundations in the Ottoman Empire*, 67–68.

[57] Inalcik, "Military and Fiscal Transformation," 328. Inalcik comments that "Thus, no matter how rich the individual *mültezim*, the security stipulations created great interdependence among the *ayan*, leading to the emergence of a closely-knit group of very wealthy people with growing

Ottoman state, for the patriarchal tax farm is, perhaps, one of the most interesting. Who provided surety for such large financial obligations? It is clear that individual hierarchs depended on the wealthy economic Greek elite who were themselves involved in many other kinds of tax farms in Anatolia and the Balkans.

The details surrounding the case of the aforementioned Patriarch Raphael the Serb (1475–76) are quite intriguing regarding surety. The *Historia Patriarchica* explains that

> as he received the patriarchal throne, where he had promised to pay 2,000 florins as *haratzion*, the end of the year had come and he was to hand it over. And the pashas called him to the divan and requested from him the *haratzion*, just as he had promised to give it. And he neither had the *haratzion* nor did he have anybody to aid him, neither from among the clerics, nor from the *archons* nor from the people. And the pashas, seeing that he had fooled them, put him into jail. And thus, a few days passed and he asked the pashas to grant him a request, to be released from jail, and to wander gathering alms from Christians, so as to be released from his debt to the throne. And they commanded this, and instead of vestments, (*epitrahilion* and *omophorion*), they placed on him heavy iron chains, and they also gave him a Turk (to accompany him). And the latter led and protected him. And wherever he went with his chains, begging, whatever he gathered, he ate and drank it, and the severely strained man died badly.

When Patriarch Raphael turned to the Greek community of Istanbul for help, he found that there was no one who would provide him with the amount that he owed to cover his debt. Patriarch Raphael could not get local support in Istanbul, because he was reviled. This was, perhaps, due to his ethnicity and his inability to speak Greek. The *Historia Patriarchica* describes him as having proclaimed that he hated "diphthongs and triphthongs." He was also perceived as a drunkard, having been reported as showing up to Church at the Good Friday service drunk, unsteady, and unable to conduct the services properly.[58] Because he could not provide the appropriate surety, he paid the price that other unsuccessful tax farmers paid by going to jail. Patriarch Raphael was released, however, and forced to spend the remainder of his life in chains begging for alms from Christians to pay back his debt.

In another important example, the Kantakouzenos family (described at greater length in the following chapter) made their fortune from the salt works concession in Ahyolu (Anchialos), shipbuilding and the luxury fur trade with Russia. This family was very involved in patriarchal politics, as well. The infamous Michael Kantakouzenos, also known as *Şeytanoğlu* (the devil's son), engineered the elevation and deposition of two patriarchs. His connection to the Grand Vizier Mehmet Sokullu Pasha was such that each candidate needed the Grand Vizier's approval before being allowed to become patriarch. Each successful candidate had to pay a certain amount to Kantakouzenos for his support and benefaction. He was, in a

influence on local and state affairs." 328. The emergence of the *archons* depends very much on this dynamic.

[58] *Historia Patriarchica*, ed. Bekker, 114–115.

sense, brokering the patriarchal appointments. In the case of Patriarch Metrophanes III (1565–72, 1579–80), he was repaying 2,000 florins a year to Kantakouzenos in addition to what he had already paid to the Imperial Treasury. Kantakouzenos, of course, handed much of this over to Mehmet Pasha. An Ottoman document describes the amount of 16,000 that was to be paid by Patriarch Metrophanes to Kantakouzenos over eight years.[59] Even from these examples one can question who had control over the hierarchy, the ecclesiastical personalities who held the offices, or the wealthy financiers who backed them. Prominent among the wealthy financiers were some Byzantine families who were able to make adjustments under Ottoman administration and return to increase their wealth, power, and prominence. Clearly, they were the ones who helped the hierarchs secure or lose their positions.[60]

ILTIZAM REVENUE OF THE IMPERIAL TREASURY

Iltizam specifically refers to the collection of taxes for the imperial domains rather than the *mukata'a*, which refers to any other kind of rent.[61] *Iltizam* appears in the Ottoman documents to describe the situation of tax collecting by a patriarch who submitted that which he gathered directly to the Imperial Treasury.

The issue of ecclesiastical taxes boils down to the question of who has ownership of the ecclesiastical land and properties, and in what system they should be taxed. Treating Church property as imperial (*miri*) property meant that the revenue derived from it would go directly to the state. The *iltizam* structure was perhaps the more convenient and practical than the *timar* to direct Church revenue from vineyards, orchards, and cultivated fields to the state as patriarchal tax (*patriklik rüsûmu.*) However, payment to the state was not in kind but in cash. The cash lump sum, termed *mâktu'*, covered the revenues from the productive use of state owned land. Each low level prelate was obligated to pay a small investiture fee or *berât* tax and then an annual assessment of *mâktu'*. To understand the structure of this taxation, one must consider that "the sultan was not supposed to give *mâktu'* directly to the Imperial Treasury, but to the agency of the patriarch, who paid for the whole patriarchate."[62] The widely dispersed holdings of the Church made payment in kind very impractical for the Church and for the Imperial Treasury. Payment as a cash lump sum was the most practical and offered the best terms to the Church. As the sultan ultimately owned the land,

59 Başbakanlıl Osmanlı Arşivi, *Mühimme Defterleri* (MD), 28: 154.

60 Zachariadou, *Deka Tourkika engrapha*, 68–70. For these families investing in tax farms see below Chapter 6 on the Kantakouzenos family in terms of lineage, wealth, and involvement both in the state and with the Church.

61 F. Müge Göçek, "Mültezim," *Encyclopedia of Islam*, 2nd ed., VII (1990), 550b.

62 Dušanka Bojanić, "Sultansk Povelje Iz Manastira Hilandara (Sultanic Acts from the Hilandara Monastery)," *Hilandarski Zbornik* 9 (1991), 171.

hierarchs had to pay for the privilege of land use, which took the form of a classic tax farm.[63]

The numerous Ottoman documents concerning ecclesiastical matters all appear to center around the collection of taxes. It was extremely important to possess the necessary document or *berât* of appointment that gave the patriarch the permission to collect taxes. There is tremendous significance in the fact that the patriarch constantly went to the Imperial Divan to secure these documents and confirmation of rights. The documents themselves stated not only that they were collecting imperial taxes but also that they were to be submitted to the Imperial Treasury. Besides using the term *mültezim*, the documents also describe the collection of the imperial tax (*mal-i miri rüsûmu*) that was to be surrendered to the Imperial Treasury (*hızane-i amireye teslim eylemek içün*).[64]

To pay for the whole patriarchate, the patriarch needed to collect the full sum from those in his own jurisdiction. Gerlach observed that during one such time, the younger Zygomalas, Theodosios, went together with the patriarch to Macedonia and the Morea to visit the Greek churches and monasteries in order to collect from the ecclesiastical officials the yearly tribute of over 4,000 *ducats*, which he had to pay to the Turkish sultan. He needed to collect this money by himself, or through his representative (*vekil*) yearly from the Greek Churches, as well as funds for his and his staff's maintenance.[65]

The patriarch and his officials were all very much aware of their obligations to the Imperial Treasury. In a patriarchal letter dated September 1578, Jeremiah II granted authority to Theodosios Zygomalas, the *Protonotarios* of the patriarchate, and to a priest named Savvatianos, who was the Keeper of the Laws (*Nomophylaka*), to travel through the regions of the Aegean islands and western Anatolia in order to collect ecclesiastical taxes. It is supposed that the tax collectors would not only carry the document prepared by the patriarch written in Greek, but would also carry a document prepared by the Imperial Divan similar to the ones seen in the 1544 series, granting the tax collecting rights to a representative (*vekil*) of the patriarch. The present 1578 document of Jeremiah II explains to the metropolitans, abbots, priests, and monks, as well as to the "noble *archons*" that in order to ease the constant burden of "immeasurable expenses," of the patriarchate to preserve the "Church of God," the patriarch feels pressured, not a little, most recently, to demand the *imperial haraç*. And demanding this, in addition, the interest and the urgent and required gifts. ..." The two individuals were to be considered as "universal exarchs," who are,

> obliged and have every permission to gather and receive the imperial *haraç,* and all other fees due to us according to our patriarchal register given to them in the 4th and 5th indiction, the tembakia, that is, all the obligations and all the other fees due us for a long time ... The hierarchs are obediently and without fail, to yield our *haraç* (pl.) to them, and exhibit to them every hospitality, assisting them and in every way helping and cooperating in the patriarchal appeal. The priests and the laity obey

[63] Bojanić, "Sultansk Povelje Iz Manastira Hilandara, 171.
[64] Ahkâm Defteri 62, f. 396; f. 503; f. 553; f. 665.
[65] Gerlach, *Tagebuch*, 33–34.

gladly and eagerly to that which we wrote to you in order that they may completely enjoy the reward from God. The honor and reception and obedience to them passes on to my humble person, likewise, to the contrary.[66]

The problematic subject of ecclesiastical taxes still raises many questions, including the use of the term *haraç* that is placed upon the Church to exploit revenues coming from the large landholdings.[67] While the term itself hearkens back to early Islamic times, even, some historians argue that it is connected etymologically to the Greek terminology, being derived from the Greek *choregia* via the Syriac with the root, *kh. r. dj* attached by the Arabs. It tends to be used as a word for tax in general, usually describing a land-based tax levied on non-Muslims, though Cahen admits there is much confusion concerning the term in the legal and technical literature in the Islamic world.[68]

The term is sometimes used interchangeably at times with the non-Muslim head tax (*ciyze*), though the Greek sources sometimes confuse the situation as well. While the meaning of the term haraç indicates primarily the tax on land, it was used at different times to indicate *cizye*.[69] As the *Historia Patriarchica* shows, however, that the patriarch is collecting an "imperial *haraç*." In other words, he is obliged to collect a sum for the Imperial Treasury that includes fees on metropolitans and the clergy and laity of the region.

The bishops had income partly from the estates that border on the churches such as wine plantations and fields, partly from alms, and taxes from their churches and communities.[70] Others scholars say that this tax is based on the Byzantine model of the *kanonikon*, a tax paid by local clergy and laity to the local bishop which the Church had previously been allowed to collect.[71] The principle behind the *kanonikon* was that it represented the gathering of customary gifts offered after marriages and baptisms, and became regulated by imperial and patriarchal legislation by the twelfth century.[72] This payment to the Byzantine imperial throne became a form of tax gathered from the bishop's pastoral work to the laity and from fees from the ordination of priests. However, the *kanonikon* tax was not grounded in canon law and was subject to uneven and confused enforcement. At times, imperial chrysobuls clearly laid out the rates to be paid, and, at other times it was hardly noticed by villages or families. As a result of the ineffectiveness of this tax, the bishop was often poverty stricken, and was forced

[66] Emile Legrand, *Notice Biographique sur Jean et Théodose Zygomalas*, vol. 2, *Recueil de Textes et de Traductions* (Paris: 1889), 185.

[67] Zachariadou, *Deka Tourkika Engrapha*, 100–101. *Historia Patriarchica* (C.S.H.B. edition) uses "*haratzion*" (*haraç*).

[68] N. Oikonomides, "Le Haradj Dans L'empire Byzantine Du XVe Siecle," in *Actes Du Premier Congrès International Des Études Balkaniques Et Sudest Europeénes*, 1966, 684. Claude Cahen, "Kharadj," *Encyclopedia of Islam* 2nd ed., IV (1997), 1053–1055.

[69] Zachariadou, *Deka Tourkika engrapha*, 79.

[70] Gerlach, *Tagebuch*, 60.

[71] Scheel in his article on 17th century documents on the Church holds this perspective. H. Scheel, *Die Staatsrechtliche Stellung der Ökumenischen Kirchenfürsten in der alten Türkei* (Berlin: Berlag der Akademie der Wissenschaften, 1943). See also J. M. Hussey and Andrew Louth, *The Orthodox Church in the Byzantine Empire* (Oxford: Oxford University Press, 2010), 333.

[72] Hussey and Louth, *The Orthodox Church in the Byzantine Empire*, 333.

to consider other opportunities to finance his sustenance and to maintain his episcopal office.[73]

Another speculation about the ecclesiastical tax is that it is the institutionalization of the *pişkeş*, the investiture gift to the sultan for the office. Taxes were, therefore developed so that hierarchs could afford to pay *pişkeş* to the sultan. This amount then became a yearly obligation.[74]

Gerlach records the comments of John Zygomalas that describe in detail the method of collecting taxes used by the local Ottoman officials, but also mentions that, after the Christian tribute had been paid to the Ottomans, then the patriarch's taxes would also be collected. This is a very telling piece of information, as it describes the patriarchal tax as something collected over and above the other taxes collected by the state. The state official, whether it was a *sipahi*, a *kadi*, or a *çavuş* would visit each village with the register containing lists of all people divided into categories of rich, moderate, and poor. The rich person was required to give 3–5 ducats, while the moderately rich person gave 80–100 *aspers*, and the poor person gave 30–40 *aspers*. If an individual could not give cash for this amount, then they would give a material item. It was after this collection that the patriarch's collection took place.[75] Zygomalas reveals that each metropolitan and bishop was to collect from all houses, according to their ability, 20–30 *aspers*. This they either did in person, or they contracted with individual collectors, to whom they might give a fee of 10–12 ducats for collecting the taxes of a region, depending on its wealth.[76]

Halil Inalcik discussed the absorption of the institution of the Church into the administration of the Ottoman state. Depending to a great extent on the documents provided by Josef Kabrda, Inalcik described the fiscal relationships of the patriarch with the Porte. Among the main issues is the payment of *pişkeş* as a yearly amount, which is termed *patriklik rüsûmu*. Inalcik conjectured that this was simply the conservative nature of Ottoman taxation practice institutionalizing the *pişkeş*. Yet how this occurs he was unable to explain.

The institutionalization of the *pişkeş* in conjunction with the Church began earlier than the first extant documentary account of 1483. However, the terms for acquiring an ecclesiastical tax farm were clearly laid out for historians for the first time in this late fifteenth century document. The same formulas were followed in

[73] Michael Angold, *Church and Society in Byzantium under the Comneni, 1081–1126* (Cambridge: Cambridge University Press, 1995), 61–61. See also, Josef Kabrda, *Le système fiscal de l'Église orthodoxe dans l'Empire ottoman d'après les documents turcs*, 1st ed. (Brno: Universita J. E. Purkyné, 1969), 67.

[74] Inalcik stresses the importance of the *pişkeş* because in his documents which are of a later period, he sees the investiture fee listed. Interestingly, Konortas uses these fees to make an assessment and analysis of the fiscal health and crisis of the Church in the late sixteenth century. P. Konortas, "Les Contributions Ecclésiastiques: Patriarchikè Zèteia' et 'Basilikon Charatzion" Contribution À l'Histoire Économique Du Patriarcat Oecuménique Aux XVe et XVIe Siècles," in *Actes Du IIe Colloque International d'Histoire: Économies Méditerranéenes Équilibres et Intercommunications XIIIe-XIXe Siecles*, vol. III (Athens: Center de Recherches Néohelléniques de la Fondation Nationale de la Rechereche Scientifique, 1986), 217–255.

[75] Gerlach, *Tagebuch*, 396.

[76] Gerlach, *Tagebuch*, 393.

subsequent documents concerning the patriarchate. Because this is such an early document, it seems highly unlikely that the *pişkeş* could have been institutionalized into a tax so quickly after it was supposed to be established. Rather, there was either an earlier Byzantine tax that was absorbed and later became this *patriklik rüsûmu* or the Ottomans realized the fiscal opportunity and simply institutionalized it.[77]

The *Historia Patriarchica* described the yearly tax that was paid by the patriarch to the Porte as *haratzion* or *haraç*.[78] The chronicle mentioned *haratzion* for the first time in the short vita of the Patriarch Raphael. Zachariadou concludes that the *haratzion* was not a tax that was initially issued by the sultan, but suggests that its origin lies in those individuals surrounding the patriarch who wished to see their candidate enthroned as patriarch.

In spite of its origins and the confusion of its meaning, both for Ottomans and for the Greek chronicles, the term *haraç* was by the sixteenth century understood to be a patriarchal tax obligation to the state.[79] This is significant because the tax was described as being paid at Easter (or around the time of St. George Day, right after Easter) at the time when the *haraç* typically was paid.[80]

The fact that *haraç* is a land tax explains why vineyards, orchards, and fields were mentioned in these types of documents dealing with collecting the *patriklik rüsûmu*. The sum submitted (*mâktu'*) was collected to cover the revenues from the usufruct on the state's property. To help us understand the structure of the taxation, an explanation by historian Dušanka Bojanić clarifies some of these issues when analyzing a similar *berât* given to Andrija, Metropolitan of Pançevo, issued in Istanbul on April 3, 1582.

Bojanić writes,

> The sultan was not supposed to give *mâktu'* or *kesim* directly to the Imperial Treasury, but to the agency of the patriarch, who paid *mâktu'* or *kesim* for the whole patriarchate. Whoever possessed the landed property with proper registration (*tapu*) had to pay the State or the owner of the land (*Sâhib-i erz*), who was entitled by the state to the *Sharia* tithes (*öşür*) in kind, extracting from the raw produce of the property. Only by the ruler's special privilege could other arrangements be made.

Perhaps because the Ottoman state was eager for payment in cash, they required the tax obligations to be paid in *mâktu'*. Since these were purely cash transactions, we can conclude with Bojanić that "a pure tax-farming relationship emerged between the prelates as land-possessors and the state as owner with eminent

77 Zachariadou, *Deka Tourkika engrapha*, 82–88.

78 *Historia Patriarchica*, ed. Bekker, 114.

79 Apostolos Vakalopoulos, *The Greek Nation: 1453–1669*, trans. Ian and Phania Moles (New Brunswick, NJ: Rutgers University Press, 1976), 118. In her chapter on the *haratzi*, Zachariadou discusses the complexity of the taxation, while she cites instances where this term was in fact used. Zachariadou, *Deka Tourkika engrapha*, 79–89. On the institutionalization see 101, and note 11; Konortas, "Les Contributions Ecclésiastiques: Patriarchikè Zèteia" et "Basilikon Charatzion," 235–243.

80 See Zachariadou, *Deka Tourkika engrapha*, 85 and note 25. She discusses the significance of the feast of St. George in April as the time to collect the *haraç*.

dominion."[81] The widely dispersed holdings of the Church made payment in kind impossible, which also made cash the preferred payment.

At the request of Stephen Gerlach, who wished to accompany Theodosios Zygomalas on his collection journeys but was denied for fear of raising suspicions with the authorities, Theodosios Zygomalas wrote to Gerlach to describe the basic details of the journey and a listing of the households, the number of bishops and priests, and the size of the communities. This valuable list of information only covers the Aegean islands and parts of Rumeli. Table 4.1 summarizes his information, giving a listing for the year 1578 of approximate Greek Orthodox households in each of the regions. During this trip, Zygomalas estimated that there were approximately 106,450 households. If each of these households gave as taxes to the patriarchal delegation an average of 25 *aspers* each, this would mean Zygomalas had collected 2,661,250 *akçe* or 45,106 ducats (1 ducat/59 *akçe* from 1560–74). This amount is approximately equal to half of the tribute paid to the Ottoman Treasury by Wallachia (104,237), and approximately equal to the tribute of Moldavia (50,000).[82] This did not account for the whole of the amount, either, as Anatolia was not represented in its entirety.

In addition to tax on land production, there were a variety of other taxes for which the Church hierarchy was responsible. These developed out of the everyday life of the Church and were fees that were assessed on the services the clergy provided. Therefore, fees were paid to the cleric for the services of marriage and baptism, for example. From this amount, the local priest would be responsible for handing over a percentage to the patriarchal tax collector. Gerlach's observations are also helpful in understanding how ecclesiastical finances worked. First, however, he commented that, "All Greek clergy are trained to get money. There are different ways to fish for it." He then describes how when a priest hears a confession, the layperson pays the priest "10, 20, or 30 *aspers,* a *thaler,* or a *ducat*" in return for forgiveness of his or her sins. When laypersons wish to order a special liturgy to be said for themselves, they send the priest candles, bread, wine, and also money, so that the priest will remember them in the liturgy by name. Another source of income for the priest, mostly in Istanbul, is when an individual becomes ill and is in danger of dying, according to Gerlach he gives the priest 300–500 ducats to hold as a down payment on his good health. If the person dies, then the priest says liturgies for him for forty days, keeping much of the money as payment, and sends what remains to the family. Zygomalas had informed Gerlach that a couple of monks that he knew at a church of St. George earned 200 ducats every year by hearing confessions, special mass readings, funerals, baptisms, weddings, confirmations, etc.[83]

[81] Dušanka Bojanič "Sultansk Povelje Iz Manastira Hilandara (Sultanic Acts from the Hilandara Monastery)," *Hilandarski Zbornik* 9 (1991).

[82] Inalcik, *Economic and Social History of the Ottoman Empire*, 67. Based on the study by M. Maxim, Recherches sur les circonstances de la majoration du Kharadj de la Moldavie entre les anneés 1538–1574, in *Association Internationale d'Etudes du Sud-Est Européen*, Bulletin XII (2), 233–261.

[83] Gerlach, *Tagebuch*, 477.

Table 4.1. Estimated Number of Households and Clergy in Patriarchal Jurisdiction

Place	Homes	Number of Priests
Halki	100	1
Gelibolu	1,000	10
Sestus and Abydos	200	2/ previously only 1
Tenedos	200+	4
Mitylene	6,000	100, 2 metropolitans
Chios	300, 1 metropolitan	
Andros	1,000	50 priests, 1 bishop
Tenos	1,000	~50 priests, 1 bishop
Leros, Kalymnos	~1,000	~50 priests, 1 bishop
	~1,000	~50 priests, 1 bishop
Karpathos, Phournai, Patmos, Karia, Samos	4,000	100
Rhodes	3,000	100
Imbros	500	30, 1 metropolitan
Lemnos		80, 1 metropolitan
St. Eustratios, Tzia +5	"some"	"some"
Skiathos, Skopelos, Skyrou	2,000	50–60
Salamis and islets	"some"	"some"
Athos	24 monasteries	
Cassandra	2,000	60, 1 bishop
Thessalonike	20,000	600 bishops and priests
Thebes	8,000	100
Euripos	10,000	200
Athens		160 bishops and priests
Corinth	7,000	100 bishops and priests
Nauplion	4,000	150
Monembasia	8,000	400 bishops and priests
Palaion Patron	7,000	300 bishops and priests
Lacedemonia	6,000	200 bishops and priests
Christianoupolis	10,000+	300
Ephesus	0 (disaster)	
Province	1000	63
Thyra		4
New Phokaia		10
Magnesia		3
Tamasalikion		2
St. Constantine		4
other villages combined		~40
Kesareia	1,000	30, 1 bishop
Herakleia	400–500	10
Approximate Total	106,450	3,715, 18 bishops

(The mark "~" signifies approximate estimate.)
Source: Theodosios Zygomalas' Letter to Stephen Gerlach, 1578. Emile Legrand, *Notice Biographique sur Jean et Théodose Zygomalas*, 187–196.

Fig. 4.1. The daily dress of the Patriarch of Constantinople and his court. (Source: Codex Vindobonensis 8626, Vienna: Österreichische Nationalbibliothek, fol. 152)

The amounts collected by the numerous services would go to the bishop or metropolitan and eventually would be included in the amount submitted to the sultan as *mal-i miri rüsûmu*. Other payments came from the profits of the village feast (*panayir resmi*) or from money collected at the distribution of holy water (*ayazma resmi*) and beeswax candles and other revenue producing services.[84] Each of these incomes was considered in the amount collected for the *patriklik rüsûmu* and *metropolidlik rüsûmu* and was collected from local parishes in addition to the *mâktu'* payments.[85]

The duties of the patriarch and the ecclesiastical hierarchy also included judicial functions. In general, the ecclesiastical juridical system was supposed to deal with issues of family and religious practice, which were under direct supervision

[84] See Kabrda for a more detailed discussion of these taxes: Kabrda, *Le Système Fiscal de l'église Orthodoxe dans l'empire Ottoman (d'Aprés les documents turcs).*
[85] Gerlach, *Tagebuch*, 477. MD 36, 350.

Fig. 4.2. The daily dress of Greek Orthodox priests. (Source: Codex Vindobonensis 8626, Vienna: Österreichische Nationalbibliothek, fol. 153)

of the Church. For instance, marriage and inheritance were to be dealt with by the patriarch and the hierarchs, except in cases where those deciding the cases are involved, and then it would go before the *kadi*.[86] The state, however, did not always grant the Church autonomy even in administering this area of communal life, especially with regard to issues of inheritance. In *berâts* of investiture, there are comments about the inheritance of clergy who died without a will and possessed wealth and property worth over and under 5,000 florins. The state articulated in what measure this was to be collected.[87] Perhaps it is for this reason that, among the sixteenth-century documents that survive in the Codex A' of the archive of the Ecumenical Patriarchate, there are numerous examples of individual hierarchs

[86] Zachariadou, *Deka Tourkika engrapha*, 93; For a developed discussion of marriage and family matters see N. Pantazopoulos, *Church and Law in the Balkan Peninsula during the Ottoman Rule* (Thessalonike: Institute for Balkan Studies, 1967).
[87] Ahkâm 62, 503.

bequeathing to the patriarchate valuable religious vessels made of precious metals and textiles used in religious services as well as cash and homes.[88]

It was the duty of the patriarch during his journeys to collect taxes throughout his jurisdiction, to visit the churches, talk to the people, and judge their disputes.[89] Jeremiah II, in his letter granting authority of representation to Theodosios Zygomalas and the priest Savvatianos, exhorted the people to

> bring forward, as if to our own person, the ecclesiastical crises and issues to be considered impartially and correctly and to be placed aright ... whomever they discipline, we hold to be disciplined. Those whom they excommunicate, we hold them as excommunicated. Those whom for good reason they forgive, and when they return and repent, are forgiven by God the Ruler of All.[90]

INVIOLABILITY OF *ILTIZAM*

The state could interfere with an *iltizam* by annulling a contract if the amount agreed upon was deemed insufficient. This aspect aptly explains the growing turnover rate in the office of patriarch. An individual wishing to become patriarch or metropolitan simply needed to offer a higher bid and better terms to the Porte in order to receive a *berât* of appointment. The Archbishop of Ohrid, Prohor, had appeared before the Divan to promise 100 extra florins for the right to govern this region. When Jeremiah I heard this, he himself went before the Divan. He was forced to pay 4,100 florins (an increase of 100 florins) to match the bid from Archbishop Prohor who purchased the right to this jurisdiction only a month earlier. Clearly, for the sake of an increase in cash, someone in the administration had an interest in not prohibiting this competition.

Not only did the state intervene to protect the rights of the tax farmer, but it also intervened on behalf of those who were taxed. For instance, on December 19, 1559, a group of non-Muslims (*zimmi)* from Edirne came to the Porte to present a petition to complain about the activities of the Metropolitan of Edirne. The nature of the abuse is unclear, but the state felt compelled to investigate the complaint before taking more action.[91] As there are abundant complaints about taxation in the *Mühimme Defterleri,* it is likely this is the case. The state also was concerned with preserving the rights of the *mültezim* against claims by former tax farmers. Only from this perspective can we understand the following *Mühimme* decision of May 23, 1573. The state had a vested interest in making sure the former patriarch did not undermine the legitimate patriarch.

[88] Archives of the Ecumenical Patriachate of Constantinople, *Codex A'*, Istanbul. See also, Mache Paize-Apostolopoulou, *Aphieromata kai dorees ton 16o ai. ste M. Ekklesia: thesmikes opseis tes euseveias*, (Athena: Ethniko Hidryma Ereunon, 2002).

[89] Gerlach, *Tagebuch*, 393.

[90] Legrand, *Notice Biographique sur Jean et Théodose Zygomalas*, 185.

[91] MD 3: 627.

The major conflict in the 1570s between competing patriarchs was between the Patriarch Jeremiah II and the former Patriarch Metrophanes III.[92] Patriarch Metrophanes III had been deposed and was supposed to have been banished to Mt. Athos but was seen by agents of the Patriarch Jeremiah II in Üsküdar. Patriarch Jeremiah II petitioned the sultan and sought assistance from the state by asking that the state intervene to help him protect his position. As a result, the Divan decreed that Metrophanes should be sent to Mt. Athos and issued two copies, one to the *kadi* of Üsküdar and the other to the *kadi* of Selanik and Sidrekapısı. Not only was Patriarch Jeremiah concerned about the presence of Metrophanes, but the state also was concerned with maintaining Jeremiah in his position as patriarch and *mültezim*.[93]

Gerlach described another instance of a conflict between two bishops in the form of competition for an office. He describes a counteroffer that was, however, unsuccessful only due to the preventative efforts and counter-payment of the patriarchate. He says,

> Just today, the patriarch and the suitable officials of the patriarchate conducted in my presence the election of a Metropolitan of Mytilene. For many inhabitants of that island have come here and want ... a pious man to be their metropolitan. As an opponent, a bad man has promised 500 *ducats* to a Turk at the sultan's Divan, if he would help him get the position. Since, however, he had not sought the office first from the patriarch, as he should have, but rather tried to buy it from the Turk, also otherwise, was a disagreeable person and the people refused to accept him, the patriarch denied him the consecration. Because, however, the Turks use their powers to carry out such matters, he sent 100 *thalers* to the Turk, and filled his mouth and hands so that he did not assist this bad man. Such things happen often all over Greece ... The above-mentioned 100 *thalers*, however, which the patriarch sent to the Turk, have to be paid back to the patriarch by the candidate whom he and the people had wanted and who was put into office.[94]

SUBDIVISION OF *ILTIZAM*

The *iltizam* could be subdivided into smaller units and sold to secondary *mültezims*. Because the taxes for the Church were paid in cash and in a preferred lump sum, *mâktu'*, as opposed to being paid in kind, there was opportunity for the local prelate as well as for the patriarch to profit from the collection.[95] In a sense the patriarch had the metropolitans as agents upon whom he relied to collect the taxes and they often found it in their own interest to disregard the established hierarchical structure.

[92] This conflict will be expanded in the chapter on the Kantakouzenos family.

[93] MD 22: 20; MD 22: 21.

[94] Gerlach, *Tagebuch*, 502–503.

[95] Darling, *Revenue-raising and Legitimacy*, 104, n. 62, and 105. The work of Venzke on the Sancak of Aleppo also contains an interesting discussion concerning the *mâktu'* assessment; see Margaret Leigh Venzke, "The Sixteenth-Century Ottoman Sanjaq of Aleppo: A Study of Provincial

This was also the case in the extensive *mukata'a* holdings covering large territories. As the structure of the Church was spread out over a wide geographic expanse, the sultans were considered to be subcontractors of the patriarchal *iltizam*, while at the same time being *mültezim* in their own right. Each prelate was responsible for collecting the ecclesiastical taxes of a local area and was issued a *berât* independently of the patriarch's intervention stipulating the amount of the *pişkeş* and the yearly amount to be submitted to the imperial treasury.

In the Ottoman conception, the Church constituted one huge *iltizam*. The ecclesiastical organization fitted naturally into the administrative organization of a tax farm because the main *mültezim* was the patriarch, and the secondary *mültezim*, the local hierarchs. An example of a *berât* subdividing the patriarchal *iltizam* was sent to the *sancakbeys* and *kadis* of Rumeli announcing the appointment of the local metropolitan of Siroz as *mültezim* in order to collect the *mal-i miri* for Patriarch Dionysios in Istanbul. However, it was not only ecclesiastical figures or Christian lay people who collected the ecclesiastical taxes. Muslim agents also collected these taxes and submitted them to the prelates. For example, in 1483 an *ulufeci* named Ahmet recorded a receipt for the 27 florins collected from the Metropolitan of Thessalonike to be submitted to the patriarch.[96] In another example from 1544, a janissary named Yusef, and an imperial guard (*solak*) named Abdelkerim collected ecclesiastical taxes on behalf of the archbishop of Ohrid.[97]

After the local *mültezim* or ecclesiastical officials had collected the taxes it was necessary to submit them to the patriarch. On occasion, as we shall see, the patriarch would collect the money in person. Often, however, he would send a *vekil*, or representative, in his stead to collect the taxes, and bring them back to Istanbul. He also had to rely on local individuals who knew the terrain and the people. For example, when Theodosios Zygomalas was collecting from the island of Lemnos, he knew that there were nearly seventy villages and a large town on the island. After collecting the amounts due, Zygomalas and the other tax collectors received donations for the patriarch, and also took 10–12 ducats for their own efforts. The local metropolitan also took his share, as did the other servants of the patriarchate including the Great Logothetis, and the Great Chartophylax, each skimming an appropriate amount for their own share of the work.[98]

Taxation" (Ph.D., Columbia University, 1981), 216–218. Essentially, this is a favorable arrangement for both the collector and the payer. For the collector, it is a quick and easy method to gather taxes and can easily be subdivided to the various individuals who will take a cut. For the payer it is advantageous because he is not responsible for packing payment in kind onto carts and losing time transporting them. P. Konortas also makes an educated guess concerning the relationship as a tax farm. In a roundtable discussion, he states that he believes this to be the way things work, and that there would reasonably be profit attached to the responsibility of tax farmer. He does not make definitive remarks towards this position, however. See "Discussion" in *Actes du IIe Colloque International d'Histoire: Économies Méditerranéenes Équilibres et Intercommunications XIIIe–XIXe siecles* (Athens: Centre de Recherches Néohelléniques de la Fondation Nationale de la Rechereche Scientifique, 1986).

96 Zachariadou, *Deka Tourkika engrapha*, 163.

97 BOA, Ahkâm Defteri 62, f. 885.

98 Gerlach, *Tagebuch*, 403.

Another example of a tax collector is the monk Mattheos, who previously had been the teacher of the Patriarch Jeremiah II. The patriarch sent him twice as tax collector to the Anatolian churches, and he, in addition to delivering the taxes to the patriarchate, earned for himself nearly 500 ducats. Gerlach reported that, "Besides the tax that the bishops and metropolitans have to send to the patriarch, they have to donate 10–15 ducats to the tax collector."[99]

STATE INTERVENTION AND COERCION

The state provided the *mültezim* with coercive power to assist him in the collection process.[100] The accepted wisdom has been that tax collection by the Church was the result of direct coercion by the state, usually at the hands of janissaries displaying oppressive behavior towards the prelates. Yet because the office of the patriarch was considered a form of property, individual office holders made investments and were determined to protect them. Therefore, we can assume that the prelates that were being challenged earnestly called for the intervention of the state to coerce non-payers to submit their obligation. An example of the patriarch seeking state intervention is the aforementioned document describing Patriarch Jeremiah I's complaint in 1544. Patriarch Jeremiah I went to the sultan to complain that his representative (*vekil*) had been to the Biromori monastery in Epirus and the monks would not hand over the required *rüsûm*.[101] The *berât* decreed that they were to pay their required amount and that no excuse to withhold any amount would be tolerated. In this instance, and in other cases, the state clearly intervened by confirming the right of the individual hierarch to collect taxes, by informing the local Ottoman authority of the misconduct and the ruling, and by threatening to bring down the power of the state on those individuals about whom the complaint was issued. This becomes clear in every document issued from the Imperial Divan. The decrees are mostly addressed to the *Sancak Beys* of Rumeli and Anadolu, and to the local *kadi* of the region. The requested action is the recognition of rights of an individual, backed by the coercive power of the state.

While it is clear that the patriarch had been given the right to collect the *mal-i miri* from among the Greek Orthodox communities, there are few opportunities to allow a glimpse into how this process worked in practice. On October 8, 1573 a decree issued to the *Rumeli Beylerbeyi* describes the *Rum Patriği* requesting an inquiry to be made about certain metropolitans who were dismissed from office and held in custody for interfering in the collection of the customary taxes.[102] These metropolitans were obligated to submit *mâktu'* to the patriarch, but did not do so, and thus interfered with the collection of the taxes. The patriarch came into direct conflict with his hierarchical administration, the supposed sub-contractors of the *iltizam*, and by the power of the state had them dismissed. He had given

[99] Gerlach, *Tagebuch*, 270.
[100] Inalcik, "Military and Fiscal Transformation," 328.
[101] BOA, Ahkâm Defteri 62 f. 565a. [102] MD 23: 109.

surety for delivering the taxes to the Imperial Treasury and did not wish to risk losing it and perhaps even be incarcerated for his debts. In this case, it is not known why the metropolitans wished to interfere with the tax, but their actions certainly placed the patriarch in an awkward and potentially dangerous situation.

Six months after this conflict with the metropolitans, Patriarch Jeremiah II was seen traveling through Rumeli collecting taxes accompanied only by a janissary. Perhaps he went in person because it was a journey to collect larger lump sum payments in arrears, or because he could no longer trust the sultans under his jurisdiction to collect without incident, or because the low level prelates did not readily pay what was required to patriarchal representatives. Nevertheless, he did go in person to collect taxes. This decree of April 25, 1574 from the *Mühimme Defterleri* was directed to the *kadi* of Tırhala (Trikala,) located in the plains of central Greece. As Patriarch Jeremiah II himself traveled through Rumeli to collect the *mal-i miri*, he arrived in a local village near Tırhala. The villagers attacked with weapons both the patriarch and the janissary accompanying him, wishing to kill them and to steal their goods and money. Fortunately for both of them, the local *gendarme* (*subaşı*) foiled the attack and took those responsible into custody to be punished. They were then to be sent to the governor of Inehbati (Nafpaktos/Lepanto) to be punished and forced to become galley slaves in the Ottoman fleet, and the goods and money were to be returned.

In this stunning example, the patriarch was at complete odds with his own flock. However, rather than being a case of insurrection against the patriarchal office, it is more likely to have been a case of robbery. Whether a patriarch or designated representative, a *vekil*, collected the taxes, carrying large amounts of cash could be quite hazardous. The presence of the janissary attests to the perceived dangers of traveling through Rumeli with a coffer full of coins. When Patriarch Jeremiah II arrived in the village to collect taxes, the villagers reacted against him, perhaps rejecting his mission as a tax-collecting agent from the capital attempting to exploit them. Would they have dared to act in this manner against a local Ottoman feudal lord? Even the janissary did not convince the villagers that he represented the coercive power of the state. The one who did represent this power was the local enforcer, the *subaşı*. He was responsible for apprehending the villagers and sending them off to be punished. This event is instructive in two important ways. First, we see that the patriarch, after his conflict with the metropolitans, did not want any more middlemen to interfere in the collection of the taxes or to disregard his authority and jurisdiction. This explains why Patriarch Jeremiah II went in person. Secondly, whatever the motive for the attack might have been, it is clear that the patriarch did not inspire awe and reverence among common villagers in a place where Christians were in a clear majority, in central Rumeli. Rather, the patriarch represented wealth and a ready opportunity for the villagers to enrich themselves at his expense. This, therefore, can be considered a commentary on the patriarch's role and function as perceived from a small Balkan village.

Apparently, the state was willing to intervene and defend the patriarch's stated rights to those revenues. It is unclear what happened to those metropolitans in

Fig. 4.3. Greek Orthodox metropolitans in liturgical vestments. (Source: Salomon Schweigger, *Ein newe Reyssbeschreibung auss Teutschland nach Constantinopel und Jerusalem* (Nürnberg: In Verlegung Johann Kramers, 1664), 215: Rare Books Division, Department of Rare Books and Special Collections, Princeton University Library)

Fig. 4.4. Greek Orthodox Patriarch with villagers. (Source: Salomon Schweigger, *Ein newe Reyssbeschreibung auss Teutschland nach Constantinopel und Jerusalem* (Nürnberg: In Verlegung Johann Kramers, 1664), 215: Rare Books Division, Department of Rare Books and Special Collections, Princeton University Library)

the previous account after they were removed from office. Others who were more trusted or more sympathetic to the goals of Patriarch Jeremiah II, however, would undoubtedly replace them. Was Patriarch Jeremiah II trying to consolidate the institution of the patriarchate and establish the patriarch as the authority over the Greek Orthodox people, or was he simply en route collecting taxes? These examples explain little about a Church attempting to consolidate a Christian community. Indeed, they say little about what the community actually is except to say that there was a divide between the patriarchate and the local villagers. From the Ottoman perspective, the chief concern was the fiscal obligation to the state.

These issues lie at the heart of the *millet* system debate. This system assumes that the administrative hierarchical structure was in place and that the patriarch had enough authority (symbolic or coercive) to govern the Greek Orthodox population. Even if on one level there was an well established administrative structure within the Greek Orthodox community, and individuals held Church positions making it appear as if a hierarchy was well developed, there were many individuals who were willing to challenge the authority of the Patriarchate of Constantinople.

In 1579, Patriarch Jeremiah II had trouble with another of his appointments for the Metropolitan of the Morea and Athens. In this case, Jeremiah had made the son of Papa Dimo into a metropolitan of the district of Athens. There were complaints made by an unnamed party, perhaps common lay people, or maybe other metropolitans, and a request was made for another person to take this position, stating that Papa Dimo's son was wicked while the other individual was very capable and competent. As a result of this complaint, Papa Dimo's son, the Metropolitan of Athens, was put into prison.[103]

The plaintiffs in this case are unknown, but it is possible that they are either disgruntled members of the Greek community or were metropolitans who formed an opposition to Patriarch Jeremiah II's faction. Patriarch Jeremiah had appointed Papa Dimo's son as metropolitan and earlier had no complaints against him. In fact, the complaints were about his personal administration and ultimately about the administration of the patriarchate. In this case, the patriarch was not successful in preventing his own agent from being removed and put into prison.

Possessing a *berât* issued by the state was extremely important for two reasons. First, those collecting the taxes could be regulated in terms of what they owed the state and which prevented abuse of the tax farm. Secondly, the *berât* represented state power to convince those who were supposed to pay not to withhold any amounts owed. A decree from March 29, 1572 was written to the *kadi* of Tırnova and to Hüseyin çavuş, the local administrator of the town, about a group of six monks who had set off on a journey to collect money.[104] These monks had been put in prison because they had not been able to produce the appropriate papers given to them by the patriarch that granted them permission to collect

[103] MD 37: 1811.
[104] MD 16: 541 f. 284.

money from the various villages on their journey. At the time of inspection, they were asked for this permission and explained that there had been an understanding about their journey with the patriarch who granted them permission and had issued a document to that effect. That permission apparently had been lost, because they were unable to produce it. Furthermore, the area in which they were sent was the *Dar-ül-Harb*, a term which literally means the "abode of war" but in this context represented all lands held by non-Muslims, lands outside of the Ottoman Empire, such as to the northern, Slavic regions. After intercession by the patriarch, the Divan ordered them to be released.

This document illustrates both the concerns of the state, and the internal functioning of the Church. It was addressed to both the *kadi* and the *çavuş* of Tirnova, who apparently were responsible for detaining this group of six monks. We are given no details about the interrogation of the monks, but it appears that the local Ottoman officials might have become suspicious of six monks traveling through their town and the surrounding villages, even if it were on a common transit route north to Russia or north-west into Hungary and Austria. Whether they attempted to collect money on their journey or not is unclear. In all probability, they had attempted to collect money, otherwise discussion of permission to do so would not have arisen. Their claim was that the patriarch had sent them and that there was an understanding with him about their journey. The Divan in Istanbul made the decision for their release, although with seemingly little justification. It appears that someone from the patriarchate had learned about this incident and had petitioned the Divan for the release of the six monks, which was granted.

Although journeys by clerics to raise funds was a quite common occurence, local authorities were appropriately alarmed by a group of six monks who were taking money from the Christians in their district. Both the *kadi* and the *çavuş* would have known who had the legal rights to collect taxes from Christians, including the regular state taxes as well as any Church taxes and extraordinary levies. Thus, these men became immediately suspect.

This document reveals other interesting aspects of the aims and policies of the Church, particularly about the patriarchate's claims to universal authority. These monks have Greek names, Niko and Yorgo, and Slavic names, Köseç, Şerovade, and Bankoloçko. This combination seems odd at first glance, because we tend to think of the vast separation between ethnic groups even in the realm of the Church. But, in the administrative practice of the Church, the patriarch had continually claimed the right of governance over all Orthodox Christians. Here he is exercising this right over the group of ethnically mixed monks. The ethnic mix could have been a practical strategy so as to have enough people with various linguistic skills to be able to communicate with Greek and Slavic speakers. That the group was large indicated that they were on a mission to collect money and wished to ensure the security and safety of the mission. We are not told of other servants, but there may also have been others as part of the retinue.

The claim of governance over all Orthodox Christians is more of an issue when considering the actual destination of the journey. It would not have been conceivable to send monks out as ecclesiastical representatives to collect funds outside the lands of the Ottoman Empire unless there was some perceived notion that the patriarchate was entitled to do so. It is not unheard of for princes and prelates to travel to the West or even to Russia appealing for monetary assistance. A group of monks, however, even six monks, does not have the same authority as the patriarch, or princes, and would not have been recognized as having jurisdiction over the areas to which they were traveling in order to raise money.

It is not clear what was meant by the term *Dar-ül-Harb* and whether it was used by the monks or simply by the Ottoman officials who were describing this area outside of Ottoman domains out of habit or common usage. This term could imply one of two things. First, it could imply the land outside of Ottoman control northward into Hungarian and Austrian territory. More likely, however, it meant Russia, the region to which the monks journeyed in order to collect donations and alms from the tsar's court.[105] It was practice to search for economic support from the empire that was emerging as the only Orthodox Christian kingdom, and that was also seeking to enlarge its own footing. Mt. Athos was especially well connected to Russia in this regard, as we see from a document of September 1583. In this decree the beys and *kadis* on the borders with Poland are told that they are not to interfere with Yuvan Meşni, the man who completed his duty of bringing alms (*sadaka*) on behalf of the Tsar Ivan (*Yuvan*) to Mt. Athos. He was to be allowed to pass freely on his return.[106]

The following examples also demonstrate how the state did not shirk from using coercive power to control ecclesiastical offices that now can be considered as *iltizam*. The state was primarily on the lookout for inappropriate and illegal activities concerning the financial aspect of the ecclesiastical administration and used its power to correct these.[107] On April 17, 1577 a ruling of the Imperial Council recorded the case of the Metropolitan of Chios (*Sakız Metropolidi Gavri*). The complaint to the Divan had been that the metropolitan had committed shameful acts and accepted bribes from the priests. For this reason he was removed from his position and expelled from his see and the island. Although the Ottoman source reported the financial aspect of the case, Gerlach reported that both he and the Metropolitan of Athens were removed on account of their attempt to revolt against the patriarch. Stephan Gerlach reported that it was well known that each of the bishops had led abominable lives. Rumor had it that the Metropolitan of Chios, Gabriel, was a molester of children. Their behavior had been tolerated for so long, that, when at last there was an attempt to remove them from their sees, they approached one of the Ottoman officials with bribes in order to allow them

[105] See Borys A. Gudziak, *Crisis and Reform: The Kievan Metropolitinate: The Patriarchate of Constantinople, and the Genesis of the Union of Brest* (Cambridge, MA: Harvard University Press, 1992), 91. Also, Constantine Sathas, *Viographikon Schediasma peri Patriarchou Hieremia II (1572–1592)* (Athens: Typographeion A. Ktena kai S. Oikonomou, 1870), presents Pseudo-Dorotheos' account of Jeremiah II's journey to Russia and the events leading to the creation of the Moscow Patriarchate in 1589.

[106] MD: 52: 192. [107] MD 30: 96.

to stay in their positions. The patriarch was, therefore, forced to go to the sultan to explain that allowing them to stay in those positions would be contrary to ecclesiastical rules which did not tolerate sinful behavior. They were, thus, removed, and sent into exile to the Holy Mountain, rather than to a desolate place. It was reported to Gerlach that the patriarch was providing them with up to 1,000 *aspers* a year for their maintenance.[108]

In another case, the Divan sent a decree to the *kadi* of Selanik and *bey* that the Metropolitan of Varna was to be removed because of illegal activities and forced into exile to Mt. Athos. He escaped from exile and went to Istanbul to continue his malicious and intriguing activities. He was brought into custody again and was confronted by Patriarch Jeremiah II in the presence of the *kadi*. He was to be returned to the aforementioned island (Mt. Athos) and placed in the named monastery It was ordered that he not be accessible nor be allowed to leave from there. The punishment was exile on Mt. Athos, which for someone used to urban life meant the edge of the world.[109]

Another case shows that the place of exile, rather than being Mt. Athos, was even further away from Istanbul, at Rhodes (Rodos). This time a patriarch was sent to Rhodes to be held in a castle on the island and not to be released ever.[110] Finally, there is another case of the Istanbul Rum Patriği being forced into exile on the island of Cyprus. In each case, the distance gets further and further from the center.[111] Exile seemed to be the punishment of choice to get rid of individual prelates who were charged with and found guilty of committing crimes against the patriarchate. The state certainly was willing to assist in the punishment, and even used its own resources to that effect.

Not only did the patriarch use the coercive power of the Ottoman state, but he also used the coercive power of the Venetian state when dealing with problems on Crete. Gerlach reported that Patriarch Jeremiah II had recently excommunicated two priests on the island of Crete, Papas Johannes Nathanail and the priest Peter Rodios. The patriarch had sent his tax collectors to Crete as he usually did, every three to four years. Over the course of time, a considerable sum of money, about 2,000 ducats, had been bequeathed to the patriarchate from people who had died. These two priests attempted to embezzle this money, and they, therefore, resisted the patriarchal tax collector.

The two priests were said to have lived and kept company with the Franks on the island, and the patriarch had them deposed. In order to realize this deposition, however, the patriarchal representatives asked the Venetian *Bailo* on Crete to intercede for them in order to prevent a major schism from taking place among those who were loyal to the two local priests and those loyal to the patriarchate. Theodosios Zygomalas was mediator, and the patriarch eventually was convinced to remove the excommunication under the condition that they would have to suffer the same or worse punishment should they again steal from the Patriarch of Constantinople. They were to report to Constantinople and should not prevent

108 Gerlach, *Tagebuch*, 323.
109 MD 31: 821.
110 MD 55: 271; MD 55: 272.
111 MD 58: 333.

the tax collectors sent by the patriarch to do their collecting, but rather should support them.[112]

CONCLUSION

The goal of this chapter has been to discuss the significance of tax farming in the Ottoman Empire and to argue that the Church played a particularly suitable and important role for the state as a cash-rich tax farm. Considering the feudal beginnings of the state, the Ottoman Imperial Treasury was always in need of cash, both for the service of the sultan's court and also to pay for the growing standing army of janissaries that became a major presence from the mid-fifteenth century. Any exploitable institution that could produce revenue for the state was tapped and adapted to the fiscal administrative structure. Thus, we have seen the ways in which the Church became a formal fiscal institution in Ottoman eyes. It is now clear that the Church was treated as an imperial tax farm, and likewise how it functioned internally with the characteristics of the *iltizam*. Bishops competed with one another, and attempted to outbid each other for the episcopal throne. The state's interest was to have a smooth and steady stream of income, and, therefore, exercised its coercive power when asked by hierarchs to intervene. In the end, as in most cases, the Ottoman Empire was the real winner, because it had transformed what has been described as a religious national and ethnic institution into a fiscal administrative institution that served the state.

112 Legrand, *Notice Biographique sur Jean et Théodose Zygomalas*, 187–196.

PART III

CONTESTED POWER AND AUTHORITY

5

Competition and Corruption

Sultan, Patriarch, and Greek Elite

THE ROLE OF THE ELITES

In a fictional dialogue, the *Dialogos*, written by a sixteenth-century bishop of the Church, an abbot of a monastery and a bishop were talking about the state of the Church. The bishop, unable to contain his sorrow, complained "Woe to our suffering. We enjoy influence peddling, and are shamed by the *archons* and the wealthy. We enjoy gifts and our unjustness, and we judge according to the gifts [we receive]. ..."[1] These words written by Damaskenos the Stoudite articulate the contemporary human dilemma faced by sixteenth-century bishops. Material gifts and influence offered by the wealthy and *archons*, the leading men of the day, led to great enjoyment; but they also led, at least in Damaskenos' mind, to the breaking of moral codes, injustice, Church canons, and to a state of suffering for the Church.

An important voice for sixteenth-century ecclesiastical affairs, and a critic of the corruption of bishops, Damaskenos the Stoudite was himself a bishop and prolific writer. Born in Thessalonike, he was educated in Constantinople and became a monk and preacher in the famous Monastery of Stoudion. After he had become a monk, he preached a number of sermons, which were published in Venice in 1558. He was ordained the Bishop of Lites and Rendines (near Thessalonike) and later was installed as Metropolitan of Naupauktos and Arta in 1574 where he served until his death in 1577.[2] His other important work was his *History of the Patriarchs of Constantinople*, the manuscript that had formed the basis of the standard *Historia Patriarchica* by Manuel Malaxos.

The *Dialogos* was meant to criticize the contemporary ecclesiastical hierarchy. In the course of a lengthy conversation between the abbot and bishop, written in

[1] E. Kakoulikou-Panou, "Damaskenou Stoudite 'Dialogos'," *Dodone* 3 (1974): 443–458. Dialogos, 450, f. 10.

[2] Marios Philippides, "Makarios Melissourgos-Melissenos," in *Historians of the Ottoman Empire*, ed. Cemal Kafadar, Hakan Karateke, and Cornell Fleischer, 2008. <http://www.ottomanhistorians.com>.

the style of a theatrical script, Damaskenos illustrated the mistakes, faults, and evils of his brethren in the sixteenth century.[3]

The *Dialogos* opens with the abbot asking how the bishop had become a righteous man. The bishop responded humbly that he was not, in fact, righteous, but that he was troubled by human weakness. The abbot responded, "And I believed that it was only in you [bishops] that goodness (*eudaimonia*), good will (*kalorizikia*), and good fortune (*eutychia*) is found, that which Plato said was only found in the blessed, and you tell me that life is full of misfortune and sorrow?"[4] The abbot, by using the term *eudaimonia*, a philosophical term that means ultimate goodness and virtue, clearly described an idealized version of a bishop's life that was full of goodness. In an effort to emphasize this notion of highest human good, a concept that hearkens back to antiquity, he called the ancients, including Plato directly, into action. The bishop responded,

> Not only do I call it misfortune and travail, this life that we hierarchs have, but it is also full of mania, and insanity, and now agitation. And may Your Holiness consider my words, because if you would wish to see our first oblivion and dishonor, and deficiency that we had—the same as Pausonias [A gambler and beggar from Aristophanes' *Plutus*] whom the historians describe, who was the most insane and unsteady and poor person,—and if you consider our success and you want to understand our worth, you will see that we are not even like the Megarans, who were despised by the Athenians for their baseness, and they were not allowed in the council, nor were they taken into account. "The wretched Megarians are dishonorable and have one fate" the prophet says.—Of these things you must also now consider us, o Holy Abbott, because we have risen to the height of the hierarchy, we think that we talk with God, and thus we say, and in truth, we are not even worthy to speak with that [unruly] beggar Iros of Kephallonia, whom Homer describes, or to be compared to him or be shown to be better than him.[5] And for these reasons, how do you not want to call our lives, just as I describe them, full of great misfortune.[6]

The abbot wondered how the bishop could be so sorrowful and pessimistic about his situation, and why he did not just thank God who "placed the poor in the midst of the kings and *archons*, and is worthy of praise."[7] After a brief exchange concerning the general human condition and reiterating the perceptions that people have of the righteousness of bishops, the bishop then embarked on a lengthy exposition outlining the weaknesses and villainies of hierarchs, explaining that they are "hierarchs in name only."[8] Having the power to bind and loose

[3] This is the same individual who wrote the *History of the Patriarchate* which was likely copied by Manuel Malaxos. Marios Philippides, "Patriarchal Chronicles of the Sixteenth Century," *Greek, Roman and Byzantine Studies* 25 (1984): 87–94. Damaskenos was born in Thessalonike, educated in Constantinople, and became a monk and preacher in the monastery of Stoudion. His sermons were published in Venice in 1558.

[4] Dialogos, 447, f. 4.

[5] Homer, *Odyssey* 18: 1–115.

[6] Dialogos, 447, f. 4–5v.

[7] Dialogos, 448, f. 4.

[8] Dialogos, 450, f. 8.

sins, the bishops instead get drunk, enjoy injustice, and are lovers of gold, while they say they are lovers of Christ.

> Woe to our archpriesthood, which we sell with silver. We do not teach the people. We become the form of evil to the people and whatever we do, they learn and they also do these things. We are hurdles and stumbling blocks of the people, to trip the people and they are scandalized by us. We are friends of wine and wine drinkers and drunkards, slanderers, we beat, we strike, we love money, and we profit from the ugly and illegitimate actions, and we are not ashamed of black profit, I leave the rest, which God alone knows."[9]

Damaskenos wrote that the bishops were worthy only to be sent to Hades. They continually face temptations the vexation from "leading men (*afentades*) through flattery that they hope for, and they wish to have the *archons* on their good side so as to have influence over other bishops."[10]

In the *Dialogos*, the bishop identified numerous canons and synodal decisions that contemporary hierarchs were consistently disobeying. Among the first he identified was a canon from the First Ecumenical Council of Nicea, which forbade the election of a bishop without a conciliar decision. This issue dealt with the major ecclesiastical problem of the day. Deciding to ordain bishops without synodal decision not only broke ecclesiastical law, but also led to the powerful *archons* rising in influence, deciding, for their own purposes, who should become the next bishop. Political pressure leading to sketchy unilateral decisions went against canonical Orthodox tradition.

Damaskenos continued his critique when he described other canons that were ignored. The 25th chapter of the council of Chalcedon stated that a see of a deceased bishop should be filled within three months of his death, while at the present time, according to the bishop, a see could be vacant for six months or a year, and only when gifts were given would another be elected bishop.[11] Other criticisms based on breaking the canons included gaining sees as a result of direct intervention from *archons*, being ordained a bishop under the legal age of 35, failing to teach the clergy and laity correctly concerning the Holy Scriptures, and continually wishing to move from a poorer eparchy to a wealthier one. The bishops, rather than being deposed for not fulfilling their obligations, continued to rule tyrannically and undeposed.[12] Later in the *Dialogos*, a critique of monasticism was also made, in which Damaskenos criticized monasteries being built by lay people, on the foundations of earlier Metropolitan churches, but with complete disregard to the spirit of monasticism and the communal life. The bishops allowed the money that people gave the Church to be used up in all the decorative arts and church vessels and utensils rather than to go to feed the poor, orphans, and widows. They also consented to random resignations of metropolitans because they wished to put others in their place to gain money. The patriarch himself accepted these

[9] Dialogos, 451, f. 11. [10] Dialogos, 451, f. 12.
[11] Dialogos, 452, ff. 14r and 14v. [12] Dialogos, 455, f. 21.

immoral conditions and even sent bishops away to other places to vacate sees, a crime that the character of the bishop said would not be forgiven. The abbot, hearing all these things replied, "Woe, what wonder! How horrible is this, my lord, so many canons of the Holy Apostles and Holy Fathers are violated. And then you say you are living a blessed life?"[13] The *Dialogos* then drew to a close, but with all the negative things having been taken in by the abbot and ultimately the reader.

It was clear to Damaskenos that there were severe problems in the Church due to the intervention and involvement of people and unscrupulous bishops. His critique was couched in the form of a dialogue, yet it was an extremely poignant response to a number of very real issues of the day. Damaskenos was writing from the standpoint of a conscientious religious person. He was dissatisfied with the state of the bishops and the Church. He saw how money and power corrupted the true nature of the Church; the hierarchs were easily tempted and fell prey to the schemes of the Greek elite. When the abbot became discouraged, the bishop responded,

> Have courage, o friend, do not fear where there is nothing to fear, because the faith of the Christians, has not been made worthless or lost because we, who have the name of hierarch, have become worthless and luckless, but the faith remains in those who have fear of God, and in those who hope in His name ...[14]

The challenge with this type of source is the prominence of such a steady account of corruption and immoral behavior. It is not always possible to understand what the underlying social dynamic was that created the environment for this bad behavior. To appreciate Damaskenos the Stoudite's concerns better, it is useful to consider them within the broader Ottoman context.[15] During the mid-sixteenth century, one may recognize many of the same sentiments and complaints listed by Damaskenos that were lodged by Ottoman Muslim subjects against members of the Ottoman bureaucracy. The same concepts of scandal, corruption, office buying, influence peddling, injustice, and unrestrained power were evident in the Ottoman imperial context. The complaints recorded dissatisfaction with a broken system, moral failings of individuals, and essentially an Ottoman decline. It is interesting that the social dynamics and critiques within the Greek Orthodox community reflected similar social dynamics of Ottoman society.

Sources detailing corruption and abuse of power existed in the Ottoman literature of the sixteenth and seventeenth centuries. Among the most important is the mirror of princes advice literature (*nasihatname*). According to historian Rifa'at Abou-El-Haj, the authors of this genre of Ottoman writing emphasize the individual moral dimension of serving the state. Abou-El-Haj argues that in presenting the ills of the state in black-and-white terms, and contrasting the

[13] Dialogos, 457, f. 23v. [14] Dialogos, 450, f.8–9.

[15] The tradition of social criticism and critique of the "obtuseness" of hierarchy exemplified by Damaskenos continued in later periods as well. See Paschalis Kitromilides, *Enlightenment and Revolution: The Making of Modern Greece* (Harvard University Press, 2013), 36.

Fig. 5.1. The procession of the Great Entrance during the Greek Orthodox Divine Liturgy. (Source: Lambert de Vos, *Kostümbuch*: Codex Ms. Or. 9, Bremen: Staats- und Universitätsbibliothek Bremen, fol. 101)

immorality of one group with the morality of their own group, the writers were in fact promoting their own political agenda and ideology.[16] Of course, in the Ottoman context, the condemnations were largely against corrupt and rapacious *devşirme* officials who rose through the ranks not through their meritorious service but through bribery and monetary compensation. Unless there was a return to the old *sipahi* order in the days of the well-run *timar* system, the state was in danger of complete chaos and collapse.

[16] R. A. Abou-El-Haj, *The Formation of the Modern State: The Ottoman Empire, Sixteenth to Eighteenth Centuries* (Albany: State University of New York Press, 1992), 20–28. Kenan Inan, "Remembering the Good Old Days: The Ottoman Nasihatname [Advice Letters] Literature of the 17th Century," in *Institutional Change and Stability Conflicts, Transitions and Social Values*, ed. Andreas Gémes, Florencia Peyrou, and Ioannis Xydopoulos (Pisa: Pisa University Press, 2009), 111–127. R. A. Abou-El-Haj, "The Ottoman Nasihatname as a Discourse over Morality," in *Mélanges Professeur Robert Mantran*, ed. A. Temini (Zaghouan, Tunis: Centre d'Etudes et de Rechereches Ottomanes, Morisques, de Documentation et d'Information, 1988), 23. C. H. Fleischer, "From Seyhzade Korkud to Mustafa Ali: Cultural Origins of the Nasihatname," in *Proceedings of the Third Congress on the Social and Economic History of Turkey*, ed. H. Lowry (Istanbul: Isis Press, 1990), 67–77. For a more recent treatment of the *nasihatname* literature see D. A. Howard, "Genre and Myth in the Ottoman Advice for Kings Literature," in *The Early Modern Ottomans: Remapping the Empire*, ed. Virginia H. Aksan and Daniel Goffman (Cambridge: Cambridge University Press, 2007), 137–166.

A contemporary example of *nasihatname* literature is the *Counsel for Sultans* by Mustafa Ali of Gelibolu (1541–1600).[17] Mustafa Ali, a mid-level Ottoman administrator, wished to impress upon his readers that the state of the Ottoman Empire was on a slippery slope of moral and administrative decline. Decline can be seen most clearly in the structure of his work. Key among the problems was the Ottoman Empire's deviation from the correct "old order" based on meritocracy, and the weakening, mismanagement and abuse of the system in which the sultan was unable to control his underlings.

Mustafa Ali offered a detailed history of his own education and training in order to emphasize the injustice of being deprived of higher rank. He described the many trials and tribulations that he, personally, faced which prevented him from ascending to positions he felt he deserved. The primary theme that he stresses is the preservation of Justice that can only survive with the vigilance of the sultan. Corruption was the result of lack of vigilance, and as Mustafa Ali shows, it takes on a variety of forms. To understand properly the moral discourse presented in this type of text, we need to broaden our scope and look at the wider transformations taking place in the Ottoman Empire and to attempt to see the text as a reflection of these changes. Among such changes were social fatigue generated by long and protracted warfare, economic crises that produced high inflation, and a peasantry that was moving to the city, removing themselves as a tax base.[18] Mustafa Ali specifically commented on these latter two issues.

However, if we look even more broadly than this, we can see a larger transformation that was taking place. The Ottoman state was undergoing its own transformation into an early modern state with a distinctive centralizing political policy. The sultan and the elite ruling class (*askeri* class) were rapidly being separated from public affairs, and there was a specialization within the bureaucracy that narrowed the roles of certain offices, ensuring that the old ruling elite could not easily re-enter the scene. For Mustafa Ali, this appeared to be the most devastating effect of the changes. Previously the *askeri* class included men of sword, men of the pen and men of learning. These different professions made up both the administrative institution of the empire, and were also the coercive force of the state and were reserved for extremely few people. The ground rules for entering this class, however, were changing. The emergence of independent career tracks created broader access to these positions. What had once been reserved for elites trained in elite schools, was now open for anyone with either enough personal connections (*intisap*), or enough money to purchase an office.

A similar shift appears in the separation of the state from the economy. Before, the state as the sole "owner" of Ottoman lands was able to extract revenue in the

[17] Cornell H. Fleischer, *Bureaucrat and Intellectual in the Ottoman Empire: The Historian Mustafa Ali (1541–1600)* (Princeton, NJ: Princeton University Press, 1986), 101. Mustafa bin Ahmet Âlî, *Mustafā Ali's Counsel for Sultans of 1581: Edition, Translation, Notes*, Forschungen Zur Islamischen Philologie Und Kulturgeschichte Bd. 6–7 (Vienna: Verlag der Österreichischen Akademie der Wissenschaften, 1979).

[18] Cornell H. Fleischer, *Bureaucrat and Intellectual in the Ottoman Empire*, 101.

form of direct taxation. In time, however, much of the land that supported the central administration was held privately and it became more difficult for the state to assess these properties and to collect their taxes. The solution was the implementation of tax farming, which became far more prevalent in the mid-sixteenth century. Tax farming requires a cash economy, and a commercialization of production in order to collect taxes in cash. According to Mustafa Ali such commercialization affected the administrative offices themselves and undermined good Ottoman order.

Clearly, Mustafa Ali was not alone in identifying and objecting to the changes that were taking place. Others also saw similar trends happening. But Mustafa Ali's work is significant because in the process of identifying the minute offending details and creating lifelike images of the good *sipahi* and the bad bureaucrat, he also outlines the ideals that he and his fellow class members held. As a result, Abou-El-Haj argues that the *nasihatnameler* "are best approached as ideological tools for arguing the case for one political faction or another of the ruling class. As such they are only oversimplifications, and therefore seem to be handy devices for the conduct of political discourse."[19]

The parallels between the attitudes of Mustafa Ali and Damaskenos the Stoudite are striking.[20] In each case, they are critiquing the proper functioning of their respective institutions. The impetus for this critique is the disaffection caused by what they see as the proliferation of influence peddling, personal connections, office buying, and general corruption. These unsavory activities led to their observing the state and the Church in a condition of decline. While the historiography of Ottoman decline is relatively extensive, the historiography dealing with simony and corruption in the Church during this period is comparatively limited, for example considered in only a cursory way by Runciman. The isolated consideration of simony in the Church has prevented Church historians from making the connections between the Ottoman and ecclesiastical cases and also from seeing office buying as emanating from a common social context.[21]

The involvement of the Greek elites in the patriarchal tax farming system affected the way in which the Church became the object of intense competition. The competition for the office of bishop or patriarch was linked to political groups or factions being willing to finance individuals wishing to gain ecclesiastical offices, including that of the patriarch. There are several examples worth mentioning which describe the direct involvement of lay people in ecclesiastical affairs.

[19] Abou-El-Haj, "The Ottoman Nasihatname as a Discourse over Morality," 23.

[20] Linda T. Darling, *Revenue-raising and Legitimacy* (Leiden: E. J. Brill, 1996), 2–8.

[21] B. Lewis, "Ottoman Observers of Ottoman Decline," *Islamic Studies* I/1 (1962): 71–87. N. Itzkowitz, "Eighteenth Century Ottoman Realities," *Studia Islamica* XVI (1962): 73–94. R. A. Abou-El-Haj, "The Expression of Ottoman Political Culture in the Literature of Advice to Princes (*Nasihatnameler*) Sixteenth to Twentieth Centuries," in *Sociology in the Rubric of Social Science*, ed. R. B. a. A. K. Ghosh (India: Department of Culture, Government of India, 1995), 282–292. S. Runciman, *The Great Church in Captivity* (Cambridge: Cambridge University Press, 1968).

In addition to Damaskenos the Stoudite, the patriarchal chronicles observe decline. A note just below the title of the *Historia Patriarchica Constantinopoleos* of Martin Crusius states,

> Concerning the patriarchs who served in this catholic great Church of Constantine's city after the Sultan Mehmet received it and what things they did in their respective times, and who was the first to give the so-called *peskion* and the *haratzion* to him, and who increased it, to the point where it exists until today, and in whose sultan's times these things occured. . . .[22]

This note suggests that the text is not only concerned with the patriarchs who served, but records the payments they made to the Ottoman state. While these two subjects, of the patriarchs and of the payments to the state were not explicitly linked for each patriarch, the idea that the patriarchs gave *pişkeş* and *haraç* appears throughout the text, and leads to charges of simony and scandal. Even before the conquest of Constantinople in 1453, Patriarch Gennadios Scholarios reacted against the practice of office buying. In fact, as early as 1451, Patriarch Gennadios who was then monk George Scholarios, composed a letter to the Emperor Constantine XI Palaiologos that later was collected and titled *Concerning Simony*.[23] The letter was a condemnation of the practice from the late Byzantine period, at a time when the emperor was still in control, though the Church had fallen into chaos, and did not even have a sitting patriarch. The last to serve was Patriarch Gregory III Mamas, a pro-Unionist, who fled Constantinople for Rome in 1451.[24] The fact that the monk George Scholarios considered simony a major problem indicates that simony was rampant even prior to the final Ottoman takeover of Constantinople. The period when he was actually patriarch, however, posed even more of a challenge. Having been called into service by Sultan Mehmet II, Patriarch Gennadios could no longer tolerate the "many and great scandals" and on three separate occasions, he resigned from the patriarchal office and went into retirement.[25] The community, who saw his virtue, called him back into service and twice he was willing to return. Attempting to understand the reason behind Patriarch Gennadios' retirement raises the question about the scandals, themselves. What were they about, and how does simony figure into this story? Why does it appear to be such a problem at this time? The answer has to do with the nature of the office of the bishop and patriarch, as conditioned by Ottoman administrative practice; it was an object of competition, and it was not simply the focus of communal leadership.

While the chronicles generally wish to portray the Church in a positive light, they face a real dilemma when describing patriarchs and bishops who gained

[22] Immanuel Bekker, ed., *Historia politica et patriarchica Constantinopoleos: Epirotica*, Corpus Scriptorum Historiae Byzantinae (Bonn: Impensis Ed. Weberi, 1849), 78.

[23] Patriarch Gennadius II Scholarios, "Contre La Simonie (1451)" in *Georgiou Tou Scholariou Apanta Ta Euriskomena = Oeuvres Complètes De Georges Scholarios*, ed. Louis Petit, Xenophon Siderides, and Martin Jugie, vol. 1 (Paris: Maison de la bonne presse, 1928) 239–251.

[24] Marios Philippides and Walter K. Hanak, *The Siege and the Fall of Constantinople In 1453* (Farnham: Ashgate, 2011), 130 n. 151.

[25] *Historia patriarchica*, ed. Bekker, 94.

their positions through "corrupt" or "scandalous" practices of laymen. Patriarch Ioasaph Kokkas who had served as the third patriarch in the succession after Patriarch Gennadios, and threw himself in a well to try to kill himself, suffered at the hands of the famous layman George of Trebizond. However, after he recovered, he continued to suffer due to the actions of the patriarchal court. Theodoros Agallianos, a bishop and prominent member of that court, condemned Patriarch Ioasaph, citing first and foremost the charge of simony, or office buying. Historian Christos Patrinelis who studied Theodoros Agallianos, also known as Theophanes, Bishop of Medea, revealed the inner workings of the post-conquest institution. In citing a number of letters written by Agallianos, Patrinelis notes that among them are various complaints of people who gained bishoprics through simony.[26] One case that Theodoros Agallianos recorded concerns two individuals, George Galesiotes and Manuel Christonymos. George Galesiotes had served in the position of secretary (*Notarios*) of the Byzantine Emperor, and under Patriarch Gennadios he became Grand Keeper of Liturgical Vessels (*Megas Skevophylax*). Galesiotes' friend, Christonymos had served as tutor to the children of the *archon* Demetrios Apokaukos-Kyritses, the secretary to the sultan since 1446, since before the conquest. Manuel Christonymos had set his sights on becoming Grand Sacristan (*Megas Ekklesiarches*), one of the more prominent offices at the patriarchate. Through Apokaukos-Kyritses' intervention in the patriarchate, he was able to attain the position even though Patriarch Gennadios himself opposed the appointment. Through financial payments, Apokaukos-Kyritses managed to place Manuel Christonymos as Grand Ecclesiarch. The patriarchal synod was swayed to support the appointment. This action, directed at the patriarchal court was a direct act of office buying. Agallianos' disgust was apparent in his condemnation that castigated both Christonymos and Apokaukos-Kyritses. He called upon the various Church canons that condemn simony saying that, if any person gained by means of money his position of priest or deacon, he should be defrocked. He noted that the canon condemned using "*kosmikois archousi*" or lay leadership, and according to the canon, the offending party ought to be punished by being defrocked.[27] The culture at the patriarchate, however, allowed for individuals to gain hierarchical positions through purchase. The moral code was broken, though there were individuals such as Patriarch Gennadios and bishops like Theodoros Agallianos and Damaskenos the Stoudite who rightfully condemned these acts.

To understand these condemnations of fellow clergy, it is important to consider, once again, the economic and social forces transforming Ottoman society that clearly affected the economic and social elites within the Greek community as well. Many of the leading Greek elite in the Ottoman period gained wealth in

[26] C. G. Patrinelis, *Ho Theodoros Agallianos Tautizomenos Pros Ton Theophanēn Mēdeias Kai Hoi Anekdotoi Logoi Tou: Mia Nea Historike Pēgē Peri Tou Patriarcheiou Konstantinoupoleos Kata Tous Protous Meta Ten Halosin Chronous* (Thessaloniki: Aristotle University of Thessaloniki, 1966), 103–107.

[27] Patrinelis, *Ho Theodoros Agallianos*, 107.

large economic enterprises outside the Church by farming taxes and by holding state monopolies.

At the end of the Byzantine Empire much of the Patriarch of Constantinople's jurisdiction was already under Turkish rule.[28] As early as 1382, we see a layperson, Anastasios Kallistos, collecting taxes for the patriarch from the region of Bursa, which had been taken by the Ottomans in 1326. There were lay people who understood how to deal with the Ottomans as they took control of the Balkans as well.[29] *Archons* had understood how to preserve and gain wealth by farming taxes and by holding state monopolies. In order to get these positions, however, one had to previously have been wealthy. Therefore, there were many families in the late Byzantine period who hid their wealth until they could figure out how to work within the new system, and then they were able to gain desirable positions. These wealthy Greeks, most likely the descendants of important Byzantine families, and originating from places such as Edirne, Filibe, Gelibolu, and Bursa, became a new aristocracy who managed to keep their previous wealth and to increase it. Thus, the notable Byzantine families were given a new lease on life.[30]

The concept of *archon* survived from antiquity to denote a magistrate, while in Byzantine times *archon* was synonymous with the *dynatoi* (the powerful) bureaucratic officials and landowners who played authoritative roles in Byzantine society. In other instances, the term *archon* was used to denote the emperor's servants and friends who had personal contact with the monarch. Technically speaking, *archon* also indicated a governor and was used to describe district administrators or independent princes.[31] *Archons* had been in vigorous competition with the hierarchy in the Byzantine provinces well before the conquest of Constantinople. A study on decentralization in medieval Morea showed that *archons* and local hierarchs were in a constant battle for control over the provincial communities.[32] The *archons* who were identified in the sixteenth-century texts were, to some degree, those individuals who maintained their status under Ottoman control, or who used the opportunities presented to them by the Ottoman system to enrich themselves.

Beginning in the late seventeenth century, the Greek Orthodox elite class became known as *Phanariots*, a class of wealthy non-Muslims, many of whom were Greek, and who lived in the Phanar district of Istanbul where the patriarchate was located,

[28] Elizabeth Zachariadou, "Wealthy Greeks and the Patriarchate of Constantinople c. 1453" (unpublished papers presented at The Business of Change: Merchants and the Fall of Constantinople, 1994); See also Chapter 4, "Hoi Hyschyroi Hypodouloi" in Elizabeth A. Zachariadou, *Deka Tourkika engrapha gia ten Megale Ekklesia: 1483–1567* (Athens: Ethniko Hidryma Ereunon, Institouto Byzantinon Ereunon, 1996), 63–77; Elizabeth Zachariadou, "Les Notables Laïques et le Patrarcat Oecuménique après la Chute de Constantinople," *Turcica* 30 (1998): 119–134.

[29] Zachariadou, "Wealthy Greeks and the Patriarchate," 1.

[30] Zachariadou, "Wealthy Greeks and the Patriarchate," 3.

[31] Alexander Kazhdan, "*Archon*" *The Oxford Dictionary of Byzantium* (New York: Oxford University Press, 1991) I, 160.

[32] Constantine G. Hatzidimitriou, "The Decline of Imperial Authority in Southwest Central Greece and the Role of 'Archontes' and Bishops in the Failure of Byzantine Resistance and Reconquest 1180–1297 AD." (Ph.D. Diss., Columbia University, 1988).

in palaces on the Golden Horn.[33] These families included the Kantakouzenos and Mavrokordatos families, whose members attained high positions in the service of the sultan, even becoming princes (*voyvodes*) of Wallachia and Moldavia in the eighteenth century. More attention has been paid, however, to the latter group of *Phanariots* than to the earlier group of post-conquest *archons*. As Byzantine historian Klaus-Peter Matschke rightly concludes when commenting on the historiography on the Phanariots, it is not helpful to call the sixteenth-century *archons* "pre- or proto-Phanariots."[34] This earlier group of *archons* did play a significant role in the sixteenth century and for this reason, they register clearly in the contemporary Ottoman and Greek sources.[35]

The first general study to deal with post-1453 *archons* as a class is Nicolae Iorga's *Byzance après Byzance* which devotes an entire, but fairly cursory, chapter to them. With little mention of the Byzantine great family lineages of the *archons* or of the origins of the *archons* as a class of wealthy Greeks, Iorga's account concentrated on the *archons* in the sixteenth century. For the most part he stressed the attachment and relationship with the patriarchate, as was clear when he began his description of the *archons* with the election of the Patriarch Jeremias of Larissa, who was supported by the Holy Synod and the "very holy noble *archons*." The most important sources for Iorga's chapter was the *Historia Patriarchica* and Stephan Gerlach's *Tagebuch* from which information about the lives of notable *archons* were taken. Both of these works were written at about the same time in the late sixteenth century and show the *archons* as a group of wealthy commercial families that sought to become masters of the only remaining formal Byzantine institution, the Greek Orthodox Patriarchate. Neither source examined the *archons* critically, to identify how they originated as a commercial class, or what they did to earn money in the Ottoman Empire, or even how they dealt with the state.

Clearly, members of the Byzantine royal families adjusted to the new regime by playing an important administrative, commercial, and economic role in Ottoman society. Members of families such as the Palaiologoi, Kantakouzenoi, Chalkokondyloi, and Rhalle became prominent Ottoman tax farmers. As tax farmers played an indispensible role in state finances, these individuals became powerful figures in the Ottoman economic and political spheres and, for the

[33] For the traditional background and historiography of the Phanariots see, Institute for Balkan Studies, *Symposium L'Époque Phanariote, 21-25 Octobre 1970: à La Mémoire De Cléobule Tsourkas* (Thessaloniki: Institute for Balkan Studies, 1974); Vasilis Sphyroeras, *Hoi Dragomanoi Tou Stolou; Ho Thesmos Kai Hoi Phoreis* (Athenai, 1965); Andrei Pippidi, *Hommes et ideés du Sud-Est européen à l'aube de l'âge moderne* (Bucureşti: Editura Academiei Republicii Socialiste România; Paris: Editions du C.N.R.S., 1980). For a revisionist account of the enigmatic Phanariot community on the verge of intergration into Ottoman governance see Christine Philliou, "Communities on the Verge: Unraveling the Phanariot Ascendancy in Ottoman Governance," *Comparative Studies in Society and History* 51/1 (2009): 151–181, and her larger treatment on the Phanariots, Christine Philliou, *Biography of an Empire: Governing Ottomans in an Age of Revolution* (Berkeley: University of California Press, 2011).

[34] Klaus-Peter Matschke, "Transition to Tourkokratia: The Byzantinist Standpoint," in *The Ottomans and the Balkans: A Discussion of Historiography*, ed. Fikret Adanır and Suraiya Faroqhi (Leiden: E. J. Brill, 2002), 108.

[35] Nicolae Iorga, *Byzance Après Byzance* (Paris: Editions Balland, 1982), 117–129.

Greek community, in the ecclesiastical sphere. Tax farms were extremely profitable. For instance, the Istanbul customs zone, which included Istanbul and all the Aegean ports of western Anatolia, was acquired through the combined efforts of "Palologoz of Kassandros," "Lefteri son of Galyanos of Trabzon," "Andriya son of Halkokondil," and "Ya'kub a new convert," and "Manul Palologoz." These individuals then directly competed for the tax concession against a Turkish consortium, and between October 1476 and December 1477 a group of Jewish and Italian financiers. Each time one of these groups increased their bids, and so the revenue promised to the state, the customs zone changed hands. The correlation between the success of the Greek group and the influence that Hass Murat and Mesih Pasha enjoyed with Mehmet II was probably a key factor. Inalcik called the group of former Byzantine noble families that had assembled in the sultan's service "the Greek faction" and concluded that there was, indeed, such a correlation between this group and Greeks controlling the Istanbul customs zone in the 1470s.[36]

Some of the most famous Byzantine aristocrats survived the conquest and maintained elite status by becoming Ottoman officials. Hass Murat Pasha and Mesih Pasha, both members of the Palaiologos family, converted and became viziers under Mehmet II.[37] These members of the Greek faction were identified by Theodore Spandounes, a cousin of the last Palaiologan emperor and member of the Kantakouzenos Byzantine imperial family whose parents emmigrated to Venice from Ottoman lands in the mid sixteenth century. Spandounes wrote an account of the history of the Ottoman Emperors as a plea to Western audiences, and he counted among his sources for this history members of his family who were in the service of the sultan. He said,

> I felt qualified by the fact that I had long experience of the country and that I was able to consult two of the nobility who were on most intimate terms with the Emperor of the Turks; they were among my closest friends and my relations, men of rare talent and great knowledge of these matters.[38]

One of these members was Mesih Pasha about whom Spandounes stated,

> Mesit Pasha (Messit bassa), who was of the house of Palaiologos. He was a brother of my father's mother. At the capture of Constantinople he had been taken by the Turks

[36] H. Inalcik, ed., *An Economic and Social History of the Ottoman Empire 1300–1914* (Cambridge: Cambridge University Press, 1994), 209–211. See N. Beldiceanu, *Les actes des premiers sultans conservés dans les manuscrits turcs de la Bibliothèque Nationale à Paris, I, Actes de Mehmet II et de Bayezid II du MS. Fonds turc ancien 39*, vol. I, II (Paris and The Hague: Mouton et Co., 1960), and Halil Inalcik, "Notes on N. Beldiceanu's Translation of the Kanunname, fond turc ancien 39, Bibliothèque Nationale, Paris," *Der Islam* 43, 1–2 (1967): 139–157.

[37] Inalcik, "Hass Murad Pasha," *Encyclopedia of Islam*, 2nd ed. Other members included Herzegzade Ahmed Pasha and Mamud Pasha; Mahmud Pasha was also related to the Angelović family of Novo Bordo and was cousins with George Amiroutzes, the first minister and imperial advisor to David Komnenos of Trabzon.

[38] Theodoros Spandouginos, *Discorso di Teodoro Spandugino Cantacusino Gentil'homo Constantinopolitano Dall'origine de'principi Turchi. Theodore Spandounes: On the Origins of the Ottoman Emperors*, trans. Donald M. Nicol (Cambridge: Cambridge University Press, 1997), 3–4.

along with his brothers. He was only ten at the time, and they were all made Turks. Mesih rose to the rank of Pasha . . .[39]

Heath Lowry argues that the "degree to which the Ottomans subsumed members of the Byzantine and Balkan nobility into the highest reaches of their own administration" becomes evident when examining how many of them became high ranking viziers in the late fifteenth and early sixteenth century. Lowry calls this period the "last phase of Ottoman syncretism" in which the former aristocracy was absorbed into the Ottoman ruling elite. Hass Murat Pasha and Mesih Pasha were prominent Byzantine examples, but there were several other Grand Viziers that included Byzantine, Serbian, Bosnian, and Albanian nobility. Individuals included Grand Veziers such as Mahmud Pasha (Angelović, 1453–68, 1472–74, Byantino-Serbian), Gedik Ahmed Pasha (1474–76, Byzantine or Serbian), Hersekzade Ahmed Pasha (1497–98;1502–06;1511;1512–14;1515–16, Bosnian), Hadim ʿAli Pasha (1501–02, Bosnian), Dukaginzade Ahmed Pasha (1514–15, Albanian), Hadim Sinan Pasha (1515; 1516–17, Bosnian).[40]

The Palaiologoi were certainly present among the ranks of Ottoman viziers, and it appears that as Ottoman officials, they were actively promoting the purchase of monopolies and tax farms among their family members. Appearing in the account of the *Historia Politike*, the Despot Demetrios Palaiologos, the son of Manuel II Palaiologos, capitulated to Sultan Mehmet II and in 1460 went to stay in Edirne where he was granted Ainos, the city in Thrace near Edirne which is on the banks of the Evros (Meriç River).[41] The chronicle describes him as receiving the administration of the salt works of Ainos to provide half of his sustainance.[42] While this area is not extremely famous for its salt production, this episode is interesting for the way in which it was described. Having received this source of revenue and being disposed to being a spendthrift, and to enjoy hunting, he was accused once of stealing *aspers* from the saltworks, which he denied doing. However, when the sultan learned that in fact, money was stolen with the knowledge and consent of Demetrios, he sent Mahmud Pasha to dispossess him of the salt works and every other income.[43] Even though the *Historia Politike* was written 100 years after the events, and the facts about the case cannot be verified, the legacy of granting favors and income-producing monopolies to Byzantine nobility was still present. In this case, the Byzantine imperial family member Demetrios Palaiologos was granted the salt works, but none other than the former Byzantine imperial family member, Mahmud Pasha, also deprived him of it. The account's

[39] Spandouginos, *Discorso di Teodoro Spandugino Cantacusino,* 46 and 164. The other was Ahmed Herzegzade Pasha, brother of the Duke of St. Sava in Bosnia.

[40] H. W. Lowry, *The Nature of the Early Ottoman State* (Albany: State University of New York Press, 2003), 120–122.

[41] Timothy E. Gregory, "Ainos," *The Oxford Dictionary of Byzantium* (New York: Oxford University Press, 1991) I, 41–42.

[42] S. I. Voutoras, I. A. Vretou, and G. Vafeiadou, *Lexicon Historias kai Geographias* (Constantinople: I.A. Vretou, 1869), vol. 1, 187 note that Ainos had a decent but underutilized harbor and that their main products included cotton, silk, camel hairs, and other items, but not salt.

[43] *Historia Politike,* Bekker, ed., 36.

purpose was more likely to suit the sixteenth-century social context. It served, in a sense, as a warning to the Greek economic elite to take care not to abuse their own resources, which could be taken away as easily as they were granted. This chronicle deliberately described the incident involving a salt works to send a direct message to the major figure of the 1570s, Michael Kantakouzenos, who was also in charge of salt works.

In contrast to the fourteenth and fifteenth centuries, when non-Muslims could enter Ottoman service while remaining Christians, in the sixteenth century there were many more limitations placed upon ambitious and wealthy Greeks.[44] Two outlets were readily available, however. First, Greeks could cultivate their interests in the world of Ottoman finances. There were many types of concessions that the state sold the rights to in order to gain a quick cash return that could be purchased by non-Muslims. Greeks were very active in purchasing these rights, and amassed fortunes supervising the tax collections on silver mines, customs duties and many other types of revenue producing institutions. Second, Greeks were able to involve themselves in the administration of the Church. This was particularly true for wealthy Greeks in Istanbul, where the Patriarchate of Constantinople retained a prominent place due to its claims of being the Ecumenical Patriarchate and because it was located in the Ottoman capital.

In addition to the symbolic elevated status the patriarchate provided to members of the Greek community, there were many important tangible benefits that the institution could provide for an enterprising patron. These included the economic benefits of the ecclesiastical tax farm. As we have seen, individual hierarchs and priests paid to be invested in office, and in order to do so they needed a financial backer. In turn, the backer benefitted directly from the tax collection process as the sums collected were significant enough to create competition among wealthy Greeks.

Greek elites who worked the Ottoman tax farms such as those of the customs zones yielded millions of *akçe* in revenue, showing amazingly high profits. By the same token, the patriarchate, because of its wide jurisdiction as a tax farm, also yielded healthy profits. The competition for the office over time, therefore, can be linked to competing political groups willing to finance an individual to become patriarch. There are several notable examples, which describe the intervention of lay people.

The process whereby the Ottoman state absorbed the Greek Orthodox Church hierarchy into its fiscal organization offered a variety of choices and opportunities to members of the Greek elite, as well as to the Greek Orthodox hierarchy. Clearly, there were hierarchs who served the Church with sincerity, and meant to fulfill the true mission of the Church. Others were more practical and saw that in order to serve the church it was necessary to use wealth and power to gain ecclesiastical positions. By the mid-sixteenth century, various Greek elite factions attempted to assert authority over the Church and, by extension, over the Greek

[44] Lowry, *The Nature of the Early Ottoman State.*

community of Istanbul, and vigorously competed for control and influence over its most prominent institution.

THE KANTAKOUZENOS FAMILY

Perhaps the wealthiest and most powerful family among the *archons* of the sixteenth century was the Kantakouzenos family, the most famous and prominent of whom was Michael Kantakouzenos, also known as Son of Satan (*Şeytanoğlu*). Şeytanoğlu represented a class of people who claimed to be scions of Byzantine imperial families; they became enormously wealthy through their activities in Ottoman finances and sought prominence in the only surviving and fully functioning Byzantine institution, which was the Church. As will become evident from the sources, this family was extremely involved in ecclesiastical affairs as well as in Ottoman tax farming concessions. It would be an interesting project to investigate and determine Şeytanoğlu's psychological make-up. The first step, however, to understanding Şeytanoğlu the person is to understand his social and economic class and, the historical and material context of his life. Understanding the types of activity in which he engaged, as well as piecing together clues as to why he was in the end executed by the sultan and reviled by the Church will be made clear.

Two centuries after Michael Kantakouzenos was executed in Ahyolu, a short history was written about another important Greek figure who was executed while serving the Ottoman Porte in the Danubian principalities in the mid-eighteenth century, a man named George Stavrakis. The significant aspect of this story is the way in which it begins. It recalls the height to which Michael Kantakouzenos rose, his goodness, wealth, power, seriousness, opposition to tyranny, and his goodwill to his fellow man. Michael Kantakouzenos suffered and was executed at the hands of those individuals who hated him and were haters of the Greek nation. The description continues by saying that two hundred years later, another such man was also executed, in the same manner and for some of the same reasons. While the biography of Stavrakis meant to demonstrate the latter's virtue—and, perhaps, innocence—the deliberate decision of the author to recall the memory of Kantakouzenos must have meant that he was a legendary figure in the collective imagination of the Greek community.[45]

Michael Kantakouzenos' presence in the collective imagination appears in another more vivid poem specifically about him that was included in the collection *Vivlos Vasileion* (The Book of Kings), written in the eighteenth century by Constantine Dapontès, secretary of the Prince Constantine Mavrokordatos.[46]

[45] Iorga, *Byzance après Byzance*, 118–121. See also Runciman, *Great Church in Captivity*, 197–8, and Lambros Kamperidis, *The Greek Monasteries of Sōzopolis: XIV–XVII Centuries* (Thessalonike: Institute for Balkan Studies, 1993), 29, n. 36.

[46] The poem was included as an appendix to an unrelated work and as an addendum to the work of Emile Legrand, *Recueil de poëmes historiques en grec vulgaire relatifs à la Turquie et aux principautés danubiennes*, vol. 5, Ecole des langues orientales vivantes (Paris: E. Leroux, 1877), appendix.

Although it cannot be used as a historical source per se, it does offer an impression about the legendary qualities that were attributed to Şeytanoğlu.

The poem explained that Michael Kantakouzenos, whom they called *Çelebi*, (well-born), was so wealthy that his farms *(çiftliks)* spread out throughout the whole of the Danube valley. Ottoman officials, the *ağas, pashas*, and viziers, attended him as if they were apprentices *(çıraks)*, and each stood up when Michael entered the room. One day, the imperial imam (*şeyh-ül-islam*) was present among a number of these officials at the home of one of them. As they stood up to greet Kantakouzenos, the *şeyh-ül-islam* was quite surprised and disturbed that they would call an infidel (*giaour*) by an honorific title like *çelebi*, and that they, as Ottoman officials, would stand to honor him. When Michael departed from the gathering, the *şeyh-ül-islam* scolded them all for their impiety. One of the *pashas* was troubled by this and told his household treasurer (*hazinedar*) to go directly to Michael to report what the *şeyh-ül-islam* said. Michael, being the clever man that he was, responded by requesting permission from the *pasha* to see if he could change the *şeyh-ül-islam's* mind about him. He wanted to make the *şeyh-ül-islam* call Michael *"çelebi."* The *pasha*, delighted by this sly proposal, consented with great anticipation. Then Michael went quickly to the *şeyh-ül-islam*'s home, and, not finding him home, asked the *şeyh-ül-islam*'s servant (*kehaya*), "In a year, how much butter does your master use? And how much honey, and candle-wax, and wood and oats does he need in his house, so that he might receive it?" The *kehaya* asked who this man was to offer these things and he said, "I am the one whom the imperial imam saw yesterday at the *pasha's* house where I was speaking with the *pasha* and other officials. They told me that the *şeyh-ül-islam* asked something concerning me." The *kehaya* took out the account book that recorded all the provisions and gave it to Michael. Michael filled one of his crafts, a Black Sea boat, full of the provisions, and went to deliver it to the *şeyh-ül-islam*. The *şeyh-ül-islam*, when he saw Michael coming with the load of goods, cried out, "Welcome, *Çelebi* Mihal," and warmly greeted him. After some time, Michael was again invited to attend a reception where they had all first gathered. He had planned to go when he was certain the *şeyh-ül-islam* was already present. When Michael entered, and before any other *pasha* could say a single word to greet him, the *şeyh-ül-islam* leaped forward and shouted with a great voice in front of everyone: "Welcome, the most well born of the *çelebi*, Mihal." And he said this two or three times and began to make an encomium for him, saying to the *pasha* how Michael was so succesful and worthy, and had many wonderful aspirations, and how such good people are in great demand in the empire. The *pasha*, whose home it was and who was curious to see how it would turn out, smiled, as he could not believe what had happened. When the imam departed, the *pasha* turned to Michael, laughing and in a loud voice, said, "'*ya seytansin, ya seytan oğlusun*,' either you are the devil, or the son of the devil."[47]

[47] Legrand, *Recueil de Poèmes historiques en grec vulgaire, appendix.*

Although this is a legendary account of how Michael Kantakouzenos received his nickname *Şeytanoğlu*, it reveals a common perception about Kantakouzenos' access to Ottoman circles and his influence upon Ottoman officials. While the historical record is not as vivid or colorful as the legendary account, in reality Kantakouzenos did have a strong ally in Mehmet Sokollu Pasha, who supported him and benefited from Kantakouzenos' ventures. With as much interaction as took place between him and the Ottoman officials, it is not hard to imagine that such a scene could take place. His friendship with Mehmet Sokollu Pasha, however, was not above suspicion or slander by competing court factions. The executions of Kantakouzenos and Mehmet Sokollu Pasha were, in effect, linked to the perception that they were forming an oppositional faction to the Sultan Murat III.

This story also shows that the Ottoman officials accepted Michael Kantakouzenos into their circle, although he was an infidel (*giaour*). In the early Ottoman period of expansion, being a non-Muslim was not an obstacle to joining the Ottomans military force and being rewarded with fiefs (*timars*). However, in accord with Islamic religious theory, non-Muslims were inherently discriminated against through the imposition of non-Muslim poll taxes, including the *cizye* and *ispence*. However, non-Muslims were allowed freedom to rise in the economic arena and gain wealth, as we have seen from the example of Michael Kantakouzenos.

The third observation that one can gain from this story is that Kantakouzenos used his wealth effectively to curry favor and wield real influence and power. Gerlach reported that Kantakouzenos was in the custom of providing to the Ottoman *pashas* honorariums of gold, wood, salt, iron, lead, and whatever they needed in their whole households.[48] His influence was also directed towards the Church, where he was recognized as the "maker" of bishops and patriarchs. His active involvement in the Church is particularly fascinating. What were the motivating factors for this invovlement if he had such good relations among Ottoman officials? The answer to this question is complicated. Certainly, the Church provided an open outlet for his desire for prestige. Even though the Patriarchate of Constantinople by no means resembled the form it took in its imperial Byzantine past, it was still the most prominent Greek institution with Byzantine roots that received Ottoman imperial sanction. Moreover, the awareness of the real economic benefits attached to the Church—the large sums of money that could be made in the brokering of ecclesiastical sees and tax farms—were surely strong attractions to Kantakouzenos. In all his dealings, Kantakouzenos' legacy was that of a wealthy, highly visible, and powerful patron who could intersect with various circles of society.

As Michael Kantakouzenos was one of the most powerful Greeks in the mid-sixteenth-century Ottoman Empire, it is sometimes hard to discern the legend from the historical record when describing the life and activities of such a complicated and multifaceted person. Among the more difficult tasks is uncovering if he was in fact the scion of the Byzantine imperial family that his name

[48] S. Gerlach. *Stephan Gerlachs Des Aelteren Tagebuch* (Frankfurt-am-Main, 1674), 463.

Fig. 5.2. The Greek Orthodox Christian brother of Alexander II, the Voivode of Wallachia, on horseback serving as an envoy (*müteferrika*) with a Turkish envoy on horseback. (Source: Lambert de Vos, *Kostümbuch*: Codex Ms. Or. 9, Bremen: Staats- und Universitätsbibliothek Bremen, fol. 17)

suggested. It is much easier to piece together the records of his business ventures and dealings with official Ottoman imperial administration, as well as with the Church. Michael Kantakouzenos is clearly visible in different sources: the Ottoman archives, in the patriarchal chronicles, and in the diary of Stephan Gerlach.

While it is possible that Kantakouzenos came the imperial family of the same name, there are some parts of his lineage that are not confirmed. At first glance, the name Kantakouzenos implies imperial aristocratic roots that go back to the person of John VI Kantakouzenos, who ruled as emperor in the mid-fourteenth century. However, in the late Byzantine period, imperial family names were rather unstable, and individuals could absorb these names, using as justification the slightest contact with the family.

A similar process was evolving in Cyprus, where a new class of wealthy Greeks, rising to prosperity from modest households, began acquiring economic and social prominence. Historian Angel Nicolaou-Konnari argues that establishing family lineage is extremely difficult, and

> There is no way of knowing whether persons with identical or similar names belonged to the same family. Furthermore, the identification of Byzantine names found in later sources, especially of names that go back to the Komnenian aristocracy, is a dangerous endeavor. . . .[49]

Similarly, in the Ottoman context, major family names continued to appear in Ottoman and Greek sources such as the above cited. The Kantakouzenos family has been studied extensively by scholars such as Donald Nicol and has been included in the *Prosopographisches Lexicon der Palaiologenzeit*.[50] Unfortunately, they do not establish the pedigree for Michael, who had the connection to the Black Sea coast city of Anchialos (Ahyolu).

Evaluating Michael Kantakouzenos' ancestry reveals the certainty of the name of his father, Demetrios Kantakouzenos. This information appears in a poem in honor of Michael and his son Andronikos written by the priest George the Aetolian (1525–1580), who was a learned cleric and admirer of the Kantakouzenos family.[51] He may have learned of the father's name through talking with the Kantakouzenos family members. However, it is also possible that George the Aetolian used one of the written sources such as the *Historia Patriarchica Constantinopoleos*, in which case he would have learned of the name of Demetrios Kantakouzenos. It

[49] Angel Nicolaou-Konnari, "Greeks," in *Cyprus: Society and Culture 1191–1374*, ed. Christopher Schabel and Angel Nicolaou-Konnari (Leiden: E. J. Brill, 2005), 43.

[50] E. Trapp, ed., *Prosopographisches Lexicon der Palaiologenzeit* (Vienna: Österreichischen Akademie der Wissenschaft, 1976–).

[51] George the Aetolian wrote two eulogies, composed in popular verse, one for Michael and the other for his son, Andronikos; see Georgiou tou Aitolou, Duo anekdota stihourgemata eis Mihael kai Andronikon tous Kantakouzenous, *Neon Hellenomnemon*, v. 9, n.3 259–264. These poems are short eulogies highly praising Kantakouzenos and his son but without real historical significance. They are more significant only if we explore who George the Anatolian was and why he wrote these, and for whom. On George the Aetolian see Bruce Merry, "George the Aetolian," *Encyclopedia of Modern Greek Literature* (Westport, CT: Greenwood Publishing Group, 2004).

is, therefore, possible that he concluded from this source that Michael's father was Demetrios Kantakouzenos who intervened with the *Archon* Xenakis in 1523 during Süleyman's attempt to take over the Christian Church properties.

The Romanian historian I.C. Filitti, in an attempt to uncover the lineage of the Romanian branch of the Kantakouzenos family who later became the *voyvodes* of Wallachia and Moldavia, traced the lineage through Michael's son, Andronikos. Filitti argued that the family descended from Manuel, the Byzantine protostrator of the Morea in 1420–29, and was given the nickname Jin by the Albanians. Filitti explains that Manuel had a son, Demetrios, who fled as a refugee to Hungary in 1474. In the following generation, though not necessarily in direct lineage, there is another Demetrios, who is known to have made a donation of a candelabra to the church of Mesemvria (Misivri), an ancient seaside town the Bulgarian Black Sea coast, in 1493.[52]

Donald Nicol identified the same Demetrios Kantakouzenos but described him as coming from the Serbian side of the family, from Novo Bordo in the years 1468–69. Novo Bordo had a large contingent from the Kantakouzenos family, who maintained their positions during the occupation by the Ottomans. However, in 1477, there was a mass execution of the Kantakouzenos family in Istanbul, though it is said that the Demetrios identified by Nicol survived and was said to have died in Mesemvria (Misivri). This Demetrios was also the same writer of religious verse in Old Serbian and collector of manuscripts.[53] Nothing more can be said about him for certain.

There are other links between the Kantakouzenos family and Misivri as well as the other important and ancient towns on the Bulgarian coast of the Black Sea, Sozopol (Ottoman: Sözebolu, Greek: Sōzopolis), and Pomerie (Ottoman: Ahyolu, Greek: Anchialos). There is the recording of the interment of Matthissa Kantakouzenos Palaiologina, who was buried in the Church of the Analepsis in Misivri in 1441. Her interment is marked by an inscription, connecting the family of the Kantakouzenos to the area of Misivri. However, it was not possible to identify her further, beyond the inscription and her family name.[54] The family of Michael Kantakouzenos had clear connections to Sözebolu that are visible in the ecclesiastical context. There is a clear trail of powerful Kantakouzenos support leading back to Sözebolu, Misivri, and Ahyolu. While there is no proof that Michael Kantakouzenos was an actual descendant of a Byzantine family, his importance as a post-conquest archon in the sixteenth century was enormous.

[52] Jean C. Filitti, *Notice sur les Cantacuzène du XIe au XVIIe siècles* (Bucharest: Geller, 1936), 8–9. For more on the Romanian branch of the Kantakouzenos family, see Jean Michel Cantacuzène, *Mille Ans dans les Balkans: Chronique des Cantacuzène dans la Tourmente des Siècles* (Paris: Editions Christian, 1992).

[53] Donald M. Nicol, *The Byzantine Family of Kantakouzenos (Cantacuzenus) c. 1100–1460: A Genealogical and Prosopographical Study*, vol. 11, *Dumbarton Oaks Studies* (Washington: Dumbarton Oaks Center for Byzantine Studies, Trustees for Harvard University, 1968), 226–227. See also Donald M. Nicol, "The Byzantine Family of Cantacuzenus," *Dumbarton Oaks Papers* XI (1968). Nicholas Kanatakouzenos was the customs officer ("*gabelotto*") who was allowed to remain in his office during the first Ottoman occupation of 1441–1444.

[54] Nicol, *Byzantine Family*, 230.

Possessing great wealth and power within the ecclesiastical institution and serving and influencing Ottoman imperial officials made him a formidable figure in Greek and Ottoman society.

Michael Kantakouzenos appears very prominently in the *Mühimme Defterleri* of the Ottoman archives because of his involvement in four business ventures. First, he was a master (*emin*) of a tax farm of a salt works in Ahyolu. Second, he directed the Ahyolu shipyard (*tershane*), and third, he was an imperial merchant (*hass tucarı*) arranging the importation of furs from Moscow for the Ottoman court. The fourth business venture is his involvement in the institution of the Church.

Salt was an important commodity and provided a steady income for whoever controlled the monopoly on the concession. The tax farms of salt works were prime concessions that non-Muslims could purchase. As mentioned previously, the former Despot of the Morea, Demetrios Palaiologos, was offered a tax farm of the salt works of Ainos. After he had been removed, there was vigorous competition among the numerous *archons* who approached the sultan for this salt works concession and the income attached to it. This example shows that salt works were desirable enterprises and that there was a tradition for Greek elites acquiring the rights to them.[55]

Salt was also essential for the survival of the population, particularly in cities where provisioning was always a greater issue than in the countryside. For this reason, salt works were state property. As the state did not want to get into the salt business, it allowed individuals to purchase the rights to produce salt and run the business as a concession. The requirement was for the individual to give the state one-fifth of its production, and the master could sell the rest of the product to cover expenses and for profit. It therefore functioned as a tax farm, where the individual tax farmer was responsible for all aspects of the tax farm administration. The state, however, would ensure that there was a steady supply of labor and protect the salt works from illegal activities.[56]

Michael Kantakouzenos' Ahyolu salt produced on the Black Sea coast of present-day Bulgaria, near Sözebolu and Misivri, was not of poor quality like other Danubian salt that was said to be black and hard so that it needed to be shattered in order to be processed.[57] Although Ahyolu was not the biggest salt works (those of Selanik and Kaffa were by far larger) it was important to the Ottomans because it provided salt directly to the Istanbul market. Like the salt works in Kaffa which provided the majority of salt to Istanbul, it also contributed to provisioning the capital.[58] Information from a 1490s register of Ahyolu salt works reveal that, at that time, there were 1,047 men working at the site. In 1580, it produced a moderate 153,000 *akçe* in state revenues from the sale of the salt.[59] On October 18,

[55] See Lütfi Güçer, "XV.-XII. Asırlarda Osmanlı İmparatorluğunda Tüz İnhisarı ve Tüzların İşletme Nizami," *İstanbul Üniversitesi İktisat Fakültesi Mecmuası* 23 (1962–63): 397–416.

[56] Inalcik, *Economic and Social History of the Ottoman Empire*, 60.

[57] Gerlach, *Tagebuch*, 303.

[58] Inalcik, *Economic and Social History of the Ottoman Empire*, 63.

[59] Güçer, "XV.–XII." Asırla102.

1576 an urgent decree was sent to the *kadi* of Varna and Ahyolu to go in person to Ahyolu in order to find out how much salt was being produced, and it would be sent by ship to Istanbul, because there was a great need for salt in Istanbul.[60]

It is not clear when Michael Kantakouzenos acquired the rights to the salt works monopoly in Ahyolu. Since his family was most likely from the area, the possession of the salt works could have been held by his family for a long time prior to the 1570s. However, the first reference to him as the master of the salt works appeared in the *Mühimme Defterleri* on November 11, 1571. An edict directed from the Imperial Divan to the kadis of Ahyolu mentioned the "*Ahyolu tüz emini Mihal*," and on Novermber 27, to the Voyvode Alexander of Wallachia, he is again clearly identified as the "*tüz emini Mihal*."[61]

Kantakouzenos' business was much greater than simply that of a holder of a monopoly on the Ahyolu salt works concession. This operation involved the transport as well as the extraction of salt. For this Kantakouzenos needed ships, and there is a clear indication that he also produced ships, both for his own business purposes and for the Ottoman state purposes. Crimean salt was transported to Istanbul by Greek ship-owners and captains.[62] Wallachian salt needed transport to Istanbul, and Kantakouzenos is reported to have controlled almost all the salt trade in Wallachia and Moldavia.[63] He received this trade privilege from Mehmet Sokollu Pasha, to whom he paid several thousand ducats each year.[64] For a period of time, he also held the position of the salt master and inspector in Istanbul.[65] In this case, Kantakouzenos oversaw all salt imported into Istanbul, the most populous city and imperial capital. Gerlach reported that the location for the sale of salt was near the fish market, where a small building was located in which Kantakouzenos had his office. This position, however, was taken away from Kantakouzenos after the treasurer (*defterdar*) discovered corrupt activity and appointed to the position a "Turk" who annually payed the sultan 1,000 ducats.[66]

The Ahyolu salt works, however, would stay in the family into the seventeenth century. Even after the execution of Michael in March of 1578, when all his property was confiscated, Michael's brother and son Andronikos gathered enough money to pay the large debts owed to the imperial treasury. Kantakouzenos' immediate family managed to regain the rights to be the *emin* of the Ahyolu salt works.[67]

As mentioned, part of the opportunity of possessing a salt works was the benefit of transporting salt from the Black Sea ports to Istanbul. Since Kantakouzenos had control over the Danubian salt trade, he also had a large fleet of boats. Apparently, he had the facilities to build the boats in Ahyolu. Every year, he built twenty or thirty galleys at his own expense for the sultan, mostly for trading purposes.[68]

[60] Başbakanlıl Osmanlı Arşivi, *Mühimme Defterleri* (MD): 457, 195.
[61] MD 16: 116. [62] Inalcik, *Economic and Social History of the Ottoman Empire*, 63.
[63] Gerlach, *Tagebuch*, 395. [64] Gerlach, *Tagebuch*, 303.
[65] Gerlach, *Tagebuch*, 95. [66] Gerlach, *Tagebuch*, 454. [67] MD 40: 385, 174.
[68] Gerlach, *Tagebuch*, 59.

However, in 1570 and 1571, there are numerous entries in the *Mühimme Defterleri* about the building of ships in Ahyolu. Between September 1570 and May 1571, there are thirty-six decrees (*hüküms)* that commanded the building of a fleet of ships for the Ottoman navy.[69] These were orders for wood, building materials, and craftsmen to be sent immediately to the shipyards of Ahyolu for the building of ships for the sultan. This was an important state matter, as Kantakouzenos was supplying about sixty ships to the Ottoman navy in preparation for what would be the battle at Lepanto in 1571.[70] Kantakouzenos provided more than one-quarter of the 206 Ottoman galleys for the Ottoman naval operation.[71] Many of these ships were certainly lost in the dramatic defeat against the Holy League's alliance in October of 1571. The impact of the victory at Lepanto for the West was an iconic battle that significantly lifted European morale, as they had just defeated the greatest threat to European Christendom. For the Ottomans, it was a stinging loss where 200 of the the empire's 230 ships sent into battle were destroyed.[72] But it was a loss that was quickly overcome with the rebuilding of the fleet, an effort that would again engage Kantakouzenos' shipyards.

The third major enterprise that Michael Kantakouzenos was involved in was as an imperial merchant bringing furs from Russia.[73] Gerlach reports that Mehmet Sokollu Pasha was the one responsible for making Kantakouzenos an imperial merchant, granting him 60,000 ducats annually to purchase furs from trading counterparts from Moscow. Kantakouzenos would bring all kinds of precious furs to the sultan so that the sultan could offer them as gifts to his *Viziers, pashas, beylerbeys*, and other important officials as well as to the women of the imperial family.[74] A *ferman* confirming Michael Kantakouzenos' right to be an imperial merchant was sent by Murat III in March 1576 to the Anadolu *sancakbeys* and *kadis*, stating that the imperial merchant Michael was to be assisted and not impeded on his departure and return to Russia to purchase furs for the state.[75]

Kantakouzenos received the right of free passage through the empire, as well as in the subject principalities. Imperial Ottoman merchants going to Moscow with gold currency and returning with fur needed to be quite cautious and were often the subject of robberies and attacks. In June 1565, a group of thirteen Muslim and Christian merchants had traveled to Moscow, and on their return through an area of Poland were attacked by a band of robbers who killed seven of their party. The sultan sent a decree to the Polish king (*Leh Kralı*) to ensure that the culprits were captured and punished and the goods restored.[76] Other orders and commands were

[69] MD 16: 106; MD 16: 105–111; MD 16: 116; MD 16: 103.

[70] Gerlach, *Tagebuch*, 60.

[71] Jack Beeching, *The Galleys at Lepanto* (London: Hutchinson & Co., 1982), 209.

[72] Jeremy Black, *War in the Early Modern World, 1450–1815* (New York: Taylor & Francis, 2012), 162–163.

[73] MD 35: 211. [74] Gerlach, *Tagebuch*, 453.

[75] Ismet Binark et al., *Osmanlı fermanları/Ottoman fermans* (Ankara: T.C. Başbakanlık Devlet Arşivleri Genel Müdürlüğü, 1994), No. 134, 14.

[76] MD 6: 1283.

directed to the Tatar Khan, the Voyvodes of Buğdan, and Wallachia, and were issued as documents to the individual merchants themselves as receipts for free passage through those lands. It is unclear whether Kantakouzenos' role as a merchant also included diplomacy and gift giving on behalf of the sultan. However, despite the lack of direct evidence for the 1560s and 1570s, there is evidence from the Russian Archives from almost fifty years later. Thomas Kantakouzenos, a descendant of Şeytanoğlu, served as head of an Ottoman embassy to Moscow in 1621, 1627, 1630, and 1633.[77] During each visit he brought the tsar valuable gifts of precious metal covered objects such as adorned horse bridles, writing sets with precious jewels, and ruby and diamond encrusted religious plaques.[78] It is likely, just as in the case of the salt works, that the role of imperial fur merchant/diplomat remained within the family.

MICHAEL KANTAKOUZENOS AND THE CHURCH

Michael Kantakouzenos' main business enterprises involving salt, ships, and furs served the social, economic, and military fabric of the Ottoman state. With his financial success in the Ottoman economic sphere, the growth of amazing wealth translated into real power in one other important social sphere, that of the Church. Michael Kantakouzenos was highly influential among ecclesiastical officials, and he was very active in getting his way among bishops and patriarchs. There is evidence that even prior to Michael's activities in the 1560s and 1570s, the Kantakouzenos family of Ahyolu, Misivri, and Sözebolu was involved directly with the ecclesiastical institution during the second quarter of the sixteenth century.

The first sign that there was a powerful force from this region appears during the deposition of Patriarch Jeremiah I, who was the subject of the 1544 *Ahkâm Defteri* documents. He was deposed in favor of Ioannikios, the Metropolitan of Sōzopolis. Ioannikios was made patriarch through the support of only a few *archons* and against a broad-based opposition. In order to acquire the patriarchal throne, he had to be able to raise the *pişkeş* of 500 florins. Without a broad base of support, he needed the vigorous aid of a few individuals. Although this small group of supporters was not named, they were influential and wealthy enough to install a highly unpopular Metropolitan from Sōzopolis onto the patriarchal throne. With support coming from his home territory, Patriarch Ioannikios likely relied on a member of the Kantakouzenos family of Ahyolu. The episode of Patriarch Ioannikios was very brief; he came to the patriarchal throne quickly and

[77] Massumeh Farhad et.al., *The Tsars and the East: Gifts from Turkey and Iran in the Moscow Kremlin* (Washington DC: Arthur M. Sackler Gallery/Smithsonian, 2009), 10. See also J. C. Filitti, *Notice sur les Cantacuzène Du XIe Au XVIIe Siècles* (Bucharest: Geller, 1936), 8–9. I. I. Vishnevskaya, "The Royal Court and the Orthodox Church in the Seventeenth Century," in Mark Suttclifee, ed., *Treasures of the Czars: From the State Museums of the Moscow Kremlin* (London: Booth-Clibborn Ed., 1995).

[78] Farhad et al., *The Tsars and the East*, Cat. n. 35, 36, 48, 64.

was removed quickly. Patriarch Ioannikios was deposed for illegally and illegitimately taking the patriarchal throne. Patriarch Jeremiah I was lawfully restored to the throne and was able to live out his second term as patriarch in office. The Kantakouzenos family are not actually visible in the sources during this episode, but because the tensions between factions vying for control of the patriarchate were long-lasting, one can see the Kantakouzenos family present in the immediate aftermath of Patriarch Jeremiah I's reign.[79]

After Patriarch Jeremiah I died, Dionysios II was elected patriarch, in large measure through the intervention of an *archon* named Kantakouzenos, though he was known as "Monoraitos." The *Vivlion Historikon* explains, "And the Galata natives were cooperative, because he [Dionysios] was a Galata native, born and bred. And the majority of bishops did not want him, neither did the *archons* of the City, only Kantakouzenos the *Monoraitos*. . . ."[80] This individual was identified as Antonios Kantakouzenos. In another instance the same Antonios Kantakouzenos the *Monoraitos* conspired directly with Michael Kantakouzenos (*Şeytanoğlu*) to remove another subsequent patriarch. In this instance, Antonios Kantakouzenos supported Patriarch Dionysios II, perhaps as a reaction against the popular Patriarch Jeremiah I, to whom Patriarch Ioannikios, Kantakouzenos' first candidate, lost the throne.

Patriarch Ioasaph II, succeeded Dionysios II and reigned for about nine years (1556–65). The *Vivlion Historikon* reveals that he consciously styled himself as the "Magnificent" (*Megaolprepos*), perhaps in imitation of the Sultan Süleyman. Both of their reputations included ruling justly, reforming laws, and stamping out all manner of illegitimate practice. Ioasaph, however, did not have the unrestricted power of the Ottoman Sultan to protect him. When he opposed Michael Kantakouzenos' uncanonical marriage, the latter conspired with the above-mentioned Antonios *Monoraitos* Kantakouzenos to depose Ioasaph. They then took it upon themselves to inspect all Ioasaph's patriarchal finances in order to charge him with financial impropriety. They eventually managed to depose him by ironically charging him with the crime of simony.[81] Interestingly, the *Historia Patriarchica* has full descriptions of the horrors of simony especially during the period of *Şeytanoğlu's* peak activity in the 1560s and 1570s. In fact, this chronicle devotes large discussions to the sin of simony, making special mention of *Acts of the Apostles* and the condemnation of Simon Magus, after whom simony received its name.[82]

Patriarch Ioasaph was succeeded by Patriarch Metrophanes III, who was ordained by Patriarch Dionysios II, the partisan of Antonios *Monoraitos*

[79] *Historia Patriarchica,* ed. Bekker, 153–157, and Zachariadou, *Deka Tourkika engrapha*, 174–177, no. 7.

[80] C. Sathas, "Apospasma ek tou Chronographou Dorotheou Monemvasias," in *Viographikon Schediasma Peri Patriarchou Hieremia B' (1572–1592),* ed. C. Sathas (Athens, 1870), 8.

[81] (Pseudo)Dorotheos, *Vivlion Historikon Periechon En Synopsei Diaphorous Kai Exochous Historias* (Venice: Nikolaos Glykeis, 1750), 895; also see Gerlach, *Tagebuch*, 60.

[82] *Historia Patriarchica* (C.S.H.B. edition), 197. On simony, see Nicholas Aloysius Weber, *A History of Simony in the Christian Church* (Baltimore, MD: J. H. Furst, 1909).

Table 5.1. Mid-Sixteenth Century Patriarchs supported by the Kantakouzenous family

Patriarch	Accession	End of Reign	Kantakouzenos support
Jeremiah I	31 December 1522	13 January 1546	No
Joannikios I (illegitimate)	1524	1525	Yes
Jeremiah I (illegitimate)	1524	1525	No
Dionysios II	17 April 1546	July 1556	Yes
Ioasaph II	Summer 1556	January 1565	No
Metrophanes III	January 1565	4 May 1572	Yes
Jeremiah II	5 May 1572	23 November 1579	No
Metrophanes III (second term)	23 November 1579	9 August 1580	Yes
Jeremiah II (second term)	August 1580	22 February 1584	Yes
Pachomios II (illegitimate)	22 February 1584	Mid-February 1584	No

Kantakouzenos, and later by Patriarch Jeremiah II, who was from the city of Ahyolu, Şeytanoğlu's hometown. Thus, we can see that from the mid-1540s to the end of the 1570s each of these patriarchs had connections to the Kantakouzenos family, and those who did not were deposed.

Table 5.1 contains the names of the mid-sixteenth-century patriarchs of Constantinople that indicates whether they were partisans of the Kantakouzenos family.[83]

From 1522 to 1584, five of ten patriarchs had direct support from Michael Kantakouzenos. Stephan Gerlach commented that Michael Kantakouzenos was directly involved in the selection process of bishops and patriarchs who would

> buy this position from the *Bassa*, the *defterdar*, Michael Kantakouzenos, and the clergy. A rich metropolitan would have to give to Michael *Şeytanoğlu*, (that's how Turks and Greeks call the aforementioned Kantakouzenos), 1,000 [*ducats*], to the priests, of whom there are many, each 10, to the *logotheti*, 10 *ducats*, and so forth. Only the patriarch would not get anything.[84]

Gerlach's description was rather harsh, making Michael Kantakouzenos the chief decision maker of the Church. The "rich metropolitans" had to pay Michael Şeytanoğlu an exorbitant sum of 1,000 ducats, and then to the patriarchal court officials much smaller sums. This financial exchange demonstrates the command that Şeytanoğlu had over the patriarchate. The funds would be given to Kantakouzenos, and Gerlach explained that the patriarch himself would not get

[83] Ecumenical Patriarchate of Constantinople, *Hemerologion tou Oikoumenikou Patriarcheiou*, vol. 2. (Thessalonike: Asprovalta, 1999), 741–742.

[84] Gerlach, *Tagebuch*, 290.

any money from the exchange. The control by the layman was so complete, that there was little to no consideration of the patriarch.

The financial indebtedness by members of the lower clergy to Şeytanoğlu was extreme, but beyond the initial financial obligation to get the office, it grew to include the installation ceremonies as well. Gerlach reported that those priests or monks needed money to give

> bribes in order to take some other innocent man's job, and make themselves bishops or metropolitans. They are ambitious and jealous fellows, and as the Orator [John Zygomalas] says, 'uneducated asses.' In addition, once they received the appointment they desired, they had to pay for all of the installation ceremonies, and entertaining connected to it.[85] If he didn't have the money, he would have to borrow it. Therefore, their whole aim is to get together the money to become bishop or metropolitan. And if someone has reached that goal, he will scratch from his subordinates within three or four years the money to repay what he had borrowed and given to Kantakouzenos.[86]

Clearly, Kantakouzenos was in direct control of the patriarchate and the appointment to ecclesiastical offices, just as if it were a monopoly that he held on the salt concession. No one could gain a position, or an opportunity to profit from the position, without first offering him payment and essentially purchasing the right. If someone went into debt to gain an ecclesiastical position, he would in turn put pressure on his subordinates, to be able to gather funds enough funds to repay Kantakouzenos.

The *Vivlion Historikon* explains that the Metropolitan of Caesarea Metrophanes became Patriarch of Constantinople through an agreement that he had with the clerics, and with Michael Kantakouzenos, and that he was "to always be at their disposal." This chronicle described how the principles and ethics of the patriarchate had been entirely destroyed, that the patriarchate was completely devastated, simony was in the open, and "people who were demons became hierarchs, because the clerics and Kantakouzenos commanded, and every illegality and immorality took place."[87]

Clearly, Patriarch Metrophanes III was put into office through the influence of Michael Kantakouzenos. However, things between the two men were not harmonious, and it is clear that Michael worked to remove Patriarch Metrophanes III, just as he had installed him. One of the main reasons was financial. Patriarch

[85] Gerlach, *Tagebuch*, 291. [86] Gerlach, *Tagebuch*, 267.

[87] Pseudo-Dorotheos, *Vivlion Historikon*, 895. Elizabeth Zachariadou introduced the fact that there are two known variants of this text that were authored by Pseudo-Dorotheos of Monemvasia. The most frequently cited version was one with the title *Vivlion Historikon*, published in Venice in 1631, and again in 1805. A second variant is found in Manuscript Codex 215 at the University of Michigan Library which includes a very lengthy excursus upon the early career of Metrophanes. While the majority of the characterizations in the *Vivlion Historikon* are critical of Metrophanes, this version offers a response to criticisms concerning his interactions at Rome and the aftermath. Zachariadou suggests that this was probably composed at the time of Dionysios II, by compatriots of Zygomalas who was from Nauplion. See E. A. Zachariadou, "He Patriarcheia Tou Dionysiou B' Se Mia Parallage Tou Pseudo-Dorotheou," *Thesaurismata Tou Hellenikou Institoutou Byzantinon Kai MetaVyzantinon Spoudon* 1, no. 1 (1962): 142–161.

Metrophanes III was supposed to pay Kantakouzenos 2,000 ducats yearly in addition to the 4,000 ducats he was to pay to the sultan. When Kantakouzenos demanded more money, up to 3,000 or 4,000 ducats, Metrophanes said that he was paying too much. He had already given Kantakouzenos 16,000 ducats over eight years.[88]

Since battle lines were drawn between Patriarch Metrophanes III and Michael Kantakouzenos, Patriarch Metrophanes had been cultivating allies among other influential people outside of the Greek community, perhaps with one of Michael Kantakouzenos' chief rivals, the aforementioned Don Josef Nasi, the Duke of Naxos, a wealthy Sephardic Jew originally from Portugal who controlled state monopolies on wine and possessed incredible wealth. There is a curious and anomalous document written by Patriarch Metrophanes III in 1568, a decree to the Greek Orthodox people of the island of Crete, stating that no Greek Orthodox Christian person living on the island should harass any of the Jewish people living there.[89] Although Crete was still in Venetian hands, the patriarchate did have ecclesiastical jurisdiction over the island. Patriarch Metrophanes, when he was still Metropolitan of Caesarea, had been appointed patriarchal exarch and was sent in 1546 to Venice on Church business.[90] After he became patriarch, he reached out again to cooperate with the Venetians, this time with the *bailo* of Crete. However, Patriarch Metrophanes was possibly motivated to issue such a decree to curry favor with the chief Jewish financier of the Ottoman Empire, Don Joseph Nasi. The connection becomes clear when one remembers that Nasi was the customs officer for all wine produced and imported into the Ottoman Empire. In March 1568, the sultan granted him the privilege of exclusive control of the trade in Cretan wines that were to be imported to Moldavia.[91] This meant that he had long-term economic interests in the wine produced on Crete and certainly would have been aware of the plight of the Jews living there. Patriarch Metrophanes would certainly have been aware of Nasi's situation and clear opportunity to gain favor. Surely this could counterbalance the overwhelming strength of Kantakouzenos in Ottoman society.

Kantakouzenos eventually drove Patriarch Metrophanes III out of the patriarchate in 1572 and in his place installed Patriarch Jeremiah II, the Metropolitan of Larissa. As Gerlach said, "Kantakouzenos was master in everything, governing after his liking, and the patriarch would not be allowed in the least to contradict him, because he is the *Bassa's* [Pasha] big friend with whom he shares the blood money."[92] John Zygomalas, the Grand Orator (*megas rhetor*) of the

[88] MD: 28: 154; Gerlach, *Tagebuch*, 233.

[89] George C. Papademetriou, "An Encyclical of the Ecumenical Patriarch Metrophanes III, 1520–1580," *Journal of Ecumenical Studies* 26/2 (1989): 338–340.

[90] Konstantinos Moustakas, "Metrophanes III of Constantinople,"*Encyclopaedia of the Hellenic World, Asia Minor*<http://www.ehw.gr/l.aspx?id=8066>.

[91] Victor Eskenasy, "Jews, Romanians, and Ottomans in the Middle Ages: Joseph Nassi and Moldavia," *Communication at XIX Spring Symposium of Byzantine Studies* (University of Birmingham, March 23–26, 1985), 358.

[92] Gerlach, *Tagebuch*, 267.

patriarchate, was perhaps sympathetic to Patriarch Metrophanes because Patriarch Metrophanes previously had good relations with his compatriots from Nauplion, but also because he disliked the strong-arm tactics of Kantakouzenos and those who cooperated with him. He therefore agreed that it was Kantakouzenos' fault that Patriarch Metrophanes had been deposed.

After Metrophanes had been deposed, he was removed to Mt. Athos for three years and was essentially in exile for about seven years. Because he was originally from Istanbul, he had many contacts and people who supported him. He also re-established the monastery of Holy Trinity on the island of Heybeliada (Halki) where he stayed for a period of time.[93] Metrophanes was never far from the action, however, and continuously made his successor, Patriarch Jeremiah II, nervous that he would return to claim the patriarchal throne. Shortly after his exile, he was seen in Üsküdar and was clearly not staying put on Mt. Athos. Patriarch Jeremiah went to the Divan to complain, and there was a decree sent out to the *kadis* of Üsküdar, Selanik, and Sidrekapisi stating that if he is still to be found in the area of Üsküdar, then he should be apprehended and sent again to Mt. Athos forever.[94] Patriarch Metrophanes' reappearance was not unusual. It was fairly common in Ottoman administration for deposed Ottoman officials to sit out for a period of time after being removed for some charge that was leveled, and then re-emerge onto the scene in the same or another similar position when the political winds became friendlier. Certainly, the same could be true for deposed patriarchs.

On another occasion, when the threat of former Patriarch Metrophanes' return became more imminent, Patriarch Jeremiah II called all the priests, monks, and dignitaries of the community, and told them that, if they were dissatisfied with him, then he would relinquish the position to Patriarch Metrophanes. However, if they were satisfied, then they should send a petition to the sultan stating their satisfaction with him as patriarch. The sultan received over 500 petitions on behalf of Patriarch Jeremiah II, and about fifty on behalf of Patriarch Metrophanes.[95] Patriarch Jeremiah II went to the Divan in order to confirm his position, but in the meantime the agents of Metrophanes also appeared. They explained to the Ottoman officials at the Imperial Divan that Metrophanes had no design against Patriarch Jeremiah II but only wished to make petitions and complaints against Michael Kantakouzenos. They complained that Kantakouzenos had extorted 16,000 ducats over the course of eight years, or 2,000 per year. It was this amount that Metrophanes wished to retrieve. Both Gerlach and the Ottoman documents record the same information.[96]

Gerlach reports that Metrophanes was born in a village or suburb on the other side of the Golden Horn (*Halıç*) from the Phanar and the patriarchate. He was from Hasköy (St. Paraskevi) located beneath the arsenal and one of the sultan's gardens. As he was from Istanbul, he had many noble friends who wanted him to regain his position. When he arrived back in Istanbul after his brief stay on Mt.

[93] Gerlach, *Tagebuch*, 59.
[94] MD 22: 20; MD 22: 21.
[95] Gerlach, *Tagebuch*, 233.
[96] MD 28: 359.

Athos, Patriarch Jeremiah II sent five or six of his monks to welcome Patriarch Metrophanes amicably in Patriarch Jeremiah II's name, to ask the reason for his journey, and whether he wanted to complain about Patriarch Jeremiah II to the sultan. Patriarch Metrophanes responded that he had returned only to request something from the sultan, and that he could not reveal it to them. Patriarch Metrophanes had well over 2,000 supporters in the city of Istanbul, and many friends who benefited during his reign as patriarch. Gerlach assessed that Patriarch Jeremiah II was, in fact, in great danger of losing his position because Metrophanes had even asked his friends, the Jewish doctors, to help him in this matter. He reasoned that these counselors were often with the sultan and only had to mention to the sultan that Patriarch Metrophanes should have the patriarchate and Patriarch Jeremiah II would be deposed. As is clear from the episode concerning the Cretan Jews, Patriarch Metrophanes had been cultivating friendships with the Jewish elites. Even to a foreign observer like Gerlach, this was great ammunition in the battle between Patriarch Metrophanes versus Kantakouzenos and Jeremiah II.[97] Realizing this threat, Patriarch Jeremiah II had promised to give to Patriarch Metrophanes 300 ducats yearly if he would simply leave the city and go anywhere else. Patriarch Jeremiah II was further worried that since he had to depart from Istanbul himself to go on one of his tax-collecting journeys, Patriarch Metrophanes would find opportunity to take over the throne.[98]

Patriarch Jeremiah II himself was from Ahyolu, although he had last served as Metropolitan of Larissa. He was well educated, which was fortunate because he was called to respond to the German Lutheran Reformers, who had descended on the Patriarchate of Constantinople with the hope of developing a strong alliance against the papacy. They sent Patriarch Jeremiah II a copy of the *Augsburg Confession of Faith*, and he and his staff in Istanbul had failed to respond in a timely manner. Patriarch Jeremiah II and his staff were reluctant to get involved in exchanges on principles of faith, because Patriarch Jeremiah II believed that such issues had been solved in the ancient Ecumenical Councils. In the end these exchanges, or lack thereof, were disappointing to the Lutheran theologians and philosophers. Michael Kantakouzenos attempted to become involved in the matter by promising to have the *Augsburg Confession of Faith* translated into vernacular Greek. This never materialized. However, German scholars like Stephan Gerlach and Martin Crusius were very curious and became interested in Kantakouzenos' rich library. Kantakouzenos had collected a significant number of manuscripts; more than half of the works were scientific and medical manuscripts as well as other classical Greek texts, plus many theological texts. Gerlach noted that after Kantakouzenos was executed, the Germans who had been involved in the Protestant-Orthodox dialogue, as well as numerous monks from Mt. Athos, showed up at Kantakouzenos' palace in Ahyolu to buy whatever they could at the auction of his goods and properties. The sultan was aware of the richness of

[97] Gerlach, *Tagebuch*, 247.
[98] Gerlach, *Tagebuch*, 403.

his library and of the Germans' interest in the collection. Upon Kantakouzenos' execution, the Ottoman officials surprised the German embassy with a generous gift of many of the books from this library.[99]

While Michael Kantakouzenos' continual involvement in ecclesiastical matters reached the highest level of ecclesiastical administration at the patriarchate in Istanbul, he was also very active in administering local ecclesiastical matters closer to his home in Ahyolu. He personally intervened and administered church matters at the local monasteries near his home in Sōzopolis. Kantakouzenos became a benefactor of the small and previously abandoned St. Anastasia monastery, and controlled its administration. In the meantime, he had decided that, because it was a small entity, it would be better served if it were to become part of the holdings of St. John the Baptist Monastery, which was *stavropegion*, meaning that it was directly under the jurisdiction of the patriarchate.[100] A patriarchal letter written by Patriarch Jeremias II in June 1575 confirmed the transfer, stating that this deed likened Kantakouzenos to a physician who cared for the "foundation of the monasteries." The translation from Kamberides reads as follows:

> The physician, who can forsee the symptoms of an illness and prescribe the necessary cure before it takes hold of the patient and causes an untimely death, is indeed praiseworthy and wise. If we praise the physician, who tends to the needs of the body, we should also commend the person who cares for the foundation of the monasteries, for the monasteries do not only provide health but also the necessary things for material subsistence as well as the salvation of the souls of those who take refuge in them. The most noble among the *archons*, the Grand Domestikos Michael Kantakouzenos, and our beloved spiritual son, having crossed to the monastery of St. Anastasia and found its affairs by those who administer it but also due to the unfavorable conditions of the place and its poverty, as well as the lack of water, he could not bring himself as a devout man to allow this to happen, but as a wise physician, in order to cure it from complete disintegration he discussed this with the Metropolitan of Sōzopolis Akakios and Nikodemos, who care of the welfare of this little monastery of St. Anastasia. He could not find any other cure against its annihilation, but to place it under the administration of the monastery of St. John the Baptist, which is managed in a sound way and it is not deprived of material wealth, being able to provide the necessary needs to those who lead a monastic life in it, and is in a position to care about St. Anastasia. The same *archon* Michael Kantakouzenos has also written to us, reminding us of the state of affairs of all the above.

In this account, Kantakouzenos was referred to as the "most noble among the *archons*, the Grand Domestikos, Michael Kantakouzenos, and our beloved

[99] G. K. Papazoglou, *Vivliothekes Sten Konstantinoupole Tou [16] Aiona (Kod. Vind. Hist. Gr. 98)* (Thessalonike, 1983).

[100] For Sakkelion's publication of these documents see Kamperidis, *The Greek Monasteries of Sōzopolis*, 15–17. For an excellent discussion of lay patronage of monasteries in the late Komnenian period, see Michael Angold, *Church and Society in Byzantium under the Comneni, 1081–1261* (Cambridge: Cambridge University Press, 1995), 333–345, where the advantages and conflicts of *stavropegion* are described in detail.

spiritual son."[101] Whether Michael Kantakouzenos was interested in saving St. Anastasia, building up St. John the Baptist, or linking them in order to have influence on them both is not clear. The latter option, however, would be the most practical way for Kantakouzenos to gain control over the well-established monastic institutions in Sōzopolis that were very prominent in his region. He handed over the smaller monastery to gain control of the larger.

There were very clear advantages to be gained for *stavropegion* monasteries. Technically, these monastic institutions came under the direct authority of the Patriarchate of Constantinople. In reality, however, they were generally far enough removed from Istanbul that there was little administrative control, especially in cases like this where there was such an influential patron involved. Generally, a monastery desires *stavropegion* status because it means that it can avoid the control of the local bishop.

In the case of the Sōzopolis monasteries, the patriarchate confirmed Kantakouzenos' donation. *Stavropegion* monasteries generally are confirmed in their status with documentation, but in this case the patriarch may have been attempting to show his authority. Michael Kantakouzenos and other *archons* always posed a challenge to his authority, as was clear in an earlier 1567 document written by Patriarch Metrophanes III. He granted the monastery of St. John the Baptist full autonomy as a *stavropegion* institution. The document reads, "The aforesaid monastery, with all its attendant houses (metochia) and properties, as well as the assets found there, is declared autonomous. It should not be influenced or disturbed from any person, whether clergyman or layman, under pain of suspension or excommunication."[102] This warning reflects the fact that clergymen and laymen could and did interfere with the management of monasteries. Furthermore, the only recourse is to excommunicate the offenders, a punishment with consequences, perhaps, in the afterlife, but without real temporal effect.

The next turn of events occurred when Kantakouzenos' monastery of St. Anastasia tried to appropriate for itself the *metochion* of St. Nicholas, a smaller monastery of which had always been a *metochion* of the monastery of St. John the Baptist. This unusual sequence of events can only be understood as Kantakouzenos' way of trying to consolidate his power over the monasteries in his area. While the St. John's Monastery still had *stavropegion* status, he could attempt this maneuver of granting the one and taking both. This was strongly resisted, but it was only after the death of Michael Kantakouzenos that the patriarchate could address the issue in two other important patriarchal letters. The first was written by Patriarch Jeremiah II in July 1579 where he confirmed that St. Nicholas was, in fact, a *metochion* of St. John the Baptist.[103] In the second letter, written in February 1580, Patriarch Metrophanes during his second term openly condemned Kantakouzenos. He wrote that through the violence of Kantakouzenos' actions, the monks of St. Anastasia had appropriated the *metochion* of St. Nicholas, and destroyed the

[101] Kamperides, *The Monasteries of Sōzopolis,* 147.
[102] Kamperides, *The Monasteries of Sōzopolis,* 88 (No. 5).
[103] Kamperides, *The Monasteries of Sōzopolis,* 112–116.

monastery, leaving very little except a small vineyard. The letter commanded that things be corrected, and followed this with a formulation of excommunication and further threats that Kantakouzenos will be "damned to eternity."[104]

Since Patriarch Metrophanes' reign was very short, and did not last past August 1580, Patriarch Jeremiah II, when he returned to the throne, also felt obliged to add his condemnation in conjunction with the Holy Synod. Patriarch Jeremiah II meant to conclude the matter once and for all. In September 1580, he wrote,

> Nevertheless, those of St. Anastasia, abusing the assistance of a secular power [Kantakouzenos] seized it and destroyed many of its possessions, leaving only a small vineyard which was planted and dedicated by a certain monk Anthimos, at his own expense, and whose name was written in the Eucharistic commemoration (*prothesis*). Thence, those of St. John the Baptist, requested that the older state of affairs should be respected and that the monastery of St. Nicholas be again attached to the monastery of St. John the Baptist. . . . the monastery of St. Nicholas, with all its possessions, the aforesaid vineyard, real estate and movable goods, to be a metochion of the monastery of St. John the Baptist, without being hindered by anyone. . . . Those of St. Anastasia must detach themselves, as well as any other person whether clergyman or layman, from the metochion of the monastery of St. Nicholas, so that the aforesaid metochion is counted among the possessions of St. John." [The official condemnation is heightened here.] ". . . he shall be excommunicated in both the present and the future time and damned and unforgiven by God, even after his death, and shall have the curses of the 318 Holy Fathers [of Nicaea], as being the cause of the desolation of the monastery.[105]

The implication of these documents is that lay authority, the *archons*, and specifically Michael Kantakouzenos in this instance, were challenging patriarchal authority. While he was alive, there was little that they could do to counter his aggressive appropriation. The one letter issued by Patriarch Jeremiah II simply confirmed that St. Nicholas was indeed a proper *metochion* of St. John the Baptist. The second letter appears to be much stronger in tone, and perhaps filled with resentment stemming from the tension between Kantakouzenos and Patriarch Metrophanes. Patriarch Jeremiah II, during his second term, then let loose in harsh tones as if warning against anyone else trying this, and threatened excommunication by bringing down the curses of the 318 Holy Fathers.

Besides having the threat of excommunication hanging over him, Michael Kantakouzenos also was in trouble with the Ottoman state. It had come to the attention of the Ottoman officials that Kantakouzenos owed a significant amount of money to the Imperial Treasury, amounts that he had amassed through the advances to finance the imperial fur trade. Part of Kantakouzenos' conflict with Patriarch Metrophanes had to do with the latter's being forced to pay over 2,000 ducats a year. It is unclear whether Patriarch Metrophanes had directly caused Kantakouzenos' demise, but at the very least he certainly contributed to it by making formal charges to the Divan.

[104] Kamperides, *The Monasteries of Sōzopolis*, 92–100.
[105] Kamperides, *The Monasteries of Sōzopolis*, 117–125.

The sultan had planned to execute Michael Kantakouzenos. Through the intervention of Mehmet Sokollu Pasha, he was granted a reprieve, however, since Mehmet Sokollu Pasha simply told the sultan that Kantakouzenos was worth more alive than dead: alive, he could be forced to pay dearly to the Imperial Treasury both what he owed, and also a penalty. This tactic saved his life once, but not twice.

Gerlach gives an excellent account of Michael Kantakouzenos' execution, the escape of his son Andronikos, and how Andronikos was able to survive his father's downfall and not be dragged down. On the last day of February 1578, the sultan sent the *kapısı pasha* (*Kapısı Bassa*) Ali Bey to Ahyolu with a number of his servants in order to execute Kantakouzenos. Ali Bey had sent two messengers on ahead to make sure Kantakouzenos was present at home, to inform him not to leave, and that Ali Bey, who was traveling to Moldavia, had become ill and wished to stay with him. When the messengers arrived, Michael, his brother Constantine, and Andronikos were all together and they realized then that there would be trouble. Unable to escape, Ali Bey gave the command to have Michael killed. Then Kantakouzenos asked to talk to a priest, to make his confession, and make his will. Ali Bey did not permit this and immediately hanged him at the door of his home. Afterward, he sent for the *kadi* of Ahyolu to send the women out of the house and set a guard on the house until he returned from Moldavia. Ali Bey took ten horses from Kantakouzenos' stables and left for Moldavia. He sent a message to the sultan that he had accomplished his mission.[106] Kantakouzenos' son, Andronikos, had slipped away and escaped and took a boat to Istanbul. He stayed with one of his friends, and then proceeded to see Mehmet Sokollu Pasha to report what had happened.

On hearing the news, Mehmet Sokollu Pasha was greatly surprised, and he asked when this had happened and who had done it. The sultan had forbidden Ali Bey on penalty of death from mentioning his mission, even to the highest *pashas*. Sokollu Pasha then told Andronikos to go to his friends and that he would protect him. The sultan had wanted to strangle Andronikos, too, but Sokollu Pasha reportedly said, "The son is still young, and had nothing to do with the matter," and sent him together with his father's steward to a stone galley to hide until he would be safe again. Stephan Gerlach commented on Andronikos' fate, but critiqued the Ottoman system of punishments and rewards when he stated,

> That's how it is in Turkey with rewards and punishments. If they are not dealt out immediately, they may sink into oblivion. Like if someone doesn't obtain at the Divan his salary, or what he should have in yearly or daily payments, immediately, nothing will come of it. Also, someone will get a grand appointment if the *Bassa* is merry, another one gets nothing. Therefore, if someone is accused or condemned to some punishment which is not carried out on the spot, he may well still have hope.

[106] Gerlach, *Tagebuch*, 465.

Had Andronikos remained, he would have been hanged. Meanwhile, however, the sultan's fury passes.[107]

Kantakouzenos had left three sons. First was Andronikos, who was twenty-five years old and in 1576 had married the daughter of a wealthy Greek named Rhalle, who was a merchant at Edirne. Second was Demetrios, who was twelve years old, and third was Ioannes, who was eight years old. Michael owned a large palace in Ahyolu which had cost him 20,000 ducats to build, but which was offered for sale for 5,000 ducats. On the estate he had many buildings his family, attendants, steward, administrator, secretary and several scribes plus servants, of which there were up to one hundred. In addition, he had slaves, and nearly forty young pages, children from noble families captured in Cyprus or from Italy or France, and also noble maidens, whom he had bought and kept. Gerlach concluded that in all things, he had been like an Ottoman *pasha*, possessing great riches, both living and material.[108]

Kantakouzenos' death was also recorded in the *Mühimme Defterleri*. In a document from December 1578, a *hüküm* was sent to the *kadis* of Ahyolu and Aydos explaining that all his possessions were to be sold to pay his debt to the Imperial Treasury.[109] In January 1579, he was described as an imperial merchant (*Hassa tacir*) and again another *hüküm* was sent to the same *kadis* concerning not selling "*Şeytanoğlu's*" goods too cheaply.[110]

The state was so concerned with the repayment of the imperial debt that the documents continue until the following November, 1579.[111] In October 1579, a *hüküm* to the İnoz *kadi* stated that following the death of the "*Ahyolu tüz emini*" his debt passed onto his brother and sons.[112] His brother, however, continued the imperial fur trade with Russia as he can be found receiving 4,000 florins for the purchase of furs in November and December 1579.[113] By the 1590s Andronikos had secured for himself and his family the Ahyolu salt works. Thereafter, the Kantakouzenoi found their fortunes in the Danubian principalities, and in the late eighteenth century members of the family become *voyvodes* of Eflâk and Karaboğdan. *Şeytanoğlu's* legacy of maneuvering in the Greek ecclesiastical world and the world of Ottoman finances, however, would remain part of the legend of what was possible for a clever Greek even a hundred years after the conquest of the Byzantine Empire.

The intervention of the Greek elite in ecclesiastical politics was not something new to the post-Byzantine experience. There were real benefits to placing one's candidate in a bishopric or even on the patriarchal throne. However, to accomplish this required two things: money and power (i.e., connections with influence at the Divan). The *archons* had connections to powerful Ottoman figures. While the patriarch was seen as a somewhat symbolic authority, the *archons*, by virtue of their experience and connections to Ottoman power and their wealth, understood how real power in the Greek community was administered.

[107] Gerlach, *Tagebuch*, 466. [108] Gerlach, *Tagebuch*, 466.
[109] MD 35: 1018. [110] MD 36: 38. [111] MD 36: 549; MD 39:5.
[112] MD 40: 385. [113] MD 39: 15; MD 39: 27.

6

Conclusion

Continuity Beyond the Sixteenth Century

Between 1453 and 1500, the office of the Patriarch of Constantinople changed hands eighteen times with an average of a one patriarch every 2.4 years. Between 1500 and 1600 it changed thirty-two times with an average of one patriarch every 3.1 years, and between 1500 and 1600 it changed fifty-three times with an average of one patriarch every 1.9 years. A quick examination of the names of individual patriarchs shows individuals were elevated, deposed, and reappointed, in one case up to seven times. The Patriarchate of Constantinople in the era after 1453 appeared to be fragile and vulnerable. As the only surviving institution from the Byzantine era, it was an institution in a state of flux. The rapid change of leadership raises the question of how much authority did the patriarch actually have over the Greek community.

The answer is complicated, when one considers that the instability of the office was caused largely because the broader lay Greek community intervened in the appointments and depositions of bishops. Doctrinal issues certainly played a role in depostions, and there are examples of patriarchs and bishops being challenged in their faith, and affirming their confession of faith in the Orthodox religion. However, the practice of condemning an opponent for unsound theology did not become common practice until the seventeenth century. One such challenge to the faith occurred in the 1560s and 1570s when the German Lutherans, Martin Crusius, and Stephan Gerlach, visited the court of Patriarch Jeremiah II Tranos. They were ultimately rebuffed by the Patriarch Jeremiah II though they became friends with members of the patriarchal court. The lack of cooperation from the sixteenth-century patriarchal hierarchs and theologians did not prevent inroads from being made by Protestants and Roman Catholics in the seventeenth century. Among the most famous cases of a patriarch who was elevated and deposed multiple times ostensibly for doctrinal reasons is Patriarch Cyril Loukaris (1612, 1620–23, 1623, 1623–33, 1634–35, 1637–38). Patriarch Cyril Loukaris held the patriarchal throne of Alexandria and Constantinople seven times between the years 1612 and 1638. Loukaris was known to be sympathic to the Calvinist doctrine, and became a proponent of translating the scriptures into the commonly used Greek language of the day. Patriarch Loukaris was caught between the intrigue of his pro-Calvinist acquaintances, and the Jesuits, who undermined him in the sultan's court. He was eventually killed, having been strangled and tossed into the Bosphorus. However, aside from this major episode there were few major doctrinal disagreements responsible for patriarchal succession in the seventeenth century.

The underlying reasons for many of the depositions of patriarchs were more often than not associated with power struggles over the ecclesiastical office. The rapid patriarchal successions show an increase in competition for patriarchal power. As bishops of the Church, patriarchs were not only subject to the vicissitudes of a dominating imperial state, but they also were subject to the machinations and designs of ambitious members of the Greek community.

If one continues to accept the *millet* system paradigm to describe Ottoman rule of non-Muslim communities, then this power struggle was purely a political struggle, in which churchmen were vying for the leadership position of the *Rum millet-i*. This view, however, does not take into account the interests of the members of the Greek community, who were made up of merchants, artisans, as well as ecclesiastical personalities.

Since according to the *millet* system non-Muslim religious leaders in the Ottoman Empire served as both spiritual and temporal leaders, it would be understood that the Porte issued laws and ruled the non-Muslim populations through the religious leaders of the Greek, Jewish, and Armenian communities. While this description is tidy and neat, and even though there might have been heavy politics involved in religious leadership succession, the notion of the *millet* system must, once again, be challenged.

An alternative, and perhaps more productive explanation should replace the *millet* system paradigm. Ecclesiastical offices offered an economic benefit to their holders, as they functioned as tax farms and became an object of intense competition for members of the Greek Orthodox community. Because these offices could only be purchased, power was spread into the hands of the wealthy lay people. This new description counters the received wisdom that the patriarch was the leader of the Greek *millet*, having both religious and civil authority over the non-Muslim Greek Orthodox Christian community.

If the focus changes from a political story to an economic one, a fuller, more contoured, and variegated picture of the Greek community in Ottoman society develops. One result is a better understanding of incidents such as the rapid turnover in the office of the patriarch and of other hierarchs. In the course of examining Ottoman and Greek ecclesiastical documents, the one common element that continually appeared throughout the study was the distinctive fiscal relationship between Church hierarchs and the Ottoman state.

From an examination of Byzantine and Ottoman evidence that extends from the earliest Ottoman times in the fourteenth century to the beginning of the seventeenth century, a clear trend was established. The Ottomans identified the Greek Orthodox ecclesiastical hierarchy as a resource for cash income. They became known primarily as tax farmers (*mültezim*) for cash income derived from the Church's widespread holdings. The Ottoman state granted individuals the right to take their positions as hierarchs in return for yearly payments to the state. To gain those positions, the hierarchy enlisted the services of members of the Greek economic elite to purchase the ecclesiastical tax farm (*iltizam*), and to alienate the Church's revenues. As a result, the hierarchical positions became highly prized for their economic aspects and, as tax farms, became subject to increased forces of competition, just as a customs zone tax or any other tax farm might be.

This practice continued into the seventeenth century, where we find the continuity of ecclesiastical tax farming. With this explanation, the work of previous historians becomes eminently more accessible and understandable. Multiple examples of this process are visible in the minutes of the patriarchal synod of the Patriarchate of Constantinople. Codex Beta and Codex Gamma cover the years 1612–1761 and contain numerous references to the tax collecting obligations of the bishops and of the patriarchate.[1] For instance, in 1624, Patriarch Cyril Loukaris and the Holy Synod proposed defrocking Metropolitan Neophytos of Corinth, who had refused to pay the *haraç* (land tax), the *zeteia* (an irregular collection applied similarly to *avariz*), and the *vakia* (monies overdue from the *zeteia*). He was defrocked because he refused to heed the warning of the synod and ignored a previous suspension.

The problem that a metropolitan such as Neophytos posed to the patriarch was that he would not pay his share; this meant that the patriarch found himself in the difficult position of trying to gather enough money himself to pay the Imperial Treasury the agreed yearly amount. This recalls the episode of Patriarch Raphael, and of numerous patriarchs, metropolitans, and bishops thereafter. Time and again, the Ottoman state responded to requests from petitioning clergy by coming to their aid, and using the state's coercive authority, to make sure that the payments were made. Even though this was the state's response, each patriarch most likely dreaded and feared the moment he was forced to clamp down on his metropolitans and bishops through state authority to ensure their loyalty and continued payment of the ecclesiastical revenues. The documentary records in Codex Beta and Gamma are full of such references.

However, an unusual development took place in the beginning of the seventeenth century. As historian Phokion Kotzageorgis explains, it appears that by the beginning of the seventeenth century, there was a "transformation of the *haraçl mâktu'* into *zara-i kassabiye*" or payment of provisions of meat for the imperial gardeners corps.[2] The form of payment and system by which it was collected appears to have changed. Nevertheless, the patriarchs and the Holy Synod continued to focus attention on the financial responsibilities of individual

[1] Nomikos Michael Vaporis, ed., *Codex (B') Beta of the Ecumenical Patriarchate of Constantinople: Aspects of the History of the Church of Constantinople* (Brookline, MA: Holy Cross Orthodox Press, 1975). Nomikos Michael Vaporis, ed., *Codex Gamma of the Ecumenical Patriarchate of Constantinople* (Brookline, MA: Holy Cross Theological School Press, 1974).

[2] Phokion Kotzageorgis, "On the Fiscal Status of the Greek Orthodox Church in the 17th Century," *Turcica: Revue d'Etudes Turques* 40 (2008): 78. See also: P. Konortas, *Othomanikes Theoreseis Gia to Oikoumeniko Patriarcheio: Beratia Gia Tous Prokathemenous Tes Megales Ekklesias (17os-Arches 20ou Aiona)* (Athens: Ekdoseis Alexandreia, 1998), 171–173.

patriarchs toward the state. Because the Holy Synod became more involved in reviewing the financial position of individual bishops, and of the institution of the Patriarchate of Constantinople in general, it appears that the patriarchate was trying to consolidate its corporate authority over individual bishops. This was, perhaps, a first step in consolidating authority within the Church, and a first step toward developing real authority over the Greek community or *millet*.[3]

In response to these financial pressures and problems, Patriarch Cyril Loukaris' rival and three-time successor Patriarch Cyril II Kontares (1633, 1635–36, 1638–39), in May 1635 appointed a financial committee to develop a solution to the "great indebtedness weighing heavily on the Great Church." The patriarch and Holy Synod enacted a number of measures to deal with this enduring problem. First, they established a financial committee composed of five hierarchs that was to have complete control over all revenues of the Church. These revenues included the alms, *zeteia*, inheritances, ordination gifts, monastic revenues and fees charged to lower clergy. Second, no clergy except the patriarch, in consultation with other hierarchs, had permission to interfere or depose anyone. The desire of clergy seeking these positions promoted a sort of hyperactive misbehavior, where scandals and charges of scandals were meant to bring down hierarchs. Third, no election of a metropolitan or archbishop could be made without the approval of the financial committee. Fourth, no collection of any kind could take place in the province without the direct permission of the financial committee, and fifth, bishops could not transfer their sees without very good reason. The patriarch and his synod meant to rein in the local clergy and hierarchy and to place them under the direct supervision of the patriarchate. The fact that a committee was established to prohibit these activities indicates that these must have been a rampant problem.

The overriding concern for Patriarch Cyril II Kontares was that the Church was under a huge financial burden that needed to be lifted. Because of this, the rapid deposition and succession produced the burden of the *pişkeş*. However, the problem with collecting the annual taxes was also extremely challenging. Patriarch Cyril II Kontares, in a sense, created an auditing committee that was intended to stop any individual from exploiting his ecclesiastical office and the perks associated with it. The problem would persist for the patriarchate, as is evident in another attempt to rein in misbehaving hierarchs at the end of the century

In May 1697, Patriarch Kallinikos II, along with Patriarch Dositheos II of Jerusalem and other hierarchs and *archons*, met to reaffirm the independence and autonomy of the patriarchates of Alexandria, Antioch, Jerusalem, the Archbishoprics of Cyprus and Ohrid and Peç.[4] They had gathered together to

[3] In her unpublished dissertation, Elif Bayraktar Tellan explores the process of consolidating authority in the eighteenth century with special emphasis on the non-fiscal role of the Patriarchate. See Elif Bayraktar Tellan, "The Patriarch and the Sultan: The Struggle for Authority and the Quest for Order in the Eighteenth-Century Ottoman Empire" (unpublished Ph.D. Diss., Bilkent University, 2011).

[4] Vaporis, *Codex Gamma*, Document 24, 54.

confirm their autonomous status, as there was a recent attempt to purchase the offices of the Church by "certain disciples of the devil" who were not named in the document out of embarrassment. One of these "disciples of the devil" was the Metropolitan of Thessalonike Methodios, who appears to have made a dangerous proposal, perhaps directly to the Divan, to purchase the ecclesiastical offices as *mukata'a* and *malikâne*.[5] According to the patriarchal document 56, the plan was to purchase the tax farm and subsequently reap financial reward by offering the offices to the highest bidder.

In order to avoid the selling of offices, Patriarch Kallinikos II called on the other patriarchs and archbishops both to affirm their independence and to render financial assistance to the Church. In the document, after the problem was laid out, it stated that, "an appeal was made to the government, money was spent, and thus common destruction was avoided." Being a formidable challenge to their authority, the above named hierarchs banded together to petition the Porte to disregard the new offer, and to ensure that the state would comply. They made a counteroffer and "spent money," most likely a considerable amount, and were assured the continuity of the office-holders.

This example confirms the existence, even at such a late date as May 1697, of a form of tax farming in the ecclesiastical sphere. The interesting development is the use of the terminology of *mukata'a,* which is a generic term for a tax farm that does not indicate the relationship with the Imperial Treasury that the term *iltizam* does. What is surprising in this document is that it carries the tone of frustration both with the individual who attempted to exploit the institution and also with the regime that allowed the institution to be exploited.

While the present study does not extend into the seventeenth century, it attempts to offer background, context, and explanation with which to better understand the previously published examples and studies including: the aforementioned ecclesiastical examples from the patriarchal archives, the work presented by Halil Inalcik on the *Piskopos Mukata'a Kalemi* that covered the years 1641–51, Josef Kabrda's examination of the Bulgarian hierarchy from 1635 to the mid-nineteenth century, the 1678 account of Sir Paul Rycaut that even included a *berât* of appointment to a Latin bishop of Chios, and the study by Helmut Scheel that focused on the Metropolis of Trebizond between1732 and 1830. It is certain this list will continue to grow as a more vigorous examination of the seventeenth and eighteenth centuries uncovers even more documents issued to ecclesiastical figures by the Ottoman state.

While the purpose of the present work has been to offer the history and context of a seemingly unique fiscal system—which in reality was not unique from the Ottoman fiscal administrative point of view—it has also attempted to offer social and cultural context. Beginning with the earliest interactions with Turkmen tribes, the Greek Orthodox bishops of Anatolia met multiple challenges

[5] Metropolitan Methodios of Thessalonike was one of those seeking to purchase the offices. See Vaporis, *Codex Gamma*, 56, n. 3.

in maintaining their flocks. Their practical financial arrangements with Turkmen overlords allowed them to maintain a presence in their ecclesiastical see, despite suggestions from the patriarchal synod of Constantinople that they were being disloyal or disobedient. When the Ottomans formally took over, it became evident that the Church posed certain challenges to governance, considering the Islamic restraints on taxing religious institutions. Therefore, the transition from Byzantine to Ottoman control saw a development of an ecclesiastical tax farm that became an important way to exploit an unconventional resource for income.

In the process of demonstrating how this ecclesiastical *iltizam* system worked, the Church was considered by the Ottomans as a fiscal institution, which can best be understood from within an Ottoman economic and social context. In turn, this context sheds light on many of the the dramatic elements of Greek Church life in the Ottoman era that have always thrilled readers of this history, such as the scandals and intrigues of the bishops, the rapid succession of patriarchs, the economic and political considerations of the Greek community, and the decision making of the Ottoman government. An awareness of the Ottoman economic and social context also sheds light on the actions of the Greek community, especially by enigmatic individuals such as Michael Kantakouzenos. It is to be hoped it will also be helpful for historians researching later periods leading into the nineteenth century and the period of the Tanzimat reforms, giving them a clearer understanding of the continuities and changes that took place in the Greek Orthodox Patriarchate of Constantinople and the Greek Orthodox community.

It is only from the context and vantage point offered in the present work that one can understand the fact that the priests, bishops, metropolitans, and patriarchs of the Greek Orthodox Church in the Ottoman Empire, from their earliest interactions, knew well and responded to the command to render unto the sultan what is the sultan's and unto God what is God's.

Glossary

ahl-i kitab People of the Book—terminology used to describe Christians, and Jews

akçe Ottoman coinage

archons wealthy and influential Greek Christian laymen

avariz extraordinary taxes

berât sultanic decree granting power or privilege (property)

çavuş a low ranking administrator enforcing justice

cema'at community, congregation, or religious community

cizye a head-tax (capitation) or poll tax paid by all non-Muslims

defter notebooks, or registers in which Ottomans kept their records

devşirme the Ottoman system by which young Balkan Christian boys aged 12–18 were taken by into the service of the Sultan, converted to Islam, and trained to serve militarily or in the bureaucracy

Divan-i Hümayun Ottoman Imperial Council

ferman imperial command directed to the office and not an individual and sealed with a sultanic seal

giaour Ottoman terminology for infidel

gomonoslar abbots

hadith traditions of the sayings of the Prophet that make up Sharia or Islamic law

hagiasmoz holy water—referring to taxes on holy water

haraç (haratzion) land tax

hazine-i 'amir Imperial Treasury

hüküms order or decree

iltizam tax farm

İstimâlet a term to describe Ottoman conquests as accommodationist. Term means trying to persuade; a gaining goodwill, a coaxing

janissaries Christian child levy who were trained to serve the Sultan in military units

kadis Islamic judges

kanonikon, the tax made up of various church related collections to meet the expenditures of the local church, which in the Ottoman period was identified as the *zitiye.*

kanun sultanic law

kata logon epidoseon for reasons of sustenance

kefere infidels

keşişler monks

kethüda guild warden

mâktu' lump sum payment to Imperial Treasury for yearly taxes

medrepolidler metropolitans

Megas Ekklesiarches Grand Sacristan of the Greek Orthodox Church

Megas Logothetes Grand Chancellor

metochia dependent monastic houses

millet başı/ethnarch national (ethnic) leader, head of the millet

millet system, a system wherein the Church governed as a state within a state, with the religious leader serving as civic leader

miri rüsûmu imperial tax

Mühimme Defterleri Register of Important Affairs

mülk freehold property

mültezim tax farmer

Mukata'a rent

mukata'a kalemi Ottoman bureau overseeing the tax farm concession system

panayir fairs

papaslar priests

patriklik rüsûmu patriarchal tax

piskoposlar bishops

pişkeş investiture gift usually given to sultan

protovestiarios Byzantine prime minister

reaya Ottoman subjects/peasantry—includes Christians and Muslims

Rum millet-i Greek Orthodox community

sancak bey military and administrative commander of a district (sancak)

Sharia Islamic religious law

sheyh-ül-islam chief Ottoman Islamic scholar/leader

stavropegion status of monastery directly under control of the Patriarchate of Constantinople

tahrir defter record of Ottoman fief

tâ'ife a group, people, class, body of men, or tribe

timar Ottoman fief

Tourkokratia Greek term for describing Ottoman rule over Greeks

ulema Islamic scholars and religious leaders

vakıf/evkaf Islamic pious endowments

Bibliography

UNPUBLISHED ARCHIVAL SOURCES

Kepeci Tasnifi Divani Hümayun Ahkâm Defteri 62.

Mühimme Defteri: Nos. 3, 6, 16, 22, 23, 28, 30, 31, 35, 36, 37, 39, 40, 52, 55, 58.

Codex A', Archives of the Ecumenical Patriarchate of Constantinople, Istanbul, Turkey.

PUBLISHED PRIMARY SOURCES

Âlî, Mustafa bin Ahmet. *Mustafā Ali's Counsel for Sultans of 1581: Edition, Translation, Notes.* Forschungen Zur Islamischen Philologie Und Kulturgeschichte Bd. 6–7. Wien: Verlag der Österreichischen Akademie der Wissenschaften, 1979.

Ashiq Pashazade. *Ashiq Pashazade Tarihi.* Istanbul, 1913–14.

Asiq-Pasha-zade. *Vom Hirtenzelt Zur Hohen Pforte.* Translated by Richard F. Kreutel, *Osmanische Geschichtschreiber.* Graz, Austria: Verlag Styria, 1959.

Ayverdi, E. H. *Istanbul Vakiflari Tahrir Defter 953(1546) Tarihli [Istanbul Vakif Records, Being Dated from 953 (1546)].* Vol. 61. Istanbul: Baha Matbaasi, Istanbul Fetih Cemiyeti, Istanbul Enstitütü, 1970.

Binark, Ismet, Necati Aktaş, and Necati Gültepe. Osmanlı Arşivi Daire Başbakanlığı. *12 Numaralı Mühimme Defteri, (978–979, 1570–1572).* Ankara: T.C. Başbakanlık Devlet Arşivleri Genel Müdürlüğü, 1996.

Binark, Ismet, Necati Aktaş, and Nihal Somer. Osmanlı Arşivi Daire Başbakanlığı. *Osmanlı Fermanları/Ottoman Fermans.* Ankara: T. C. Başbakanlık Devlet Arşivleri Genel Müdürlüğü, 1994.

Binark, Ismet, Necati Gültepe, and Necati Aktaş. Osmanlı Arşivi Daire Başbakanlığı. *3 Numaralı Mühimme Defteri, (966–968, 1558–1560).* Ankara: T. C. Başbakanlık Devlet Arşivleri Genel Müdürlüğü, 1993.

Binark, Ismet, Necati Gültepe, and Necati Aktaş. Osmanlı Arşivi Daire Başbakanlığı *5 Numaralı Mühimme Defteri, (973, 1565–1566).* Ankara: T. C. Başbakanlık Devlet Arşivleri Genel Müdürlüğü, 1994.

Binark, Ismet, Necati Gültepe, and Necati Aktaş. Osmanlı Arşivi Daire Başbakanlığı. *6 Numaralı Mühimme Defteri, (972, 1564–1565).* Ankara: T. C. Başbakanlık Devlet Arşivleri Genel Müdürlüğü, 1995.

Bompaire, Jaques, ed. *Actes De Xeropotamou.* Vol. III: Paris, 1964.

Cantemir, Dimitrie. *The History of the Growth and Decay of the Othman Empire.* Translated by Nicolas Tindal, John James, and Paul Knapton. London, 1734.

Chalkokondylas, Laonikos. *Historiarum Demonstrationes.* Edited by E. Darkó. Budapest: Sumptibus Academiae litterarum Hungaricae, 1922–27.

Crusius, Martın. *Turco-Graeciae, Lıbro Octo.* Basle, 1584.

Darrouzes, Jean, ed. *Notitiae Episcopatuum Ecclesiae Constantinopolitanae.* Geographie Ecclésiastique de l'Empire Byzantin. Paris: Institut français d'études byzantines, 1981.

Darrouzes, Jean, ed. *Les Regestes Des Actes Du Patriarcat De Constantinople.* Edited by Jean Darrouzes. Vol. I. Les Actes Des Patriarches Fasc. VII Les Regestes de 1410 à 1453, *Le Patriarcat Byzantin.* Paris: Institut francais d'etudes byzantines, 1991.

Delikanes, Kallinikos. *Ta En Tois Kodixi Tou Patriarchikou Archeophylakiou Sozomena Episema Ekklesiastika Engrapha, Ta Aphoronta Eis Tas Scheseis Tou Oikoumenikou Patriarcheiou Pros Ekklesias Alexandreias, Antiocheias, Ierousalymnon Kai Kyprou 1574–1863*. Constantinople: Ecumenical Patriarchate, 1904.

Delikanes, Kallinikos. *Ta En Tois Kodixi Tou Patriarchikou Archeophylakiou Sozomena Episema Ekklesiastika Engrapha, Ta Aphoronta Eis Tas Scheseis Tou Oikoumenikou Patriarcheiou Pros Ekklesias Rossias, Vlachias Kai Moldavias, Servias Achridon Kai Pekiou 1564–1863*. Constantinople: Patriarchal Printing House, 1905.

Dölger, F. and Wirth, P. *Regesten Der Kaiserurkunden Des Oströmischen Reiches. 5. Teil. Regesten Von 1341–1453*. Munich: C. H. Beck, 1965.

Doukas. *Decline and Fall of Byzantium to the Ottoman Turks*. Edited by Harry J. Magoulias Trans. Detroit: Wayne State University Press, 1975.

Forster, Edward Seymour, ed. *The Turkish Letters of Ogier Ghiselin De Busbecq Imperial Ambassador at Constantinople 1554–1562*. Oxord: Oxford University Press, 1927, 1968.

Gedeon, Manouel Io. *Kanonikai Diataxeis, Epistolai, Lyseis, Thespismata Ton Hagiotaton Patriarchon Konstantinoupoleos Apo Gregoriou Tou Theologou Mechri Dionysiou Tou Apo Adrianoupoleos. Vol. 7 (2 volumes), Subsidia Byzantina Lucis Ope Iterata*. Leipzig: Zentralantiquariat der Deutschen Demokratischen Republik, 1888–89.

Gedeon, Manouel Io. *Episema Grammata Tourkika Anapheromena Eis Ta Ekklesiastika Hemon Dikaia Ekdothenta Phrontidi*. Constantinople: Patriarchal Press, 1910.

Gennadius II, Patriarch of Constantinople. "Contre La Simonie (1451)." In *Georgiou Tou Scholariou Apanta Ta Euriskomena = Oeuvres Complètes de Georges Scholarios*, edited by Louis Petit, Xenophon Siderides, and Martin Jugie, 1:239–251. Paris: Maison de la bonne presse, 1928.

Georgiou Tou Aitolou. "Duo Anekdota Stihourgemata Eis Mihael Kai Andronikon Tous Kantakouzenous." *Neos Hellenomnemon* 9/3 (1912): 259–264.

Gerlach, Stephan. *Stephan Gerlachs Des Aelteren Tagebuch*. Frankfurt-am-Main, 1674.

Halasi-Kun, Tibor. "Gennadios' Turkish Confession of Faith." *Archivum Ottomanicum* 12 (1987–1992): 5–103.

Hypselantes, Athanasios Komnenos. *Athanasiou Komnenou Hypselantou Ekklesiastikon Kai Politikon Ton Eis Dodeka Vivlion [8,9] Kai [10] Etoi Ta Meta Ten Halosin (1453–1789) Ek Cheirographou Anekdotou Tes Hiearas Mones Tou Sina*. Originally published En Konstaninopupolei: I. A. Vretou, 1870 ed. Athens, 1972.

Inalcik, Halil. *Suret-i Defter-i Sancak-i Arvanid*. Ankara: Türk Tarih Kurumu Basimevi, 1954.

Kakoulidou-Panou, Elene. "Damaskenou Stoudite 'Dialogos'." *Dodone* 3 (1974): 443–458.

Korablev, B., W. Regel, and E. Kurtz, eds. *Actes De Zographou*. Vol. IV. Amsterdam: Hakkert, 1969.

Korablev, B., W. Regel, and E. Kurtz, eds. *Actes De Philothee*. Vol. VI. Amsterdam: Hakkert, 1975.

Kravari, Vassiliki, ed. *Actes Du Pantocrator*. Vol. XVII. Paris: P. Lethielleux, 1991.

Kresten, Otto. *Das Patriarchat Von Konstantinopel Im Ausgehenden 16. Jahrhundert: Der Bericht Des Leontios Eustratios Im Cod. Tyb. Mb 10: Einleitung, Text, Übersetzung, Kommentar*. 2 vols. Vienna: Österreichischen Akademie der Wissenschaften, 1970.

Kritovoulos, Michael. *History of Mehmed the Conqueror*. Translated by Charles T. Riggs. Princeton: Princeton University Press, 1954.

Kritovoulos, Michael. *Critobuli Imbriotae Historiae*. Edited by D. Reinsch. Berolini et Novi Eboraci: De Gruyter, 1983.

Lampros, Spyridon Paulou. *Ecthesis Chronica and Chronicon Athenarum*. London: Methuen & co., 1902.

Legrand, Emile. *Recueil de poëmes historiques en grec vulgaire relatifs à la Turquie et aux principautés danubiennes*. Vol. 5. Ecole des langues orientales vivantes. Paris: E. Leroux, 1877.

Legrand, Emile. *Bibliotheque Grecque Vulgaire*. Vol. 2. Paris, 1881.

Legrand, Emile. *Notice Biographique Sur Jean Et Théodose Zygomalas*. Vol. 2. *Recueil De Textes Et De Traductions*. Paris, 1889.

Lemerle, Paul, ed. *Actes De Kutlumus*. Vol. II. Paris: P. Lethielleux, 1945.

Miklosich, F. and Müller, J. *Acta et diplomata medii aevi sacra et profana*. 6 vols. Vienna, 1860–90.

Nicolay, Nicolas de. *The Navigations into Turkie*. Translated by Thomas Washington. The English Experience, Its Record in Early Printed Books Published in Facsimile, No. 48. Amsterdam, Theatrum Orbis Terrarum,1585; New York, Da Capo Press, 1968.

Neşrî, Mehmet. *Kitab-i Cihan-Nümâ Neşrî Tarihi*. Translated by Faik Reshit Unat and Dr. Mehmet A. Köymen. Vol. I. Ankara: Türk Tarih Kurumu Basimevi, 1949.

Oikonomides, Nicolas, ed. *Actes De Kastamonitou*. Vol. IX. Paris: P. Lethielleux, 1978.

Paize-Apostolopoulou, Mache. *Aphieromata kai dorees ton 16o ai. ste M. Ekklesia: thesmikes opseis tes euseveias*. Athena: Ethniko Hidryma Ereunon, 2002.

Paize-Apostolopoulou, Mache. *Episema Keimena Tou Patriarcheiou Konstantinoupoleos: Ta Sozomena Apo Ten Periodo 1454–1498*. Kentro Neoellenikon Ereunon Ethniko Hidryma Ereunon 121. Athena: Ethniko Hidryma Ereunon Kentro Neoellenikon Ereunon, 2011.

Papachryssanthou, Denise, ed. *Actes Du Protaton*. Vol. VII. Paris: P. Lethielleux, 1975.

Papachryssanthou, Denise, ed. *Actes De Xenophon*. Vol. XV. Paris: P. Lethielleux, 1986.

Papachryssanthou, D., J. Lefort, and N. Oikonomidis, eds. *Actes D'Iviron*. Vol. XVI. Paris: P. Lethielleux, 1990.

Papachryssanthou, D., P. Lemerle, A. Guillou, and N. Svoronos, eds. *Actes De Lavra: Etudes Historiques-Actes Serbes Complements Et Index*. Vol. XI. Paris: P. Lethielleux, 1982.

Petit, L., ed. *Actes Du Pantocrator*. Vol. II. Amsterdam: Hakkert, 1964.

Petit, L. and B. Korablev, eds. *Actes De Chilander*. Vol. V. Amsterdam: Hakkert, 1975.

Philippidis-Braat, Anna. "La Captivité De Palamas Chez Les Turcs: dossier et commentaire." *Travaux et Memoires* 7 (1979): 109–222.

Pseudo-Dorotheos. *Vivlion Historikon Periechon En Synopsei Diaphorous Kai Exochous Historias*. Venice: Nikolaos Glykeis, 1750.

Rycaut, Paul. *The Present State of the Ottoman Empire*. London, 1668.

Rycaut, Paul. *The Present State of the Greek and Armenian Churches, Anno Christi 1678*. London: John Starkey, 1679.

Sakelion, A. J. "Dialexis." *Soter* XV (1892): 240–246.

Sathas, Konstantinos N.. *Viographikon Schediasma Peri Patriarchou Hieremia B' (1572–1592)*. Athens, 1870.

Sathas, Konstantinos N. *Mesaionike vivliotheke epistasia K.N. Satha*. Venetia: Typois tou Chronou, 1872.

Scholarios, Gennadios. *Geōrgiou Tou Scholariou Hapanta Ta Heuriskomena = Oeuvres Complètes De Georges Scholarios*. Edited by Louis Petit, X. A. Sidéridès, and Martin Jugie. Paris: Maison de la bonne presse, 1928.

Slusser, M., ed and trans. *St. Gregory Thaumaturgus Life and Works*. The Fathers of the Church. Washington, DC: Catholic University of America Press, 1998.

Sphrantzes, George. *Chronicon Minus*. Edited by V. Grecu. Bucharest: Editura Academiei Republicii Socialiste Romania, 1966.

Sphrantzes, George. *The Fall of the Byzantine Empire: A Chronicle by George Sphrantzes 1401–1477.* Translated by Marios Philippides. 1st edition. Amherst, MA: University of Massachusetts Press, 1980.

Spandouginos, Theodoros. *Discorso Di Teodoro Spandugino Cantacusino Gentil'homo Constantinopolitano Dall'origine De'principi Turchi. Theodore Spandounes: On the Origins of the Ottoman Emperors.* Translated by Donald M. Nicol. Cambridge: Cambridge University Press, 1997.

Şener, Murat. *7 Numaralı Mühimme Defteri*, 975-976/1567-1569: Tıpkıbasım. Ankara: T.C. Başbakanlık Devlet Arşivleri Genel Müdürlüğü, 1997.

Talbot, Alice-Mary, ed. *The Correspondence of Athanasius I, Patriarch of Constantinople: Letters to the Emperor Andronicus II, Members of the Imperial Family, and Officials, Corpus fontium historiae Byzantinae. v. 7, Dumbarton Oaks Texts. 3.* Translated by Alice-Mary Talbot. Washington: Dumbarton Oaks Center for Byzantine Studies, Trustees for Harvard University, 1975.

Tietze, ed. *Mustafa Ali's Counsel for Sultans of 1581.* Vol. VI, VII. *Forshungen Zur Islmischen Philologie Und Kulturgeschichte.* Vienna: Verlag Der Österreichischen Akademie Der Wissenschaften, 1979, 1982.

Treu, M. *Matthaios Metropolit Von Ephesus, Ueber Sein Leben Und Seine Schriften.* Potzdam: Programm des Victoria-Gymnasiums zu Potsdam, 1901.

Vatopedinos, Arkadios. "Agioreitika Analekta 15. Basilike Diataghe Pros Demetrion Ton Boulioten Peri Agion Oros." *Gregorios o Palamas* 2 (1918): 152.

Vaporis, Nomikos Michael. *Codex Gamma of the Ecumenical Patriarchate of Constantinople.* Holy Cross Theological School Press, 1974.

Vaporis, Nomikos Michael, ed. *Codex (B') Beta of the Ecumenical Patriarchate of Constantinople: Aspects of the History of the Church of Constantinople.* Holy Cross Orthodox Press, 1975.

SECONDARY SOURCES

Abou-El-Haj, R. A. "The Ottoman Kanun as an Instrument of Domination." Paper presented at the International Committe of Pre-Ottoman and Ottoman Studies, Seventh Symposium, Pecs, September 7–11, 1986.

Abou-El-Haj, R. A. "The Ottoman Nasihatname as a Discourse over Morality." In *Mélanges Professeur Robert Mantran*, edited by A. Temini, 17–30. Zaghouan, Tunis: Centre d'Etudes et de Recherches Ottomanes, Morisques, de Documentation et d'Information, 1988.

Abou-El-Haj, R. A. *The Formation of the Modern State: The Ottoman empire, Sixteenth to Eighteenth Centuries.* Albany: State University of New York Press, 1992.

Abou-El-Haj, R. A. "The Expression of Ottoman Political Culture in the Literature of Advice to Princes (Nasihatnameler) Sixteenth to Twentieth Centuries." In *Sociology in the Rubric of Social Science*, edited by R. K. Bhattacharya and A. K. Ghosh, 282–292. New Delhi: Anthropological Survey of India, 1995.

Akin, Nur. "Fener." In *Dünden Bugüne Istanbul Ansiklopedisi*, edited by Ilan Tekeli and Nuri Akbayar, 279–281. Istanbul: Türkiye Ekonomik ve Toplumsal Tarih Vakfi, 1994.

Alexander, John Christos. *Toward a History of Post-Byzantine Greece: The Ottoman Kanunnames for the Greek Lands, Circa 1500–Circa 1600.* Athens: J. C. Alexander, 1985.

Alexander, John C. "The Lord Giveth and the Lord Taketh Away: Athos and the Confiscation Affair of 1568–1569." In *Athos in the 14th–16th Centuries*, (*Athonika Symmeikta*, 4) 149–200. Athens: The National Hellenic Research Foundation, 1997.

Alexandries, Alexes. *The Greek Minority of Istanbul.* Athens: Center for Asia Minor Studies, 1984.

Anastasopoulos, Antonis. "Non-Muslims and Ottoman Justice(s?)." In *Law and Empire: Ideas, Practices, Actors*, edited by Caroline Humfress and Nimrod Hurvitz, 275–292. Leiden: E. J. Brill, 2013.

Andreades, A. "De La Population De Constantinople Sous Les Empereurs Byzantins." *Metron* 1 (1920): 1–56.

Angelov, Dimiter. *Imperial Ideology and Political Thought in Byzantium (1204–1330).* Cambridge: Cambridge University Press, 2007.

Angold, Michael. *The Byzantine Empire, 1025–1204.* London and New York: Longman, 1984.

Angold, Michael. *Church and Society in Byzantium under the Comneni 1081–1261.* Cambridge: Cambridge University Press, 1995.

Angold, Michael. *Cambridge History of Christianity: Volume 5, Eastern Christianity.* Cambridge: Cambridge University Press, 2006.

Anhegger, Robert. "Beiträge Zur Osmanischen Baugeschichte I." *Istanbuler Mitteilungen* 6 (1955): 89–118.

Anhegger, Robert. "Beiträge Zur Osmanischen Baugeschichte Ii." *Istanbuler Mitteilungen* 8 (1958): 40–56.

Anhegger, Robert "Ein Christ Und Zwei Armenier Christen in Osmanischen Reich, Unter-Und Gegen-Einander." *WZKM: Festchrisft Andreas Tietze zum 70. Geburtstag gewidmet von seinen Freunded und Schülern* 76 (1986): 19–33.

Apostolopoulos, Dimitris. *To Mega Nomimon: Symvole Sten Ereuna Tou Metavyzantinou Demosiou Dikaiou.* Athens : D. Apostolopoulos, 1978.

Apostolopoulos, Dimitris. *Ho "Hieros Kodix" Tou Patreiarcheiou Konstantinoupoleos Sto B' Miso Tou Ie Aiona. Ta Mona Gnosta Sparagmata.* Athens: Ethniko Hydryma Ereunon/ Kentron Neoellenikon Ereunon, 1992.

Apostolopoulos, Dimitris. "Les Mécanismes D'une Conquête: Adaptations Politiques Et Statut Économique Des Conquis Dans Le Cadre De L'empire Ottoman." In *Actes Du IIe Colloque International D'histoire: Économies Méditerranéenes Équilibres Et Intercommunications Xiiie-Xixe Siècles*, Colloque international d'historie, 191–204. Athens: Centre de Recherches Néohelléniques de la Fondation Nationale de la Recherche Scientifique, 1986.

Arnakis, G. *Oi Protoi Othomanoi.* Edited by Nikos A. Bees. Vol. 41. *Texte Und Forshungen Zur Byzantinisch-Neugriechishen Philologie.* Athens, 1947.

Arnakis, George. "Gregory Palamas Among the Turks And Documents of His Captivity As Historical Sources." *Speculum* 26 (1951): 104–118.

Arnakis, George. "The Greek Church of Constantinople and the Ottoman Empire." *The Journal of Modern History* 23/3 (1952): 235–250.

Arnakis, George. "Gregory Palamas, the Chiones and the Fall of Gallipoli." *Byzantion* 22 (1952): 305–312.

Aruçi, Muhammed. "Islamic Authority and Its Attitude Towards Non-Muslim Groups and Minorities in Muslim Society." In *Authority, Privacy and Public Order in Islam: Proceedings of the 22nd Congress of L'Union Européenne Des Arabisants Et Islamisants*, edited by Barbara Michalak-Pikulski and Andrzej Pikulski, 249–266. Leuven, The Netherlands: Peeters Publishers, 2006.

Asdrachas, Spyros I. "Problems of Economic History of the Period of Ottoman Domination in Greece." *Journal of the Hellenic Diaspora* VI/2 (1979): 5–37.

Ayverdi, Ekrem Hakki. *Fatih Devri 855–886 (1451–1481) [Period of the Conquerer, 855–886 (1452–1481]*. Vol. 3, 4. Istanbul: Baha Matbaasi, Osmanli Mimarisinde, 1973, 1974.

Babinger, Franz. "Die Türkischen Quellen Dimitri Kantemir's." In *Zeki Velidi Toğan'a Armağan*, 51–60. Istanbul: Maarif Basimevi, 1955.

Babinger, Franz. *Mehmet the Conqueror and His Time*. Translated by Ralph Manheim. Edited by William C. Hickman. Princeton: Princeton University Press, 1978.

Babinger, Franz. *Hans Dernschwam's Tagebuch Einer Reise Nach Konstantinopel Und Kleinasien (1551/55): Nach Der Urschrift Im Fugger Archiv Herausgegeben Und Erläutert*. Berlin: Duncker and Humblot, 1923, 1986.

Bakirtzis, Nicholas. *Hagios Ioannis Prodromos Monastery on Mount Menoikeion: Byzantine Monastic Practice, Sacred Topography, and Architecture*, Princeton: Princeton University (Slobodan Ćurčić), 2005.

Balta, Evangelia. *Rural and Urban Population in the Sancak of Euripos in the Early 16th Century*. Athens: Hetaireia Euvoikon Spoudon, 1992.

Balta, Evangelia. *Les Vakifs De Serrès Et De Sa Région (Xve Et Xvie S.)*. Translated by Edith Karagiannis. Athènes: Centre De Rechereches Néo-Helléniques, 1995.

Balta, Evangelia. "The Economic Advancement of the Rum Millet as a Function of Otherness." *O Eranistis* 24 (2003): 139–160.

Bardakjian, Kevork B. "The Rise of the Armenian Patriarchate of Constantinople." In *Christians and Jews in the Ottoman Empire: The Functioning of a Plural Society*, edited by Benjamin Braude and Bernard Lewis, 89–100. New York: Holmes & Meier, 1982.

Barker, John. *Manuel II Paleologus: 1391–1425, A Study in Late Byzantine Statesmanship*. New Brunswick, NJ: Rutgers University Press, 1969.

Barnes, John Robert. *An Introduction to Religious Foundations in the Ottoman Empire*. Leiden: E. J. Brill, 1987.

Beeching, Jack. *The Galleys of Lepanto*. London: Hutchinson & Co., 1982.

Beldiceanu, N. *Les Actes Des Premiers Sultans Conserves Dans Les Manuscrits Turcs De La Bibliotheque Nationale a Paris, I, Actes De Mehmet Ii Et De Bayezid Ii Du Ms. Fonds Turc Ancien 39*. Vol. I, II. Paris-La Haye: Mouton et Co., 1960.

Beldiceanu, N. "A Propos De Deux Registres Ottomans De Recensement Des Monastères Du Mont Athos." *Byzation* 52 (1982): 496–499.

Beldiceanu-Steinherr, I. "La Population Non-Musulmane De Bythynie (Duexieme Moitie Du Xives Premier Poitie Du Xves." In *The Ottoman Emirate (*1300–1389), edited by Elizabeth Zachariadou, 7–22. Rethymnon: Crete University Press, 1993.

Bellefonds, Y. Linant de. "La Suppression Des Juridictions de Statut Personnel En Egypte." *Revue Internationale de Droit Comparé* 8/3 (1956): 412–425.

Ben abi Zimra, R. D. "Dhimmis in the Muslim Court: Legal Autonomy and Religious Discrimination." *International Journal of Middle East Studies* 31 (1999): 429–444.

Bialor, Perry A. "Greek Ethnic Survival under Ottoman Domination." In *The Limits of Integration: Ethnicity and Nationalism in Modern Europe*, edited by Oriol Pi-Sunyer, 43–76. Amherst, MA: Department of Anthropology: University of Massachusetts, 1971.

Binark, Ismet. *Istanbul, Fatih, Fetih Ve Fatih Devri Hakkinda Yazilmis Kitaplar Bibliografyasi*. Istanbul: Istanbul Fetih Cemiyeti, 1977.

Binark, Ismet, Necati Gültepe, Necati Aktaş, and Yusuf Ihsan Genç. *Başbakanlık Osmanlı Arşivi Rehberi*. Ankara: Devlet Arşivleri Genel Müdürlüğü, 1992.

Binswanger, Karl. *Untersuchungen Zum Status Der Nichtmuslime Im Osmanischen Reich Des 16. Jarhunderts Mit Einer Neudefinition Des Begriffs "Dimma"*. Vol. 23. Munich: Dr. Rudolf Trofenik, Beiträge zur Südosteuropas und des Nahen Orients, 1977.

Bîrsan, Cristina. *Dimitrie Cantemir and the Islamic World*. 1st edition. Istanbul: Isis Press, 2004.

Bisaha, Nancy. *Creating East and West: Renaissance Humanists and the Ottoman Turks*. Philadelphia: University of Pennsylvania Press, 2004.

Black, Jeremy. *War In The Early Modern World, 1450–1815*. New York: Taylor & Francis, 2012.

Bojanić, Duşanka. "Sultansk Povelje Iz Manastira Hilandara (Sultanic Acts from the Hilandara Monastery)." *Hilandarski Zbornik* 9 (1991): 201–204.

Boojamra, John Lawrence. *The Church and Social Reform: The Policies of Patriarch Athanasios of Constantinople*. New York: Fordham University Press, 1993.

Bosworth, C. E. "The Concept of Dhimma in Early Islam." In *Christians and Jews in the Ottoman Empire: The Functioning of a Plural Society*, edited by Benjamin Braude and Bernard Lewis, 37–51. New York: Holmes & Meier, 1982.

Brafman, David. "Facing East: The Western View of Islam in Nicolas De Nicolay's 'Travels in Turkey'." *Getty Research Journal* 1 (2009): 153–160.

Braude, Benjamin. "Foundation Myths of the Millet System." In *Christians and Jews in the Ottoman Empire: The Functioning of a Plural Society*, edited by Bernard Lewis and Benjamin Braude, 69–88. New York: Holmes & Meier, 1982.

Braude, Benjamin. "Venture and Faith in Commercial Life of the Ottoman Balkans, 1500–1600." *International History Review* 7/4 (1985): 519–542.

Braude, Benjamin and Bernard Lewis, eds. *Christians and Jews in the Ottoman Empire: The Functioning of a Plural Society*. 2 vols. Vol. II: The Arabic-Speaking Lands. New York: Holmes & Meier, 1982.

Braudel, Fernand. *The Mediterranean and the Mediterranean World in the Age of Philip II*. 2 vols. New York: Harper & Row, 1972.

Brown, L. Carl, ed. *Imperial Legacy: The Ottoman Imprint on the Balkans and the Middle East*. New York: Columbia University Press, 1996.

Brown, Peter. "Review of the Great Church in Captivity: A Study of the Patriarchate of Constantinople from the Eve of the Turkish Conquest to the Greek War of Independence, by Steven Runciman." In *Religion and Society in the Age of St.Augustine*. edited by Peter Brown, 154–160. Faber and Faber, 1972.

Browning, Robert. *Byzantium and Bulgaria: A Comparative Study Across the Early Medieval Frontier*. London: Temple Smith, 1975.

Bryer, A. "Greek Historians on the Turks: The Case of the First Byzantine-Ottoman Marriage." In *The Writing of History in the Middle Ages*, edited by R. Davis and J. M Wallace-Hadrill, 471–493. Oxford: Clarendon Press, 1981.

Buhl, F. "Millet." *Islam Ansiklopedisi* 8 (1958): 317.

Cahen, Claude. *Pre-Ottoman Turkey: A General Survey of the Material and Spiritual Culture and History, C. 1071–1330*. New York: Taplinger Publishing Company, 1968.

Cantacuzène, Jean Michel. *Mille Ans Dans Les Balkans : Chronique Des Cantacuzène Dans La Tourmente Des Siècles*. Paris: Editions Christian, 1992.

Cavallo, Guglielmo. *The Byzantines*. Chicago: University of Chicago Press, 1997.

Charanis, P. "The Monastic Properties and the State in the Byzantine Empire." *Dumbarton Oaks Papers* IV (1948): 51–119.

Chrisohoides, K., ed. *Mount Athos in the 14th–16th Centuries*. Vol. 4. *Athonika Symmeikta*. Athens: The National Hellenic Research Foundation Institute for Byzantine Research, 1997.

Çiçek, Kemal, Ercüment Kuran, Nejat Göyünç, and İlber Ortaylı, eds. "Istimalet." *Great Ottoman Turkish Civilization*. Istanbul: Yeni Türkiye, 2000.

Çizakça, Murat. *A Comparative Evolution of Business Partnerships: The Islamic World and Europe, With Specific Reference to the Ottoman Archives*. Leiden: E. J. Brill, 1996.

Clogg, Richard. "The Greek Millet in the Ottoman Empire." In *Christians and Jews in the Ottoman Empire: The Functioning of a Plural Society*, edited by Benjamin Braude and Bernard Lewis, 185–207. New York: Holmes & Meier, 1982.

Cohen, Amnon. "On the Realities of the Millet System: Jerusalem in the Sixteenth Century." In *Christians and Jews in the Ottoman Empire: The Functioning of a Plural Society*, edited by Benjamin Braude and Bernard Lewis, 7–18. New York: Holmes & Meier, 1982.

Cohen, A. *Jewish Life under Islam: Jerusalem in the Sixteenth Century*. Cambridge, MA: Harvard University Press, 1984.

Cohen, A. "Ottoman Sources for the History of Ottoman Jews: How Important?" In *The Jews of the Ottoman Empire*, edited by Avgidor Levy, 687–704. Princeton, NJ: Darwin Press and the Institute of Turkish Studies, 1994.

Cohen, Mark R. *Under Crescent and Cross: The Jews in the Middle Ages*. Princeton: Princeton University Press, 1994.

Cohen, M. R. "The Jews of Islam: From the Rise of Islam to Sabbatai Zevi: A Bibliographic Essay." In *Sepharidic Studies in the University*, edited by J. S. Gerber, 43–119. Madison: Fairleigh Dickinson University Press, 1995.

Croskey, Robert. "Byzantine Greeks in Late Fifteenth- and Early Sixteenth Century Russia." In *The Byzantine Legacy in Eastern Europe*, edited by Lowell Clucas, 33–56. Boulder: East European Monographs, 1988.

Cvetkova, B. "Early Ottoman Tahrir Defters as a Source for Studies on the History of Bulgaria and the Balkans." *Archivum Ottomanicum* 8 (1983): 133–213.

Darling, Linda T. "Ottoman Politics Through British Eyes: Paul Rycaut's 'The Present State of the Ottoman Empire'." *Journal of World History* 5/1 (April 1, 1994): 71–97.

Darling, Linda T. *Revenue-raising and Legitimacy*. Leiden: E. J. Brill, 1996.

Darling, Linda T. "Christian-Muslim Interaction on the Ottoman Frontier: Gaza and Accomodation in Early Ottoman History." In *The Ottoman Mosaic: Exploring Models for Peace by Re-exploring the Past*, edited by Kemal Karpat, 103–120. 1st edition. Seattle: Cune Press, 2009.

Darling, Linda T. "Nasihatnaler, Icmal Defterleri, and the Timar-Holding Ottoman Elite in the Late Sixteenth Century." *Osmanli Arastirmalari (The Journal of Ottoman Studies)* XLIII (2014): 193–226.

Davison, R. *Reform in the Ottoman Empire*. Princeton: Princeton University Press, 1963.

Dawkins, R. M. "The Crypto-Christians of Turkey." *Byzantion* VII/13 (1933): 247–275.

D'Ohsson, Ignatius M. *Tableau General De L'empire Ottoman*. Paris, 1824.

de Clercq, Charles. "La Turcograecia De Martin Crusius Et Les Patriarches De Constantinoples De 1453 a 1583." *Orientalia Christiana Periodica* 33 (1967): 210–220.

De Mendieta, Emmanuel Amand. *Mount Athos: The Garden of the Panaghia*. Edited by Trans. Michael R. Bruce. Amsterdam: Adolf M. Hakkert, 1972.

Demetriades, Vassilis. "Athonite Documents and the Ottoman Occupation." In *Mount Athos in the 14–16th Centuries*, 41–67. Athens: The National Hellenic Research Foundation, 1997.

Demetriou, Chrysostomos. "Hoi Exokatakoiloi Archontes Tes En Konstantinoupolei Megales Tou Christou Ekklesias." *Texte und Forschungen zur Byzantinisch-Neugriechischen Philologie* 7 (1927).

Dennis, George. "The Byzantine-Turkish Treaty of 1403." *Orientalia Christiana Periodica* 33 (1967): 72–88.

"Discussion." In *Actes Du IIe Colloque International d'Histoire: Économies Méditerranéenes Équilibres et Intercommunications XIIIe-XIXe Siècles*, 217–255. Athens: Centre de Recherches Néohelléniques de la Fondation Nationale de la Recherche Scientifique, 1986.

Ecumenical Patriarchate of Constantinople. *Hemerologion Tou Oikoumenikou Patriarcheiou*. 2 vols. Thessalonike: Asprobalta, 1999.

Engelzakis, Benedict. *Studies and Documents Relating to the History of the Church of Cyprus from the Fourth to the Twentieth Centuries*. Translated by Norman Russell. Brookfield, VT: Variorum, 1995.

Enverî. *Le Destan d'Umur Pacha (Düstûrnâme-i Enveri)*. Edited by Irene Melikoff-Sayar. Bibliothèque Byzantine. Documents. 2. Paris: Presses universitaires de France, 1954.

Epstein, Mark Alan. *The Ottoman Jewish Communities and Their Role in the Fifteenth and Sixteenth Centuries*. Frieburg: Klaus Schwarz, 1980.

Epstein, Mark A. "The Leadership of the Ottoman Jews in the Fifteenth and Sixteenth Centuries." In *Christians and Jews in the Ottoman Empire: The Functioning of a Plural Society*, edited by Benjamin Braude and Bernard Lewis, 101–115. New York: Holmes & Meier, 1982.

Ercan, Yavuz. "Türkiye'de Xv. Ve Xvi. Yüzyillarda Gayrimüslimlerin Hukuki, Içtimai Ve Iktksati Durumu." *Belleten* 47/188 (1983): 1119–1149.

Eskenasy, V. "Jews, Romanians, and Ottomans in the Middle Ages: Joseph Nassi and Moldavia," In *Communication at XIX Spring Symposium of Byzantine Studies*, 358. Birmingham, England: University of Birmingham, 1985.

Esterházy, Miklós and Lajos Fekete. *Türkische Schriften Aus Dem Archive Des Palatins Nikolaus Esterházy 1606–1645, Redigiert Von Ludwig Fekete. Mit 10 Tafeln Und 1 Karte*. Budapest: Druck der Königlichen ungarischen universitätsdruckerei, 1932.

Faroqhi, Suraiya. "In Search of Ottoman History." In *New Approaches to State and Peasant in Ottoman History*, edited by Halil Berktay and Faroqhi Suraiya, 211–241. Frank Cass: London, 1992.

Faroqhi, Suraiya. "Book Review: Gilles Veinstein, Etat Et Societe Dans L'empire Ottoman, Xvie-Xviiie Secles. La Terre, La Guerre, Les Communautes." *Turcica* XXVII/16 C. (1995): 286–289.

Faroqhi, Suraiya. *Approaching Ottoman History: An Introduction to the Sources*. Cambridge: Cambridge University Press, 1999.

Faroqhi, Suraiya. *Subjects of the Sultan: Culture and Daily Life in the Ottoman Empire*. London: I.B.Tauris, 2005.

Fattal, Antoine. *Le Statut Legal des Non-Musulmans en Pays d'islam*. Vol. X. *Recherches Publiées sous la Direction de l'Institut de Lettres Orientales de Beyrouth*. Beirut: Imprimerie Catholique, 1958.

Fekete, Lajos. *Die Siyaqat-Schrift in Der Türkischen Finanzverwaltung*. Budapest: Akadémiai Kiadó, 1955.

Filitti, J. C. *Notice sur les Cantacuzène du XIe Au XVIIe Siècles*. Bucharest: Geller, 1936.

Fine, John V. A. *The Late Medieval Balkans*: Ann Arbor: University of Michigan Press, 1987.

Fleet, Kate. "The Effect of the Fall of Constantinople on Ottoman-Genoese Trade Relations." *The Business of Change: Merchants and the Fall of Constantinople* (Unpublished Papers, 1994).

Fleischer, Cornell H. *Bureaucrat and Intellectual in the Ottoman Empire: The Historian Mustafa Ali (1541–1600).* Princeton, NJ: Princeton University Press, 1986.

Fleischer, C. H. "From Seyhzade Korkud to Mustafa Ali: Cultural Origins of the Nasihatname." In *Proceedings of the Third Congress on the Social and Economic History of Turkey*, edited by H. W. Lowry and R. S. Hattox, 67–77. Istanbul: Isis Press, 1990.

Foss, C. *Ephesus after Antiquity: A Late Antique, Byzantine and Turkish City.* Cambridge: Cambridge University Press, 1979.

Fotic, A. "The Official Explanation for the Confiscation and Sale of Monasteries (Churches) and Their Estates at the Time of Selim II." *Turcica* 26 (1994): 33–54.

Frazee, Charles. *Catholics and Sultans: The Church and the Ottoman Empire 1453–1923.* Cambridge: Cambridge University Press, 1983.

Friedrichs, Christopher R. *The Early Modern City, 1450–1750.* London: Longman, 1995.

Gedeon, Manouel. *Patriarchikoi Pinakes.* Konstantinoupolis, 1885–90.

Gedeon, Manouel. *Patriarchikai Ephemerides. Eideseis Ek Tes Hemeteras Ekklesiastikes Historias, 1500–1912.* Athens: Sergiadou Printing Press, 1935.

Gedeon, Manouel. "Tetrakosieteris Patriarchikes Doreas (1538–1938)." *Archeion tou Thrakikou Laographikou kai Glossikou Thesaurou* 25 (1957): 221–222.

Gedeon, Manouel Io. *Chronika Tou Patriarchikou Oikou Kai Tou Naou.* Constantinople: Patriarchal Printing Press, 1884.

Gedeon, Manouel Io. *Vracheia semeiosis peri ton ekklesiastikon hemon dikaion hypovletheisa te 12 Dekembriou 1908 to Panagiotato Oikoumeniko Patriarche.* En Konstantinoupolei: Ek tou Patriarchikou Typographeiou, 1909.

Genç, Mehmet and Osman Oykar. "Osmanlı Maliyesinde Malikâne Sistemi." In *Türkiye Iktisati Semineri.* Ankara: Hacettepe Üniversitesi Yayınları, 1975.

Gerber, Haim. "Jewish Tax-Farmers in the Ottoman Empire in the 16th and 17th Centuries." *Journal of Turkish Studies* 10 (1986): 143–154.

Gerber, Haim. *State, Society, and Law in Islam: Ottoman Law in Comparative Perspective.* Albany: SUNY Press, 1994.

Gervers, Michael and Ramzi Jibran Bikhazi, eds. *Conversion and Continuity: Indigenous Christian Communities in Islamic Lands Eight to Eighteenth Centuries, Papers in Mediaeval Studies 9.* Toronto: Pontifical Institute of Mediaeval Studies, 1990.

Gibbon, Edward. *The History of the Decline and Fall of the Roman Empire.* Edited by J. B. Bury. Vol. VII. Methuen & Co., 1900.

Gibbons, H. A. *The Foundation of the Ottoman Empire.* Oxford: Clarendon Press, 1916.

Giese, Friedrich. "Die Geschichtlichen Grundlagen Für Die Stellung Der Christlichen Untertanen Im Osmanischen Reich." *Der Islam* 19 (1931): 264–277.

Glara, Eleni. "In Search of Communities in Seventeenth Century Ottoman Sources: The Case of the Kara Ferye District." *Turcica* 30 (1998): 135–162.

Göçek, F. M. "Mültezim." *Encyclopedia of Islam: Second Edition.* Leiden: E. J. Brill, 1993.

Goffman, D. *Izmir and the Levantine World.* Seattle: University of Washington Press, 1990.

Goffman, Daniel. "Ottoman Millets in the Early Seventeenth Century." *New Perspectives on Turkey* 11 (1994): 135–158.

Gradeva, Rossitsa. "Orthodox Christians in the Kadi Courts: The Practice of the Sofia Sheriat Court, Seventeenth Century." *Islamic Law and Society* 4/1 (1997): 37–69.

Güçer, Lütfi. "XV.–XII. Asırlarda Osmanlı İmparatorluğunda Tüz İnhisarı ve Tüzların İşletme Nizami." *İstanbul Üniversitesi İktisat Fakültesi Mecmuası* 23 (1962–63): 397–416.

Hacker, J. R. "Ottoman Policy toward the Jews and Jewish Attitudes toward the Ottomans during the Fifteenth Century." In *Christians and Jews in the Ottoman Empire: The Functioning of a Plural Society*, edited by B. Braude and B. Lewis, 117–126. New York: Holmes & Meier, 1982.

Hacker, J. R. "Jewish Autonomy in the Ottoman Empire: Its Scope and Limits. Jewish Courts from the Sixteenth to the Eighteenth Centuries." In *The Jews of the Ottoman Empire*, edited by A. Levy, 153–202. Princeton, NJ: Darwin Press and the Institute of Turkish Studies, 1994.

Haldon, John. "'Jargon' Vs. 'the Facts'? Byzantine History-Writing and Contemporary Debates." *Byzantine and Modern Greek Studies* 9 (1984): 95–132.

Haldon, John. "Merchants and the Byzantine State: Contradiction, Competition, or Complementarity?" *The Business of Change: Merchants and the Fall of Constantinople* (Unpublished Papers, 1994).

Hammer-Purgstall, Joseph. *Histoire de l'Empire ottoman : depuis son origine jusqu'a nos jours.* Paris : Impr. de Béthune et Plon, 1844. <http://www.archive.org/details/histoiredelempir01hamm>.

Harvey, Alan. "The Monastic Economy and Imperial Patronage From the Tenth to the Twelfth Century." In *Mount Athos and Byzantine Monasticism: Papers from the Twenty-Eighth Spring Symposium of Byzantine Studies, Birmingham, March 1994*, edited by Mary Cunningham and Anthony Bryer, 99–111. Birmingham: Variorum, 1996.

Hasluck, F. W. *Christianity and Islam under the Sultans.* Edited by Margaret M. Hasluck. 1929. Vol. I. New York: Reprint, Octagon Books, 1973.

Hathaway, Jane. "Book Review: Ronald C. Jennings, Christians and Muslims in Ottoman Cyprus and the Mediterranean World, 1571–1640." *The Turkish Studies Association Bulletin* 18/2 (1994): 176–180.

Hattox, Ralph S. "Mehmed the Conqueror, the Patriarch of Jerusalem, and Mamluk Authority." *Studia Islamica*, 90 (2000): 105–123.

Hatzidimitriou, C. G. "The Decline of Imperial Authority in Southwest Central Greece and the Role of 'Archontes' and Bishops in the Failure of Byzantine Resistance and Reconquest 1180–1297 A.D." Ph.D. Dissertation: Columbia University, 1988.

Hendy, M. F. *Studies in the Byzantine Monetary Economy, C. 300–1450.* Cambridge: Cambridge University Press, 1985.

Hering, Gunnar. "Das Islamische Recht Und Die Investitur Des Gennadios Scholarios (1454)." *Balkan Studies* 2/2 (1961): 231–256.

Heyd, Uriel and V. L. Ménage. *Studies in Old Ottoman Criminal Law.* Oxford: Clarendon Press, 1973.

Hopwood, K. "Low-Level Diplomacy between Byzantines and Ottoman Turks: The Case of Bythinia." In *Byzantine Diplomacy*, edited by J. Shepherd and S. Franklin, 151–155. London: Variorum, 1992.

Howard, Douglas A. "Genre and Myth in the Ottoman Advice for Kings Literature." In *The Early Modern Ottomans: Remapping the Empire*, edited by Virginia H. Aksan and Daniel Goffman, 137–166. Cambridge: Cambridge University Press, 2007.

Hussey, J. M. *The Orthodox Church in the Byzantine Empire.* Oxford: Clarendon Press, 1986.

Imber, Colin. *The Ottoman Empire 1300–1481.* Istanbul: Isis Press, 1990.

Imber, Colin, Keiko Kiyotaki, and Rhoads Murphey. *Frontiers of Ottoman Studies*. London: I.B.Tauris, 2005.

Inalcik, Halil. "Stefan Duşan'dan Osmanlı Imparatorluğuna: Asırda Rumeli'de Hristiyan Sipahiler ve Menşeleri." In *60. Doğum Yılı Münasebetiyle Fuad Köprülü Armağanı*, 207–248. Istanbul: Dil ve Tarih Coğrafya Fakültesi Yayını, 1953.

Inalcik, Halil. "Ottoman Methods of Conquest." *Studia Islamica* II (1954): 104–129.

Inalcik, Halil. *Fatih devri üzerinde tetkikler ve vesikalar*. Ankara; Türk Tarih Kurumu Basimevi, 1954.

Inalcik, Halil. "The Problem of the Relationship between Byzantine and Ottoman Taxation." In *Akten Des XI Internationalen Byzantinisten Kongresses Munich 1958*, edited by H.G. Beck, 237–242. Munich: C. H. Beck, 1960.

Inalcik, Halil. "Notes on N. Beldiceanu's Translation of the Kanunname, Fond Turc Ancien 39, Bibliotheque Nationale, Paris." *Der Islam* 43/1–2 (1967): 139–157.

Inalcik, Halil. "Suleiman the Lawgiver and Ottoman Law." *Archivum Ottomanicum* I (1969): 105–138.

Inalcik, Halil. "Ottoman Policy and Administration in Cyprus after the Conquest." *Ayyildiz Matbaasi* (1969): 5–23.

Inalcik, Halil. "The Policy of Mehmet II toward the Greek Population of Istanbul and the Byzantine Buildings of the City." *Dumbarton Oaks Papers* 23–24 (1969–70): 231–249.

Inalcik, Halil. "Hawala." *Encyclopedia of Islam: Second Edition*. Leiden: E. J. Brill, 1971.

Inalcik, Halil. *The Ottoman Empire: The Classical Age 1300–1600*. Translated by N. Itzkowitz and C. Imber. Second edition. New Rochelle, NY: Aristide D. Caratzas, Orpheus, 1973.

Inalcik, Halil. "Military and Fiscal Transformation in the Ottoman Empire, 1600–1700." *Archivum Ottomanicum* 6 (1980): 283–337.

Inalcik, Halil. "Ottoman Archival Materials on Millets." In *Christians and Jews in the Ottoman Empire: The Functioning of a Plural Society*, edited by Benjamin Braude and Bernard Lewis, 437–449. New York: Holmes & Meier, 1982.

Inalcik, Halil. "The Appointment Procedure of a Guild Warden (Kethüda)." *Wiener Zeitschrift für die Kunde des Morgenlands* 76, Festscrhift Andreas Tietze (1986): 135–142.

Inalcik, Halil. "Istanbul: An Islamic City." *Journal of Islamic Studies* 1 (1990): 1–23.

Inalcik, Halil. "Djizya." *Encyclopedia of Islam: Second Edition*. Leiden: E. J. Brill, 1991.

Inalcik, Halil. "The Status of the Greek Orthodox Patriarchate under the Ottomans." *Turcica* 21–23 (1991): 407–436.

Inalcik, Halil. "Tax Collection, Embezzlement and Bribery in Ottoman Finances." *The Turkish Studies Association Bulletin* 15/2 (1991): 327–346.

Inalcik, Halil. "Ottoman Galata, 1453–1553." In *Première Rencontre Internatinale Sur L'empire Ottoman Et La Turquie Moderne*, edited by E. Eldem. Istanbul: Isis Press, 1991.

Inalcik, Halil. "Greeks in the Ottoman Economy and Finances, 1453–1500." In *To Hellenikon: Studies in Honor of Speros Vryonis, Jr.*, edited by J. Stanojevich Allen, John S. Langdon, and Stephen W. Reinert, 289–365. New Rochelle, NY: Aristide D. Caratzas, 1993.

Inalcik, Halil. "State, Sovereignty and Law during the Reign of Süleymân." In *Suleyman the Second and His Time*, edited by Cemal Kafadar and Halil Inalcik, 203–210. Istanbul: Isis, 1993.

Inalcik, Halil, ed. *An Economic and Social History of the Ottoman Empire 1300–1914*. Cambridge: Cambridge University Press, 1994.

Inalcik, Halil. "Istanbul." *Encyclopedia of Islam: Second Edition*. Leiden: E. J. Brill, 1997.

Inan, Kenan. "Remembering the Good Old Days: The Ottoman Nasihatname [Advice Letters] Literature of the 17th Century." In *Institutional Change and Stability Conflicts, Transitions and Social Values*, edited by Andreas Gémes, Florencia Peyrou, and Ioannis Xydopoulos, 111–127. Pisa: Pisa University Press, 2009.

Institute for Balkan Studies (Greece). *Symposium L'époque phanariote: 21–25 octobre 1970.* Thessaloniki: Institute for Balkan Studies, 1974.

Iorga, Nicolas. *Despre Cantacuzini.* Bucharest: Institutul de Arte grafice si Editura Minerva, 1902.

Iorga, Nicolas. *Byzance Apres Byzance.* Paris: Editions Balland, 1982.

"Istimalet." *Redhouse Yeni Türkçe Ingilizce Sözlük.* Istanbul: Redhouse Yayinevi, 1968.

Itzkowitz, N. "Eighteenth Century Ottoman Realities." *Studia Islamica* 16 (1962): 73–94.

Jakelić, Slavica. *Collectivistic Religions: Religion, Choice, and Identity in Late Modernity.* Farnham, Surrey, England; Burlington, Vt.: Ashgate Publishing, Ltd., 2010.

Jeannin, Pierre. *Merchants of the 16th Century.* Translated by Paul Fittingroff. New York: Harper and Rowe, 1972.

Jennings, Ronald C. *Studies on Ottoman Social History in the Sixteenth and Seventeenth Centuries: Women, Zimmis and Shari'a Courts in Kayseri, Cyprus and Trabzon, Analecta Isisiana; 39.* Istanbul: The Isis Press, 1999.

Kabrda, Josef. *Le Système Fiscal De L'église Orthodoxe Dans L'empire Ottoman (D'aprés Les Documents Turcs).* Brno: Universita J. E. Purkyné, 1969.

Kafadar, Cemal. *Between Two Worlds: The Construction of the Ottoman State.* Berkeley: University of California Press, 1995.

Kamperides, Lambros. "The Notion of Millet in Mavrokordatos' Philotheou Parerga and His Perception of the Enlightened Ottoman Despot." *Journal of the Hellenic Diaspora* 18/1 (1992): 67–78.

Kamperidis, Lambros. *The Greek Monasteries of Sōzopolis: XIV-XVII Centuries.* Thessalonike: Institute for Balkan Studies, 1993.

Kane, Thomas Aloysius. *The Jurisdiction of the Patriarchs of the Major Sees in Antiquity and in the Middle Ages: A Historical Commentary.* Washington, DC: Catholic University of America Press, 1949.

Karaca, Zafer. "Rum Ortodoks Kiliseleri." In *Dünden Bugüne Istanbul Ansiklopedisi*, 349–353. Istanbul: Türkiye Ekonomik ve Toplumsal Tarih Vakfi, 1994.

Karpat, Kemal H. "Millets and Nationality: The Roots of the Incongruity of Nation and State in the Post-Ottoman Era." In *Christians and Jews in the Ottoman Empire: The Functioning of a Plural Society*, edited by Benjamin Braude and Bernard Lewis, 141–169. New York: Holmes & Meier, 1982.

Kastritsis, Dimitris J. *The Sons of Bayezid: Empire Building and Representation in the Ottoman Civil War of 1402–1413.* Leiden: E. J. Brill, 2007.

Kazhdan, Alexander P., ed. *The Oxford Dictionary of Byzantium.* 3 Volumes. New York: Oxford University Press, 1991.

Kazhdan, Alexander P. "Archon." In *The Oxford Dictionary of Byzantium*, Vol. 1, edited by Alexander P. Kazhdan, 160. New York: Oxford University Press, 1991.

Kazhdan, Alexander P. "Protovestiaros." In *The Oxford Dictionary of Byzantium*, Vol. 1, edited by Alexander Kazhdan, 1749. New York: Oxford University Press, 1991.

Kazhdan, Alexander P. and Aristeidis Papadakis. "Patriarchates." In *The Oxford Dictionary of Byzantium*, Vol. 3, edited by Alexander P. Kazhdan, 1599–1600. New York: Oxford University Press, 1991.

Kazhdan, Alexander P. and Alice Mary Talbot. "Zeaolts." In *The Oxford Dictionary of Byzantium*, Vol. 3, edited by Alexander P. Kazhdan, 2221–2222. New York: Oxford University Press, 1991.

Kenanoğlu, M. Macit. *Osmanli millet sistemi : mit ve gerçek*. Aksaray Istanbul: Klasik, 2004.

Kermeli, Eugenia. "The Right to Choice: Ottoman Justice Vis-À-Vis Ecclesiastical and Communal Justice in the Balkans, Seventeenth-Nineteenth Centuries." In *Studies in Islamic Law: A Festschrift for Colin Imber*, edited by Andreas Christmann and R Gleave. Oxford: Published by Oxford University Press on behalf of the University of Manchester, 2007.

Kiel, M. "Remarks on the Administration of the Poll Tax (Cizye) in the Ottoman Balkans and Value of Poll Tax Registers (Cizye Defterleri) for Demographic Research." *Etudes Balkaniques* 4 (1990): 70–99.

Kitromilides, Paschalis. *Enlightenment and Revolution: The Making of Modern Greece*. Cambridge: Harvard University Press, 2013.

Knös, B. *L'histoire De La Litterature Neo-Grecque. La Periode Jusqu'en 1821*. Uppsala: Acta Universitatis Upsaliensis, 1962.

Kolovos, Elias. "Christian Influence and the Advent of the Europeans: Negotiating for State Protection: Çiftlik-Holding by the Athonite Monasteries (Xeropotamou Monastery, Fifteenth-Sixteenth C." In *Frontiers of Ottoman Studies*, edited by Colin Imber, Keiko Kiyotaki, and Rhoads Murphey, 197–210. London: I. B.Tauris, 2005.

Konidares, Gerassimos I. "Review Article" the Oecumenical Patriarchate in the Orthodox Church." *Balkan Studies* 14/2 (1973): 331–351.

Konortas, Paraskevas. "He Exelixe Ton 'Ekklesiastikon' Beration Kai to 'Pronomiakon Zetema'." *Historia*: 42–51.

Konortas, Paraskevas. *Les Rapports Juridiques Et Politiques Entre Le Patriarcat Orthodoxe De Constantinople Et L'administration Ottomane De 1453 a 1600 (D'après Les Documents Grecs Et Ottomans). These De Cycle 2 Tomes*. Paris : Universite de Paris, 1985.

Konortas, Paraskevas. "'Les Contributions Ecclésiastiques: Patriarchikè Zèteia' Et 'Basilikon Charatzion' Contribution à L'histoire Économique Du Patriarcat Oecuménique Aux XVe Et XVie Siècles." In *Actes du IIe Colloque International D'histoire: Économies Méditerranéennes Équilibres et Intercommunications XIIIe–XIXe Siècles*, 217–255. Athens: Centre de Recherches Néohelléniques de la Fondation Nationale de la Recherche Scientifique, 1986.

Konortas, Paraskevas. "Discussion." In *Actes du IIe Colloque International d'histoire: Économies Méditerranéennes Équilibres et Intercommunications XIIIe–XIXe Siècles*, 217–255. Athens: Centre de Recherches Néohelléniques de la Fondation Nationale de la Recherche Scientifique, 1986.

Konortas, Paraskevas. "Les Contributions Ecclésiastiques 'Patriarchikè Zèteia' Et 'Basilikon Charatzion'. Contribution à l'histoire Économique du Patriarcat Oecuménique aux XV Et XVI ss." In *Économies Méditerranéennes: Équilibres et Intercommunications, XIIIe–XIXe Siècles*, 217–255. Athens, 1986.

Konortas, Paraskevas. *Othomanikes Theoreseis Gia to Oikoumeniko Patriarcheio: Beratia Gia Tous Prokathemenous Tes Megales Ekklesias (17os-Arches 20ou Aiona)*. Athens: Ekdoseis Alexandreia, 1998.

Konortas, Paraskevas. "From *Tâ'ife* to *Millet*: Ottoman Terms Concerning the Ottoman Greek Orthodox Community." In *Ottoman Greeks in the Age of Nationalism: Politics, Economy, and Society in the Nineteenth Century*, edited by Dimitri Gondicas and Charles Issawi, 169–180. Princeton, NJ: Darwin Press, 1999.

Köprülü, M. Fuad. *The Origins of the Ottoman Empire.* Edited by Gary Leiser Trans. Albany, NY: State University of New York, 1992.

Kostes, Kostas. "Koinotetes, Ekklesia Kai Millet Stis 'Ellenikes' Periohes Tes Othomanikes Autocratorias Kata Ten Periodo Ton Metarrythmiseon." *Mnemon* 13 (1991): 57–75.

Kotzageorgiou, Phokion. *He Athonike Mone Aghiou Pavlou Me Vase to Archeio Tes (14os Ai.– 1830): Oikonomike Epiviose, Koinonike Dynamike Mesa Sto Othomaniko Kratiko Systema.* Thessalonike: Aristotle University of Thessalonike, 1999.

Kotzageorgis, Phokion. "On the Fiscal Status of the Greek Orthodox Church in the 17th Century." *Turcica: Revue d'Etudes Turques* 40 (2008): 67–81.

Kunt, Ibrahim Metin. "Ethnic-Regional (Cins) Solidarity in the Seventeenth-Century Ottoman Establishment." *International Journal of Middle Eastern Studies* v (1974): 233–239.

Kunt, Ibrahim Metin. "Transformation of Zimmi into Askeri." In *Christians and Jews in the Ottoman Empire: The Functioning of a Plural Society*, edited by Benjamin Braude and Bernard Lewis, 55–67. New York: Holmes & Meier, 1982.

Kunt, Ibrahim Metin. "State and Sultan up to the Age of of Süleyman." In *Süleyman the Magnificent and His Age: The Ottoman Empire in the Early Modern World*, edited by Ibrahim Metin Kunt and Christine Woodhead, 3–29. London: Longman, 1995.

Laiou, A. E. "In the Medieval Balkans: Economic Pressures and Conflicts in the Fourteenth Century." In *Byzantina Kai Metabyzantina*, edited by Speros Vryonis Jr, 137–162. Malibu: Undena Publication, 1985.

Lambton, Ann. "Mongol Fiscal Administration in Persia." *Studia Islamica* 64 (1986): 79–99.

Lambton, Ann. "Pishkash: Present or Tribute." *Bulletin of the School of Oriental and African Studies* 57 (1994): 144–158.

Lambton, A. "Pishkash." *Encyclopedia of Islam: Second Edition,* 8. Leiden: E. J. Brill, 1995.

Lampros, Spyrid on Paulou. *Ecthesis Chronica and Chronicon Athenarum.* London: Methuen & co., 1902.

Lampros, Spyridon Paulou. *Neos Hellenomnemon.* Vol. 1–21; Mar. 1904–Dec. 1927. Athens: B. Gregoriadès, 1969.

Lemerle, P. E. "Le Juge Généneral Des Grecs et La Réforme Judiciare d'Andronic III." In *Mémorial Louis Petit; Mélanges D'histoire et D'archéologie Byzantines*, edited by Archives de l'Orient chrétien, 292–316. Paris: Institut français d'études byzantines, 1948.

Lemerle, P. E. "Recherches Sur Les Institutions Judiciares À L'époque Des Paléologues, II. Le Tribunal Du Patriarcat Ou Tribunal Synodal." In *Mélanges Paul Peeters,* 68: 318–333. Analecta Bollandiana. Brussels: Société des Bollandistes, 1950.

Lemerle, P. E. *L'emirat d'Aydin, Byzance et l'Occident; Recherches Sur La Geste d'Umur Pacha.* Vol. 1. Paris: Presses universitaires de France, 1957.

Lemerle, P. E. "Documents et Problèmes Nouveaux Concernant Les Juges Généraux." *Deltion Tes Hristianikes Archaiologikes Hetaireias* 4/4 (1964).

Lemerle, P. and P. Wittek. "Recherches Sur L'histoire Et Le Status Des Monasteres Athonites Sous La Domination Turque." *Archives d'Histoire du Droit Oriental* 3 (1947): 411–471.

Lewis, B. "Ottoman Observers of Ottoman Decline." *Islamic Studies* 1/1 (1962): 71–87.

Levy, A. *The Sephardim in the Ottoman Empire.* Princeton, NJ: The Darwin Press, 1992.

Levy, Avgidor, ed. *The Jews of the Ottoman Empire.* Princeton, NJ: Darwin Press and the Institute of Turkish Studies, 1994.

Lewis, Bernard. *The Jews of Islam.* Princeton: Princeton University Press, 1984.

Leykin, A. K. *The Tsars and the East: Gifts From Turkey and Iran in the Moscow Kremlin.* Washington: Arthur M. Sackler Gallery, Smithosonian Institution, 2009.

Lowry, Heath W. "A Note on the Population and Status of the Athonite Monasteries under Ottoman Rule (Ca. 1520)." *Wiener Zeitschrift fur die Kunde des Morgenlandes* 73 (1981): 229–246.

Lowry, Heath W. "Polemique à Propos D'un Compte Rendu Paru Dans Byzantion LII." *Byzantion* 55 (1982): 403–414.

Lowry, Heath W. *The Ottoman "Tahrir Defters" as a Source for Urban Demographic History: The Case Study of Trabzon (Ca. 1486-1583).* Ann Arbor: University Microfilms International, 1984.

Lowry, Heath W. "From Lesser Wars to the Mightiest War.' The Ottoman Conquest and Transformation of Byzantine Urban Centers in the Fifteenth Century." In *Continuity and Change in Late Byzantine and Early Ottoman Society*, edited by Anthony Bryer and Heath W. Lowry, 323–338. Birmingham and Washington, DC: University of Birmingham and Dumbarton Oaks, 1986.

Lowry, Heath W. "The Ottoman Tahrir Defterleri as a Source for Social and Economic History: Pitfalls and Limitations." Paper presented at the Turkische Wirtschafts- und Sozialgeschichte (1071–1920): Akten des IV. Internationalen Kongresses, Munchen, 1986.

Lowry, Heath W. "The Role of Byzantine Provincial Officials Following the Ottoman Conquests of Their Lands." In *IIIrd Congress on the Social and Economic History of Turkey, Princeton University, 1983*, edited by H. W. Lowry & R. S. Hattox, 261–267. Istanbul: Isis Press, 1990.

Lowry, Heath W. "From Trabzon to Istanbul: The Relationship between Süleyman the Lawgiver and His Foster Brother (Süt Karindasi) Yahya Efendi." *Osmanlı Arastirmaları/ Journal of Ottoman Studies* 10 (1990): 39–48.

Lowry, Heath W. "The Fate of Monastic Properties under the Ottomans: Examples from Mount Athos, Limnos and Trabzon." *Byzantinische Forschungen* 16 (1991): 275–311.

Lowry, Heath W. "The Island of Limnos: A Case Study on the Continuity of Byzantine Forms under Ottoman Rule." In *Studies in Defterology: Ottoman Society in the Fifteenth Cenuturies*, edited by H. W. Lowry, 165–180. Istanbul: Isis Press, 1992.

Lowry, Heath W. "Priviledge and Property in Ottoman Machuka in the Opeining Decades of the Tourkokratia: 1461–1553." In *Studies in Defterology: Ottoman Society in the Fifteenth Cenuturies*, edited by H. W. Lowry, 123–130. Istanbul: Isis Press, 1992.

Lowry, Heath W. "Süleyman's Formative Years in the City of Trabzon: Their Impact on the Future Sultan and the City." In *Süleyman the Second and His Time*, edited by Halil Inalcik and Cemal Kafadar, 21–36. Istanbul: Isis Press, 1993.

Lowry, Heath W. "When Did the Sephardim Arrive in Salonica? The Testimony of the Ottoman Tax-Registers, 1478–1613." In *The Jews of the Ottoman Empire*, edited by Avgidor Levy, 153–202. Princeton, NJ: Darwin Press and the Institute of Turkish Studies, 1994.

Lowry, Heath W. *The Nature of the Early Ottoman State.* Albany: State University of New York Press, 2003.

Lowry, Heath W. *Islamization and Turkification of the City of Trabzon (Trebizond), 1461–1583.* Istanbul: Isis Press, 2009.

Lowry, Heath W. *Trabzon Sehrinin Islamlasmasi ve Türklesmesi, 1461–1583 Trabzon Şehrinin İslamlaşma ve Türkleşmesi, 1481–1583.* 4th revised. Istanbul: Bosphorus University Press, 2010.

Lowry, Heath W. "Early Ottoman Period." In *The Routledge Handbook of Modern Turkey*, edited by Metin Heper and Sabri Sayari, 5–14. New York: Routledge, 2012.

Lowry, H and A. Bryer, eds. *Continuity and Change in Late Byzantine and Early Ottoman Society.* Birmingham and Washington, DC: University of Birmingham and Dumbarton Oaks, 1986.

Lybyer, Albert Howe. *The Government of the Ottoman Empire in the Time of Suleiman the Magnificent.* Vol. 18. *Harvard Historical Studies.* Cambridge, MA: Harvard University Press, 1913.

Mango, Cyril. "Review of The Great Church in Captivity: A Study of the Patriarchate of Constantinople from the Eve of the Turkish Conquest to the Greek War of Independence by Steven Runciman." *The American Historical Review* 74/5 (1969): 1576–1578.

Mantran, Robert. "Foreign Merchants and the Minorities in Istanbul during the Sixteenth and Seventeenth Centuries." In *Christians and Jews in the Ottoman Empire: The Functioning of a Plural Society*, edited by Benjamin Braude and Bernard Lewis, 127–137. New York: Holmes & Meier, 1982.

Mardin, Ebül'ula. "The Development of Shari'a under the Ottoman Empire." In *Law in the Middle East*, edited by M. Khadduri & H. Liebesny. Washington, DC: Middle East Institute, 1955.

Maropoulou, M. "L'Économie: Moyen de Transgression Ou d'Adaptation Sociale? Le Témoinage de Gennadios Scholarios." In *Actes du IIe Colloque International d'Histoire: Économies Méditerranéenes Équilibres et Intercommunications XIIIe-XIXe Siècles*, 257–268. Athens: Centre de Recherches Néohelléniques de la Fondation Nationale de la Recherche Scientifique, 1986.

Martels, Z. "Impressions of the Ottoman Empire in the Writings of Augerius Busbequius (1520/2–1591)." *Journal of Mediterranean Studies* 5/2 (1995): 209–221.

Matschke, Klaus Peter. "Some Merchant Families in Constantinople before, during and after the Fall of the City, 1453." *The Business of Change: Merchants and the Fall of Constantinople* (Unpulished Papers, 1994).

Matschke, Klaus-Peter. "The Notaras Family and Its Italian Connections." *Dumbarton Oaks Papers: Symposium on Byzantium and the Italians, 13th-15th Centuries.* 49 (1995): 59–72.

Matschke, Klaus-Peter. "Transition to Tourkokratia: The Byzantinist Standpoint." In *The Ottomans and the Balkans: A Discussion of Historiography*, edited by Fikret Adanır and Suraiya Faroqhi, 79–113. Leiden: E. J. Brill, 2002.

Maxim, Mihai. "Recherches Sur Les Circonstances de La Majoration Du Kharadj de La Moldavie Entre Les Anneés 1538–1574." *Association Internationale d'Etudes Du Sud-Est Européen Bulletin* X/2 (1972): 233–261.

Maxim, Mihai. "Les Relations Des Pays Roumans Avec L'archevêché D'ohrid à Lumière De Documents Turcs Inédits." *Revue Études Sud-Est Europeen* XIX (1981): 653–671.

Maxim, Mihai. "Demetrie Cantemir (1673–1623)." Edited by Cemal Kafadar, Hakan Karateke, and Cornell Fleischer. *Historians of the Ottoman Empire*, 2006. <http://www.ottomanhistorians.com>.

Merry, Bruce. "George the Aetolian." In *Encyclopedia of Modern Greek Literature.* 158–159, Westport, CT: Greenwood Publishing Group, 2004.

Metropolitan Maximos. *The Oecumenical Patriarchate in the Orthodox Church: A Study in the History and Canons of the Church.* Translated by Gamon McLellan. Vol. 24. *Analekta Vlatadon.* Thessalonike: Patriarchal Institute for Patristic Studies, 1976.

Meyendorff, John. "Byzantine Views of Islam." *Dumbarton Oaks Papers* 18 (1964): 115–132.

Meyendorff, John. *The Byzantine Legacy in the Orthodox Church*. St Vladimir's Seminary Press, 1982.

Meyendorff, John. *Imperial Unity and Christian Divisions: The Church, 450–680 AD*. St. Vladimir's Seminary Press, 1989.

Minkov, Anton. *Conversion to Islam in the Balkans: Kisve Bahas Petitions and Ottoman Social Life, 1670–1730*. Leiden: E. J. Brill, 2004.

Moačanin, Nenad. "The Poll-Tax and Population in the Ottoman Balkans." In *Frontiers of Ottoman Studies*, edited by Colin Imber, Keiko Kiyotaki, and Rhoads Murphey, 77–89. London: I. B.Tauris, 2005.

Moravcsik, G. *Byzantinoturcica*. Second edition. 2 vols. Berlin: Akademie-Verlag, 1958.

Moustakas, Konstantinos. "The Logic of Historical Thematology in *The Historia Politica Constantinopoleos* and the *Historia Patriarchica Constantinopoleos*." In *Festschrift in Honor of Ioannis P. Theocharides: Studies on the Ottoman Empire and Turkey*, edited by Evangelia Balta, Georgios Salakides, and Theoharis Stavrides, 2: 363–374. Istanbul: Isis Press, 2014.

Necipoğlu, Gülrü. *Architecture, Ceremonial, and Power: The Topkapi Palace in the Fifteenth and Sixteenth Centuries*. New York and Cambridge, MA: Architectural History Foundation and MIT Press, 1991.

Necipoglu, Nevra. "Byzantium between the Ottomans and the Latins: A Study of Political Attitudes in the Late Palaiologan Period 1370–1460." Ph.D., Harvard University, 1990.

Nicol, Donald M. "The Byzantine Family of Cantacuzenus." *Dumbarton Oaks Papers* XI (1968): 309–315.

Nicol, Donald M. *The Byzantine Family of Kantakouzenos (Cantacuzenus) Ca. 1100–1460: A Genealogical and Prosopographical Study*. Washington: Dumbarton Oaks Center for Byzantine Studies, 1968.

Nicol, Donald M. *The Despotate of Epiros, 1267–1479: A Contribution to the History of Greece in the Middle Ages*. Cambridge: Cambridge University Press, 1984.

Nicol, Donald M. "Byzantine Political Thought." In *The Cambridge History of Medieval Political Thought C.350-c.1450,* edited by J. H. Burns. Cambridge: Cambridge University Press, 1991.

Nicol, Donald M. *The Last Centuries of Byzantium: 1261–1453*. Cambridge: Cambridge University Press, 1993.

Nicolaou-Konnari, Angel. "Greeks." In *Cyprus: Society and Culture 1191–1374*, edited by Christopher David Schabel and Angel Nicolaou-Konnari, 13–62. Leiden: E. J. Brill, 2005.

Obolensky, D. *The Byzantine Commonwealth: Eastern Europe* 500–1453. London: Weidenfeld and Nicolson, 1971.

Oikonomides, Nicholas. "Le Haradj Dans l'empire Byzantine du XVè Siècle." In *Actes du Premier Congrès International Des Études Balkaniques et Sudest Europeénes*, 681–688, 1966.

Oikonomides, N. "Les Archives Medievales Du Mont Athos: Etat Actuel de L'inventaire et Programme de Publication." In *Proceedings of the XIII International Congress of Byzantine Studies*, edited by J. M. Hussey, D. Obolensky, and S. Runciman, 44: 489–493. London: University Press, 1967.

Oikonomides, Nicholas. "Monasteres Et Moines Lors De La Conquete Ottomane." *Südost-Forschungen* 36 (1976): 1–10.

Oikonomides, Nicholas. "Ottoman Influence on Late Byzantine Fiscal Practice." *Südost-Forschungen* 45 (1986): 1–24.

Oikonomides, Nicholas. "Patronage in Palaiologan Mt. Athos." In *Mount Athos and Byzantine Monasticism: Papers from the Twenty-Eighth Spring Symposium of Byzantine Studies, Birmingham, March 1994*, edited by Anthony Bryer and Mary Cunningham, 99–111. Birmingham: Variorum, 1996.

Orhonlu, Cengiz. "Kharadj." *Encyclopedia of Islam: Second Edition*. Leiden: E. J. Brill, 1997.

Ostrogorsky, George. *History of the Byzantine State*. Translated by Joan Hussey. New Brunswick, NJ: Rutgers University Press, 1969.

Ozil, Ayse. *Orthodox Christians in the Late Ottoman Empire: A Study of Communal Relations in Anatolia*. Oxford: Routledge, 2013.

Paize-Apostolopoulou, Mache. *Aphieromata kai dorees ton 16o ai. ste M. Ekklesia: thesmikes opseis tes euseveias*. Athena: Ethniko Hidryma Ereunon, 2002.

Pakalin, M. Z. "Millet Başı." *Osmanlı Tarih Deyimleri ve Terimleri Sözlüğü*. Vol. II (1946–54): 535.

Palmer, Andrew, Sebastian Brock, and Robert Hoyland. *The Seventh Century in the West-Syrian Chronicles*. Vol. 15. *Translated Texts for Historians*. Liverpool: Liverpool University Press, 1993.

Pamuk, Sevket. *A Monetary History of the Ottoman Empire, Cambridge Studies in Islamic Civilization*. New York: Cambridge University Press, 2000.

Pantazopoulos, N. *Church and Law in the Balkan Peninsula during the Ottoman Rule*. Thessalonike: Institute for Balkan Studies, 1967.

Papademetriou, G. C. "An Encyclical of the Ecumenical Patriarch Metrophanes III, 1520–1580." *Journal of Ecumenical Studies* 26/2 (1989): 338–340.

Papadopoullos, Theodore H. "Orthodox Church and Civil Authority." *Journal of Contemporary History* 2/4 (1967): 201–209.

Papadopoullos, Theodore H. *Studies and Documents Relating to the History of the Greek Church and People under Turkish Domination*. Second edition. London: Variorum, 1990.

Papazoglou, Georgios K. *Vivliothekes Sten Konstantinoupole Tou [16] Aiona (Kod. Vind. Hist. Gr. 98)*. Thessalonike, 1983.

Patrinelis, Christos G. *Ho Theodoros Agallianos Tautizomenos Pros Ton Theophanen Medeias Kai Hoi Anekdotoi Logoi Tou: Mia Nea Historike Pege Peri Tou Patriarcheiou Konstantinoupoleos Kata Tous Protous Meta Ten Halosin Chronous*. Athens: C. G. Patrinelis, 1966.

Patrinelis, Christos G. "Chronologika Zetemata Tes Patriarcheias Tou Hieremiou A' (1522–46)." *Mnemosyne* 1 (1967): 249–262.

Patrinelis, Christos G. "The Exact Time of the First Attempt of the Turks to Seize the Churches and Convert the Christian People of Constantinople to Islam." *Actes du 1er Congrès International des Etudes Balkaniques et Sud-Est Europe'ens* III (1969): 567–574.

Patrinelis, Christos G. *Demosieumata Manouel Gedeon: Analytike Anagraphe*. Athens: Academy of Athens: Rescearch Center of Medieval and Modern Greece, 1974.

Petmezas, Socrates. "L'organisation Ecclésiastiques Sous Les Ottomans." In *Conseils Et Mémoires De Synadinos Prête De Serrès En Macédoine (Xviie Siècle)*, edited by S. Asdrachas, Paolo Odorico, T. Karanastassis, K. Kostis and S. Petmezas, 487–569. Paris: Editions de l'Association "Pierre Belon," 1997.

Philippides, Marios. "Patriarchal Chronicles of the Sixteenth Century." *Greek, Roman and Byzantine Studies* 25 (1984): 87–94.

Philippides, Marios. "Makarios Melissourgos-Melissenos." In *Historians of the Ottoman Empire*, edited by Cemal Kafadar, Hakan Karateke, and Cornell Fleischer, 2008. <http://www.ottomanhistorians.com>.

Philippides, Marios. "Damaskenos the Studite." In *Historians of the Ottoman Empire*, edited by Cemal Kafadar, Hakan Karateke, and Cornell Fleischer, n.d. <http://www.ottomanhistorians.com>.

Philippides, Marios and Walter Hanak. *The Siege and the Fall of Constantinople in 1453: Historiography, Topography, and Military Studies*. Farnham, England and Burlington, VT: Ashgate, 2011.

Philliou, Christine. "Communities on the Verge: Unraveling the Phanariot Ascendancy in Ottoman Governance." *Comparative Studies in Society and History* 51/1 (2009): 151–181.

Philliou, Christine May. *Biography of an Empire: Governing Ottomans in an Age of Revolution*. Berkeley: University of California Press, 2011.

Pippidi, Andrei. *Hommes et Idées Du Sud-Est Européen À L'aube de L'âge Moderne*. Bucureşti: Editura Academiei Republicii Socialiste România ; Éditions du C. N. R. S, 1980.

Raby, Julian. "Mehmet the Conqueror's Greek Scriptorium." *DOP* 37 (1983): 15–35.

Rahn, Markus. *Die Entstehung des Armenischen Patriarchats von Konstantinopel*. LIT Verlag Münster, 2002.

Reinert, S. W. "Orhan." *The Oxford Dictionary of Byzantium*. Vol. 3, edited by Alexander P. Kazhdan, 1533. New York: Oxford University Press, 1991.

Reinert, Stephen W. "The Palailogoi, Yildirim Bayezid and Constantinople: June 1389–March 1391." In *To Hellenikon: Studies in Honor of Speros Vryonis, Jr.*, edited by J. Stanojevich Allen, John S. Langdon, and Stephen W. Reinert, 289–365. New Rochelle, NY: Aristide D. Caratzas, 1993.

Rozen, Minna. "Individual and Community in the Jewish Society of the Ottoman Empire: Salonica in the Sixteenth Century." In *The Jews of the Ottoman Empire*, edited by Avgidor Levy, 215–73. Princeton, NJ: Darwin Press and the Institute of Turkish Studies, 1994.

Runciman, Stephen. "Lucas Notaras, 'Gambros Tou Basilevs'." In *Polychronion: Festschrift Franz Dölger Zum 75. Geburstag*, edited by Peter Wirth. 447–449, Heidelberg: Carl Winter-Universitätsverlag, 1966.

Runciman, Stephen. "Rum Milleti: The Orthodox Communities under the Ottoman Sultans." In *The Byzantine Tradition after the Fall of Constantinople*, edited by John J. Yiannias, 1–15. Charlottesville: University Press of Virginia, 1992.

Runciman, Steven. "Byzantine Historians and the Ottoman Turks." In *Historians of the Middle East*, edited by B. Lewis and P. M. Holt, 271–276. London: Oxford University Press, 1962.

Runciman, Steven. *The Great Church in Captivity*. Cambridge: Cambridge University Press, 1968.

Sadat, Deena. "Rumeli Ayanlari: 18th Century." *Journal of Modern History* 44/3: 346–363.

Sahillioğlu, Halil. "Bir Mültezim Zimem Defterine Göre XV Yüzyil Sonunda Osmanlı Darphane Mukata'a ları." *Iktisat Fakültesi Mecmuasi* 23/1–4 (1963): 1–74.

Sahillioğlu, Halil. "The Role of International Monetary and Metal Movements in Ottoman Monetary History 1300–1750." In *Precious Metals in the Later Medieval and Early Modern Worlds*, edited by J. F. Richards, 269–304. Durham: Carolina Academic Press, 1983.

Sahillioğlu, Halil. *Studies on Ottoman Economic and Social History*. Istanbul: Research Centre for Islamic History Art and Culture (IRCICA), 1999.

Said, E. W. *Orientalism*. New York: Vintage Books, 1978.

Sakel, Dean. "Three Tales for a Sultan? Three Tales on Mehmed the Conqueror and Patriarch Gennadius." *British Journal of Middle Eastern Studies* 35/2 (2008): 227–238.

Semavi, Eyice. "Galata: Osmanli Dönemi." In *Dünden Bugüne Istanbul Ansiklopedisi.* Edited by Nuri Akbayar, 6, 349–354. Istanbul: Türkiye Ekonomik ve Toplumsal Tarih Vakfi, 1994.

Salakides, Georgios. *Sultansurkunden Des Athos-Klosters Vatopedi Aus Der Zeit Bayezid II. Und Selim I.* Thessalonike: Institute for Balkan Studies, 1995.

Savory, R. M. "Kīzīl-Bāsh." *Encyclopedia of Islam.* 2nd Edition. Leiden: E. J. Brill, 1990.

Schacht, J. "Al-Halabi, Burhan Al-Din Ibrahim B. Muhammad B. Ibrahim." *Encyclopedia of Islam.* 2nd Edition. Leiden: E. J. Brill, 1990.

Scheel, H. *Die Staatsrechtliche Stellung Der Ökumenischen Kirchenfürsten in Der Alten Türkei.* Berlin: Berlag der Akademie der Wissenschaften, 1943.

Seng, Yvonne J. "The Sher'iye Sicilleri of the Istanbul Müftülüğü." *The Turkish Studies Association Bulletin* 15/2 (1991): 307–324.

Ševčenko, Ihor. "Society and Intellectual Life in the Fourteenth Century." In *Actes Du XIVe Congrès International Des Études Byzantines, Bucarest, 6-12 Septembre 1971*, edited by M. Berza and E. Stănescu, 1: 69–92. Bucharest: Editura Academiei Republicii Socialiste România, 1976.

Ševčenko, Ihor. *Society and Intellectual Life in Late Byzantium.* London: Variorum Reprints, 1981.

Sharp, Andrew. *Orthodox Christians and Islam in the Postmodern Age.* Leiden: E. J. Brill, 2012.

Shaw, Stanford. "The Aims and Achievements of Ottoman Rule in the Balkans." *Slavic Review* 21 (1962): 617–632.

Sidarous Bey, Sésostris. *Des Patriarcats Dans l'Empire Ottoman et Particulièrement En Egypte.* Paris: Rousseau, 1907.

Skendi, Stavro. "Crypto-Christianity in the Balkan Area under the Ottomans." *Slavic Review* XXVI (1967): 227–246.

Skendi, Stavro. "The Millet System and Its Contribution to the Blurring of Orthodox Identity in Albania." In *Christians and Jews in the Ottoman Empire: The Functioning of a Plural Society*, edited by Bernard Lewis and Benjamin Braude, 243–257. New York: Holmes & Meier, 1982.

Sphyroeras, Vasilis. *Hoi Dragomanoi Tou Stolou; Ho Thesmos Kai Hoi Phoreis.* Athenai, 1965.

Spiridonakis, B. G. *Essays on the Historical Geography of the Greek World in the Balkans During the Turkokratia.* Thessalonike: Institute for Balkan Studies, 1977.

Staurinidou, Nikolaos S. *Metaphraseis Tourkikon Istorikon Engrafon: Aphoronton Eis Ten Istorian Tes Kretes.* Vol. A. 1657–72 and Vol. B. 1672–94: Herakleion, Crete: Ekdidontai dapane Ypourgeiou Politismou kai Epistemon, 1976.

Stavrianos, L. S. *The Balkans since 1453.* New York: Holt, Rinehart and Winston, 1963.

Stavrides, Théoharis. *The Sultan of Vezirs: The Life and Times of the Ottoman Grand Vezir Mahmud Pasha Angelovic'(1453–1474).* Leiden: E. J. Brill, 2001.

Talbot, Alice Mary. *Amiroutzes, George.* Vol. 1, edited by Alexander P. Kazhdan, 77–78. Oxford: Oxford University Press, 1991.

Talbot, Alice Mary and Alexander P. Kazhdan. "*Stauropegion.*" Vol. 3, edited by Alexander P. Kazhdan, 1946–1947. Oxford: Oxford University Press, 1991.

Tellan, Elif Bayraktar. "The Patriarch and the Sultan: The Struggle for Authority and the Quest for Order in the Eighteenth-Century Ottoman Empire." Ph.D. Dissertation: Bilkent University, 2011.

Theolin, Sture. *The Torch of the Empire : Ignatius Mouradgea d'Ohsson and the Tableau général of the Ottoman Empire in the Eighteenth Century = Imparatorlugun mesalesi:*

XVIII. yüzyilda osmanli imparatorluğunun genel görünümü ve Ignatius Mouradgea dOhsson. Istanbul: Yky, 2002.

Thomas, John Philip. *Private Religious Foundations in the Byzantine Empire*. Washington, DC: Dumbarton Oaks Research Library and Collection, 1987.

Thomas, John, Angela Constantinides-Hero, and Giles Constable. *Byzantine Monastic Foundation Documents A Complete Translation of the Surviving Founders' Typika and Testaments*. Vol. 3. Washington, DC: Dumbarton Oaks Research Library and Collection, 2000.

Trapp, E., ed. *Prosopographisches Lexicon Der Palaiologenzeit*. Vienna : Österreichischen Akademie der Wissenschaft, 1976.

Turan, O. "Les Souverains Seldjoukides Et Leurs Sujets Non-Musulmans." *Studia Islamica* 1 (1953): 65–100.

Ursinus, Michael. "Zur Diskussion Um "Millet" Im Osmanischen Reich." *Südost-Forschungen* 48 (1989): 195–207.

Ursinus, Michael. "Millet." *Encyclopedia of Islam*. 2nd Edition. VII (1990): 61–64.

Ursinus, Michael. "Petitions from Orthodox Church Officials to the Imperial Diwan, 1675." *Byzantine and Modern Greek Studies* 18 (1994): 236–247.

Vakalopoulos, A. E. *History of Macedonia:* 1354–1833. Edited by Trans. Peter Megann. Thessaloniki: Institute for Balkan Studies, 1973.

Vakalopoulos, Apostolos. *The Greek Nation:* 1453–1669. Translated by Ian and Phania Moles. New Brunswick, NJ: Rutgers University Press, 1976.

Van der Velden, Eva De Vries. *L'elite Byzantine Devant L'avance Turque a L'epoque De La Guerre Civile De 1341–1354*. Amsterdam: J. C. Gieben, 1989.

Vaporis, N. M. *Witnesses for Christ: Orthodox Christian Neomartyrs of the Ottoman Period, 1437–1860*. Crestwood, NY: St. Vladimir's Seminary Press, 2000.

Venzke, M. L. "The Sixteenth-Century Ottoman Sanjaq of Aleppo: A Study of Provincial Taxation." Ph.D. Dissertation: Columbia University, 1981.

Vishnevskaya, I. I. "The Royal Court and the Orthodox Church in the Seventeenth Century." In *Treasures of the Czars: From the State Museums of the Moscow Kremlin*. Booth-Clibborn Editions, 1995.

Visvisis, J. "L'administration Communales Des Grecs Pendant La Domination Turque." In *Le Cinq-Centieme Anniversaire De La Prise De Constantinople.*, 217–238. Athens: Imprimerie nationale, 1953.

Vlasto, A. P. *The Entry of the Slavs into Christendom: An Introduction to the Medieval History of the Slavs*. Cambridge: Cambridge University Press, 1970.

Voulgares, Apostolos. "O Ethnarchikos Rolos Tou Oikoumenikou Patriarcheiou." In *Anafora Eis Mnemen Metropolitou Sardeon Maximou* 1914–1986, edited by Alkibiades K. Kalyvopoulos, 335–346. Geneva: Iera Metropolis Elvetias, Idryma dia ten christianiken enoteta Atef Danial, 1989.

Voutyras, Stauros I. *Lexikon historias kai geographias*. Vol. 1. Constantinople: Typois I. A. Vretou, 1869.

Vryonis, Speros, Jr. *The Decline of Medieval Hellenism in Asia Minor and the Process of Islamization from the Eleventh through the Fifteenth Century*. Los Angeles: University of California Press, 1971.

Vryonis, Speros, Jr. "The Greeks under Turkish Rule." In *Hellenism and the First Greek War of Liberation (1821–1830): Continuity and Change*, edited by N. Diamandouros et. al., 97–109. Thessalonike: Institute for Balkan Studies, 1976.

Vryonis, Speros, Jr. "Problems in the History of Byzantine Anatolia." In *Byzantina Kai Metabyzantina: Studies on Byzantium, Seljuks, and Ottoman*, edited by Speros Vryonis, Jr., I. Malibu: Undina Press, 1981.

Vryonis, Speros, Jr. "The Byzantine Legacy and Ottoman Forms." In *Byzantina Kai Metabyzantina: Studies on Byzantium, Seljuks, and Ottoman*, edited by Speros Vryonis, Jr., XIII. Malibu: Undina Press, 1982.

Vryonis, Speros, Jr. "Decisions of the Patriarchal Synod in Constantinople as a Source for Ottoman Religious Policy in the Balkans Prior to 1402." In *Byzantina Kai Metabyzantina: Studies on Byzantium, Seljuks, and Ottoman*, edited by Speros Vryonis, Jr., XVI. Malibu: Undina Press, 1982.

Vryonis, Speros, Jr. "Religious Changes and Patterns in the Balkans, 14th–16th Centuries." In *Byzantina Kai Metabyzantina: Studies on Byzantium, Seljuks, and Ottoman*, edited by Speros Vryonis, Jr., X. Malibu: Undina Press, 1982.

Vryonis, Speros, Jr. "Religious Change and Continuity in the Balkans and Anatolia from the Fourteenth through the Sixteenth Century." In *Byzantina Kai Metabyzantina: Studies on Byzantium, Seljuks, and Ottoman*, edited by Speros Vryonis, Jr., XI. Malibu: Undina Press, 1982.

Vryonis, Speros, Jr. "The Experience of Christians under Seljuk and Ottoman Domination, Eleventh to Sixteenth Century." In *Conversion and Continuity: Indigenous Christian Communities in Islamic Lands Eight to Eighteenth Centuries*, edited by Michael Gervers and Ramzi Jibran Bikhazi, 185–216. Toronto: Pontifical Institute of Mediaeval Studies, 1990.

Vryonis, S. "Byzantine Constantinople and Ottoman Istanbul: Evolution in a Millenial Imperial Iconography." In *The Ottoman City and Its Parts*, edited by R. Abou-El-Haj, Irene A. Bierman, and Donald Preziosi, 13–52. New York: Aristide C. Caratzas, 1991.

Vryonis, Speros, Jr. "The Byzantine Patriarchate and Turkish Islam." *Byzantino-Slavica* 57/11 (1996): 69–111.

Vucinich, W. S. "The Nature of Balkan Society under Ottoman Rule." *Slavic Review* 21/4 (1962): 616–622.

Ware, Timothy. *Eustratios Argenti: A Study of the Greek Church under Turkish Rule, by Timothy Ware.* Oxford: Clarendon Press, 1964.

Ware, Timothy. *The Orthodox Church.* 2nd edition, New York: Penguin, 1993.

Weber, Nicholas Aloysius. *A History of Simony in the Christian Church: From the Beginning to the Death of Charlemagne (814).* Baltimore: J. H. Furst Company, 1909.

Wittek, Paul. "De La Defaite D'ankara a La Prise De Constantinople." *Revue des Etudes Islamiques* 12 (1938): 1–34.

Wittek, P. *The Rise of the Ottoman Empire.* Second edition. London: The Royal Asiatic Society of Great Britain and Ireland, 1938, 1971.

Yeor, Bat. *The Decline of Eastern Christianity Inder Islam: From Jihad to Dhimmitude.* New Jersey, NY: Fairleigh Dickinson University Press, 1996.

Yerasimos, S. *La Fondation De Constantinople Et De Sainte-Sophie Dans Les Traditions Turques.* Paris: Jean Maisonneuve, 1990.

Yerasimos, Stefanos. *Les Voyageurs Dans L'empire Ottoman, Xive-Xvie Siècles: Bibliografie, Itinéraires et Inventaire des Lieux Habités.* Ankara: Société turque d'histoire, Atatürk Kültür Merkezi, Türk Tarih Kurumu, 1991.

Yerasimos, Stephanos. "La Communaute Juive D'istanbul a La Fin Du Xvie Siècle." *Turcica* XXVII (1995): 101–133.

Zachariadou, E. A. "Mia Italike Pege Tou Pseudo Dorotheou Gia Ten Historia Ton Othomanon." *Peloponnesiaka* 5 (1961): 46–59.

Zachariadou, E. A. "He Patriarcheia Tou Dionysiou B' Se Mia Parallage Tou Pseudo-Dorotheou (the Patriarchate of Dionysios B' in a Variant of Pseudo-Dorotheos)." *Thesaurismata* 1/1 (1962): 142–161.

Zachariadou, E. A. "Early Ottoman Documents of the Prodromos Monastery (Serres)." *Sudost-Forschungen* 28 (1969): 1–12.

Zachariadou, E. A. "Ottoman Documents from the Archives of Dyonisiou (Mt. Athos) 1495–1520." *Sudost-Forschungen* 30 (1971): 1–36.

Zachariadou, E. A. "Süleymnan Çelebi in Rumeli and the Ottoman Chronicles." *Der Islam* 60 (1983): 268–296.

Zachariadou, E. A. *Trade and Crusade: Venetian Crete and the Emirates of Menteshe and Aydin (1300–1415)*. Vol. 11. Venice: Instituto Ellenico di Studi Bizantini e Postbizantini (Library of the Hellenic Institute of Byzantine and Post-Byzantine Studies), 1983.

Zachariadou, E. A. "Holy War in the Aegean." In *Latins and Greeks in the Eastern Mediterranean after 1204*, edited by Bernard Hamilton, Benjamin Arbel, and David Jacoby, 212–225. London: Frank Cass, 1989.

Zachariadou, E. A. "The Neomartyr's Message." *Deltio Kentrou Mikrasitikon Spoudon* 7 (1990–91): 51–63.

Zachariadou, E. A., ed. *The Ottoman Emirate (1300–1389)*. Rethymnon: Crete University Press, 1993.

Zachariadou, E. A. "Wealthy Greeks and the Patriarchate of Constantinople Ca. 1453." Paper presented at the "The Business of Change: Merchants and the Fall of Constantinople" (Unpublished Papers, 1994).

Zachariadou, E.A. "The Worrisome Wealth of the Çelnik Radic." In *Studies in Ottoman History in Honour of Professor V. L. Menage*, edited by C. Imber and C. Heywood, 383–397. Istanbul: Isis Press, 1994.

Zachariadou, E. A. "Ta Logia Kai O Thanatos Tou Louka Notara." In *Rodonia Time Ston M. I. Manoysaka*, edited by Chrysa Maltezou, Theocharis Detorakis and Christoforos Charalampakis, 135–146. Rethymno: Panepistimio Kretes, 1995.

Zachariadou, E. A. *Deka Tourkika engrapha gia ten Megale Ekklesia: 1483–1567*. Athens: Ethniko Hidryma Ereunon, Institouto Byzantinon Ereunon, 1996.

Zachariadou, E. A. "A Safe and Holy Mountain: Early Ottoman Athos." In *Mount Athos and Byzantine Monasticism: Papers from the Twenty-Eighth Spring Symposium of Byzantine Studies, Birmingham, March 1994*, edited by M. Cunningham and A. Bryer, 127–132. Birmingham: Variorum, 1996.

Zachariadou, E. A. "Some Remarks About Dedications to Monasteries in the Late 14th Century." In *Athos in the 14–16th Centuries*, edited by Ethnikon Hidryma Ereunon, 27–31. Athens: The National Hellenic Research Foundation, 1997.

Zachariadou, E. A. "Co-Existence and Religion." *Archivum Ottomanicum* 15 (1997): 119–129.

Zachariadou, E. A."Les Notables Laïques Et Le Patrarcat Oecuménique Après La Chute De Constantinople." *Turcica* 30 (1998): 119–134.

Zachariadou, E. A. and V. Demetriades. "Serbian Ladies and Athonite Monks." *Wiener Zeitschrift fur die Kunde des Morgenlandes* 84 (1994): 35–55.

Zakythenos, D. A. *The Making of Modern Greece: From Byzantium to Independence*. Oxford: Basil Blackwell, 1976.

Index

Page numbers in italics followed by 'f' as in *196f5.2* refer to figures.
Page numbers in italics followed by 't' as in *162t4.1* refer to tables.
Unless otherwise noted, references to patriarchs refer to patriarchs of Constantinople, i.e., the Ecumenical Patriarchate of Constantinople.

Abou-El-Haj, Rifa'at A., 182–183, 185
Actes de Lavra, 98–99
Acts of the Apostles, sin of simony discussed in, 203
Ahkâm Defteri 62. *See Kâmil Kepeci Tasnifi Ahkâm Defteri*
ahl-i kitab "people of the book," 20–21
Ahyolu (Anchialos)
  Kantakouzenos's palace in, 208–209
  salt works, 155, 199–200, 213
  ship building, 155, 200–201
  and Sōzopolis, 121n29
    See also Sōzopolis
Alexander II (Voyvode of Wallachia), *196f5.2,* 200
Alexandria, patriarchate of, 122, 131, 214, 217
Amiroutzes, George
  and the Angelović family of Novo Bordo, 190n37
  and Komnenos (Emperor of Trebizond), 5–6
  Ottoman connections of, 5–6
  personal history of, 5–6
Anatolian emirates (*beyliks*), and the Byzantine State, 68
Andronikos II Palaiologos, 68, 89, 99
Angold, Michael, 72, 77, 209n100
Antioch
  Ignatius of, 71
  patriarchate of, 81, 122, 131, 217
Apostolopoulos, Dimitris
  on Greek submission to the Ottomans, 51–52
  on Patriarchal Synodal decrees related to Patriarch Symeon of Trebizond, 113–115
Archbishop of Ohrid, Prohor
  independent status of, 50
  rights to collect taxes from Eflâk and Karaboğdan, 126, 129–134, 137, 165
Archbishop of Peç, independent status of, 50
archons (leading men of Greek society)
  in Byzantine society, 18, 52, 188–189
  experience with and connections to Ottoman power, 12, 17, 52, 213–216
    See also Historia Politike
  individual. *See* Amiroutzes; Kantakouzenos; Kritovoulos; Notaras; Palaiologoi
  mentioned, 6, 26
  post-1453 studied as a class, 189
Arnakis, George
  anachronistic explanations of, 38
  and the *berât* issued to Metropolitan Leontios of Larissa, 38–39
Aşıkpashazade, 27, 42
Athonite monasteries
  in the *Actes du Protaton,* 90, 98n110
  idiorythmy promoted in, 90
  independent status of, 90–91, 93, 134
  monastic documents of, 91–92n81
  Ottoman occupation of, 93, 99–101
  and the Palaiologos family, 90, 93, 95–97
  Stavronikita monastery founded by Patriarch Jeremiah I, 125
avariz (extraordinary taxes), 141, 216

Balta, Evangelia, 88, 94
Bayezid. *See* Sultan Bayezid
berâts for the right to collect the tax (*mal-i miri*), in the *Ahkâm Defteri. See Kâmil Kepeci Tasnifi Ahkâm Defteri* 62
Biromori (Geromeri) monastery in Epirus
  Ahkâm Defteri document No. 10, 127, 134–135
  stavropegion status, 134–135, 168
Bisaha, Nancy, 30
bishops (*episkopos*)
  and Byzantine imperial administration, 66–67, 72–75
    See also Patriarchal *iltizam*
  income from *kanonikon* taxes, 45, 158–159
  individual. *See* Archbishop of Ohrid, Prohor; Damaskenos the Stoudite; Theodoros Agallianos
  and local Turkish rulers, 67, 74–78, 81–85
  tradition of authority of, 71
    See also metropolitans
Black Death of 1348–49, 70–71
Bojanič, Dušanka, 156–157nn62–63, 161
Bosworth, C.E., 20
Brankoviç, Maria (Mara), 112–113, 150
Braude, B enjamin
  on the *millet* system as a myth, 11, 46–48, 49, 50, 61
  on the Notaras episode/sixteenth century contests for power, 26n13, 28–29
  "patina of self-serving tradition" of the Greek community described, 24

Brown, Peter, 5, 71
Busbecq, Ogier Ghiselin de, *Turkish Letters* of, 30
Byzantine exile governments, and Latin imperial administration of Constantinople, 69
Byzantine period
  and Anatolian emirates (*beyliks*), 68–70, 78–80, 92
  civil war. *See* Second Palaiologan Civil War
  and the Ecumeniucal Patriarch of Constantinople, 3, 4–5, 9
    Ephesus, 78–80
  glorification of, 4–7
  maritime trade, 70, 78
  and Ottoman fiscal administration, 142–143
  state and Church relations during, 3, 4–5, 9–10, 51–52, 66–67, 70–74

Çandarlı Halil Pasha (Sultan Mehmet II's Grand Vizier), execution of, 27
Cantemir, Demetrie
  as a historian and commentator on the Ottoman Empire, 34
  The History of the Growth and Decay of the Othman Empire, 31–32
çavuş (low ranking administrator enforcing justice as tax collection agents), 159, 171–172
çelebi (well-born), Michael Kantakouzenos referred to as, 94
Chalkokondyloi, 189
Chiones (Ottoman subjects), 64
cizye (poll tax) paid by non-Muslims, 100, 111, 112, 128, 141–142, 158, 195
Codex A', 164
Codex Beta and Gamma, 216–217
confiscation of Athonite properties, 100–101
corporate organization of Ottoman society, 48, 59
Crete, ecclesiastical jurisdiction over, 106, 174–175
Crusius, Martin, 16, 16n25, 186, 208, 214

Damaskenos the Stoudite (sixteenth-century bishop)
  chronicles used as historical sources, 16, 16n25, 179
  Dialogos of, 179–182
  personal history of, 179
  simony condemned by, 185, 187
Darling, Linda T., 20n1
  on Ottoman revenue raising, 141–142, 142n8
Demetrios Palaiologos, 19, 191–192
devşirme (child-levy), 6, 112, 183
Divan-i Hümâyûn (Ottoman Imperial Council)
  documents of. *See Kâmil Kepeci Tasnifi Ahkâm Defteri*
  and sultanic rulings on ecclesiastical administrative matters, 110
  in the *Historia Politike,* 113
  See also Patriarch Jeremiah II
D'Ohsson, Ignatius Moradgea (Muradcan Tosunyan) (1740–1807)
  anachronistic understanding of the non-Muslims in Ottoman society, 34–36
  conception of *Rum millet-i* (Greek Orhodox Community), 14, 41
  personal history of, 34
Düstûrnâme-i Enverî, 68n11, 79

Ebu's-su'ud Efendi (*sheyh-ül-islam*), 42, 101
ecclesiastical tax farms. *See* Patriarchal *iltizam*
Ecumenical Patriarchate of Constantinople. *See* Patriarchate of Constantinople
Ecumenical Patriarchs
  authority in 1453 of, 11
  and the example of Tagaris, 82
  individual. *See* Patriarch Cyril Loukaris; Patriarch Gennadios; Patriarch Ioasaph; Patriarch Metrophanes III
  as *millet başı*/ethnarch (national (ethnic) leader), 10, 14, 28n19, 37, 50, 54
Edirne
  Greek elite families in, 188, 191, 213
  Metropolitan of Edirne, 165
  Patriarch Dionysios II's captivity in, 113
  salt work of Ainos in, 191
Emperor Basil I, 9
Emperor Basil II, 131
Emperor Constantine XI Palaiologos, 8
  and Patriarch Gennadios's letter *Concerning Simony,* 186
  and the political role of Christian bishops, 71
  and Sultan Mehmet, 107–108
Ephesus, 78–80
Epirus (Delvine)
  Biromori (Geromeri) monastery in, 127
  Byzantine exile government in, 69

gâzi (holy war) thesis
  deconstructed by Lowry, 20, 56–57
  and evidence from the *timar* and *tahrir* defters of Rumeli, 55–57
  and the Ottoman practice of accommodation. *See istimâlet*
  as the prevailing narrative for the rise of the Ottoman Empire, 19–20, 79
Gedeon, Manouel Io, 28n19, 38, 39
Gerlach, Stephen
  on clerical corruption associated with papist system, 152–153, 173–174

on Michael Kantakouzenos, 195, 204–205, 208, 212–213
personal history of, 17
Tagebuch as a historical source, 152, 189
on the tax collection activities of the Zygomalas family, 152–153, 157, 159, 161–163, *162t4.1*, 167–168
Germans and Germany
Protestant-Orthodox dialogue, 208–209
scholars. *See* Crusius; Gerlach; Giese; Scheel
Gibb, H.A.R. and Harold Bowen, paradigm of the *millet* system, 11, 47–48
Gibbon, Edward, 3, 32–33
Giese, Friedrich, 41–43
Goffman, Daniel, 49
Greek economic elite. *See archons*
Greek Orthodox economic elites
Patriarchal *iltizam* as a competitive activity of, 142
See also archons (leading men of Greek society)
Greek Orthodox Patriarchate. *See* Patriarchate of Constantinople
Gregory Palamas (Archbishop of Thessalonike)
on the Church and society under Ottoman rule, 15, 63–66
debate with Ottoman subjects, 63, 64–65
Ottomans first encountered by, 70

haraç (*haratzion*) land tax, 216
in the *Actes de Lavra,* 98–99
in early Islamic times, 158
in the *Historia Patriarchica,* 160
imperial haraç collected by Theodosios Zygomalas, 157–158
and John VI Kantakouzenos's submission to Umur Pasha, 68
and Manuel II's administration of Mount Athos, 96–97
role of kings in the institution of, 114
Hass Murat Pasha, 190–191
Hendy, Michael F., on the *Notitiae Episcopatuum,* 77, 77n37
hesychasam (silent meditation), 63, 90
Historia Patriarchica Constantinopoleos by Manuel Malaxos
on Archbishop Prohor's rights to collect taxes, 132–133
and the chronicles of Damaskenos, 16, 179
haraç (*haratzion*) as a term in, 155, 158, 160, 186
importance as a historical source, 16–17, 32–33
on the investiture of Patriarch Gennadios, 23–26, 108
mentioned, 197
on Patriarch Jeremiah I's collection of taxes, 125, 132–133
pişkeş as a term in, 150, 186
on the sin of simony, 203
Historia Politike
legacy of granting favors to the Byzantine nobility in, 191–192
pişkeş as a term in, 113, 120n25
holy war. *See gâzi*

Ibrahim Pasha (Grand Vizier), 121, 122
idiorythmy, 90
Ilkhanids
financial administration, 143
pişkeş (investiture gifts), 150–151
iltizam (tax farms)
and Byzantine fiscal administration, 142–143
the Church as a revenue-producing institution, 140–141
ecclesiastical administration of. *See* Patriarchal *iltizam*
and Ilkhanid fiscal administration, 143
jailing of unsuccessful tax farmers. 155. *See also* Patriarch Raphael
as lucrative operations, 125, 144–145, 189–190
and the *malikâne* system, 154
negative image of, 144
in Ottoman state documents, 15, 147–148, 156–158
berât issued to Patriarch Symeon, 116–117
and property rights, 150
term/periods of, 153–154
Inalcik, Halil
on the fiscal status of the Greek Orthodox Church, 58, 59–60, 148–149, 159, 218
on *istimâlet,* 54–55, 57
on rights and legal status of the Church hierarchy, 58–60, 111
on timars granted to bishops, 87–88
investiture fees. *See pişkeş* (investiture gifts)
investiture of Patriarch Gennadios (George Scholarios). *See* Patriarch Gennadios
Iorga, Nicolae, *Byzance après Byzance,* 189
Ismail I (Safavid ruler), 109
istimâlet (practice of accommodation)
and the early Ottoman period, 57, 75, 101, 103, 109
introduced by Inalcik, 54–55, 57
and *timar,* 87, 93–94

janissaries (*yeniçeri),* ecclesiastical tax collection by Yusef, 137, 167
Jerusalem
community of Franks in, 49
kadi of, 49
Patriarchate of, 38, 52n101, 122, 217
and Paul Tagaris, 81–82
Patriarch Jeremiah I's pilgrimage to, 121–122

Jews
  and Chiones, 64n3
  financiers, 144, 189, 190
  forced resettlement in Istanbul of, 28
  on the island of Crete, 206, 208
  and the *millet* system, 46, 48, 215
  Yahud milleti (Jewish millet), 48
John VIII Palaiologos, 67–68
John VII Palaiologos, 96, 98
John VI Kantakouzenos, 64, 67–68, 197
  Ottomans enlisted in military campaigns of, 70
John V Paliologos, 67–68, 93

Kabrda, Josef, 44–45, 159
kadis (Islamic judges)
  cizye (poll tax) registers of, 141
  documentation of decrees related to
    in the *Ahkâm Defteri,* 126–127, 132, 135–136
    in the *Mühimme Defterleri,* 17, 213
  kadi of Jerusalem, 49
Kâmil Kepeci Tasnifi Ahkâm Defteri 62
  fourteen Ottoman documents listed, 126–128
  Ottoman management of Church administration, 15–16, 130–131
Kâmil Kepeci Tasnifi Ahkâm Defteri 62—individual documents
  Document No. 1, 126, 130–132
  Document No. 2, 126, 130–132
  Document No. 3, 126, 132
  Document No. 4, 126, 135–136
  Document No. 5, 126, 132
  Document No. 6, 126, 133–134
  Document No. 7, 127
  Document No. 8, 126, 127, 134
  Document No. 9, 127, 134
  Document No. 10, 127, 134–135
    See also Biromori (Geromeri) monastery in Epirus
  Document No. 11, 127, 135
  Document No. 12, 127, 135
  Document No. 13, 136
  Document No. 14, 127, 137
kanonikon (customary fees)
  emvatoikion paid to bishops upon ordination and appointment, 115
  and marriage taxes, 45, 158–159
  and *patriklik rüsûmu* (patriarchal tax), 45, 60
Kantakouzenos, Andronikos, 212–213
Kantakouzenos, Antonios (*Monoraitos*), Patriarch Dionysios II supported by, 126, 203–204
Kantakouzenos family
  ancestry, Romanian/Mesemvria (Misivri) branch of, 198
  ancestry of, imperial family roots, 197
  individuals. *See* John VI Kantakouzenos; Kantakouzenos, Andronikos; Kantakouzenos, Antonios (*Monoraitos*); Kantakouzenos, Michael; Kantakouzenos, Thomas
  wealth and status of, 193, 195, 197, 202–204
    See also individual family members
Kantakouzenos, Michael
  ecclesiastical influence, 202–210, *204t5.1*
  epithet *Şeytanoğlu* given to, 193–195
  execution of, 193, 208–209, 211–213
  as an imperial merchant, 200–202
    and the Ahyolu Salt works, 155, 199–200, 213
  poems about
    by Constantine Dapontès, 193–194
    by George the Aetolian, 197–198
  uncanonical marriage of, 201
Kantakouzenos, Thomas, 202
kata logon epidoseon (for reasons of sustenance), 77, 84
Kenanoğlu, M. Macit *Ottoman Millet System: Myth or Reality,* 61–62
kethüda (guild warden), 59, 148–149, 152
Komnenos, David (Emperor of Trebizond), and Amiroutzes, 5–6
Konortas, Paraskevas, 38n51, 52–54, 159n74, 167–168n95
Kotzageorgis, Phokion, 237
Kral George (ruler of Serbia), 119
Kritovoulos, Michael (Kritovoulos of Imvros), 21–23, 24, 26–28, 27n15, 150

Lambton, 150–151
Lemerle, Paul, 94
Lewis, Bernard, 46
Lowry, Heath W., *gâzi* (holy war) thesis deconstructed by, 20, 56–57

Mahmud Pasha Angelović (1456–68 and 1472–74), 6, 190n37, 191
mâktu' (lump sum payments to the Imperial Treasury), 85, 141, 156, 160–161, 163, 167, 168, 216
Malaxos, Manuel
  personal history of, 16, 180n3
  writing. *See Historia Patriarchica Constantinopoleos*
malikâne (tax farms)
  ecclesiastical offices purchased as, 218
  system of, 154
Manuel II Palaiologos
  and the administration of Mount Athos, 90, 95–98
  Ottoman tax policies maintained by, 96–99
marriage and family issues
  Amiroutzes's divorce, 6

and clerical fees, 158–159, 161
and the ecclesiastical juridical system, 40, 117, 124, 163
forbidden between believers and unbelievers, 44
as a "liberty" granted to the Greeks by the Ottomans, 33–34
Michael Kantakouzenos's uncanonical marriage, 203
Mavrokordatos family, 189
Prince Constantine Mavrokordatos mentioned, 193
Mavrozoumis (Greek leader in Biga), 63–64, 65
Mehmet Sokollu Pasha (Grand Vizier), 129
and Michael Kantakouzenos, 155, 195, 200, 201, 212
Melissourgos-Melessinos, Makarios, *Chronicon Maius,* 23, 30, 33
Mesih Pasha, 190–191
Metrophanes. *See* Patriarch Metrophanes III
metropolitans (*medrepolidler*)
and Byzantine state administration, 72
disruption of system of, 76–77
illegitimate ordination by Tagaris, 81–82
interference in tax collection by individuals dismissed from office, 168–169
in liturgical vestments, *170f4.3*
and the Patriarchate of Constantinople, 116, 117, 118, 124
metropolitans (*medrepolidler*) by metropolis
Metropolitan of Attaleia, assumed by the Metropolitan of Germanoupoulos, 81
Metropolitan of Attaleia-Perge, Theophilos, 82–84
Metropolitan of Caesarea, Metrophanes, 205
as Patriarch. *See* Patriarch Metrophanes
Metropolitan of Chalcedon (Kadiköy), 83–84
Metropolitan of Corinth, Neophytos, 216
Metropolitan of Edirne, 165
Metropolitan of Ephesus, Matthew, 78–80
Metropolitan of Germanoupolis, 81
Metropolitan of Larissa
installed as Patriarch Jeremiah II by Kantakouzenos, 189, 206–207, 208
Leontios, 38–39, 38
Metropolitan of Myra, Matthew, 82–84
Metropolitan of Peritheorion, Dorotheos, 81
Metropolitan of Siroz, 120, 146–147, 167
Metropolitan of Sōzopolis
Akakios, 209
Ioannikios, 202
Metropolitan of Thebes, 16
Metropolitan of Thessalonike
encroachment on rights of, 133
Methodios considered a "disciple of the devil," 218
receipt for taxes paid by, 60, 167
Metropolitan of Trebizond, Ananias, 43–44, 218
Metropolitan of Tyre, 81, 82
Metropolitan Theophylaktos, 119
Metropolotan of Varna, 174
Michael VIII Palaiologos, 69
millet başı/ethnarch (national (ethnic) leader), 10, 14, 28n19, 37, 54
millet system
Gibb and Bowen's paradigm of, 11, 47–48
and the Greek community under Ottoman rule, 11–13, 140
Patriarch Gennadios Scholarios 1454 investiture, as the founding moment of, 10–11, 14, 21, *25f1.1*
periodization of, 57–58
tâ'ife as a term for, 47, 49
and Tanzimat reforms, 39, 42, 43, 47, 48, 53, 57, 219
monasteries
independent status of. *See stavropegion* status
of Mt. Athos. *See* Athonite monasteries
Pammakaristos, 24, 117, *118t3.1*
as *vakif*/*evkaf* (pious endowments), 85, 88, 94, 101, 117, 125
Mt. Athos
direct Ottoman rule of, 95
Manuel II's *Prostagma of 1404,* 96–98, 96n99
Metrophane's exile to, 207
Metropolitan of Varna's exile to, 174
monasteries on. *See* Athonite monasteries
Mühimme Defterleri ("Register of Important Affairs")
content of, 17
iltizams in, 142n8
Michael Kantakouzenos' business ventures in, 199
tax assessment and collection complaints, 145, 165–166
term *millet* in, 48
mukata'a (rent)
collection, 145–147
defined, 145n25
ecclesiastical holdings of, 146–147, 167
ecclesiastical offices purchased as, 218
iltizam distinguished from, 156
and Mongol fiscal administration, 143n13
mültezim (tax farmer) domains distinguished from, 146, 218
Ottoman bureau of episcopal rents (*Piskopos Mukata'a Kalemi*), 58, 148–149, 218
and the *timar* system, 138–139

mukata'a kalemi (Ottoman bureau overseeing tax farm rental concessions), 148–149
mültezim (tax farmers)
Metropolitan from Siroz as, 120, 146–147, 167
patriarchs and bishops as. *See* Patriarchal *iltizam*
rent (*mukata'a*) distinguished from, 146, 218
requirements of, 145–146
Mustafa Ali of Gelibolu (Otoman administrator), *Counsel for Sultans,* 184–185

Nasi, Don Josef (Duke of Naxos), 206
New Testament
Church and state in, 8
offices identified in, 71
Nicolay, Nicolas de, 30–31
non-Muslims under Ottoman rule, 30, 33, 46
Benjamin Braude on. *See* Braude
legal status of described by D'Ohsson, 34–35
See also ahl-i kitab "people of the book"; Jews; *zimmi* (non-Muslims)
Notaras, Lucas
execution of, 29
historical representation of, 28–29
political authority of, 29
and Sultan Mehmet II, 26–28
Notitiae Episcopatuum, 76–77

Orhan. *See* Sultan Orhan
Ottoman dynasty
conquest period, 51–52, 54, 65–66
See also gâzi (holy war) thesis; *istimâlet* (practice of accommodation)
dominance over emirates in Anatolia, 69–70
foundational myth of, 19
rulers. *See* Sultan
society. *See* Ottoman society
Ottoman society
authority and power of the state, 126
archons connection to, 192, 213
and Catholics and Protestants, 49
competition and corruption of, 17–18, 182
corporate organization of, 48, 59
daily dress of Greek Orthodox priests, *164f4.2*
D'Ohsson's anachronistic understanding of the non-Muslims in Ottoman society, 34–36
in the European popular imagination, 30–31
Greek community as constituent elements of, 8, 10, 14, 18, 29, 53, 65–67, 191–192
See also archons; *istimâlet* (practice of accommodation); pişkeş (investiture gifts)
Ottoman tax farming
detailed. *See iltizam*; Patriarchal *iltizam*
documentation of. *See Kâmil Kepeci Tasnifi Ahkâm Defteri*
rent. *See mukata'a*
summarized, 142–144
tax farmers. *See mültezim* (tax farmers)

Palaiologoi
conversion of Hass Murat Pasha and Mesih Pasha, 190–191
individuals. *See* Andronikos II Palaiologos; Demetrios Palaiologos; Emperor Constantine XI Palaiologos; John VIII Palaiologos; John VII Palaiologos; John V Paliologos; Manuel II Palaiologos; Michael VIII Palaiologos
in the Ottoman ruling elite, 190–191
as Ottoman tax farmers, 189–190, 199
Second Palaiologan Civil War, 65, 67–68
Palamas. *See* Gregory Palamas
Pantazopoulos, Nicholas, 74, 111n9
Pantocrator monastery, 90, 99n113
Papadopoullous, Theodore H., 16n25, 36–38, 39, 39n54, 40, 41
Patmos
berât in the archive of the Monastery St. John the Theologian on, 123–124
judicial decision recording the resignation of a priest from, 60
patriarachal zitiye (patriarchal alms), as imperial taxation identified, 53
Patriarchal *iltizam*
bidding for, 147–148
bishops as state tax collectors, 66–67, 125, 132–133, 140, 142, 146, 147–148
described in 1483 *berat* to Patriarch Symeon, 117–118
exploitation by elites, 142
mentioned, 103, 110
and pişkeş (investiture gifts), 150–152
Patriarchal Synodal Acta
lack of discipline in the hierarchy and clergy in, 76–78
on Metropolitan of Ephesus, Matthew, 78
on Metropolitan of Peritheorion, Dorotheos, 81
on the Metropolitan of Tyre, 81, 82
on negotiation and accommodation by local bishops, 11–12, 15, 75–76
on Patriarch Matthew I, 84–85
on Paul Tagaris, 81–82
Patriarchate of Alexandria, 122, 131, 214, 217
Patriarchate of Antioch, 81, 122, 131, 217
Patriarchate of Constantinople
Acta. See Patriarchal Synodal Acta

archives of, v, 11, 165, 216–217
dress of priests and patriarchs, *163f4.1*, *170f4.4*
and the hierarchical structure of the Orthodox Church, 50, 192
legal status of, 43–45, 53
legal status of. *See* rights and privileges of the patriarchate under Ottoman rule
and Michael Kantakouzenos, 202–211, *204t5.1*
millet system championed by, 10, 25f1.1
monasteries directly under the control of. *See stavropegion* status
monastery of Pammakaristos, 24, 117, *118t3.1*
Pope of Rome compared with, 11
turnover rate for Patriarchs, 153–154
Patriarchate of Constantinople—re-establishment
and Church power to govern the Greek community, 24–25
fiscal system as a means to consolidate local power and authority, 52–53, 159–160
See also pişkeş (investiture gifts)
and Istanbul resettlement, 27, 28
Patriarchate of Jerusalem, 38, 122
individual. *See* Patriarch Athanasios; Patriarch Dositheos II
Patriarch Athanasios of Jerusalem, 119
Patriarch Cyril II Kontares, and the indebtedness of the Great Church, 217–218
Patriarch Cyril Loukaris, 214–217
Patriarch Dionysios II, 113–123, 125–126, 203
and the Metropolitan from Siroz, 120, 146–147, 167
Patriarch Dositheos II of Jerusalem, 217
Patriarch Gennadios (George Scholarios)
investiture of, 10–11, 14, 21–22, 25–26, *25f1.1*
avoided by D'Ohsson, 34
documentation of privileges of, 22–23, 107–108, 137–138
letter *Concerning Simony,* 186
and post-conquest church/state relations, 14, 26, 58, 103
letter to Kral George (Serbian ruler), 119
Patriarch Ioakeim, 120
Patriarch Ioannikios, 122–123, 202–203
Patriarch Ioasaph II
and Amiroutzes, 5–6, 7
as "Magnificent" (Megaolprepos), 203
and Michael Kantakouzenos, 203
suicide attempt of, 3–4, 5, 187
Patriarch Jeremiah I
as a subject of 1544 *Ahkâm Defteri* documents, 126–127, 132–135, 165
deposition and reinstatement of, 122–123, 202–203
installation of, 121
and Stavronikita monastery on Mt. Athos, 125
Patriarch Jeremiah II, and Patriarch Metrophanes III, 206–207
Patriarch Kallinikos II, 217–218
Patriarch Markos Xylokaraves, 112, 150
Patriarch Matthew I, and Ottoman ruler Bayezid, 84–85
Patriarch Metrophanes III
and Michael Kantakouzenos, 155–156, 206–208, 210
personal history of, 203, 207–208
Patriarch Neophytos VII, 36
Patriarch of Jerusalem, Paul Tagaris, 82
Patriarch Pachomios, 61, 120
Patriarch Prokopios, 36
Patriarch Raphael the Serb, investiture fee case of, 113, 116, 155, 160, 216
Patriarch Symeon of Trebizond
berât of Bayezid II issued to, 60, 116–117
investiture fees paid by, 112–114, 115, 150
mültezim collected by, 117, 146
Patriarch Theoleptos
documentation of administrative rights and authority of, 137–138
documentation of rights and privileges of the Greek Orthodox community, 107–108, 137–138
patriklik rüsûmu (patriarchal tax)
as an imperial tax, 53, 120, 145–146, 147, 156, 163–164
pişkeş (investiture gifts) viewed as, 60, 159–160
Patrinelis, Christos G., 108, 187
pişkeş (investiture gifts)
and guild wardens. *See kethüda* (guild warden)
and the integration of the local non-Muslim communities into the Ottoman system, 53, 111, 150–152, 159–160
in medieval Persian society, 151
paid by Symeon and his successors in Trebizond, 112–116, 150
paid by the metropolitan of Trebizond, 43–44
under Ilkhanid rule, 150–151
Piskopos Mukata'a Kalemi (1641–51), 58, 148–149, 218
Pope Pius II (Aeneus Silveas Piccolomini), 30
Prohor. *See* Archbishop of Ohrid
Prosopographisches Lexicon der Palaiologenzeit, 197

Rhalle family, 189, 213
Rhodes (Rodos)
capture of, 124, 128–129
exile to, 174
Patriarchal Jurisdiction of, 123, *162t4.1*

rights and privileges of the patriarchate under Ottoman rule
and capitulation, 76
documentation of, 60–62, 107–108, 134, 137–138
See also Kâmil Kepeci Tasnifi Ahkâm Defteri 62
D'Ohsson on, 35–36
Inalcik on, 58–60, 111, 148–149, 218
Kritovoulos on, 22–23
and the monasteries of Mt Athos, 99
Papadopoullos's distortion of, 37–38, 39
purchasing of, 192
Runciman's description of, 39–40
Roman Catholics
and the Greek Orthodox community, 70, 214
millet, 48
and Ottoman society, 49
Rum millet-i (Greek Orthodox Community), 38, 41, 50, 54
Runciman, Steven, 4–5, 6, 8n10, 39–41, 39n54, 40n55, 41n56, 185
Rycaut, Sir Paul, 31, 34, 218

St. Anastasia Monastery, 209–211
St. John Prodromos in Serres, 26, 88, 92, 93–94, 94n90
St. John the Baptist Monastery, *stavropegion* status of, 209, 210
sancak beys (military and administrative commander of a district)
independence of, 99, 99n116
and metropolitans as *timar,* 87, 100
of Rumeli and Anadolu, 168
Scheel, Helmuth, 158n71
on the Metropolis of Trebizond, 43–44, 218
Second Palaiologan Civil War, 65, 67–69
Serres (Siroz), metropolitan of, 120, 146–147, 167
Şeytanoğlu (the devil's son). *See* Kantakouzenos, Michael
Sharia Islamic religious law
and the Athonite properties confiscation crisis, 100–101
and the Ottoman state, 13, 20, 42, 107
and *zimmis,* 48, 58
sheyh-ül-islam (chief Ottoman Islamic scholar/leader)
Ebu's-su'ud Efendi (*sheyh-ül-islam*), 42, 101
judicial decree issued by(1521), 109
Simon Magus, 115, 203
simony
condemned by Dameskenos, 182, 187
condemned by the church, 115, 125, 203
by elite figures not condemned by Patriarch Gennadios, 52n101
Patriarch Symeon accused of, 112, 115
sipahi (standing cavalry)
as *cizye* collection agents, 141–142, 159
and sipahi tâ'ife, 127, 136
and the *timar* system, 85–86, 87, 183–185
Sōzopolis
and the Kantakouzenos family, 121n29, 210
Metropolitan Akakios of, 209
monasteries. *See* St. Anastasia; St. John the Baptist Monastery
Sphrantze, George, *Chronicon Minus,* 23, 27, 42
stavropegion status
of Athonite monasteries, 89
of Biromori (Geromeri) monastery in Epirus, 134–135, 168
granting of, 89, 210
of St. John the Baptist Monastery, 209
Süleyman Çelebi of Rumeli, 95–96, 95n5
Süleyman I, the "Magnificent". *See* Sultan Süleyman
Sultan Ahmed I, *berât* issued to Metropolitan Leontios of Larissa, 38–39
Sultan Bayezid I
financial bureaucracy and administration, 97, 143n12
siege of Constantinople, 84, 95
Sultan Bayezid II
berât awarded to Patriarch Maximos, 60
berât awarded to Patriarch Symeon, 60, 116
receipt for taxes paid by the Metropolitan of Thessalonkike, 60, 167
Sultan Mahmud I, enthronement of, 42, 43
Sultan Mahmud II, *berât* awarded to Parthenios by, 43
Sultan Mehmet II (1451–81)
Grand Vizier of. *See* Çandarlı Halil Pasha
investiture of Patriarch Gennadios. *See under* Patriarch Gennadios
patriarchate re-establishment. *See* Patriarchate of Constantinople—re-establishment
stepmother. *See* Branković, Maria (Mara)
and Trebizond, 5–6, 112–113, 150
Sultan Murat I, *hüküm* granting tax exemption, 93–94
Sultan Murat II (1421–51), *timar* rights during reign of, 55, 86
Sultan Murat III
and Michael Kantakouzenos' execution, 195
and Michael Kantakouzenos' rights as an imperial merchant, 201
Sultan Orhan ("Great Emir"), 64–65, 92–93
Sultan Selim I (Sultan Yavuz), 19, 60, 109
Sultan Selim II (r.1566–1574)
berât issued by Bishop Kallistos confirmed by, 61
confiscation of Athonite properties atttempted by, 100–101
pictured, *102f2.1*

Sultan Selim III, 43
Sultan Süleyman (Süleyman I, the "Magnificent"), 198, 203
conquests of, 128–129
and patriarchate involvement in the Imperial Divan, 137
and the rights and privileges of the Greek Orthodox community, 107–108
tax collection records during the reign of, 15

tahrir defter
monastic rights and privileges documented in, 100, 137
Tahrir Defteri of Rumeli, 55–57, 86, 87–88
Tapu *Tahrir Defteri,* 3, 88, 94n90
tâ'ife
non-Muslim (*zimmî*) community described as, 47
sipahi (*sipahi tâ'ife*), 127, 136
as a term for *millet,* 47, 49
Tanzimat reforms, 39, 42, 43, 47, 48, 53, 57, 219
taxation
Actes de Lavra tax register from Thessalonike, 98–99
cizye (poll tax) paid by non-Muslims, 100, 111, 112, 128, 141–142, 158, 195
clerical fees for marriage and baptism, 45, 158–159, 161
irregular taxes. *See avariz*; *zeteia*
land tax. *See haraç* (*haratzion*)
Ottoman tax policies maintained by Manuel II, 96–99
patriarchal tax. *See patriklik rüsûmu*
taxation collection activities
Gerlach on. *See* Gerlach
by layperson, Anastasios Kallistos, 188
by the monk Mattheos, 168
Patriarchs as. *See under* Patriarchs
of the Zygomalas family. *See* Zygomalas, Ioannes; Zygomalas, Theodosios
tax collection agents. *See çavuş*; *kadi*; *sipahi*
tax farms. *See iltizam*; Patriarchal *iltizam*
Tellan, Elif Bayraktar, 217n3
Theodoros Agallianos (or Theophanes, Bishop of Medea), 187
Thessalonike
Actes de Lavra tax register, 98–99
Archbishop of. *See* Gregory Palamas
timar system
bishops as *timariots,* 87–88, 101
Christian aristocracy integrated with, 55–56, 110, 195
and Christian monasteries, 87–88, 94, 94n90
iltizam as more practical than, 110, 139–140, 144, 156
institution of, 128, 139
sipahi order as an ideal, 85–86, 87, 183–185
Tindal, Nicolas, 31–32
Tourkokratia (Ottoman rule), *See also* Ottoman dynasty; Ottoman society
Trebizond (Trabzon)
archons of, 112
Greek Christian émigrés from viewed as traitors, 5–7, 150
Komnenian Emperor of. *See* Komnenos, David
Metropolitan Ananias of, 43–44
Patriarchate of. *See* Patriarch Symeon of Trebizond

Umur Pasha (Aydınoğulları ruler of Smyrna)
in the *Düstûrnâme-i Enverî,* 68n11, 79
land tax (*haraç*) levied on John VII Kantakouzenos, 68
and Metropolitan of Ephesus, Matthew, 68, 78–80
Ursinus, Michael, 48

Vakalopoulos, Apostolos, 7, 150
Venetians
and the Byzantine-Turkish Treaty of 1403, 96
and Crete, 124, 174, 206
holdings in Morea, 129
maritime trade concessions with the Byzantine state, 70
and Thessalonike, 99
Vivlion Historikon, 121, 203, 205, 205n87
Vivlos Vasileion (The Book of Kings) by Constantine Dapontès, 193–194
von Hammer, Joseph, 33–34
Vryonis, Speros, Jr.
on the disappearance of bishoprics, 76, 77
on Metropolitan Matthew of Ephesus, 78, 80n47
on the Turko-Islamic political and cultural ascendance, 74n30

Wittek, Paul, 94

Zachariadou, Elizabeth
on Metropolitan of Ephesus, Matthew, 80
Ten Turkish Documents Concerning the Great Church (1483-1567), 60–61
on textual variations of *Vivlion Historikon,* 205n87
zeteia (irregular taxes), 216, 217
zımmi (non-Muslims)
conversion of, 44
and early Islamic experience, 20, 41, 48
and profitable tax farming posts, 142, 165
and Sharia law, 48, 58
and special treatment awarded for voluntary submission, 58
tâ'ife as a term for, 47

tax collection from, 44
See also Jews; non-Muslims under Ottoman rule
Zygomalas, Ioannes (or John Zygomalas)
clerical corruption reported by, 153
personal history of, 17, 152
on tax collecting methods of local Ottoman officials, 159
Zygomalas, Theodosios (Grand Orator (*megas rhetor*) of the patriarchate)
clerical corruption observed and adjudicated by, 163, 174–175, 205, 206–207
household estimates of, 161, *162t4.1*
personal history of, 152
tax collection activities of, 152, 157–158, 165, 167–168

The manufacturer's authorised representative in the EU for product safety is Oxford University Press España S.A. of el Parque Empresarial San Fernando de Henares, Avenida de Castilla, 2 – 28830 Madrid (www.oup.es/en or product.safety@oup.com). OUP España S.A. also acts as importer into Spain of products made by the manufacturer.

www.ingramcontent.com/pod-product-compliance
Lightning Source LLC
Chambersburg PA
CBHW050548240126
38706CB00003B/135
* 9 7 8 0 1 9 8 7 1 7 8 9 8 *